We work with leading authors to develop the
strongest educational materials in law,
bringing cutting-edge thinking and best learning
practice to a global market.

Under a range of well-known imprints, including
Longman, we craft high quality print and
electronic publications which help readers
to understand and apply their content,
whether studying or at work.

To find out more about the complete range of our
publishing, please visit us on the World Wide Web at:
www.pearsoneduc.com

Tort Law

Third Edition

Catherine Elliott
and Frances Quinn

An imprint of **Pearson Education**

Harlow, England · London · New York · Reading, Massachusetts · San Francisco
Toronto · Don Mills, Ontario · Sydney · Tokyo · Singapore · Hong Kong · Seoul
Taipei · Cape Town · Madrid · Mexico City · Amsterdam · Munich · Paris · Milan

Pearson Education Limited,
Edinburgh Gate,
Harlow,
Essex CM20 2JE,
United Kingdom

and Associated Companies throughout the world

Visit us on the World Wide Web at:
www.pearsoneduc.com

First published 1996
Second edition published 1999
Third edition published 2001

ISBN 0582–43811–X

British Library Cataloguing-in-Publication Data
A catalogue record for this book is available from the British Library

10 9 8 7 6 5 4 3 2 1
05 04 03 02 01

Set by 69 in Baskerville
Printed in Great Britain by Henry Ling Ltd., at the Dorset Press,
Dorchester, Dorset.

Contents

Preface

Tort is an area of English law which rarely stands still for long, and the period since publication of our last edition has been no exception. As ever, negligence has provided many of the new cases examined here, including **Reeves** *v* **Commissioner of Police for the Metropolis** (1999); **Barrett** *v* **Enfield** (1999); **Phelps** *v* **Hillingdon** (1999) and **Hall** *v* **Simons** (2000), while the European Court of Human Rights case, **Osman** *v* **UK** (1999), looks set to have a profound effect on the issue of immunities in negligence. Other key cases have included **Reynolds** *v* **Times Newspapers** (1999) in defamation; **Holbeck Hall Hotel** *v* **Scarborough Borough Council** (1999) in nuisance; **DPP** *v* **Jones** (1999), **R** *v* **Bournewood Community and Mental Health NHS Trust, ex parte L** (1998) and **R** *v* **Governor of Brockhill Prison** (2000) in trespass; and **Trotman** *v* **Yorkshire County Council** (2000) on vicarious liability. As well as these and many other new cases, this edition includes a completely new chapter covering product liability, and expanded coverage of breach of statutory duty and liability in negligence for omissions and acts of third parties. A further change in this edition is that, following the change in terminology put in place as part of Lord Woolf's reform of the civil justice system, the party bringing an action is now referred to as the claimant, rather than the plaintiff (except in direct quotations from cases decided before the change).

As with the previous editions, our aim is to provide a clear explanation of the law of tort. As well as setting out the law itself, we look at the principles behind it, and discuss some of the issues and debates arising from tort law. We hope that the material here will allow you to enter into some of that debate and develop your own views as to how the law should develop.

One of our priorities in writing this book has been to explain the material clearly, so that it is easy to understand, without lowering the quality of the content. Too often, law is avoided as a difficult subject, when the real difficulty is the vocabulary and style of legal textbooks. For that reason, we have aimed to use 'plain English' as far as possible, and explain the more complex legal terminology where it arises. There is also a glossary of technical terms at the back of the book. In addition, chapters are structured so that material is in a systematic order for the purposes of both learning and revision, and clear subheadings make specific points easy to locate.

Although we hope that many readers will use this book to satisfy a general interest in the law, we recognize that the majority will be those who have to sit an examination in the subject. Therefore, each chapter features typical examination questions, with detailed guidance on answering them, using the material in the book. This is obviously useful at revision time, but we recommend that when first reading the book, you take the opportunity offered by the Questions sections to think through the material that you have just read and look at it from different angles. This will help you both understand and remember it. You will also find a section at the end of the book which gives useful general advice on answering exam questions on tort law.

This book is part of a series that has been written by the same authors. The other books in the series are *The English Legal System*, *Criminal Law* and *Contract Law*.

We have endeavoured to state the law as at 1 March 2001.

Catherine Elliott
and Frances Quinn
London 2001

▶ Addendum

Z *v* United Kingdom, TP & KM *v* United Kingdom (2001) unreported

Just as this book was going to press, the European Court of Human Rights announced their decision in this case, which arose from the facts of **X** *v* **Bedfordshire** and **M** *v* **Newham**, in which it had been held that local authorities owed no duty of care to individuals in respect of their performance of their statutory social services duties. The European Court said such immunity was a violation of the right to an effective remedy under Art. 13 of the European Convention on Human Rights, and the applicants should have been given the chance to argue their case on its merits.

Acknowledgements

We are grateful to the following examination boards for permission to reproduce questions which have appeared in their examination papers.

The AQA (*AEB*) and Oxford Cambridge and RSA Examinations (OCR).

The examination boards are not responsible for the suggested answers to the questions. Full responsibility for these is accepted by the authors.

Table of cases

Table of statutes

Table of statutory instruments

Table of European legislation

1 Introduction

The law of tort covers a wide range of situations, including such diverse claims as those of a passenger injured in a road accident, a patient injured by a negligent doctor, a pop star libelled by a newspaper, a citizen wrongfully arrested by the police, and a landowner whose land has been trespassed on. As a result, it is difficult to pin down a definition of a tort; but, in broad terms, a tort occurs where there is breach of a general duty fixed by civil law.

When a tort is committed, the law allows the victim to claim money, known as damages, to compensate for the commission of the tort. This is paid by the person who committed the tort (known as the tortfeasor). Other remedies may be available as well. In some cases, the victims will only be able to claim damages if they can prove that the tort caused some harm, but in others, which are described as actionable *per se*, they only need to prove that the relevant tort has been committed. For example, landowners can claim damages in tort from someone trespassing on their land, even though no harm has been done by the trespasser.

▶ Torts distinguished from other wrongs

Torts and crimes

A crime is a wrong which is punished by the state; in most cases, the parties in the case are the wrongdoer and the state (called the Crown for these purposes), and the primary aim is to punish the wrongdoer. By contrast, a tort action is between the wrongdoer and the victim, and the aim is to compensate the victim for the harm done.

There are, however, some areas in which these distinctions are blurred; in some tort cases, damages may be set at a high rate in order to punish the wrongdoer, while in criminal cases, the range of punishments now includes provision for the wrongdoer to compensate the victim financially, though this is still not the primary aim of criminal proceedings, and the awards are usually a great deal lower than would be ordered in a tort action.

There are cases in which the same incident may give rise to both criminal and tortious proceedings. An example would be a car accident, in which the driver might be prosecuted by the state for dangerous driving, and sued by the victim for the injuries caused.

Torts and breaches of contract

A tort involves breach of a duty which is fixed by the law, while breach of contract is a breach of a duty which the party has voluntarily agreed to assume. For example, we are all under a duty not to trespass on other people's land, whether we like it or not, and breach of that duty is a tort. But if I refuse to dig your garden, I can only be in breach of a legal duty if I had already agreed to do so by means of a contract.

In contract, duties are usually only owed to the other contracting party, whereas in tort, they are owed to people in general, and while the main aim of tort proceedings is to compensate for harm suffered, contract aims primarily to enforce promises.

Again, there are areas where these distinctions blur. In some cases liability in tort is clarified by the presence of agreement – for example, the duty owed by an occupier of land to someone who visits the land is greater if the occupier has agreed to the visitor's presence. Equally, many contractual duties are fixed by law, and not by agreement; the parties must have agreed to make a contract, but once that has been done, certain terms will be imposed on them by law.

A defendant can be liable in both contract and tort. For example, if a householder is injured by building work done on their home, it may be possible to sue in tort for negligence and for breach of a contractual term to take reasonable care.

▶ The role of policy

Like any other area of law, tort has its own set of principles on which cases should be decided, but clearly it is an area where policy can be seen to be behind many decisions. For example, in many tort cases the parties will, in practice, be two insurance companies – cases involving car accidents are an obvious example. The results of such cases may have implications for the cost and availability of insurance to others; if certain activities are seen as a bad risk, the price of insurance for those activities will go up, and in some cases insurance may even be refused.

In terms of simple justice, it may seem desirable that everybody who has suffered harm, however small, should find it easy to make a claim. In practical terms, however, the tort process is expensive and it is difficult to justify its use for very minor sums. The courts have to strike a balance between allowing parties who have suffered harm to get redress, and establishing precedents that make it too easy to get redress so that people make claims for very minor harms.

There are other practical concerns too: it has been suggested, for example, that in the USA, where ordinary individuals are much less reluctant to sue than here, medical professionals are inclined to avoid new techniques, or to cover themselves by ordering costly and often unnecessary tests, because of the danger of legal action. While it is clearly a good thing that dangerous techniques should not be used, medical science has always had to take certain risks in order to make new discoveries, and it may be that fear of litigation can stunt this process.

These are difficult issues to weigh up, and traditionally English judges avoided the problem by behaving as though such considerations played no part in their decisions, referring only to established principles. However, in recent years they have been more willing to make clear the policy implications behind their decisions: certainly the 'floodgates' argument (the term used to describe fears that allowing wider liability on the part of defendants will lead to the courts being flooded with new cases) has been overtly referred to in the case law on both nervous shock and the recovery of economic loss in negligence.

▶ Tort and the requirement of fault

In addition to proving that the defendant has committed the relevant act or omission (and, where necessary, that damage has been caused as a result), it is sometimes necessary to prove a particular state of mind on the part of the defendant. This is described as a tort requiring an element of fault, and depending on the tort in question, the required state of mind may be intention, negligence or malice. Most torts require some element of fault; the few that do not are described as torts of strict liability.

Intention

'Intention' has various meanings depending on the context, but it essentially involves deliberate, knowing behaviour. So for example, if I throw a ball at a window deliberately, knowing the glass will probably break, I can be said to intend to break the window. If on the other hand, I threw the ball at a wall, unaware that there was a window in the wall, then I would not intend to break the window. Trespass is an example of a tort in which the required state of mind is intention.

Negligence

As a state of mind, negligence essentially means carelessness – doing something without intending to cause damage, for example, but not taking care to ensure that it does not. In the example above, when I threw the ball at the wall, then I may have been negligent. The term 'negligence' also describes a particular tort.

Malice

In tort, to act maliciously means acting with a bad motive. Normally, malice – and motive in general – is irrelevant in tort law. If what you do is lawful, it remains lawful whatever your reason for doing it. Similarly, if your act is unlawful, doing it with a good motive will not usually make it lawful. This was the approach taken by the House of Lords in the leading case of **Bradford Corporation *v* Pickles** (1895). The Bradford Corporation owned a reservoir on property adjoining Pickles's land. Water naturally flowed under Pickles's land and into the reservoir. Pickles wanted to force the corporation to buy his land at a high price. With this aim in mind, he dug up some of his land, in order to stop the natural flow into the reservoir. It was already settled law that it was not a tort for a landowner to interfere with the flow of underground water, but the corporation argued that although Pickles's action would normally have been lawful, his malice made it unlawful. The House of Lords rejected this argument.

However, there are a few torts for which malice is relevant. The tort of malicious prosecution involves bringing a prosecution motivated by the wrong reasons, and so malice is an essential ingredient. For defamation, certain defences will be unavailable if the defendant has acted maliciously, and in nuisance, malice can render what would have been a reasonable act an unreasonable one. For example, in **Hollywood Silver Fox Farm Ltd *v* Emmett** (1936) the defendant and claimant owned farms near each other. After a dispute between them, the defendant arranged for guns to be fired on a part of his own land which was near the claimant's land, with the intention of interfering with the breeding of the claimant's foxes. The firing did have this effect, and so the claimant sued for nuisance. The action was successful, because of the malicious motive with which the defendant acted.

Malice may also be relevant to the calculation of damages, making them higher than they would be if the same act was committed without malice.

Strict liability

A strict liability tort is committed simply by performing the relevant act or omission, without having to prove any additional state of mind at the time. The tort under **Rylands *v* Fletcher** (see p. 239) is an example of a tort of strict liability. Where the duty breached is a statutory one, proof of a state of mind such as negligence is not normally required, so if an Act simply states that something should be done, not doing it will in itself establish liability. The Consumer Protection Act 1987 has brought another area within the fold of strict liability, namely damage caused by defective products. It should be noted that while liability may be strict, it is not necessarily absolute as in many cases defences will be available.

Reasons for a requirement of fault

In practice the majority of torts do require some proof of fault, and there are several reasons why this has traditionally been thought desirable, including the following.

Control of tort actions
The fact that a claimant must usually prove fault limits the number of tort actions brought, and prevents the courts from being overloaded.

Laissez faire *policy*
The modern tort system arose in the nineteenth century, when the doctrine of *laissez faire* was prominent. This argued that individuals should be responsible for their own actions, with as little intervention from the state as possible. People were not required actively to look after each other, only to avoid doing each other harm, and they would only be expected to make amends for such harm as they could reasonably have avoided doing – in other words, not for harm caused when they were not at fault. The state would provide a framework of rules so that people could plan their affairs, but would intervene in those affairs as little as possible.

Economic policy
As we stated above, fully compensating every tort victim would result in apparently unacceptable practical results; by limiting the actions brought, and the actions won, the requirement of fault helps prevent this.

Deterrence
The requirement of fault is said to promote careful behaviour, on the basis that people can take steps to avoid liability, whereas under strict liability it would be beyond their control, leaving little incentive to take care.

Wider liability would merely shift the burden
Compensation is designed to shift the burden of harm from the person who originally suffered the harm to the person who pays the compensation. It moves, rather than cancels out, the harm, so it can be argued that it is better to let the loss lie where it falls unless some other purpose can be served by providing compensation. A fault requirement adds an additional purpose, that of punishing the wrongdoer.

Accountability
The requirement of fault is a way of making people pay for what they have done wrong, which appears to be a deep-seated social need – even

though in many cases it is actually an insurance company which pays, and not the person responsible.

Strict liability merely reverses the burden of proving fault
Almost all strict liability torts allow the defendant to plead the contributory fault of the claimant as a defence, or a factor which should reduce damages. In practice therefore, strict liability often amounts to nothing more than a reversal of the burden of proof.

Arguments against a requirement of fault

Unjust distinctions
The result of the fault principle is that two people who have suffered exactly the same injuries may receive very different levels of compensation. For example, John and Jim both lose the use of their legs in separate car accidents; in Jim's case the driver is proved to be at fault, in John's, the driver is not. They both suffer the same degree of pain, they both end up with the same disability, and the same problems. Yet John may win thousands of pounds in damages to help him cope with those problems, while the most Jim can hope to receive are benefits provided by the social security system. As we shall see further on, some countries have partially replaced tort law with no-fault compensation schemes aimed at dealing with this problem. A no-fault scheme could compensate not only accidents, but also hereditary and other disabilities and illnesses, on the basis that the problems are the same, regardless of cause.

Illogical distinctions
Even if it is admitted that the potentially huge number of tort actions has to be limited in some way, proof of fault is not the only grounds by which this could be done, nor a particularly logical choice. It appears to be the result of a policy decision that it is sometimes just to reward defendants who have been careful, by protecting them from liability for the consequences of their actions. Quite apart from the fact that fault is difficult to prove, and failure to prove fault does not mean that fault did not occur, it is difficult to see the logic of this approach when the wrongdoer is insured, and would not personally lose anything by paying damages.

Lack of deterrence
The practical deterrent effect of fault liability is debatable. First, the generalized duty to take care is too vague to influence behaviour much. Secondly, in many cases the tortfeasor will be well aware that damages will be paid by their insurance company. Motorists are obliged by law to take out insurance against accidents, as are most employers, and many professional organizations run negligence insurance schemes for their members. It can be argued that defendants also know that a claim may

result in higher premiums, but it is debatable whether this is actually much of a deterrent, especially in business situations where the cost can simply be passed on to consumers in higher prices.

Of course, cost may not be the only deterrent; bad publicity can be equally powerful, if not more so. However, large corporations with good lawyers can largely avoid such publicity by negotiating an out-of-court settlement. In such a case, claimants' chances of recovery seem to depend not on fault, but on the amount of pre-trial publicity they can drum up.

Tort should compensate and not punish
It can be argued that it is not the job of tort to punish wrongdoers; that function properly belongs to the criminal law.

Damages disproportionate to fault
Clearly there are cases in which a very minor level of fault can result in very serious consequences. There can be a huge disproportion between defendants' negligence (such as a momentary lapse in concentration) and the high damages that they subsequently have to pay.

Expense
The need to prove fault increases the length, and so the cost, of tort cases. This increases the proportion of money spent on the tort system which never reaches claimants.

Unpredictability
The fault principle adds to the unpredictability of tort cases, and increases anxiety and pressure on both sides. The practical result is that claimants may feel pressurized into accepting settlements worth much less than they could have won if they had gone to court.

Objective standard
Fault is judged by reference to an objective standard of behaviour, which ignores the knowledge or capacity of the individual; this can mean that someone is legally at fault, when we would not consider that they were at fault morally, or at least not to the degree suggested by the law. For example, the law requires an objective standard of care from drivers, and it expects this equally after 20 years of driving, or 20 minutes.

▶ Alternative methods of compensation for accident victims

A hundred years ago, the law of tort, with all its flaws, was almost the only way of gaining compensation for accidental injury, but its role has declined with the development of insurance and social security. For these the issue of fault is usually irrelevant.

The social security system

Where an employed accident victim is left unable to work, they may claim statutory sick pay for a set period; when that period runs out, they may be able to claim incapacity benefit and certain additional allowances if still unable to work.

Where an injury (or in some cases an illness) arises from an accident at work, the Industrial Injuries Scheme will pay a disablement benefit. However, this benefit is not payable for the first 15 weeks after the accident, and therefore provides no compensation for injuries with short-term effects, no matter how serious those effects may be during that time. Disablement benefit is not assessed on the basis of lost earnings, but on a standardized assessment of the level of disability. For example, regulations provide that loss of one eye amounts to a 30 per cent disability, and a victim with that disability will receive the same amount whether it has left them completely unable to work, slashed their earnings by half or not affected them at all. Since 1986 most disabilities assessed at less than 20 per cent are no longer covered by the scheme.

The social security system also provides benefits for accident victims who suffer no permanent effects of their injuries, but nevertheless lose their jobs as a result of time spent off work while recovering. In this case, unemployment benefit or income support may be payable.

The Criminal Injuries Compensation Scheme is regarded as part of the social security scheme. Administered by the Criminal Injuries Compensation Board, it compensates victims of violent crime and those injured preventing crime. Compensation is given for pain and suffering and loss of amenity, based on a tariff, with around £1,000 awarded for relatively minor injuries such as fractured bones, and at the upper end, £250,000 for serious brain damage. Most of the tariff awards are roughly comparable to the sums that would be awarded by a court for the same kinds of injury, but the amounts awarded to victims of crime causing very serious injury are considerably higher than those that are likely to be awarded by a court. The scheme also compensates victims of crime for loss of earnings and expenses, but no compensation is paid for the first 28 weeks' loss of earnings, and the total amount of compensation for loss of earnings is limited to one-and-a-half times the average gross industrial wage (currently around £29,000 a year). In practice the scheme provides a remedy where a person's rights in tort are useless because the assailant has not been identified, or would be unable to pay substantial damages if sued. After several cases were criticized by the media for the low payments made, in 1998 the Government announced plans to increase the compensation levels.

Compared with the tort system, social security looks relatively efficient. The 1978 Pearson Commission on Civil Liability and Compensation for Personal Injury found that the social security system spent £421 million a year on compensating accident victims, with over one-and-a-half million new claims resulting from accidents every year, at an operating cost of around 11 per cent of that amount. By contrast, the tort system paid out £202 million, between 215,000 accident victims, and its running costs were about 85 per cent of the value of compensation. As well as the added costs incurred by the need to prove fault, the tort system was made more expensive by medical disputes about the long-term effects of injuries, and disputes about the amount of damages to be paid.

A disadvantage of the social security scheme is that the level of benefits is low and there is often a stigma attached to those who accept the benefits – tabloid newspapers, for example, routinely describe welfare benefits as 'handouts', even though the recipients may have been contributing through tax and National Insurance for years.

Insurance

A whole range of policies provide insurance cover in many potentially dangerous situations. Two of the most important sources of accidents are road traffic and industry, and statute makes it a criminal offence for either vehicle users or employers to be without adequate insurance – the Road Traffic Act 1988 and the Employers' Liability (Compulsory Insurance) Act 1969. In addition, the Motor Insurers' Bureau, an organization set up by the insurance industry, gives money to traffic victims where the driver is either uninsured, or unidentified (as in the case of a 'hit and run' accident).

Many people take out household insurance, which usually covers occupier's liability. Three main types of policy provide compensation where accidental death or injury occurs: life assurance, personal accident insurance and permanent health insurance. The Pearson Commission looked at the impact of these policies. It found that around 10 per cent of people in their survey had either personal accident or permanent health policies, and these paid out about £50 million a year in accident compensation. Concerns about the National Health Service in recent years are likely to have increased the percentage of people holding health insurance considerably.

In many cases, employers provide a variety of benefits which may also be of use to accident victims. There may be lump sums payable under occupational pension schemes where death or injury lead to premature retirement. Some employers offer sick pay at higher rates and for longer periods than the statutory scheme, though this rarely exceeds six months on full pay.

Special funds

Highly-publicized accidents involving large numbers of victims, such as the sinking of the *Herald of Free Enterprise* ferry off Zeebrugge and the King's Cross underground fire, sometimes result in the setting up of special funds to compensate the victims.

No-fault systems

The social security and insurance arrangements run alongside the tort system in England. However, in some countries, tort liability in particular fields has been completely replaced by a general no-fault scheme of compensation. The main benefits of this are that similar levels of harm receive similar levels of compensation, regardless of whether fault can be proved, and that the money spent on administering the tort system, and providing legal aid in tort cases, can instead be spent in compensating those who have suffered harm.

The most notable scheme is that which was created in New Zealand in 1972. Their scheme covered personal injuries caused by accidents, which included occupational diseases, and was financed by a levy on employers, the self-employed, vehicle owners, health care providers and through general taxation. Tort actions for personal injury were abolished, and instead injured parties claimed through the Accident Compensation Commission.

Victims unable to work as a result of their accidents could claim weekly payments of up to 80 per cent of their pre-accident earnings, up to a statutory maximum. Those who were still able to work, but at a lower rate of pay than before, could claim 80 per cent of the difference between old earnings and new. Payments could be adjusted to reflect inflation and improvement or deterioration in the victim's medical condition. The system also allowed for lump-sum payments to compensate for pain and suffering (known as non-pecuniary loss, as it is difficult to put a price on it). However, during the late 1980s and early 1990s, the political climate in New Zealand turned against high spending on any kind of welfare and social benefits. As a result, the no-fault scheme has been dismantled and the tort system brought back into operation.

In the USA, approximately half of all the states have established no-fault schemes for victims of road accidents, though there is considerable variation between these schemes and their effect on any potential tort claim. In most of these states, motorists have to buy no-fault insurance cover up to the limit imposed by their state, and the driver and anyone else injured by the vehicle can make a claim. Non-pecuniary loss such as pain and suffering is still covered by the tort system and in some states, claims for non-pecuniary loss can only be brought if the case is particularly serious.

The US schemes seem to have led to a lowering in the cost of motor insurance, and the award of compensation to many victims who would have received no compensation under the old system.

In the Australian state of New South Wales, tort liability for transport accidents has been replaced by a scheme which only pays compensation if the accident was caused by the fault of someone, and for these purposes the victim's fault is not sufficient. The practical effect of this has simply been that cases which would in the past have been dealt with as tort cases in the civil courts are now being heard by administrative tribunals; and owing to the statutory maximum awards, a decrease in the amount of compensation for the serious cases.

Although most no-fault schemes have been created in the context of transport accidents, in Sweden there is a no-fault scheme for victims of medical accidents.

Alternative methods of making wrongdoers accountable

There are also alternatives to the tort system in terms of holding wrong-doers to account for what they have done. The criminal law is an obvious example, though it does not cover all activities which would lead to redress in tort. Highly-publicized accidents often result in public inquiries, such as the thalidomide tragedy, the sinking of the *Herald of Free Enterprise* and the King's Cross fire.

▶ Reform of the tort system

The Pearson Commission considered several alternative recommendations for reform, including a no-fault scheme, and the abolition of fault-based tort liability, to be replaced by a system which would place responsibility on the party best placed to insure against the risk. Where, for example, a pedestrian is knocked down by a car, it is obviously much more practical for the motorist to insure against such an accident than for the pedestrian to do so. Equally, it is easier for an employer to take out one insurance policy covering the whole workforce than for each employee to buy their own accident insurance. However, there will be cases where it might be reasonable to expect the victim to insure themselves against the risk, and in this case an uninsured victim would have to bear the loss.

The Commission concluded that given the social security system in England, it was unnecessary to establish a full no-fault compensation system. It recommended that the tort system should still provide accident compensation, alongside the benefits provided by the social security system, but that there should be a shift in the balance between the two towards increased social security benefits. In particular, the report advocated that benefits available under the Industrial Injuries Compensation Scheme should be increased, and a similar compensation scheme should be set up for injuries caused by motor vehicles, as these were by far the largest category of accidental injury studied by the Commission and were also likely to be serious. The scheme would be financed by a levy on petrol.

The Commission considered the idea of no-fault schemes for other particular types of accident, but given the possible difficulties in defining the scope of such schemes, and in financing them, felt there were too many practical problems to make these a sound proposition.

The idea of a general compulsory insurance was also rejected, on the ground that it would be difficult to enforce, that some might find it unaffordable, and that it was not desirable to expect people to insure themselves against harm caused by others. Such a system would retain the high operational costs of the tort system, yet lose the advantage of making wrongdoers pay for the harm they cause.

The Commission recommended that the tort system should be kept because of its deterrent effect and because '[t]here is an elementary justice in the principle of the tort action that he who has by his fault injured his neighbour should make reparation' (Pearson Report of the Royal Commission on Civil Liability and Compensation for Personal Injury, Cmnd 7054, 1978, paras 245–263). It envisaged, however, that many small tort cases would no longer be brought if its recommendations on social security benefits were put into action.

The Commission also suggested that two measures be taken to reduce tort damages. Non-pecuniary damages would be available only in the most serious cases, and the value of any social security benefits obtained as a result of injury should be offset against the damages awarded. This, it was suggested, was justified by the fact that both social security benefits and tort damages were ultimately derived from society at large, and should not be paid twice. The Pearson Commission was not a success, and its proposals were heavily criticized. The suggestion for a road accident compensation scheme, for example, was criticized as creating yet another *ad hoc* category in an already complex and fragmented system, when in fact road accident victims appeared to be one of the categories best served by the tort system. Shortly after the Pearson Commission reported, a Conservative government was elected, and rather than increase social security benefits as the Commission had suggested, it set about cutting them, so there was no real opportunity for the social security system to play a larger role in accident compensation as the Commission had envisaged. By the late 1980s, it was generally assumed in the majority of Western industrialized countries that social security spending should be curtailed, and despite a change of government in the UK, controlling expenditure on welfare benefits is still seen as a priority; against this background, the Commission's overall approach is obviously not going to be adopted. Only one significant move has been made in their direction, with the advent of legislation to allow the value of social security benefits received by accident victims to be claimed back by the state from tortfeasors (see p. 300).

ANSWERING QUESTIONS

1 How satisfactory is the present system whereby compensation for personal injuries arising from a negligent action depends on proof of fault? Are there any alternatives? *OCR*

Most of the relevant material to answer this question can be found in this chapter, and you will also find useful material at the end of the next chapter on criticisms of the law of negligence. You could first consider what fault is (p. 3), and given the wording of the question you are primarily concerned with negligence, not malice and intention. In order to decide whether the present system is satisfactory you could then point to the reasons for (p. 5) and arguments against (p. 6) the fault requirement. The second part of the question is concerned with the alternatives which are discussed at p. 7 and then you could draw your own conclusion. Note that for this question you need to do more than just discuss the law of negligence; the issue here is also the practical workings of the tort system.

2 **'The defendants' motives for their actions are generally irrelevant in assessing whether or not they have tortious liability.' How true is this statement? Illustrate your answer with specific examples.** *OCR*
This was a wide-ranging question which needed material to be taken from a range of sources. In your introduction you could point out that normally motive is irrelevant but that examples can be given of where occasionally motive is taken into account in deciding tortious liability. Ideally your introduction would specify which examples would be considered and in what order, so that the reader knows the overall structure of the essay and it does not appear to be simply a rambling list with no particular direction.

Leading from your introduction you could consider the case of **Bradford Corporation** *v* **Pickles** as the key illustration of the fact that usually motive is irrelevant. Then you could move on to your examples of when it can occasionally be relevant. Suitable examples could include malicious prosecution and that in nuisance malice can render an activity unreasonable – **Hollywood Silver Fox Farm Ltd** *v* **Emmett** is a useful illustration of this. Bad motive can prevent the defence of qualified privilege from being available in defamation and can be relevant to the defence of necessity generally. Motive is sometimes taken into account in calculating an award of damages. Where the status of an individual as a rescuer is important, such as in relation to negligence, the law is essentially taking into account the person's motive. All these issues are discussed in later chapters.

2 Negligence

Negligence is the most important tort in modern law. It concerns breach of a legal duty to take care, with the result that damage is caused to the claimant. (The tort of negligence is distinct from negligence as a state of mind, with which this chapter is not concerned.) Just a few examples of the type of case which might be brought in negligence are people injured in a car accident who sue the driver, businesses which lose money because an accountant fails to advise them properly, or patients who sue doctors when medical treatment goes wrong.

Torts other than negligence are normally identified by the particular interest of the claimant they protect. For example, nuisance protects against interference with the claimant's use and enjoyment of land, while defamation protects against damage to reputation. By contrast, negligence protects against three different types of harm: personal injury, damage to property, and economic loss (though as we shall see, it protects each of these to different extents).

The tort of negligence comprises three elements: a duty of care, breach of that duty, and damage resulting from the breach.

THE DUTY OF CARE

Negligence is essentially concerned with compensating people who have suffered damage as a result of the carelessness of others, but the law does not provide a remedy for everyone who suffers in this way. One of the main ways in which access to compensation is restricted is through the doctrine of the duty of care. Essentially, this is a legal concept which dictates the circumstances in which one party will be liable to another in negligence: if the law says you do not have a duty of care towards the person (or organization) you have caused damage to, you will not be liable to that party in negligence.

It is interesting to note that in the vast majority of ordinary tort cases which pass through the court system, it will usually be clear that the defendant does owe the claimant a duty of care, and what the courts will be looking at is whether the claimant can prove that the defendant breached that duty – for example, in the huge numbers of road accident cases that courts hear every year, it is already established that road users owe a duty to other road users, and the issues for the court will generally revolve around what the defendant actually did and what damage was caused. Yet flick through the pages of this or any other law book, and you soon see that duty of care occupies an amount of space which seems disproportionate to its importance in real-life tort cases. This is because when it comes to the kinds of cases which reach the higher courts and therefore the pages of law books, duty of care arises frequently, and that in turn is because of its power to affect the whole shape of negligence law. Every time a new duty of care is recognized (or declined), that has implications for the numbers of tort cases being brought in the future, the types of situations it can play a part in, and therefore the role which the tort system plays in society.

As a result, the law in this field has caused the courts considerable problems and we can analyse its development in three main stages: the original neighbour principle as established in **Donoghue *v* Stevenson**; a two-stage test set down in **Anns *v* Merton London Borough** (1978), which greatly widened the potential for liability in negligence; and a retreat from this widening following the case of **Murphy *v* Brentwood District Council** (1990).

▶ Development of the duty of care

The neighbour principle

The branch of law that we now know as negligence has its origins in one case: **Donoghue *v* Stevenson** (1932). The facts of **Donoghue *v* Stevenson** began when Mrs Donoghue and a friend went into a cafe for a drink. Mrs Donoghue asked for a ginger beer, which her friend bought. It was supplied, as was customary at the time, in an opaque bottle. Mrs Donoghue poured out and drank some of the ginger beer, and then poured out the rest. At that point, the remains of a decomposing snail fell out of the bottle. Mrs Donoghue became ill, and sued the manufacturer.

Up until this time, the usual remedy for damage caused by a defective product would be an action in contract, but this was unavailable to Mrs Donoghue, because the contract for the sale of the drink was between her friend and the cafe. Mrs Donoghue sued the manufacturer, and the House of Lords agreed that manufacturers owed a duty of care to the end consumer of their products. The ginger beer manufacturers had breached that duty, causing harm to Mrs Donoghue, and she was entitled to claim damages.

For the benefit of future cases, their Lordships attempted to lay down general criteria for when a duty of care would exist. Lord Atkin stated that the principle was that 'You must take reasonable care to avoid acts or omissions which you can reasonably foresee would be likely to injure your neighbour.' This is sometimes known as the neighbour principle. By 'neighbour', Lord Atkin did not mean the person who lives next door, but 'persons who are so closely and directly affected by my act that I ought to have them in contemplation as being so affected when I am directing my mind to the acts or omissions which are called in question'. The test of foreseeability is objective; the court asks not what the defendant actually foresaw, but what a reasonable person could have been expected to foresee.

Later cases established that the duty had to be owed to the actual claimant; the fact that it was owed to others would not suffice. In an American case, **Palsgraf** *v* **Long Island Railroad Co** (1928), two of the defendant's employees helped a passenger board a train. In doing so, they negligently knocked a parcel the passenger was carrying. It contained fireworks, and exploded as it dropped. The explosion shook some scales about 25 feet away, which fell and in turn hit and injured the claimant. The New York Court of Appeals held that she was not entitled to damages, explaining that a duty of care was owed to the holder of the package but not to the claimant who had been standing far away, as there was no reason to foresee that she was in any danger from the contents of the package.

The claimant does not, however, have to be individually identifiable for the defendant to be expected to foresee the risk of harming them. In many cases, it will be sufficient if the claimant falls within a category of people to whom a risk of harm was foreseeable – for example, the end user of a product, as in **Donoghue** *v* **Stevenson**. The ginger beer manufacturers did not have to know that Mrs Donoghue would drink their product, only that someone would.

In **Haley** *v* **London Electricity Board** (1965) the defendants dug a trench in the street. Their precautions for the protection of passers-by were not sufficient to protect the claimant, because he was blind. He was injured as a result, and the court held that the number of blind people who walk about on their own made it foreseeable that such a person could be injured, and therefore gave rise to a duty of care to take suitable precautions to prevent such injury.

A two-stage test

The issue of reasonable foresight was never the only criterion for deciding whether a duty of care is owed. As time went on, and a variety of factual situations in which a duty of care arose were established, the courts began to seek precedents in which a similar factual situation had given rise to the existence of a duty of care. For example, it was soon well established that motorists owe a duty of care to other road users and employers owe a duty to their employees, but where a factual situation seemed completely new, a duty of care would only be deemed to arise if there were policy reasons for doing so. 'Policy reasons' simply mean that the courts take into account not just the legal framework, but also whether society would benefit from the existence of a duty. The apparent need to find such reasons was said to be holding back development of the law.

However, in **Anns v Merton London Borough** (1978) Lord Wilberforce proposed a significant extension of the situations where a duty of care would exist, arguing that it was no longer necessary to find a precedent with similar facts. Instead, he suggested that whether a duty of care arose in a particular factual situation was a matter of general principle.

In order to decide whether this principle was satisfied in a particular case, the courts should use a two-stage test. First, they should establish whether the parties satisfied the requirements of the neighbour test – in other words, whether the claimant was someone to whom the defendant could reasonably be expected to foresee a risk of harm. If the answer was yes, a *prima facie* duty of care arose. The second stage would involve asking whether there were any policy considerations which dictated that no duty should exist.

This two-stage test changed the way in which the neighbour test was applied. Previously, the courts had used it to justify new areas of liability, where there were policy reasons for creating them. After **Anns v Merton London Borough**, the test would apply unless there were policy reasons for excluding it. This led to an expansion of the situations in which a duty of care could arise, and therefore in the scope of negligence. This expansion reached its peak in **Junior Books v Veitchi** (1983), where the House of Lords seemed to go one step further. The House appeared to suggest that what were previously good policy reasons for limiting liability should now not prevent an extension where the neighbour principle justified recovery. They therefore allowed recovery for purely economic loss (see p. 20) when previously this had not been permitted. This illustrates a problem with the **Anns** test; that it could be applied with little regard for previous case law.

The first stage being relatively easy to pass, there was also thought to be a risk that the bounds of liability would be extended beyond what was reasonable, particularly given the judiciary's notorious reluctance to discuss issues of policy – a discussion that was necessary if the second stage was to offer any serious hurdle. For example, in **McLoughlin v O'Brian** (1983) (see p. 44), Lord Scarman, refusing to impose any limit other than that of mere foreseeability for 'nervous shock', said 'the policy issue as to where to draw the line is not justiciable. The problem is one of social, economic and financial policy. The considerations relevant to a decision are not such as to be capable of being handled within the limits of the forensic process.'

The growth in liability for negligence set all sorts of alarm bells ringing, and eventually, the problems of insuring against the new types of liability, and the way in which tort seemed to be encroaching on areas traditionally governed by contractual liability, led to a rapid judicial retreat.

The law today

In 1990, the case of **Murphy *v* Brentwood District Council** came before a seven-member House of Lords. The House invoked the 1966 Practice Statement (which allows them to depart from their own previous decisions) to overrule **Anns**. They quoted the High Court of Australia in **Sutherland Shire Council *v* Heyman** (1985), a case in which the High Court of Australia had itself decided not to follow **Anns**:

> It is preferable, in my view, that the law should develop novel categories of negligence incrementally and by analogy with established categories, rather than by a massive extension of a *prima facie* duty of care, restrained only by indefinable 'considerations which ought to negative, or to reduce or limit the scope of the duty or the class of person to whom it is owed'.

The broad general principle with its two-part test envisaged in **Anns** was thereby swept aside, leaving the courts to impose duties of care only when they could find precedent in comparable factual situations.

Rejection of the **Anns** test does not mean that the categories of negligence are now closed, but the creation of new duties of care is likely to involve a much more gradual process, building step-by-step by analogy with previous cases involving similar factual situations. Issues of policy will still arise, as such consideration of policy is an inescapable result of the importance of the judge's position. Some would argue that the judges would do better to face up to this fact honestly, as **Anns** was forcing them to do, rather than often hiding this consideration behind reliance on precedents.

In **Caparo Industries plc *v* Dickman** (1990) it was stated that there were now three questions to be asked in deciding whether a duty of care was owed by the defendant to the claimant. Was the damage to the claimant reasonably foreseeable? Was the relationship between the claimant and the defendant sufficiently proximate? Is it just and reasonable to impose a duty of care? However, although this test does provide a broad framework for the establishment of a duty of care, in practice the detailed rules have come to differ according to the type of damage sustained (the three main categories being personal injury and/or damage to property, pure economic loss, and psychiatric injury); whether the damage was caused by an act or an omission; whether by the claimant or a third party; and whether the defendant(s) fall within a range of groups who have become subject to special rules.

Before we move on to look at the rules surrounding where and when a duty of care will be found, there is one important procedural point which will help you make sense of some of the cases discussed in this chapter. Where a case raises an issue of law, as opposed to purely issues of fact, the defendant can make what is called a striking out application, which effectively argues that even if the facts of what the claimant says happened are true, this does not give them a legal claim against the defendant. Cases where it is not clear whether there is a duty of care are often the subject of striking out applications, where essentially the defendant is saying that even if they had caused the harm alleged to the claimant, there was no duty of care between them and so there can be no successful claim for negligence. Where a striking out application is made, the court conducts a preliminary examination of the case, in which it assumes that the facts alleged by the claimant are true, and from there, decides whether they give rise to an arguable case in law – so in a case involving duty of care, they would be deciding whether, on the facts before them, the defendant owes a duty of care to the defendant. If not, the case can be dismissed without a full trial. If the court finds that there is an arguable case, the striking out application will be dismissed, and the case can then proceed to a full trial (unless settled out of court). The claimant will still have to prove that the facts are true, and that the complete case is made out, so a case which is not struck out can still be lost at trial. For an example of this, see **Swinney** *v* **Chief Constable of the Northumbria Police** (p. 64). A recent case brought before the European Court of Human Rights, **Osman** *v* **UK** (1999), appears to have put some limits on the use of striking out applications – see p. 77.

▶ Physical injury and damage to property

The most straightforward case as far as the existence of a duty of care is concerned (and in practice the most common) is one where the defendant physically injures the claimant, or damages their property. In these cases the **Caparo** test applies: a duty of care will exist where the damage was reasonably foreseeable, there is a relationship of proximity and it is just, fair and reasonable to impose (though it is important to remember in all negligence cases that establishing the existence of a duty is only a step towards liability; the claimant still needs to prove that the duty was breached and that the breach caused damage). Thus, for example, a motorist automatically owes a duty of care not to cause physical injury to other road users, even though they are likely to be strangers to him or her. The operation of the test can be seen in **Langley** *v* **Dray** (1998), where the claimant was a policeman who was injured in a car crash when he was chasing the defendant, who was driving a stolen car. The Court of Appeal held that the defendant knew, or ought to have known, that he was being pursued by the claimant, and therefore in increasing his speed he knew or should have known that the claimant would also drive faster and so risk injury. The defendant had a duty not to create such risks and he was in breach of that duty.

In **Watson** *v* **British Boxing Board of Control** (2000), a boxer suffered severe brain damage after being injured in a match, and evidence suggested that his injuries would have been less severe if immediate medical attention had been available at the ringside. The Court of Appeal applied **Caparo** and upheld the boxer's claim against the sport's controlling body: injury was foreseeable, the boxers' licensing system operated by the Board created a relationship of proximity, and it was just, fair and reasonable to impose a duty.

▶ Pure economic loss

Many losses resulting from tort could be described as economic; if the claimant's house is burnt down, the loss is economic in the sense that the claimant no longer has an asset they used to have. Similarly, a claimant who suffers serious injury which makes them unable to work suffers a financial loss. The law of tort has always been willing to compensate for these losses with damages.

However, economic loss also has a more precise meaning in tort. The term is usually used to cover losses which are 'purely' economic, meaning those where a claimant has suffered financial damage, but has incurred no personal injury or damage to property – as when a product bought turns out to be defective, but does not actually cause injury or damage to property. In cases of pure economic loss, the law of tort has been reluctant to allow a claim.

A case which illustrates the difference between the types of loss is **Spartan Steel** *v* **Martin** (1972). Here the defendants had negligently cut an electric cable, causing a power cut that lasted for 14 hours. Without electricity to heat the claimants' furnace, the metal in the furnace solidified, and the claimants were forced to shut their factory temporarily. They claimed damages under three heads: damage to the metal that was in the furnace at the time of the power cut (physical damage to property); loss of the profit that would have been made on the sale of that metal (economic loss arising from damage to property); and loss of profit on metal which would have been processed during the time the factory was closed due to the power cut (pure economic loss). A majority of the Court of Appeal held that the first two claims were recoverable but the third was not. The defendants owed the claimants a duty not to damage their property, and therefore to pay for any loss directly arising from such damage, as well as for the damage itself, but they did not owe them any duty with regard to loss of profit.

There are two main reasons for the traditional reluctance to compensate pure economic loss. The first is that, traditionally, contract was the means by which economic loss was compensated, and the courts were reluctant to disturb this. Contract was seen as offering certainty; defendants could only be liable for losses caused by their own failure to fulfil a freely undertaken agreement, and this clearly had benefits in the commercial world.

The second reason, linked to the first, is the much-quoted 'floodgates' argument. This reasons that while, as a general rule, an act or omission can only cause personal injury or property damage to a limited number of people, the possible economic loss from the same act may be vast and in practice incalculable. In **Spartan Steel**, for example, had the defendants been liable to compensate for profit lost as a result of the power cut, the number and amount of claims might in theory have been astronomical. Although this does not provide much of a moral reason why such losses should not be compensated, an accepted part of law's role in a market economy like ours is to provide industry and commerce with a framework within which they can plan their activities, and preventing claims for economic loss obviously assists in this.

The issue of economic loss in negligence has been the subject of much legal activity over the last 30 years or so, and the law has swung backwards and forwards over the issue. The result is that claims for pure economic loss are now allowed in certain situations, but the law surrounding them is complex, fragmented and still has an unsettled air. However, it is more easily understood if we first look at the developments that have taken place in the last three decades.

The initial position on pure economic loss in negligence was laid down in the case of **Candler** *v* **Crane, Christmas & Co** (1951). Here a firm of accountants had done some work for a client, knowing that the figures produced would also be considered by a third party. As a result of relying on the figures, the third party suffered financial loss, but the Court of Appeal (Lord Denning dissenting) held that the accountants owed no duty of care to the third party; their responsibility was only to the client with whom they had a contractual relationship.

This remained the situation until 1963, when the extremely important case of **Hedley Byrne** *v* **Heller** provided that there were some situations in which negligence could provide a remedy for pure economic loss caused by things the defendant had said, or information they had provided; essentially, there needed to be a 'special relationship' between the parties, which would arise where the defendants supplied advice or information, knowing that the claimants would rely on it for a particular purpose (the case is discussed more fully below).

Following this came the case of **Anns** *v* **Merton London Borough** (1978) which, as we discussed on p. 17, was part of the judicial expansion of negligence liability during the 1970s. The case concerned economic loss arising from the claimant's house being badly built; defective foundations had caused cracking in the walls. This might at first sight appear to be a case of damage to property, but the courts have traditionally been insistent that a defect is not the same thing as damage: where a product is defective in its manufacture, claims may be made for any personal injury caused as a result of the defect, or any damage to other property, but not for the defect itself, which is considered economic, since the loss arises from the reduced value of the object. In **Anns**, however, the House of Lords decided that the cracks in the walls could be viewed as damage to property rather than economic loss, and therefore compensated.

This was followed by the case which is generally viewed as forming the peak of the expansion in negligence liability, **Junior Books** *v* **Veitchi** (1983). The claimants in the case had had a factory built for them under a contract with the building firm. The factory needed a special type of floor in order to support the kind of machinery the claimants wanted to use, and the claimants requested that the builders use a particular flooring firm to provide this, which they did. After the floor was laid, it was found to be defective. If the factory owners had themselves contracted with the flooring company, they could have sued them in contract for the price of replacing the floor, but their only contract was with the builders; the builders had contracted with the flooring company. It was possible to make out a case that the builders had been negligent, but a possible stumbling block was that the factory owners' loss was purely economic: the defect in the floor posed no threat to safety, nor any risk of damage to the fabric of the building, and so the only loss was the cost of replacing it. However, a majority of the House of Lords held that there was nevertheless a duty of care between the builders and the factory owners with regard to the defect in the floor.

The situation after this was that claimants could recover for economic loss caused by statements under **Hedley Byrne**, and following **Anns** and then **Junior Books**, it was also possible to recover for economic loss caused by negligent acts. However, the general expansion of negligence liability was much criticized and it was at this point that the courts began to draw back, with the eventual overruling of **Anns** in **Murphy** *v* **Brentwood District Council** (1990). Like **Anns**, this concerned a defective building, and as well as laying down general principles for the way in which the law on negligence should develop, the House of Lords put a stop to the possibility that defects in products could be seen as damage to property; it reaffirmed that they were to be regarded as economic loss and that they could not be compensated in negligence.

Junior Books was not overruled in **Anns**, but in a series of later cases on defective products the courts declined to follow it. In **Simaan General Contracting Co** *v* **Pilkington Glass Ltd (No 2)** (1988), the claimants were constructing a building in Abu Dhabi. They had been asked by the building owner to ensure that the glass in the windows was a particular shade of green, the colour of peace in Islam. The claimants contracted with another firm to obtain and erect the glass, and this firm contracted with the defendants, who were to make and supply the glass. When the glass was supplied, it was the wrong colour and had to be returned and replaced, which delayed the building project resulting in economic loss to the claimants. The normal means by which they could gain compensation for the loss would be to sue the glass erecting company for breach of contract, but that firm went into liquidation soon afterwards. The claimants therefore sued the glass makers, Pilkington, but the Queen's Bench Division refused to allow liability for economic loss in the absence of a contract between the parties.

After a number of similar cases, it was generally considered that **Junior Books** was to be regarded as unique to its facts, and in particular the idea that by specifying that the flooring company should be used, the claimants created a relationship of proximity between themselves and the defendants, even though there was no contract. It was also suggested (by Lord Oliver in **D & F Estates** *v* **Church Commissioners for England** (1988), and Lord Bridge in **Murphy**, for example) that **Junior Books** could be regarded as an example of the **Hedley Byrne** principle.

Despite this suggestion, both the courts and academic commentators began to develop an approach to economic loss which distinguished between such loss when caused by negligent acts, and when caused by negligent statements or advice. Aside from the apparent anomaly of **Junior Books**, it appeared that economic loss arising from acts was not recoverable in negligence, whereas such loss arising from statements and advice was, if it could be fitted into the requirements of **Hedley Byrne**. This led to the rather bizarre situation in which surveyors or architects who negligently advise on the construction of a building that turns out to be defective are liable for economic loss caused as a result, but builders who are negligent in constructing such buildings are not.

During the 1990s, a new mood of cautious expansion has been noted in a number of cases. These have extended **Hedley Byrne** beyond liability for negligent statements or advice, and established that it can also cover negligent provision of services. This was specifically stated in **Henderson** *v* **Merrett Syndicates Ltd** (1995), and confirmed in **Williams and Reid** *v* **Natural Life Health Foods Ltd and Mistlin** (1998) (both cases are discussed below). The result now appears to be that pure economic loss is recoverable under **Hedley Byrne** principles where it is caused by either negligent advice or information, or by negligent provision of services. It is not recoverable where it is caused by defective products, where **Murphy** still applies. Nor is it recoverable when caused by negligent acts other than the provision of services. This was confirmed in **Londonwaste** *v* **AMEC Civil Engineering** (1997), a case similar to **Spartan Steel** in that the claimants, a company which burnt waste to provide electricity, lost profits as a result of being forced to close down when the defendant road menders severed a power cable. The waste company was allowed to recover for physical damage done to their power station, but not for loss of income from the sale of electricity, nor for the costs incurred from having to dispose of the waste elsewhere, since these were not the result of the physical damage done to the power station, though they were the results of the defendants' negligence.

We will now look in more detail at **Hedley Byrne** and its effects.

The Hedley Byrne **principles**

The claimants in **Hedley Byrne** *v* **Heller** (1964) were an advertising agency, who had been asked by a firm called Easipower Ltd to buy substantial amounts of advertising space on their behalf. To make sure their clients were creditworthy, Hedley Byrne asked their own bank, the National Provincial, to check on them. National Provincial twice contacted Heller, who were Easipower's bankers and were backing them financially, to inquire about Easipower's creditworthiness. Heller gave favourable references on both occasions, but each time included a disclaimer – 'without responsibility on the part of this Bank or its officials'.

The second inquiry asked whether Easipower was 'trustworthy, in the way of business, to the extent of £100,000 per annum', and Heller answered that Easipower was a respectably constituted company, considered good for its ordinary business engagements. This message was conveyed to Hedley Byrne, and, relying on that advice, they entered into a contract with Easipower Ltd. Easipower later went into liquidation, leaving Hedley Byrne to pay the £17,000 due to companies from whom they had bought advertising space. Hedley Byrne claimed this amount from Heller.

In view of the words disclaiming liability, the House of Lords held that no duty of care was accepted by Heller, and none arose, so the claim failed. However, the House also considered what their conclusion would have been if no words of disclaimer had been used, and this is where the importance of the case lies. Their Lordships stated *obiter* that in appropriate circumstances, there could be a duty of care to give careful advice, and that breach of that duty could give rise to liability for negligence. The fact that the sole damage was economic loss did not, they said, affect the question of liability.

This decision was a radical departure from previous principles in two ways. First, as **Candler** shows, liability had not previously been imposed for pure economic loss; however the House approved Lord Denning's dissenting judgment in **Candler**, and held that the majority had decided that case wrongly. Secondly, it had long been considered, on the basis of **Derry** *v* **Peek** (1889) (see Chapter 7) that a false statement could only give rise to liability if made intentionally or recklessly, and it was assumed that negligence did not suffice. This view was put to rest by the House.

The House of Lords laid down a number of requirements which claimants would need to satisfy in order to establish a duty of care under **Hedley Byrne**. There must be a 'special relationship' between the parties; a voluntary assumption of responsibility by the party giving the advice; reliance by the other party on that advice or information; and such reliance must be reasonable. The requirements are to a large extent interlinked, but some specific principles can be drawn out from the cases.

The 'special relationship'

This was described by Lord Reid in **Hedley** as arising where 'it is plain that the party seeking information or advice was trusting the other to exercise such a degree of care as the circumstances required, where it was reasonable for him to do that, and where the other gave the information or advice when he knew or ought to have known that the enquirer was relying on him'. In such circumstances, a person would generally have three options: they could say nothing; could give an answer but explain that it was being given without the careful reflection that the questioner would be relying on; or could simply give the advice or information. Anyone who chose the latter course could be deemed to have accepted responsibility for exercising the degree of care which was required in the circumstances.

Lord Morris similarly explained that a duty of care would arise where 'a person takes it upon himself to give information or advice to, or allows his information or advice to be passed on to, another person who he knows, or should know, will place reliance on it'. For such an assumption to arise, the person giving the advice would usually need to have some skill or experience in the relevant area.

Lord Reid made it plain that the 'special relationship' requirement meant that **Hedley Byrne** only covers situations where advice is given in a business context:

> Quite careful people often express definite opinions on social or informal occasions, even when they see that others are likely to be influenced by them; and they often do that without taking the care which they would take if asked for their opinion professionally, or in a business connection . . . there can be no duty of care on such occasions.

Advice given off-the-cuff in a social setting will therefore not, as a rule, give rise to a duty of care. For example, both doctors and lawyers frequently complain that as soon as they disclose their profession at parties, fellow guests want to discuss backaches or boundary disputes; they can at least take comfort that, tedious though the ensuing conversations may be, they will not result in a negligence suit if the advice given is careless. Curiously, there is however one case in which a duty of care under **Hedley** was found in a purely friendly setting. In **Chaudry v Prabhakar**

(1988), the defendant had advised the claimant, a friend, to buy a particular second-hand car, without noticing that it had been in an accident. It was in fact unroadworthy, and the claimant successfully sued for negligence. The case has however been heavily criticized, and is unlikely ever to be followed; it certainly appears wrong in the light of Lord Reid's statement.

Some cases have suggested that even in a business context, the required relationship will only exist where the defendants are in the business of providing the actual type of advice that the claimants sought. This was held in **Mutual Life and Citizens Assurance Co** *v* **Evatt** (1971), where an insurance company had carelessly given false information about a company in which the claimant had invested. The Privy Council held that there was no duty of care; the defendants were in the business of providing insurance, not providing investment advice, and could not be liable for such advice. A majority of the court held that **Hedley Byrne** should be restricted to cases involving people whose profession centres around the giving of advice, such as accountants, solicitors and surveyors.

However, in the same case, Lords Reid and Morris dissented, arguing that it was sufficient that the advice was sought from a business person, in the course of business, and on the whole it is this broader approach which has been followed. A fairly typical application can be seen in **Esso Petroleum Co Ltd** *v* **Mardon** (1976). Here the claimant had leased a petrol station on the strength of Esso's advice that he could expect to sell at least 200,000 gallons a year. In fact he only managed to sell 78,000 gallons in 15 months. The Court of Appeal held that in making the prediction, the petrol company had undertaken a responsibility to Mr Mardon, and he had relied on their skill in the petrol market; his claim was allowed.

In **Williams and Reid** *v* **Natural Life Health Foods Ltd and Mistlin** (1998), an attempt was made to establish a special relationship between the managing director of a company and the claimants who had suffered loss as a result of the company's negligence. The claimants had obtained a franchise for a health food shop from the defendant company, Natural Life. Mr Mistlin was the managing director and principal shareholder of Natural Life. Natural Life's literature included some detailed financial projections concerning the future profitability of franchises, but these turned out to be inaccurate; the claimant's business traded at a loss and was eventually forced to close. The claimants sued Natural Life, but soon it too was wound up, and they sued Mr Mistlin instead.

At first instance and in the Court of Appeal, it was held that Mr Mistlin had assumed a responsibility towards the defendants, and they had relied on his advice; therefore under the **Hedley Byrne** principle, he owed them a duty of care. However, the House of Lords rejected this view. They held that in order to fix personal liability on the director of a company which had given negligent advice, there had to be a special relationship between the claimants and the director; a special relationship between the claimants and the company was not enough. To establish a special relationship with the director, the claimants would have to prove that the director, or someone acting on his or her behalf, had conveyed directly to the claimants that the director was assuming personal responsibility towards them; and in order to establish reliance on that assumption of responsibility, the claimants had to prove not just that they had relied on it, but that it was reasonable for them to rely on a personal assumption of responsibility.

Mr Mistlin owned and controlled Natural Life; Natural Life's literature suggested that it had sufficient expertise and experience to provide reliable advice to potential franchisees, and this expertise was presented as arising from Mr Mistlin's six years' experience in the health food business. Nevertheless, the House of Lords held that this was not sufficient to make him personally liable. There had been no personal exchanges between the claimants and Mr Mistlin, and nothing Mr Mistlin had done had suggested that he was undertaking a personal liability to them; there was not even evidence that the claimants believed he was doing so. The action therefore failed.

The same issue arose in **Hale** *v* **Guildarch** (1999). Mr and Mrs Hale owned a three-bedroomed house, and had almost paid off their mortgage on it. They wanted to make some improvements to the house and to buy a new car, so they approached their mortgage company to see whether they could increase the mortgage, and were referred to a group of financial consultants called ADC Group Ltd. ADC recommended a home income plan, which involved borrowing the money needed for the car and the home improvements, plus an additional sum which would be put into an investment called a bond. The Hales were told that the bond would give a sufficient return to pay the interest on the whole loan, and the ADC adviser said that it was such a good scheme that he would recommend it to his own father.

The bond did not grow at a sufficient rate, and in fact never could have done as the amount invested was too small; the Hales had never even been warned that there was a chance it might not perform as suggested. However, in the meantime ADC had gone out of business, so the Hales attempted to sue the adviser who had sold them the plan, on the basis that he had assumed a personal responsibility towards them. The court held that this was not the case; exaggerated sales talk, including the remark about recommending the plan to his own father, could not amount to assuming a personal responsibility. Nor was there any evidence to suggest that at that time the Hales thought that he was undertaking a personal responsibility to them.

It has been established that the special relationship can arise between an employer and an employee in the situation where a reference for future employment is provided. In **Spring** *v* **Guardian Assurance plc** (1994), the claimant, Spring, had been employed by the defendant, but was sacked. When seeking a new job, he needed a reference, and the defendant wrote one saying that he was incompetent and dishonest, and as a result, Spring, not surprisingly, failed to get the job. He brought an action against the defendant in negligence for the economic loss caused by not getting the job. The trial judge found that Spring was not dishonest, and that while the defendant had genuinely believed that what he was writing was true, he had reached that conclusion negligently. The House of Lords agreed that a duty of care existed in that situation, and that the defendant had breached it.

Spring is interesting because it differs from **Hedley** in an important respect: in **Hedley** (and the other cases based on **Hedley** principles), the information at issue was given *to* the claimants; in **Spring** it was information *about* the claimant, given to someone else. How far this represents a new widening of the principles is not yet clear, although some limits were defined in **Kapfunde** *v* **Abbey National Plc** (1998). Ms Kapfunde had applied to Abbey National for a job, and supplied them with details of her medical history, including the fact that she had suffered from chest problems and sickle cell anaemia. Abbey National referred this information to a doctor, who acted as an occupational health adviser for them, and he advised them that Ms Kapfunde was likely to have a higher than average amount of sick leave and so was unsuitable for employment. Ms Kapfunde was turned down for the job. She claimed for the economic loss against Abbey National, arguing that they were vicariously liable for the doctor's advice, as his employers. The Court of Appeal found that Abbey National were not vicariously liable as the doctor was an independent contractor (see Chapter 13 on Vicarious liability), but in any case, they said, the doctor would not have owed a duty of care since there was no special relationship between him and Ms Kapfunde: there was no normal doctor–patient relationship (in fact he had never met her); he was retained to advise Abbey National and had never accepted any responsibility towards Ms Kapfunde.

In **Henderson** *v* **Merrett Syndicates Ltd** (1995), it was established that the existence of a contract between the parties did not prevent a **Hedley Byrne** special relationship arising. The case arose when the Lloyd's insurance organization made considerable losses on many of its policies. The losses had to be borne by people who had invested in Lloyd's by underwriting the policies. Known as Lloyd's names, these people were grouped into syndicates and invested on the understanding that they were assuming unlimited liability; if big losses were made, the names could lose everything they had. They were willing to take on this liability because becoming a name was seen as a sure way of making money for those who were wealthy enough to be able to invest, and in previous years it had proved to be exactly that.

However, in the early 1990s, a series of natural and man-made disasters led to unusually big claims, and the names were called upon to pay; many were ruined financially as a result. They alleged that the agents who organized the syndicates had been negligent; many of the names had entered into contracts with these managers, but by the time the actions were brought, the three-year limitation period for a breach of contract action had expired. Could they then take advantage of the longer (six-year) limitation period for tort actions? The House of Lords held that they could; the syndicate managers had assumed responsibility for the names' economic welfare, and the existence of a contract could only prevent liability in tort if such liability would contradict the terms of the contract. Lord Goff explained:

> . . . liability can, and in my opinion should, be founded squarely on the principle established in **Hedley Byrne** itself, from which it follows that an assumption of responsibility coupled with the concomitant reliance may give rise to a tortious duty of care irrespective of whether there is a contractual relationship between the parties, and in consequence, unless his contract precludes him from doing so, the plaintiff, who has available to him concurrent remedies in contract and tort, may choose that remedy which appears to him most advantageous.

Negligent misstatements often take place in a pre-contractual situation, where one party is trying to persuade the other to enter a contract. **Hedley Byrne** can apply in such situations, but in practice it has been made less important in this area by the Misrepresentation Act 1967, which imposes its own liability.

Voluntary assumption of responsibility

The voluntary assumption of responsibility is generally deemed to arise from the fact that the defendant has chosen to give advice or information (or more commonly, to allow it to be passed on to a third party), when, as Lord Reid pointed out, they also have the option to stay silent or stress that the advice should not be relied upon. This has implications in cases where the defendant has issued some kind of disclaimer (as was the case in **Hedley Byrne** itself) as this clearly suggests that they have not voluntarily assumed responsibility, nor is it reasonable for the claimant to rely on them.

However, the mere existence of a disclaimer will not necessarily prevent liability. In **Smith** *v* **Eric S Bush** (1990) (discussed below) it was stated that the existence of a disclaimer did not prevent a duty of care arising, although the disclaimer might affect liability for breach of that duty. This was further discussed in **First National Commercial Bank** *v* **Loxleys** (1996), where the court was asked to strike out a claim because the defendants argued that their disclaimer prevented a duty of care from arising. The Court of Appeal refused to strike out the action, pointing out the position in **Smith** *v* **Eric Bush**. However, it commented that in **Henderson**, stress had been placed on the assumption of responsibility as a key indicator of whether a duty of care existed, and suggested that this development might mean that it was possible for the existence of a disclaimer to mean there was no duty of care on the ground that there was no voluntary assumption of responsibility. If the existence of a disclaimer is held by the courts to mean there is no duty of care, the expansion of **Hedley Byrne** liability to cover not just advice but services, in **Henderson**, will prove to be less significant, since it could be negated by use of disclaimers.

In several cases the courts have used the assumption of responsibility concept as a means to restrict liability, by looking at who a provider of information or advice can be deemed to have assumed responsibility to. In **Hedley**, Lord Bridge talked of the claimant needing to be an individual to whom the defendant knows the information will be conveyed, or 'a member of an identifiable class', and later cases have attempted to clarify this, though not always successfully or consistently.

In **Smith** *v* **Eric S Bush**, the claimants were the purchasers of a house which had been negligently surveyed by the defendants, and was worth much less than they had paid for it. The survey had been commissioned by the building society from which the claimants had sought a mortgage, as part of its standard practice of ensuring that the property was worth at least the money that was being lent. However, such surveys were routinely relied upon by purchasers as well, and in fact purchasers actually paid the building society to have the survey done, although the surveyors' contract was always with the building society. The House of Lords held that in such situations surveyors assumed a duty of care to house purchasers; even though the surveys were not done for the purpose of advising home buyers, surveyors would be well aware that buyers were likely to rely on their valuation, and the surveyors only had the work in the first place because buyers were willing to pay their fees. An important factor was that this did not impose particularly wide liability: the extent of the surveyors' liability was limited to compensating the buyer of the house for up to the value of the house.

In **Siddell** *v* **Smith Cooper & Partners** (1999) the claimants had bought a company, B, through which they were going to buy and hold shares in other companies. The defendants were appointed as auditors to the company, and they also contracted with the claimants personally to provide them with financial advice and accountancy services. They advised them on how best to borrow the money to buy the company, and as a result of their advice, the claimants eventually put up their homes as security for the borrowing. After four years, B company was found to have serious financial irregularities which the accountants had never spotted or reported, and it became insolvent with debts of over £1 million. The claimants lost their houses, and sued the defendants for negligence in preparing the accounts. The defendants argued that as auditors, they only owed a duty to the company which employed them, B. However, the Court of Appeal held that although this was generally true of auditors, in this case, the fact that this firm was also employed as accountants to the claimants, and knew of their relationship to B, made it at least arguable that they owed a duty to them.

More complex problems arise when the claimant is not known to the defendant, but claims to be, as Lord Bridge put it 'a member of an identifiable class'. In **Goodwill** *v* **British Pregnancy Advisory Service** (1996), an attempt was made to use **Hedley Byrne** in a new factual context. The claimant, Ms Goodwill, had become pregnant by her boyfriend. Three years before their relationship began, he had undergone a vasectomy performed by the defendants. They had advised him after the operation that it had been successful and he would not need to use contraception in the future. He told Ms Goodwill this when they began their relationship, and she stopped using any contraception. In fact the vasectomy had reversed itself, and she became pregnant. She sued the defendants for negligence, claiming the cost of bringing up her daughter.

The Court of Appeal held that in order to claim successfully for pure economic loss arising from reliance on advice provided by the defendants, a claimant had to show that the defendants knew (either because they were told or because it was an obvious inference), that the advice they supplied was likely to be acted on by the claimant (either as a specific individual or one of an ascertainable group), without independent inquiry, for a particular purpose which the defendants knew about at the time they gave the advice, and that the claimant had acted on the advice to his or her disadvantage.

In the case before them, the Court of Appeal held that at the time when the advice was given, the claimant was not known to the defendants, and was simply one of a potentially large class of women who might at some stage have a sexual relationship with the patient before them. They could not be expected to foresee that years later, their advice to their patient might be communicated to and relied on by her for the purpose of deciding whether to use contraception; therefore the relationship between the defendants and Ms Goodwill was not sufficiently proximate to give rise to a duty of care. The court pointed out however that the situation might be different where a man and his partner were advised at the same time, or possibly even where their relationship was known to those giving the advice.

In common-sense terms, the distinction is a difficult one. Clearly, as Ms Goodwill pointed out, in this day and age it was not unlikely that a man of her boyfriend's age would have a sexual relationship with future partners, and while the class of possible future partners might be large, the number who would end up pregnant was not, given that once pregnancy had occurred, it would be known that the vasectomy had reversed itself. Furthermore, the purpose to which such partners would put the advice was exactly the same as the purpose for which the patient would use it: as a statement that if they had sexual relations, no pregnancy would result. What we see in cases like this one is the courts struggling to balance the need to compensate loss where justice demands it and no other means of redress is available, and yet avoid opening those much-mentioned floodgates and opening defendants to unreasonable liability. The theme is continued in the 'wills cases' discussed at p. 35 below.

Reliance by the claimant

Reliance under **Hedley Byrne** requires that the claimant depended on the defendant using the particular skill or experience required for the task which the defendant had undertaken; it is not merely general reliance on the defendant exercising care. Furthermore, a claimant cannot be said to rely on a defendant's advice unless they know that the defendant gave that advice. In **Abbott** *v* **Strong** (1998), the claimants were shareholders of a company which had been placed in receivership. Before this happened, the shareholders had been encouraged to buy shares by a circular sent to them by the company's directors, which it was later discovered contained inaccurate profit forecasts. The defendants were accountants who had helped prepare the profit forecasts, though the shareholders had not known this at the time they read the circulars. The claimants sued the accountants, but the court held that the shareholders could not be said to have relied on the statements made by the accountants, since as far as the shareholders were concerned at the time, the statements had come solely from the directors of the company.

The claimant must prove not only that they relied on the defendant, but that it was reasonable to do so, and the courts have held that this will not be the case where the claimant relies on information or advice for one purpose, when it was given for a different purpose. In **Caparo Industries plc** *v* **Dickman** (1990), Caparo made a takeover bid for a company, Fidelity, in which it already owned a large number of shares. When the takeover was complete, Caparo discovered that Fidelity was almost worthless. In assessing the likely value of Fidelity, Caparo claimed to have relied on the figures prepared for Fidelity's annual audit, which was required by the Companies Act. It showed a healthy profit which did not in fact exist. Caparo sued the auditors, but the House of Lords held that they could not succeed. The accounts were produced for the purpose laid down in the Companies Act 1985, that of ensuring that existing shareholders can exercise responsible control over the company. They were not designed to guide potential new investors, and therefore they could also not be expected to guide existing investors seeking to increase their share, like Caparo.

Lord Bridge held that there was no special relationship between Caparo as potential investors and the auditors. He drew a distinction between situations where 'the defendant giving advice or information was fully aware of the nature of the transaction which the claimant had in contemplation' and those in which 'a statement is put into more or less general circulation and may foreseeably be relied upon by strangers to the maker of the statement, for any one of a variety of purposes which the maker of the statement has no specific reason to contemplate'.

This approach was followed in **Reeman** *v* **Department of Transport** (1997). Mr Reeman was the owner of a fishing boat that required an annual certificate of seaworthiness from the Department of Transport (DoT), without which it could not be used at sea. The boat was covered by such a certificate when Mr Reeman bought it, but it was later discovered that the surveyor who inspected it for the DoT had been negligent; the certificate should not have been issued and would not be renewed, making the boat practically worthless.

Mr Reeman sued for his economic loss, but the Court of Appeal held that, following **Caparo**, the provision of information for a particular purpose could not be taken as an assumption of responsibility for its use for a different purpose. The purpose of issuing the certificate was to promote safety, not to establish a boat's commercial value. In addition, the class of person likely to rely on the statement had to be capable of ascertainment at the time the statement was made, and not merely capable of description; when the certificate was issued, there was no reason to identify Mr Reeman as someone who was likely to rely on it.

In **Machin** *v* **Adams** (1998), Mr Machin had agreed to buy a property from Mrs Adams and her husband, a builder. As part of the deal between them, the Adams were to convert the property into a nursing home and provide Mr Machin with a certificate from an architect, stating that the work had been done properly. An architect, B, was engaged to inspect the work and provide a certificate, but he did not see the contract between the Adams and Mr Machin, though he was later made aware that the certificate he was to supply would be shown to someone else. B supplied the certificate, which was given to Mr Machin. The work was later discovered to be defective, and Mr Machin attempted to sue B, as well as suing the Adams. However the Court of Appeal held that B had no duty of care towards Mr Machin, since B was ignorant of the purpose for which his advice was required and could not therefore have assumed responsibility to Mr Machin.

However, the courts are willing to look very closely at the circumstances in which advice was given, and have made it clear that the fact that a certain type of information is generally given for one particular purpose does not mean that it cannot simultaneously be given for another purpose, which the claimant reasonably relies on.

In **Andrew** *v* **Kounnis Freeman** (1999), the defendant was a company of accountants which had acted as auditors for an airline. The airline had been in financial difficulties, and the Civil Aviation Authority (CAA) had refused to renew its licence unless the accountants could supply audited accounts and information that the airline's financial position was satisfactory, by a specified date. The auditors supplied the accounts on the day before the deadline, with a letter confirming the company's financial position. Shortly afterwards, the airline went into liquidation, and the Air Travel Trust (ATT), which acts on behalf of the CAA, had to pay out over £5 million to bring stranded passengers home and fulfil the airline's bookings. As we know from previous cases, audited accounts are drawn up for the benefit of a company's shareholders, rather than any third parties who read them, but the claimant, a trustee of the ATT, nevertheless sued the accountants for negligence. He alleged that in renewing the airline's licence (and therefore laying itself open to having to pay out to the passengers), the CAA had relied on the accountants' statements about the airline, and that the letter supplied with the accounts showed that the accountants realised this and were therefore assuming a responsibility to the CAA when they supplied the accounts.

The accountants' argued that this awareness was not enough to create a duty, and the case was initially struck out. The claimant appealed, and the Court of Appeal held that a reasonable auditor, knowing the deadline date, would be aware that the CAA would have no opportunity further to investigate information supplied so close to the deadline, and that therefore the accounts would be relied upon in deciding whether to renew the licence. Therefore it was a reasonable inference that the accountants were supplying the accounts not just for the airline and its shareholders, but also for the CAA in making their decision on the licence, and the accountants could be said to have assumed a duty towards the CAA.

A close look at the facts surrounding the case led to a similar result in **Law Society** *v* **KPMG Peat Marwick** (1999). Here the defendants were accountants to a firm of solicitors, and were asked by them to prepare the annual accounts which were required by the Law Society. The accountants failed to uncover the fact that a senior partner in the firm was defrauding hundreds of clients. When the frauds eventually came to light, over 300 clients claimed compensation from a fund set up for this purpose by the Law Society, and the Law Society sued the accountants, claiming that the accounts had been prepared negligently. The accountants argued that their duty was only owed to the solicitors' firm; the Law Society held that the accountants owed a duty to them, by virtue of the Law Society's reliance on the information given in the accounts. The Court of Appeal analysed the situation using the three-step **Caparo** test. They held that if accountants' reports failed to highlight improprieties in the way a firm dealt with clients' money, it was clearly foreseeable that loss to the fund would result. There was sufficient proximity between the reporting accountant and the Law Society, and it was fair and reasonable to impose a duty. On this last point, the court made use of similar reasoning to that in **Smith** *v* **Eric S Bush** (see p. 30), pointing out that the imposition of a duty did not expose the accountants to unrestricted liability; the amount of compensation that could be claimed was restricted to the amount of clients' money that had been lost in the frauds, and the time within which it could be claimed was also limited, given that reports were delivered annually, so negligence in any one year could be uncovered by a non-negligent report the following year.

The case of **Bristol and West Building Society** *v* **Mothew** (1996) stresses that the claimant must be able to establish a causal link between the reliance and their loss. Here, Mothew was a solicitor who had acted for both the building society and a borrower in the purchase of a property. Mothew gave information to the building society concerning the borrower, and negligently failed to disclose that the buyer had taken out a second mortgage on the property. Ultimately the buyer defaulted on repayments and the property was repossessed and sold, at a loss to the building society, which tried to reclaim the loss from Mothew.

Mothew claimed that if the building society had been told of the second charge, they would still have gone ahead with the transaction and made the same loss, so that there was in fact no reliance on the negligent advice. The Court of Appeal held that the building society had to show a causal link between the negligent advice and the loss, in this case by showing what loss had been caused by the existence of the second charge. They did not, however, have to prove that they would not have gone ahead with the transaction had they known about the charge.

Recovery without reliance – the 'wills cases'

A group of cases concerning wills have introduced the possibility of recovering damages in negligence where it is difficult to see any real concept of reliance. In **Ross** *v* **Caunters** (1980), a solicitor had been negligent in preparing a client's will, with the result that it was in breach of probate law and the intended beneficiary was unable to receive her inheritance. She successfully sued the solicitor for the value of her loss.

Although the loss was purely economic, and caused by an act rather than a statement, the case was not considered especially significant at the time, since it took place in the period after **Anns** *v* **Merton London Borough** (1978), when the wider approach to the issue of a duty of care was in place, and before **Murphy** *v* **Brentwood District Council** (1990) tightened up the requirements again. However, it was followed in the post-**Murphy** case of **White** *v* **Jones** (1995). Here, two daughters had had a quarrel with their father, and he cut them out of his will. The family was later reconciled, and the father instructed his solicitors to renew the £9,000 legacies to his daughters. A month later, he discovered that the solicitors had not yet done this, and reminded them of his instructions. Some time later, the father died, and it was found that the will had still not been changed, so the daughters could not receive their expected inheritance. They sued the solicitors, and the House of Lords allowed the claim, even though the loss was purely economic and the result of negligent work rather than a negligent misstatement.

White *v* **Jones** proved somewhat difficult to explain on **Hedley Byrne** principles. Wills are prepared in order to put into practice the wishes of the person making the will (the testator), and as Lord Goff stated in **White** *v* **Jones**, in many cases, beneficiaries will not even be aware that they stand to gain, so it is hard to see how they can be said to rely on the solicitor's skill as required under **Hedley Byrne**. Clearly the solicitors in both cases had assumed the responsibility for preparing the wills correctly for the testators, but this was a contractual relationship. Could they also be said to have accepted a responsibility towards the beneficiaries? The House of Lords admitted that it was difficult to see how this could be argued, but even so, they were prepared to allow a remedy.

What appears to have swayed them was the practical justice of the claimant's case: the solicitor had been negligent, yet the only party who would normally have a valid claim (the testator and his estate) had suffered no loss, and the party who had suffered loss had no claim. As Lord Goff pointed out, the result was 'a lacuna in the law which needs to be filled'. The exact *ratio* of the case is difficult to discover, as the three judges were divided on how the assumption of responsibility problem was to be got over. Lords Browne-Wilkinson and Nolan argued that in taking on the job of preparing the will, the solicitor had voluntarily accepted responsibility for doing it properly, and it was for the law to decide the scope of that responsibility and in particular whether it included a duty to the claimants. Both held that it did. Lord Goff held that the solicitor had in fact assumed responsibility only to the testator, but that the law could and should deem that responsibility to extend to the intended beneficiaries.

However, even if the decision in **White** *v* **Jones** did no more than use practical justice to fill a loophole in the law, the case of **Carr-Glynn** *v* **Frearsons** (1998), has extended it beyond this approach. Here a testatrix had made a will leaving the claimant her share in a property. The defendants, the solicitors who had drawn up the will, had advised the testatrix that there was a problem with the ownership of the property which could result in her share automatically passing to the other part-owners on her death, so that any bequest of it would be ineffective. They told her what to do to avoid the problem, but she died before taking the advice. The claimant therefore received nothing under the will, and the estate also suffered a loss since the share in the property passed to the co-owners.

The judge of first instance found that the solicitors were not negligent, since their advice had been correct, and the testatrix had simply failed to take it, but he went on to discuss whether a duty of care would in any case have existed. In this situation, he decided, it would not. The case was different from **Ross** *v* **Caunters** and **White** *v* **Jones**, where the estate had suffered no loss and the party who had suffered loss had no claim; here, allowing a duty of care to the disappointed beneficiaries might give rise to two claims for the same loss, one from the intended beneficiaries and one from the estate. The court expressly stated that claims under the principle in **Ross** *v* **Caunters** should be limited to situations where the estate had suffered no loss, and the only person who had suffered loss had no claim. This is of course another example of the concern about creating indeterminate liability; in the circumstances envisaged by the court, liability would be restricted to manageable levels, given that the solicitor will always know of the intended beneficiaries and the level of loss they might sustain.

However, the claimant successfully appealed. The Court of Appeal held that although the estate had a claim, any damages it recovered by bringing that claim would not go to the claimant, who was therefore still left without a remedy unless the principle of **White** *v* **Jones** was extended to cover her. The Court stated such an extension was reasonable; there was a duty of care, and it required that the solicitor should have taken action herself to ensure that the will would take effect as expected.

However, some limits to the extension of the wills cases have been laid down. In **Clarke** *v* **Bruce, Lance & Co** (1988), it was made clear that the duty of care to intended beneficiaries arises from the responsibility undertaken to the testator, and so cannot apply when the interests of the testator and the beneficiary differ. Here a solicitor had failed to advise his client that transactions he was planning to make would reduce the value of a legacy left in his will to the claimant. As a result, the claimant suffered some loss, but the case was held to fall outside the **Ross** *v* **Caunters** principle; the interests of the claimant and the testator were not identical, and the solicitor's primary duty was to the interests of his client.

The limitations of **Ross** *v* **Caunters** were also stressed in **Hemmens** *v* **Wilson Browne** (1995), where a solicitor had been negligent in carrying out a client's wish to make an *inter vivos* gift (something given while the giver is still alive, rather than left in a will) to the claimant. In this case, the court pointed out that although the claimant's loss was foreseeable, and there was as much of a relationship between the solicitor and the claimant as in the wills cases, the claimant had not been left without a remedy as the claimants in those cases had; the donor of the gift was still alive and could instruct another solicitor to make the transaction, and sue the previous one for breach of contract. Similarly, in **Walker** *v* **Geo H Medlicott & Son** (1998), a claimant sued solicitors who had been instructed to include a gift to him in a client's will, but who had negligently failed to do so. However, the circumstances were such that he could take advantage of s. 20 of the Administration of Justice Act 1982 to have the will rectified to show the testator's true intention, and so the Court of Appeal held that he could reasonably be expected to mitigate his loss by doing so; he could not bring negligence proceedings against the solicitor while that alternative remedy existed.

The case of **Horsfall** *v* **Haywards** (1999), however, makes it clear that it is not necessary to bring a case for rectification where there is very little chance of such an action succeeding, or where success in getting a will rectified will not lead to the claimants gaining compensation for what they claim they should have received under the will.

Further restrictions have been applied in **Worby** *v* **Rosser** (1999). Here the claimants were the wife and children of a Mr Worby. He had made a will in 1983, leaving most of his estate to them. Some time later, he fell under the influence of his accountant, a Mr Tuli, and made a new will which left a lot of money to Mr Tuli and reduced the amount left to the Worby family under the previous will. After Mr Worby died, the family were able to take action to prevent the second will being acted upon, on the ground that, essentially, Mr Worby had not really known what he was doing (this is known as lacking testamentary capacity and is part of the law on wills). However, the action proved quite expensive, and although the court in that action had awarded them costs, the Worbys were unable to actually get those costs paid by Mr Tuli. They therefore decided to sue Mr Rosser, the solicitor who had drawn up the second will, arguing that he owed them a duty of care to ensure that Mr Worby had testamentary capacity when he made the will, and that his breach of that duty had led to them incurring the legal costs.

The Court of Appeal rejected this argument. The aim of the courts in **White** *v* **Jones** had been to achieve practical justice for a category of beneficiaries who had no other remedy available to them. This was not the case for the claimants in Worby; they could sue the estate for their costs, and the estate could in turn sue the solicitor if it could be proved that he was negligent.

Quite how far the principles laid down in **White** *v* **Jones** extend are still unclear. We do know that they apply to will-making services offered by practitioners other than solicitors (**Esterhuizen** *v* **Allied Dunbar Assurance Plc** (1998)), but what about cases involving agreements other than wills? In **Hemmens**, the attempt to use the principle in a non-wills case failed, but this was because the claimant could have had access to another remedy. In **Woodward** *v* **Wolferstans** (1997), it appeared that the **White** *v* **Jones** principle could apply to instructions given to a solicitor with regard to buying a house. The defendants were solicitors to the claimant's father, and the court held that they owed her the same duty of care that they owed to her father. However, the claim failed on the facts. We know from **Henderson** that the original **Hedley Byrne** principle can cover not just negligent misstatements, but also other negligently provided services, so it may that the line of cases from **Ross** *v* **Caunters** also spread this far. This would mean that the extended assumption of responsibility described above may apply in other three-party situations where a similar lacuna in the law may be found.

Problems with the law on economic loss

Too many restrictions – or too few?
The case of **Spartan Steel** *v* **Martin** (1972) illustrates that the distinction between pure economic loss and other kinds of loss can be a very fine one – and one that in common-sense terms is difficult to justify. The defendants' negligence caused all three of the types of loss that resulted from the power cut, and all three types of loss were easily foreseeable, so why should they have been liable to compensate two sorts of loss but not the third? To the non-legal eye, distinguishing between them seems completely illogical – as indeed it must to a claimant who is left with a loss caused by someone else, and has no redress unless they have a contract. In many cases this can be seen as allowing a defendant to get away with seriously careless behaviour, regardless of the loss caused to others.

On the other hand, it can be argued that rather than not allowing sufficient redress for pure economic loss, the tort system in fact allows too much. In most cases of pure economic loss, what we are really talking about is not loss, but failure to make a gain. This is obvious in the wills cases, for example, but also applies to cases such as **Smith** *v* **Eric Bush** (1990), where it can be argued that in buying the house the claimants were simply entering into a market transaction, and these always run the risk of creating loss as well as the possibility of making a gain. They did not have money taken from them, they simply bought a house which was worth less than they thought.

Traditionally, the role of tort law is to compensate those who have actually suffered loss; those who wish to protect their expectation of gain should do so through contract, and those who have given nothing in return for a service should not be compensated when that service lets them down financially. One answer to the latter view is that in most of the cases where claimants have not given anything in return for provision of advice or services, the defendants nevertheless gain a commercial benefit from the situation. This is most clear in **Smith** *v* **Eric Bush**, where the surveyors only had the work in the first place because house buyers were willing to pay for it, albeit indirectly, but it can also be found in less obvious situations. In **Hedley Byrne**, Lord Goff pointed out that in establishing whether the necessary special relationship existed in a particular case:

> It may often be a material factor to consider whether the adviser is acting purely out of good nature or whether he is getting his reward in some indirect form. The service that a bank performs in giving a reference is not done simply out of a desire to assist commerce. It

would discourage the customers of the bank if their deals fell through because the bank had refused to testify to their credit when it was good.

Contract and tort

The issue of the relationship between contract and tort causes particular problems, and in particular, the assertion in **Henderson** that a claimant who has a contractual remedy as well as a possible action in negligence should be able to choose between them. As well as rendering the limitation period for contractual actions essentially meaningless in these situations, it allows the claimant to pick and choose in other ways. For example, in contract a loss will only be compensated if there was a very high degree of probability that it would result from the defendant's breach of contract; is it necessarily right that a claimant who cannot satisfy that requirement should get another bite of the cherry in tort, where liability can be allowed for even extremely unlikely losses if they were reasonably foreseeable?

Lack of clarity

Perhaps the most significant practical problem in this area is that in their anxiety to avoid opening the floodgates to massive liability, yet allow redress where justice seems to demand it, the courts have resorted to over-complex and not entirely logical arguments. The wills cases are an obvious example of this, and the result is uncertainty about their scope, and the possibility of further fragmentation in the way the law treats economic loss.

The same dilemma lies behind the curious situation that, as we said earlier, architects or surveyors who give negligent advice that leads to a defective building can be sued for the resulting economic loss, yet builders who construct defective buildings cannot. In practice, however, this particular situation has been addressed by introduction of legislation: the Defective Premises Act 1972 states that builders and others who take on work 'for or in connection with the provision of a dwelling-house' may be held liable to the owners of those dwellings if they fail to carry out the work properly, and the house becomes unfit for habitation. This contrasts with other Commonwealth jurisdictions, where the common law has allowed recovery in tort for defective buildings, most recently confirmed in New Zealand in **Invercargill City Council** *v* **Hamlin** (1996).

▶ Psychiatric injury or 'nervous shock'

It is well established that physical injury can give rise to a claim in tort, but what about psychiatric damage? The concept of a duty has been used to limit recovery for psychiatric damage (often called nervous shock), in the same way as it has been used to limit claims for economic loss. In the past, where there was no physical harm the courts were slow to accept psychiatric injury alone as a head of damage in a claim for negligence. While it is now recognized as a head of damage, there are severe restrictions on when it can be claimed.

What is 'nervous shock'?

Psychiatric injury has traditionally been known by the courts as 'nervous shock', a label which adds to the confusion surrounding this area of the law by being completely misleading. The term implies that claimants can seek damages because they are shocked at the result of a defendant's negligence, or perhaps upset, frightened, worried or grief-stricken. This is not the case. In order to claim for so-called 'nervous shock', a claimant must prove that they have suffered from a genuine illness or injury. In some cases, the injury or illness may actually be a physical one, brought on by a mental shock: cases include a woman who had a miscarriage as a result of witnessing a terrible road accident (**Bourhill** *v* **Young** (1943), though the woman's claim failed on other grounds), and a man who was involved in an accident but not physically injured in it, who later suffered a recurrence and worsening of the disease myalgic encephalomyelitis (ME), also known as chronic fatigue syndrome, as a result of the shock (**Page** *v* **Smith** (1995)).

If the shock has not caused a physical injury or illness, the claimant must prove that it has caused what Lord Bridge in **McLoughlin** *v* **O'Brian** (1983) (see below) described as 'a positive psychiatric illness'. Examples include clinical depression, personality changes, and post-traumatic stress disorder, an illness in which a shocking event causes symptoms including difficulty sleeping, tension, horrifying flashbacks and severe depression. It is important to be clear that this category does not include people who are simply upset by a shock, regardless of how badly; they must have a recognised psychiatric illness, and medical evidence will be needed to prove this. Consequently we will use the term psychiatric injury from now on, though 'nervous shock' is referred to in many judgments.

Claimants who can prove such injury must then establish that they are owed a duty of care by the defendant, with regard to psychiatric injury. This will depend on their relationship to the event which caused the shock, and case law has developed different sets of rules, covering different categories of claimant. The number of categories has varied at different stages of the law's development, but since the most recent House of Lords case, **White and Others** *v* **Chief Constable of South Yorkshire** (1998), there are now three:

- those who are physically injured in the event which the defendant has caused, as well as psychiatrically injured as a result of it;

- those who were put in danger of physical harm, but actually suffer only psychiatric injury; these are termed primary victims;
- those who are not put in danger of physical injury to themselves, but suffer psychiatric harm as a result of witnessing such injury to others; these are called secondary victims. A duty of care to secondary victims will arise only if they can satisfy very restrictive requirements.

Claimants who are physically injured

An accident victim who suffers physical injury due to the negligence of another can recover damages not just for the physical injuries but also for any psychiatric injury as well. The ordinary rules of negligence apply to such cases.

Primary victims

As we have said, this category comprises those who are put at risk of physical injury to themselves, but who actually suffer only psychiatric injury as a result of the dangerous event. **White and Others** (1998) confirms that if a person negligently exposes another to a risk of injury they will be liable for any psychological damage that this may cause the other person, even if the threatened injury does not in fact happen. This was established by the leading case of **Dulieu *v* White & Sons** (1901). The claimant was serving in a public house when one of the defendant's employees negligently drove his van and horses into the premises. The claimant feared for her safety, and though she was not actually struck she was badly frightened and suffered a miscarriage as a result. The defendant was found liable even though there was no physical impact, as he could have foreseen that the claimant would have suffered such shock.

The individual characteristics of a claimant in this category can be taken into account when deciding whether their injuries were foreseeable. In **Page *v* Smith** (1995) the claimant was involved in an accident but he was not physically injured. He had previously suffered from ME for about 20 years; it had ceased at the time of the accident but the accident triggered its re-emergence. He claimed damages on the basis that the accident had made him suffer nervous shock, which had then led to the resurgence of his ME. The claim was allowed by the House of Lords.

Although a claimant can claim for psychiatric injury caused by fears for their own safety even though no physical injury actually occurred, there must be some basis for the fears. In **McFarlane *v* Wilkinson** (1997), the Court of Appeal held that the fear must be reasonable, given the nature of the risk and the claimant's situation. The case arose out of the terrible events on the *Piper Alpha* oil rig, when the rig caught fire and many people died as a result of the explosion. The claimant had been in a support boat about 50 yards from the rig, and witnessed the disaster. His claim for the psychiatric injury suffered as a result was rejected by the Court of Appeal, on the ground that the boat he was on was clearly never in any danger, and so his fear for his safety was unreasonable (for reasons which will be obvious when we look at the witness cases below, merely seeing the disaster would not have been sufficient ground for this claimant's claim). What is unclear is whether a claimant can be considered as a primary victim if they were not actually in physical danger, but had reasonable grounds for thinking that they might be. The two leading judgments in **White** differ slightly in this area: Lord Steyn says the claimant must have 'objectively exposed himself to danger or *reasonably believed* that he was doing so' (our italics); on the other hand Lord Hoffmann refers only to primary victims being 'within the range of foreseeable physical injury'. Of course, in the majority of cases the reasonable belief that the claimant was in danger will arise from the fact that they actually were, but in the throes of an emergency situation, it is not difficult to imagine making out a case for believing oneself to be in some danger when in fact there is no physical risk at all, and it is a pity that their Lordships did not make themselves clearer on this crucial point.

In **CJD Group B Claimants** *v* **The Medical Research Council** (1998), it was suggested that there might be a group which could not be considered primary victims in the usual sense, but who nevertheless should be treated in the same way. The claimants in the case had all had growth problems as children, and they had been treated with injections of growth hormone which, it was later discovered, may have been contaminated with the virus which causes Creutzfeld Jakob Disease (CJD), a fatal brain condition (this is the brain condition recognized as the human form of BSE or mad cow disease, but the events in this case have no link with the controversy over BSE-infected beef). It was established that those who had received the contaminated injections were at risk of developing CJD, but it was not possible to discover which batches had been contaminated, nor to test the recipients to discover whether a particular individual was harbouring the virus. As a result, the claimants were having to live with the fear of knowing that they might develop the disease, and some of them suffered psychiatric injury as a result of this. It was established that the defendants had been negligent in allowing the injections to continue after the risk of contamination was suspected, and the claimants claimed that they were owed a duty as primary victims with regard to psychiatric injury, as the injections they were negligently given made them more than mere bystanders, and could be compared to the car accident in which the claimant in **Page** *v* **Smith** was involved. Morland J disagreed with this analysis, holding that they were not primary victims in the normal sense, because the psychiatric injury was not actually triggered by the physical act of the injections, but by the knowledge, which came later, that they might be at risk of developing CJD. Even so, he allowed their claim, on the basis that there was a relationship of proximity between the parties, that the psychiatric injuries were reasonably foreseeable, and there was no public policy reason to exclude them from compensation.

There was no appeal from the first instance decision, and the claims proceeded, but that may not be the last we hear of the principle laid down. As the defendants pointed out, there are other situations in which people might suffer psychiatric injury as a result of knowing they run a particular risk of disease, such as those exposed to radiation or asbestos, and where such exposure is caused by another's negligence, the CJD case may provide grounds for a claim. The case was decided before **White**, but if Lord Steyn's slightly wider definition of a primary victim is the correct one, the circumstances can be easily brought within it, since the claimants' psychiatric injury was caused by the fact that they reasonably believed themselves to be exposed to physical danger.

Secondary victims

White and Others (1998) establishes that sufferers of psychiatric injury who are not either physically injured or in danger of being physically injured are to be considered secondary victims. Among the important cases which have fallen within this group are claims made by people who have suffered psychiatric injury as a result of witnessing the death or injury of friends, relatives or work colleagues; those whose psychiatric injury has been caused by them unwittingly bringing about death or injury, where the ultimate cause was someone else's negligence; and those who have suffered psychiatric injury as a result of acting as rescuers, both those who have voluntarily given assistance to others in danger, and those who have done so as a result of their jobs, such as police officers.

Until **White**, each of these groups had been subject to different treatment, but **White** establishes that they are all to be subject to the same rules, namely those developed in two key cases, **McLoughlin** *v* **O'Brian** (1982) and **Alcock** *v* **Chief Constable of Yorkshire** (1992). These established that secondary victims could only claim for psychiatric injury in very limited circumstances, and **White** confirms these limitations. In **McLoughlin** *v* **O'Brian**, the claimant's husband and children were involved in a serious car accident, caused by the defendant's negligence. One of her daughters was killed and her husband and two other children badly injured. The claimant was not with her family when the accident happened, but was told about it immediately afterwards, and rushed to the hospital. There she saw the surviving members of her family covered in dirt and oil, and her badly injured son screaming in fear and pain. She suffered nervous shock as a result, including clinical depression and personality changes.

The House of Lords allowed her claim, even though up until then, only witnesses who were actually present at the scene of a shocking incident had been allowed to recover for psychiatric injury. The decision itself was rather confused, in that Lord Bridge suggested that the sole criterion was still reasonable foresight, and the claimant could recover because her psychiatric injury was reasonably foreseeable, but Lords Wilberforce and Edmund-Davies favoured a different approach. They suggested that while psychiatric injury did have to be reasonably foreseeable, this in itself was not enough to create a duty of care towards secondary victims. Unlike other types of claimant, secondary victims would have to satisfy a series of other requirements, concerning their relationship to the primary victims of the shocking incident and their position with regard to that incident. This second approach is the one which has since found favour with the courts, and it was explained in detail in **Alcock** *v* **Chief Constable of South Yorkshire** (1992).

Alcock arose from the Hillsborough football stadium disaster in 1989. The events which gave rise to the case (and to **White and Others** *v* **Chief Constable of South Yorkshire** (1998)) took place during the 1989 FA Cup Semi-Final match between Liverpool and Nottingham Forest. All tickets for the match had been sold, and it was being shown on live television. However, play had to be stopped after six minutes because so many spectators had been allowed onto the terraces that some were being crushed against the high fences that divided the terraces from the pitch. Ninety-five people died in the tragedy that followed, and another 400 needed hospital treatment for their injuries.

The South Yorkshire police were responsible for policing the ground, and it was widely thought that the incident was caused by a negligent decision on their part, which allowed too many people into the ground. Claims for physical injury and death were settled by the police, as were others for psychiatric injury which clearly fell within the accepted categories of those who could make a claim for this type of damage. This left two further groups who claimed psychiatric injury as a result of the tragedy: relatives and friends of those injured or killed, whose claims were examined in **Alcock**; and police officers on duty for the events of that day, who were represented in **White** (the fate of their claim is discussed later).

Alcock was a test case in that the specific claimants were chosen because between them they represented a range of relationships to the dead and injured, and positions in relation to the incident at the ground, which were held by around 150 other people who claimed to have suffered psychiatric injury as a result of the tragedy. They included parents, grandparents, brothers, brothers-in-law, fiancés and friends of the dead and injured, and had either been at the stadium when the disaster occurred and witnessed it at first hand, seen it live on the television, gone to the stadium to look for someone they knew, been told the news by a third party, or had to identify someone in the temporary mortuary at the ground.

...nts argued that the test for whether they were owed a duty
...simply whether their psychological injuries were reasonably
...e, as Lord Bridge had suggested in **McLoughlin**. The House of
...ook a different view, pointing out that while it was clear that
...is and injuries commonly caused suffering that went well beyond the
...mediate victims, it was generally the policy of the common law not to
compensate third parties, and although some exceptions could be made,
they should be subject to much stricter requirements than those which
applied to primary victims.

A secondary victim must first prove that psychiatric injury to secondary
victims was a reasonably foreseeable consequence of the defendant's negligence. **White** confirms earlier cases in stating that this will only be
established where a bystander of reasonable fortitude would be likely to
suffer psychiatric injury; if the claimant only suffers psychiatric injury
because they are unusually susceptible to shock, reasonable foreseeability
is not proved. However, it was pointed out that this rule should not be
confused with the 'eggshell skull' situation seen, for example, in **Page** v
Smith, where as a result of psychiatric injury the damage is more serious
than might be expected. So long as a bystander of normal fortitude would
be likely to suffer psychiatric injury, it does not matter that that psychiatric
injury is made more serious by some characteristic personal to the claimant; but if the psychiatric injury would not have occurred at all to someone
without the claimant's particular susceptibility, there is no claim.

Once reasonable foreseeability is established, there are three further
tests which the courts must consider:

- the nature of the psychiatric injury;
- the class of person into which the claimant falls, with regard to the
  primary victim(s);
- the claimant's proximity to the shocking incident.

The restrictions which these tests place on claims can be seen in the fact
that every single claimant in **Alcock** failed on at least one of them. We will
now look at each in turn.

The nature of the psychiatric injury

Alcock confirms that a claimant must prove that their psychiatric damage
amounts to a recognised psychiatric illness. Furthermore, the psychological damage must have been caused by the claimant suffering a sudden
and unexpected shock. This excludes cases in which people suffer psychiatric illness as a result of the grief of bereavement, or the stress and
demands of having to look after a disabled relative injured by the negligence of another. As Lord Ackner said in **Alcock**, 'psychiatric illnesses
caused in other ways, such as by the experience of having to cope with
the deprivation consequent upon the death of a loved one, attract no
damages'. In **Sion** v **Hampstead Health Authority** (1994), the claimant

had developed a stress-related psychiatric illness as a result of watching his son slowly die in intensive care as a result of negligent medical treatment. It was held that as the father's psychiatric illness had not been caused by a sudden shock, he could not recover damages for it.

Lord Keith in **Alcock** thought that this element of shock would normally be lacking where the person watched a disaster on the television.

> The viewing of these scenes cannot be equated with the viewer being within 'sight or hearing of the event in question' to use the words of Lord Wilberforce [in **McLoughlin** *v* **O'Brian**], nor can the scenes reasonably be regarded as giving rise to shock, in the sense of a sudden assault on the nervous system. They were capable of giving rise to anxiety for the safety of relatives known or believed to be present in the area affected by the crush, and undoubtedly did so, but that is very different from seeing the fate of the relative or his condition shortly after the event.

The courts have held that shock might be the result, not just of injury or death to a loved one but also of damage to property. In **Attia** *v* **British Gas** (1988), British Gas were installing central heating into the claimant's house. She had spent many years decorating and improving her home and she was very attached to it. When she returned home in the afternoon she found her house on fire. It took the fire brigade four hours to get the blaze under control, by which time her house was seriously damaged. The fire was caused by the negligence of the defendants' employees. British Gas accepted their liability for the damage to the house but the claimant also sought damages for the nervous shock she had suffered as a result. The Court of Appeal accepted that she could make a claim for nervous shock resulting from the incident.

In many cases, causation will be difficult to prove, since in addition to the required shock, claimants will have experienced the grief of bereavement, which could equally well have caused their psychiatric injury. In **Vernon** *v* **Bosley (No 1)** (1996), it was made clear that so long as a sudden shock is at least partly responsible for the claimant's psychiatric injury, the fact that grief has also played a part in causing it will not prevent a claim. In that case, the claimant had witnessed his children drowning in a car that was negligently driven by their nanny. The Court of Appeal accepted that his psychiatric illness might have been partly caused by his grief at losing his children, but since the shock of witnessing the accident had also played a part, it was not necessary to make minute inquiries into how much of his illness was attributable to each cause, if indeed it was even possible to find out.

The class of person

Alcock makes it clear that relatives are the people most likely to succeed in an action for psychological damage as a secondary victim. But there is no set list of relationships; whether or not a claim succeeds will depend on the facts of each particular case. In **McLoughlin** *v* **O'Brian** Lord Wilberforce said:

> As regards the class of persons, the possible range is between the closest of family ties – of parent and child, or husband and wife – and the ordinary bystander. Existing law recognizes the claims of the first; it denies that of the second, either on the basis that such persons must be assumed to be possessed of fortitude sufficient to enable them to endure the calamities of modern life, or that defendants cannot be expected to compensate the world at large . . . other cases involving less close relationship must be very carefully scrutinized. I cannot say that they should never be admitted. The closer the tie (not merely in relationship, but in care) the greater the claim for consideration. The claim, in any case, has to be judged in the light of the other factors, such as proximity to the scene in time and place, and the nature of the accident.

On the same subject, Lord Keith said in **Alcock**:

> As regards the class of persons to whom a duty may be owed . . . I think it sufficient that reasonable foreseeability should be the guide. I would not seek to limit the class by reference to particular relationships such as husband and wife or parent and child.

He said that friends and engaged couples could potentially be included, for, 'It is common knowledge that such ties exist, and reasonably foreseeable that those bound by them may in certain circumstances be at real risk of psychiatric illness if the loved one is injured or put in peril.'

Despite these liberal-sounding statements, on the actual facts of the case, brothers, brothers-in-law, grandparents, uncles and friends were all found not to have a sufficiently close relationship with the deceased or injured person to succeed in their action. This is partly because the House of Lords emphasized that a claimant would not only have to prove that the *type* of relationship was a close one but also that the relationship was *as a matter of fact* close: there needed to be a close relationship in terms of love and affection. This point had merely been made in passing by Lord Wilberforce in **McLoughlin** *v* **O'Brian** when he said that ties had to be close 'not merely in relationship, but in care'. The result in **Alcock** was that a brother present at the stadium at the time of the disaster at which his brother was killed failed in his action because he had not supplied evidence to prove that he was as a matter of fact close to his brother. Lord Keith said that the closeness of the tie could be presumed in 'appropriate cases', giving as examples the relationship between parent and child and that between fiancé(e)s. But if the relationship of a brother is not an appropriate case it is difficult to imagine many other examples.

White dealt with two other classes of person, who, it was suggested, should be owed a duty of care with regard to psychiatric illness: rescuers and employees. The case, as stated earlier, arose from the Hillsborough disaster, and here the claimants were police officers who had been on duty at the ground on the day of the tragedy. Like **Alcock**, **White** was originally a test case in that the four claimants had performed different roles which between them represented the experiences of a number of other officers. Three of them had actually been at the scene of the crushing incident: PC Bevis had spent time attempting to resuscitate fans, who were in fact already dead, close to the fences; Inspector White had passed dead and injured fans from the fenced-in areas; as had PC Bairstow, who had also helped in giving a victim heart massage. The fourth officer, PC Glave, had moved bodies into a temporary morgue set up at the opposite end of the ground from the incident, and obtained first aid for some of the injured. The claimants claimed on two alternative grounds: first, that the police force owed them a duty of care as employees, and this covered the psychiatric injuries they had suffered (this claim is discussed below); or secondly, that they were owed a duty of care as rescuers. They argued that either of these situations meant they were not secondary victims at all, and therefore not subject to the **Alcock** restrictions. Both these arguments succeeded in the Court of Appeal (each applied to different claimants among the four), but the House of Lords rejected both. It stated that only those who were in danger of physical injury (or, according to Lord Steyn, reasonably believed themselves to be so) could be viewed as primary victims; everyone else was a secondary victim, and as such, subject to the **Alcock** tests, which clearly the officers could not pass as they had no pre-existing relationships with those killed or injured at the ground.

Until **White**, it had been assumed that rescuers, meaning people who suffered psychiatric injury as a result of helping the primary victims of a shocking incident, were a special case, on the ground of public policy – the theory being that such selfless behaviour should be encouraged and supported, and therefore not subjected to rules stricter than those of ordinary negligence. This was generally viewed as the position taken in the classic rescuer case of **Chadwick** *v* **British Railways Board** (1967), where the claimant spent 12 hours helping victims of a terrible train disaster which occurred near his home, and in which over 90 people were killed. He successfully claimed for psychiatric injury which occurred as a result of the experience.

In **White**, however, the House of Lords stated categorically that rescuers were not a special case, and were subject to the normal rules stated in **Alcock**. In looking at the question of whether the officers could recover as rescuers, the House of Lords could easily have limited itself to considering whether professional rescuers should be treated in the same way as those who volunteer their help. It would have been easy to maintain the special treatment of voluntary rescuers, yet deny the officers' claim on the grounds that the public policy reasons did not apply to them, since there should be no need to encourage them to act in ways that were already required by their jobs. However, the House chose to go further than this and consider the whole area of rescuers who suffer psychiatric shock. It stated that rescuers were not, and should not be, a special category. Where acting as rescuer put a claimant in danger of physical injury, they could claim as a primary victim, but where no risk of physical injury was caused to the rescuer, they would be a secondary victim, and therefore subject to all the restrictions in **Alcock**.

Two main reasons were given by Lord Hoffmann for the ruling. First, that allowing rescuers to be a special case would sooner or later lead to difficult distinctions: once rescuers includes those who help without putting themselves in any physical danger, the line between rescuers and bystanders may become difficult to draw. How much help would someone have to give to be considered a rescuer? Lord Hoffmann's second reason was that allowing the claims of professional rescuers would appear unjust, given that the police officers' conditions of service provided for them to be compensated in other ways for the psychiatric injury they had suffered, while on the other hand, the bereaved relatives in **Alcock** had been given nothing. While it is difficult to argue with the justice of this point, Lord Hoffmann's reasoning does not explain why volunteer rescuers should be treated in the same way as professional ones. Interestingly, Lord Hoffmann claimed that this was not a change in the law, stating that existing rescuer cases were merely examples of the standard rules on recovery for psychiatric shock, because the claimants in those cases were all at risk of physical injury to themselves and therefore primary victims. In the leading case of **Chadwick**, at least, this is debatable: while a theoretical risk of a wrecked train carriage collapsing on the claimant was mentioned in the case, it is by no stretch of the imagination a keystone of the judgment.

This reasoning makes the impact of the judgment less clear than it seems at first sight. If Mr Chadwick can be considered a primary victim on the facts of his case, it may be that what the decision actually does is to allow the courts to take a wide view of whether voluntary rescuers were subject to physical danger, and use that reasoning to allow or deny a claim, rather than explicitly mentioning public policy.

The second argument made by the police officers in **White** was that they were owed a duty of care as employees of the party whose negligence caused the shocking event. It is well established that employers owe a duty of care towards employees, which obliges them to take reasonable care to ensure that employees are safe at work, and although police officers are not actually employed by their Chief Constable, the court accepted that for the purposes of their argument, the relationship was sufficiently similar to the employer–employee relationship. The claimants in **White** claimed that this meant they could not be considered secondary victims, and were not subject to the **Alcock** restrictions. As stated above, the argument was successful in the Court of Appeal, but was rejected by the House of Lords.

The House stated that the employers' duty to employees was not a separate tort with its own rules, but an aspect of the law of negligence, and therefore subject to the normal rules of negligence. This meant that where a type of injury was subject to special restrictions on when a duty of care would exist, these rules applied where the injury was caused by an employer to an employee, just as they would normally. So, for example, just as there was no general duty not to cause economic loss to others, there was no duty for an employer not to cause economic loss to employees, by, for example, reducing opportunities to earn bonuses. In the same way, there was no special duty of care regarding psychiatric damage caused by employers to employees, just the normal rules.

These meant that an employer would be liable for causing psychiatric injury to an employee who was a primary victim, and the House of Lords acknowledged that this had happened in **Walker** *v* **Northumberland County Council** (1995), where the council had been found liable for causing psychiatric injury to an employee after he had a nervous breakdown brought on by overwork and stressful working conditions. Lord Hoffmann said Walker was a primary victim because it was the strain of the work that his employers made him do that caused his nervous breakdown. However, where the employee was a secondary victim, the employer would only be liable for their psychiatric injury if they could pass the tests laid down in **Alcock**. The claimants in **White** were secondary victims and as they could not pass the **Alcock** tests, they could not claim.

The issue was addressed again in **Cullin** *v* **London Fire and Civil Defence Authority** (1999), where the claimant was a firefighter who suffered psychiatric injury after an incident in which two colleagues became trapped inside a burning building. The claimant was among those who went into the building to attempt a rescue which proved impossible; he later witnessed their bodies being carried out. The fire authority applied to have his action struck out on the ground that the situation was similar to those of the police officers in **Frost**, in that the claimant was a professional rescuer and the risk of psychiatric injury he had been exposed to was a normal part of his job. The court disagreed, and said that this approach was too narrow. Relying on remarks made *obiter* by Lord Goff in **Frost**, they said that a professional rescuer who could establish that they were exposed to danger and the risk of physical injury, or reasonably believed that they were, even if only in the aftermath of the event, could qualify as a primary victim. In this case it was at least arguable that the firefighter had been a primary victim and so the action could not be struck out.

Unwitting agents

There remains one category of claimant whose position is left unclear in **White**, namely those who witness a shocking accident caused by someone else's negligence, and while they are in no physical danger themselves, might be considered more than mere bystanders because some action of theirs physically brings about death or injury to another. The best-known example is **Dooley** *v* **Cammell Laird** (1951). Here the claimant was operating a crane at the docks where he worked, when, through no fault of his, it dropped a load into the hold of the ship being unloaded. He successfully claimed for psychiatric injury caused through fearing for the safety of a colleague working below. Until **White**, the case, along with a couple of similar decisions, was viewed as establishing the right of an employee to recover for psychiatric injury caused by witnessing or fearing injury to colleagues as a result of their employers' negligence. In **White**, Lord Hoffmann maintains that there is no such right, and that the cases, all of which were first instance judgments, were decided on their facts, and before the **Alcock** control mechanisms were in place. However, he concedes that there may be grounds for treating unwitting agent cases as exceptional, and exempting them from the **Alcock** restrictions, though the point is *obiter* since as Lord Hoffmann points out, the facts of **White** do not raise the issue.

The issue was examined in **Hunter** *v* **British Coal** (1998). Here the claimant was a driver in a coal mine, who accidentally struck a water hydrant while manoeuvring his vehicle. He went to try to find a hose to channel the water away safely, leaving behind a colleague, C. When the claimant was about 30 metres away, he heard the hydrant explode and rushed to find the valve to turn it off, which took about 10 minutes. During that time he heard a message over the tannoy that a man had been injured, and on his way back to the accident scene another colleague told him that it looked as though C was dead. This proved to be the case, and the claimant's belief that he was responsible for his colleague's death caused him to suffer clinical depression, and when it became clear that in fact the accident had occurred because of his employer's failure to put certain safety features in place, he sued. The Court of Appeal held that in order to be owed a duty of care of psychiatric injury, the claimant would have to have either been at the scene of the accident when it happened, or see its immediate aftermath; his depression had been caused by hearing about it and that was not sufficient. The case therefore seems to suggest that unwitting agents may have a claim if they satisfy the requirements of proximity in space and time.

Other bystanders

The cases make it clear that bystanders who have no relationship with the primary victims of an accident are very unlikely ever to be able to sue successfully for psychiatric injury experienced as a result. This approach

approves the traditional position in cases such as **Bourh**
where it was held that a woman who suffered psychiat
of witnessing a horrific motorcycle accident involvi
not recover damages; the court held that an ordina.
expected to withstand the shock of witnessing such an
meant that it was not reasonably foreseeable that the claimant
fact suffer psychiatric damage as a result.

However, in **Alcock** the point was made that there might be very rare
occasions when an incident was so horrific that psychiatric damage to
even uninvolved bystanders was foreseeable, and there a duty of care
would arise. The House of Lords gave the rather lurid and imaginative
example of a petrol tanker crashing into a school playground full of
children and bursting into flames.

Proximity

Witnessing an event may consist of being present at the event itself, being
present at its immediate aftermath, seeing it on television, hearing it on
the radio, or coming upon its immediate aftermath. In **Alcock** some
claimants had seen the disaster from other stands inside the stadium; one
of the claimants was watching the match on a television nearby and when
he saw the disaster commence went to find his son who was killed; others
saw the tragedy on the television at home or heard about it on the radio.
Alcock established that to succeed in a claim for nervous shock, the witness
must have been sufficiently proximate to the accident, which normally
means that they must have been present at the scene of the accident or its
immediate aftermath; hearing it on the radio or seeing it on the television will not usually be enough.

The House of Lords was not prepared to specify exactly what was the
immediate aftermath, but the interpretation they give to the issue is narrower than that advocated in some of the *obiter dicta* in **McLoughlin** *v* **O'Brian**.
Lord Keith appears to approve of the *dicta* in the Australian case of **Jaensch**
v **Coffey** (1984), which stated that the aftermath continues for as long as the
victim remains in the state caused by the accident, until they receive immediate post-accident treatment. **McLoughlin** was considered to be a borderline case by Lord Ackner and it was stated that identifying the body of a
loved one at a temporary mortuary eight hours after the accident did not
fall within seeing the immediate aftermath of the tragedy.

The House made it clear that merely being informed of the incident by
a third party was not sufficiently proximate. This runs contrary to the
decision in **Hevican** *v* **Ruane** (1991), which was decided after **Alcock**. In
that case a boy was killed in a car accident. His father was informed of his
death at the police station and then identified his body in the mortuary. He
was able to claim damages for the nervous shock that he suffered, but in
the light of the *dicta* in **Alcock** it is unlikely that the case would be decided
in the same way today.

The House also had to deal with the question of whether watching an ...cident on television could be sufficiently proximate to impose liability to secondary victims for nervous shock, as the Hillsborough disaster had been broadcast live on television to millions of people. The pictures did not pick out individuals, as broadcasting guidelines prevented the portrayal of death or suffering by recognizable individuals. On the facts, the House of Lords did not find that watching the television broadcasts was sufficiently proximate, though it did not rule out the possibility that sometimes television viewers could be sufficiently proximate. The House of Lords drew a distinction between recorded broadcasts and live ones. The former were never sufficiently proximate to give rise to a duty of care. With the latter they said that a claim was unlikely to arise because of the broadcasting guidelines which meant that normally even live broadcasts of disasters could not be equated with actually having been present at the scene of the tragedy. Lord Jauncey stated:

> I do not consider that a claimant who watches a normal television programme which displays events as they happen satisfies the test of proximity. In the first place a defendant could normally anticipate that in accordance with current television broadcasting guidelines shocking pictures of persons suffering and dying would not be transmitted. In the second place, a television programme such as that transmitted from Hillsborough involves cameras at different viewpoints showing scenes all of which no one individual would see, edited pictures and a commentary superimposed.

If pictures in breach of broadcasting guidelines were shown, their transmission would normally break the chain of causation as a *novus actus interveniens*. This would mean that the instigator of the incident would not be liable because they could not have foreseen that such pictures would be shown, though the broadcaster may be in breach of a duty of care, an issue not dealt with by the House.

Occasionally the chain of causation would not be broken and liability on the original instigator could be imposed. The example the judges gave was of a publicity-seeking organization arranging an event where a party of children were taken in a hot-air balloon, the event being shown live on television so that their parents could watch. If the basket suddenly burst into flames, the suddenness of the tragedy might mean that it was impossible for the broadcasters to shield the viewers from scenes of distress and this would be reasonably foreseeable to the instigator of the accident.

Statutory provision

In addition to the common law remedy for nervous shock, emotional distress can occasionally be compensated under statute. For example, there is now a statutory award for bereavement contained in the Fatal Accidents Act 1976. There is no need to prove proximity to the incident that caused the death nor evidence of a medically recognized mental illness. However, it has its own limitations as it is only awarded to a very small class of people, is for a fixed sum of money and is only available on death, not serious injury.

Problems with the law on psychiatric damage

The position of rescuers

As explained earlier, until recently rescuers were thought to be a special case with regard to psychiatric shock, and a rescuer who suffered psychiatric shock as a result would not be subject to the same restrictions as a mere bystander. **White** of course changes this, and this aspect of the decision was comprehensively criticized in the dissenting judgments of Lords Goff and Griffiths in that case. Lord Hoffmann's claim that rescuers had never been a special case, and that the main authority, **Chadwick**, fitted in with his analysis because there was a danger of the train collapsing, is disputed by Lord Goff. He points out that the trial judge in **Chadwick** treated the potential danger as irrelevant, and was right to do so, because it was clearly not the threat of danger to himself that caused Mr Chadwick's psychiatric injury, but the horror of spending hours surrounded by the terrible sights and sounds that were the aftermath of the accident.

Lord Goff also pointed out that making rescuers' claims dependent on whether they were at risk of physical injury could create unjust distinctions. He gave the example of two men going to help in the aftermath of a train crash, where the situation happened to be that helping victims in the front half of the train involved some threat of physical danger, and working in the back half did not. Each of the two men might perform the same service, suffer the same trauma and end up living with the same degree of psychiatric injury, yet if they happened to be helping at opposite ends of the train, one would be able to claim compensation for his psychiatric injury and the other would not, a distinction which his Lordship said was 'surely unacceptable'.

The 'closeness of relationship' rules

As you will remember, it was established in **Alcock** *v* **Chief Constable of South Yorkshire** (1992) that one of the requirements for recovery by a secondary victim was that they should have a relationship with a primary victim that was 'close in care', meaning that it is not sufficient to establish, for example, that the primary and secondary victims were brothers; it must also be proved that the relationship between them was close in terms of the way they felt about each other.

The requirement must make the trial more traumatic for the claimant, yet quite how it contributes to the law is difficult to see. Clearly it would be ridiculous for a claimant who was the brother of a primary victim to claim damages if in fact they disliked each other intensely and rarely had any kind of contact – but in such cases, is it likely that the claimant would be able to prove that he had suffered a psychiatric illness as a result of his brother's death or injury? This requirement alone provides a limiting mechanism that makes the test of factual closeness unnecessary.

In addition, it is hard to see why this should affect the defendant's duty, which is still initially based on foreseeability; how can a defendant be said to foresee whether or not the person they injure will have a close relationship with their relatives, and therefore to owe a duty only if they do?

The proximity requirements

As you will recall, the decision in **Alcock** regarding proximity was that in order to claim for psychiatric injury, a secondary victim would have to have been present at the incident which endangered, injured or killed their loved one, or to have witnessed its 'immediate aftermath'.

In **McLoughlin**, the deciding factor seemed to be that the injured were in much the same state as when the accident happened, covered in oil and dirt, and so the implication seems to be that this made the sight of them more devastating, and therefore more likely to mentally injure Mrs McLoughlin. While it is clear that these factors could make a sight more distressing and shocking, it is difficult to make out why exactly the courts believe this should be the dividing line between experiences which can and cannot cause psychiatric injury. Sight is not the only way in which human beings perceive suffering: hearing about the circumstances of an accident, particularly when the outcome is not known, can surely be equally devastating. Similarly, the House of Lords in **Alcock** were emphatic that those seeing the incident on television could not be caused psychiatric injury by the experience, yet the claimants who saw the TV coverage would have known, right at the time when the incident was happening before their eyes, that their loved ones were there. Even if they could not identify them by sight, it is hard to see that this was less distressing than coming upon the aftermath of an accident, and if it was equally distressing, there seems no reason why it should be less likely to cause psychiatric injury.

Nor is the courts' emphasis on the time between the accident and the perception of it easy to justify. Among the **Alcock** claimants, for example, was one man who had gone to the ground and searched all night for the brother he knew had been at the match. It is difficult to see why those long hours of searching and worrying should be less likely to cause psychiatric injury than sight of a loved one immediately after an accident.

The 'sudden shock' requirement

As with the proximity requirements, it is difficult to find a rational basis for the line drawn between psychiatric injury caused by a sudden shock and the same injury caused by, for example, the stress of caring for a seriously injured relative, or the grief of being bereaved. So long as the psychiatric shock is a foreseeable result of the defendant's negligence, why should the precise aspect of the claimant's situation which triggered it off make any difference?

Take the case of **Sion** *v* **Hampstead Health Authority** (1994), for example (see p. 46). Had the son died suddenly of a fatal heart attack caused by his poor medical treatment, and his father been there to witness it, the father might very well have been able to secure compensation for any psychiatric illness he suffered as a result. Why should the fact that he watched his son die slowly, with all the stress and grief that must cause, change his situation? The defendant's treatment of his son is no less negligent; his own psychiatric injury is no less real, and nor is it less foreseeable. Clearly the law has to draw a line somewhere, but the justification for making a sudden shock the defining factor is hard to see.

Reform

The Law Commission has been looking at this area of the law for some time, and in 1995, began consulting with interested parties. The results of their consultations were published in 1998. The Commission argues that the current rules on compensation for secondary victims are too restrictive. They agree that the requirement for a close tie between primary and secondary victim is justified and should remain, but believe this alone would be sufficient; they recommend that the requirements of proximity (both in time and space, and in method of perception) should be abolished. They also suggest that the requirement for psychiatric injury to be caused by sudden shock should be abandoned.

▶ Omissions

As a general rule, the duties imposed by the law of negligence are duties not to cause injury or damage to others; they are not duties actively to help others. And if there is no duty, there is no liability. If, for example, you see someone drowning, you generally have no legal duty to save them, no matter how easy it might be to do so (unless there are special reasons why the law would impose such a duty on you in particular, such as under an employment contract as a lifeguard). This means tort law generally holds people liable for acts (the things people do), not omissions (the things they fail to do).

However, there are some situations in which the courts have recognised a positive duty to act, arising from the circumstances in which the parties find themselves. Although the categories are loose and at times overlap, the following are the main factors which have been taken into consideration.

Control exercised by the defendants

Where the defendants have a high degree of control over the claimant, they may have a positive duty to look after them which goes beyond simply taking reasonable steps to ensure that the defendants themselves do not cause injury. A key case in this area is **Reeves *v* Commissioner of Police for the Metropolis** (1999). The case was brought by the widow of a man who had committed suicide while in police custody. Although previous case law had accepted that the police had a duty of care to prevent suicide attempts by prisoners who were mentally ill, Mr Reeves was found to have been completely sane, and the police therefore argued that while clearly they had a duty of care not to cause his death, they could not be held responsible for the fact that he chose to kill himself, and had no duty to prevent him from doing so. However, the Court of Appeal held that their duty of care to protect a prisoner's health did extend to taking reasonable care to prevent him or her from attempting suicide; they accepted that to impose a positive duty like this was unusual, but explained that it was justified by the very high degree of control which the police would have over a prisoner, and the well-known high risk of suicide among suspects held in this way.

Assumption of responsibility

Although in English law people generally have no duty to actively help each other, such a duty will be implied where the courts find that one of the parties has assumed responsibility for the other in some way. A common reason for finding such an assumption is where a contract implying such responsibility exists, or where such responsibility clearly arises from the defendant's job.

In **Costello *v* Chief Constable of Northumbria Police** (1999), the claimant was a police constable, who was attacked by a prisoner in a police station cell. A police inspector was nearby, but despite her screams, he failed to come to her aid. The claimant sued the Chief Constable, alleging that the inspector had a duty of care towards her in that situation (the Chief Constable was sued as being vicariously liable – see Chapter 13). The Court of Appeal agreed; as a police officer, the inspector had assumed a responsibility to help fellow officers in circumstances like these, and where a member of the police force's failure to act would result in a fellow officer being exposed to unnecessary risk of injury, there was a positive duty to act.

A defendant may also be deemed to have assumed responsibility for another person by virtue of his or her actions towards that person. In **Barrett *v* Ministry of Defence** (1995), the Ministry of Defence (MOD) was sued by the widow of a naval pilot, who had died by choking on his own vomit after becoming so drunk that he passed out. He had been found unconscious and an officer had organized for him to be taken up to his own room, but nobody had been told to watch over him and make sure he did not choke. The court heard that extreme drunkenness was common on the remote Norwegian base where the death happened, and the officer in charge admitted that he had not fulfilled his responsibility, imposed by Royal Navy regulations, of discouraging drunkenness at the base. At trial, the judge found the defendant was negligent in tolerating the excessive drinking, but reduced the damages by one-quarter because the dead man had been contributorily negligent in getting so drunk. The MOD appealed.

The Court of Appeal disagreed with the first instance court's finding that the officer could be liable for failing to prevent drunkenness; and held that it was fair, just and reasonable to expect an adult to take responsibility for their own consumption of alcohol and the consequences of it. However, the Court held that once the officer had ordered the unconscious man to be taken up to the room, he had from that point assumed responsibility for his welfare, and had been negligent in not summoning medical help or watching over him. Bearing in mind that the defendant would never have had to assume this responsibility had it not been for the dead man's own actions, they decided that the defendant should be held only one-third to blame, and damages reduced accordingly.

Creation of a risk

Where a defendant actually creates a dangerous situation – even if this risk is created through no fault of the defendant – the courts may impose a positive duty to deal with the danger. This issue was explored in **Capital and Counties Plc *v* Hampshire County Council** (1997). The case, which is discussed more fully at p. 66, concerned the question of whether fire brigades had a duty of care towards people whose property was on fire. The court concluded that in general they did not, but said that where a fire brigade had actually done something which either created a danger or made the existing danger worse, they then had a positive duty to take reasonable steps to deal with that danger. In the case itself, this meant that a fire brigade whose employee had ordered the claimant's sprinkler system to be turned off, and thereby enabled the fire to spread more rapidly than it would otherwise have done, was liable in negligence.

▶ Liability for the acts of third parties

In general, tort law is designed to impose liability on those who have caused damage, and so it does not usually impose liability on one person or body for damage done by another. This is the case even if the defendant could have foreseen that their own acts might make it possible or likely that someone else might cause damage as a result of them. In **P Perl (Exporters)** *v* **Camden London Borough Council** (1984) the defendant council owned two adjoining buildings, numbers 142 and 144. The first was rented by the claimant, and the second was empty. There was no lock in the door of number 144, making it possible for thieves to enter, and by knocking a hole in the wall, some thieves got through to number 142 and burgled it. The Court of Appeal held that the council was not liable for negligence: they might have foreseen the risk of harm in leaving the property without a lock, but that was not sufficient to make them responsible for the acts of the burglars.

There are, however, five circumstances where a duty of care regarding the acts of third parties may arise. The first and perhaps most common is where the law imposes vicarious liability, which is discussed in Chapter 13. The other four are where there is a relationship of proximity between the claimant and the defendant, or such a relationship between the defendant and a third party who causes damage to the claimant; where the defendant has negligently created a source of danger; and where the defendant knew or had reason to know that a third party was creating a risk to others on the defendant's property. As you will see from the discussion of cases below, there are links between liability of the acts of third parties and liability for omissions, since many cases will essentially concern an omission to prevent damage being done by a third party.

The defendant–claimant relationship of proximity

The term 'relationship of proximity' is essentially legal shorthand for the existence of circumstances relating to the particular defendant and the particular claimant, which may be reasons why a duty of care should exist between them. This is a horribly slippery concept, but becomes clearer if we look at some examples.

The relationship can often arise from the existence of a contract between the parties. In **Stansbie** *v* **Troman** (1948), the defendant was a decorator, working on the claimant's premises. The claimant, leaving him alone in the house when she went out, specifically requested that he should be sure to lock the house before he left. He failed to do this, with the result that she was burgled. This was the same result as in **Perl**, but the existence of a contractual relationship between them was enough in this case to establish a relationship of proximity and so impose a duty of care.

The relationship may also arise from things the parties have said and done. This was the case in **Swinney** *v* **Chief Constable of Northumbria Police** (1996) (discussed at p. 64 below) where the police were held to have a duty of care to a particular claimant because she had supplied them with information regarding a criminal and stressed that it should be kept confidential, and it was clear that if they did not do so, there was a serious risk that the criminal who the information concerned would try to take revenge on the claimant. This case can be contrasted with **Hill** *v* **Chief Constable of West Yorkshire** (1988). In that case, the mother of one of the women killed by Peter Sutcliffe, better known as the Yorkshire Ripper, sued the police, arguing that they had been negligent in failing to catch him earlier and so prevent her daughter's murder. It was held in this case that there was no relationship of proximity between the police and the claimant's daughter, since there was no reason for them to believe she was in special danger from Sutcliffe; she was simply in the same general danger as any member of the female public in the area where the murders were being committed (in both these cases, issues of public policy were also important; these are discussed on p. 64).

The more recent case of **Palmer** *v* **Tees Health Authority** (1999) has taken up this issue again, but with no change in the approach of the courts. Here the claimant was the mother of a child murdered by a mentally ill patient of the defendant health authority. The killer had previously threatened to abduct and kill a child, and the claimant argued that he was able to do so because the health authority had been negligent in their assessment of the risk of this happening. The Court of Appeal found that, as in **Hill**, there was no proximity between the health authority and the claimant's daughter. To establish such proximity, she would at the very least have had to be identifiable as a potential victim, and even that might not necessarily be sufficient. The court suggested that when assessing whether there was proximity between the claimant and the defendant in such cases, it might be relevant to ask what the defendants could actually have done to protect the claimant. In this case, the possible steps were treatment and/or detention of the patient, or warning the victim; it was found that the first was thought unlikely to be effective, and the second was impossible since they did not know who to warn. Where there was nothing the defendants could reasonably have done, it was unlikely that there would be proximity.

The defendant–third party relationship of proximity

The main way in which a relationship of proximity can arise between the defendant and a third party who has injured the claimant is where the defendant had a right or responsibility to control the third party. However this will rarely be enough in itself to create a duty of care: in addition, the claimant will need to be someone who was at a particular risk of damage if the defendants were negligent in controlling the third party, over and above the general risk such negligence might pose to the public at large.

This can be seen in the case of **Home Office** *v* **Dorset Yacht Co** (1970). Here prison officers (employed by the Home Office) were in charge of a borstal situated on an island. Due to their negligence, some boys escaped from the borstal and took boats belonging to the claimants to try to get away from the island, damaging the boats in the process. The House of Lords found that the Home Office was liable for the acts of the boys because the boys were under the officers' control (or at least they were supposed to be!). However, that did not mean that the Home Office owed a duty to anyone who might suffer damage caused by the boys, only those at particular risk; the yacht owners were held to come into this category because it was clearly foreseeable that if the boys escaped, they would try to get off the island by stealing boats.

Creating a risk of danger

A defendant who negligently creates or allows the creation of a risk of danger may be liable if a third party's actions cause that danger to injure the claimant. An example arose in **Haynes** *v* **Harwood** (1935), where a horse was left unattended in a busy street and bolted when some children threw stones at it. The defendant was held to owe a duty of care to a police officer who, seeing the danger, ran after the horse and caught it, injuring himself in the process.

In such cases it is not sufficient that the defendant creates a situation which might make it possible for a third party to injure someone else: there must be the creation of a special risk. This can be seen in **Topp** *v* **London Country Bus (South West)** (1993), where a bus was left unattended outside a pub by the defendant's employee, with the keys left in the ignition. When the pub closed, somebody (presumably drinkers from the pub, though this was not proved), got into the bus and drove it away. There was evidence that the bus was being driven erratically and without headlights, and ultimately it hit and killed the claimant. The Court of Appeal held that the defendant's leaving the bus as he did was not sufficient to amount to creating the kind of risk which would create a duty of care as in **Haynes**. It was no more a source of danger than any other vehicle parked on the road (unlike the horse, which might well have bolted even without the intervention of the children).

Risks created on the defendant's property

Where a defendant knows, or has the means of knowing, that a third party has created a risk to others on the defendant's property, the defendant has a duty to take reasonable steps to prevent danger to others. In most such cases, the danger will be to people on adjacent land. Such a situation was the subject of **Smith** *v* **Littlewoods Organisation** (1987). Here Littlewoods were the owners of a disused cinema. While it stood empty, vandals set the building on fire, and the fire spread, causing damage to neighbouring buildings. The House of Lords held that an occupier of land could owe a duty to prevent risks caused on it by third parties, although on the facts of the case Littlewoods had not been negligent, since they had not known about the vandals and the precautions they had taken to keep trespassers out were reasonable.

▶ Special groups

A number of occupational and other groups have become subject to particular rules concerning negligence claims. This is generally because there are policy reasons why these groups should have immunity from certain types of action, and/or because there are frequently policy reasons why a duty of care should not be imposed in them in particular types of situation.

However, **Osman** *v* **UK** (1999), a case brought before the European Court of Human Rights, has raised questions about the use of such immunities. It is discussed at p. 77.

The police

In general, police officers may be liable like anyone else for damage they negligently cause while going about their duties (in practice in such cases it is the Chief Constable of the relevant area who is sued, under the principle of vicarious liability, and any damages are paid out of a special fund). However, there are some circumstances in which special rules may apply.

A distinction is made between operational matters (broadly speaking, the way in which the police actually carry out their work), and policy matters (decisions made about issues such as the allocation of resources, or the priority given to different types of work). The police can be held liable (with some exceptions, discussed below) for the former, but not the latter.

The distinction can be seen in operation in **Rigby** *v* **Chief Constable of Northamptonshire** (1985). Here a building owner sued the police for fire damage to his property, caused when the police used CS gas, which is inflammable, to oust a gunman who had taken refuge there. The court held that the police could not be held liable for equipping themselves with the gas, even though a non-flammable alternative was available, because that was a policy decision; however, they could be liable for negligence in failing to bring firefighting equipment to the scene, since this was an operational matter. As the case shows, the difference between the two is not always easy to spot.

The decision in **Hill** *v* **Chief Constable of Yorkshire** (1988) (see p. 61) was seen as providing the police with some immunity from negligence actions arising from the way in which they went about the job of preventing and dealing with crime. As well as pointing to the lack of proximity between the police and the young lady who was killed, the House of Lords indicated that there were good policy reasons for not imposing a duty of care on the police in such cases: the fear of being sued might cause the police to do their work with a view to preventing liability, which might adversely affect their performance; the decisions they made were likely to be partly policy-based; and the business of defending claims would be a waste of money and manpower, distracting the police from the job of dealing with crime.

For these reasons, it was held in **Alexandrou** *v* **Oxford** (1993), the police could not be held liable to a member of the public who was burgled after they had dismissed a message that his burglar alarm had been activated as a false alarm, and so failed to go to the scene and investigate. They owed him no duty of care even to turn up and check.

Similar policy reasons were invoked in **Leach** *v* **Chief Constable of Gloucester** (1998). The claimant here had acted as an 'appropriate adult', a role created by the Police and Criminal Evidence Act 1984, which obliges the police to invite such a person to sit in on interviews with suspects who may be mentally disordered, as a protection for those suspects. Voluntary workers often take this role, and the claimant was such a worker. She was asked by the police to sit in on interviews with a man who they thought was mentally disordered; he turned out to be Frederick West, who was accused of a number of horrific murders (and who ultimately killed himself before he could be tried). As a result of attending numerous interviews, plus being left alone with West in his cell and visiting the murder scene, the claimant suffered post-traumatic stress disorder, and claimed that the police had had a duty of care to protect her from such injury by warning her of the disturbing nature of the case, assessing her suitability for such work and providing counselling as they had done for West's solicitor. The Court of Appeal held that such a duty could not be imposed on the police, because the field of people who might act as appropriate adults was wide, and an obligation to look after the needs of all these people would make it very difficult for the police to carry out their work of investigating crime; in particular, it would be impossible to interview suspects effectively if they had to protect the psychological well-being of an appropriate adult at the same time. However, the court conceded that there might be a duty to provide counselling and gave permission for this point to go to trial.

It was made clear in **Swinney** *v* **Chief Constable of Northumbria Police (No 2)** (1999), however, that the decision in **Hill** does not give the police a complete immunity from negligence actions concerning their crime-fighting activities. The claimant in **Swinney** was a pub landlady who had given the police information concerning the identity of a hit-and-run driver who had killed a police officer. The person she identified was known to the police as a violent and ruthless criminal. The claimant made it very clear to the police that, understandably, she was giving them the information confidentially and did not want to be identified as its source, and they agreed to this. Nevertheless, the police recorded her as the informant in a document containing the details she had supplied. This document was left in an unattended police car, from where it was stolen, and eventually reached the hands of the hit-and-run driver. The result was a campaign of terrifying threats of violence against the claimant. She was so badly affected by this that she suffered psychiatric illness and was forced to give up running her pub.

When the claimant tried to sue the police for negligence concerning the information she supplied, the police argued that there was no relationship of proximity between them and the people who had made the threats that would justify making the police liable for the actions of this third party; and that there were policy reasons, similar to those described in **Hill**, why they should not be held to have a duty of care towards the claimant. The Court of Appeal disagreed.

On the proximity question, the Court of Appeal held that the case could be distinguished from **Hill**, where the claimant's daughter had not been at any special risk from the murderer, but was simply one of many women in the area who were his potential victims. In **Swinney**, it was clear that if the information was allowed to fall into the wrong hands, the claimant was in particular danger, and in recognizing and agreeing to the need for confidentiality, the police had undertaken a responsibility towards this particular person. The Court stated that informers were not to be considered merely as members of the public with regard to their relationship with the police; where someone gave information like this to the police, it created a special relationship, which gave rise to sufficient proximity to establish a duty of care.

As far as the policy issues were concerned, the Court of Appeal held such arguments were indeed relevant, but that in this case, the policy arguments favoured the claimant's case. They pointed out that the imposition of a duty of care to keep confidential information secure would encourage informants to come forward, and so help rather than hinder the fight against crime.

On the facts, it was held that the actions of the police had not in fact breached their duty of care towards the claimant, so she lost her case. However, in establishing the existence of a duty of care in this situation, the decision clearly establishes that the police immunity with regard to crime-fighting is far from absolute. The decision of the European Court of Human Rights in **Osman** *v* **UK** also addresses this issue, and is discussed at p. 77.

Similarly, in **Waters** *v* **Commissioner of Police for the Metropolis** (2000), the House of Lords held that the immunity did not apply to a negligence action brought by a police officer who claimed that she had been raped by another officer, and as a result of making a complaint about him, had been ostracized and bullied by other officers, which had resulted in her suffering psychiatric injury. She claimed that the police had failed to deal properly with her complaint, and had caused or allowed the other officers to victimize her. The House of Lords stated that the issue of whether the immunity should apply had to be considered in the light of all the relevant considerations in each case. It was true that, as in **Hill**, the negligence action would take officers and other resources away from the primary job of dealing with crime, but this had to be balanced against other issues of public interest, namely the fact that if the claimant's allegations were true, there was a serious problem with the police, which should be brought to public attention so that steps could be taken to deal with it.

Other emergency services

A number of recent cases have looked at the liability for negligence of the other emergency services – fire brigades, ambulance services and coastguards – with varying results.

The position of the fire services was examined in three cases, heard together by the Court of Appeal: **Capital & Counties plc** *v* **Hampshire County Council; John Munroe (Acrylics) Ltd** *v* **London Fire and Civil Defence Authority; Church of Jesus Christ of Latter-Day Saints (Great Britain)** *v* **West Yorkshire Fire and Civil Defence Authority** (1997). The cases were heard together because they raised similar issues of law, but their facts were each slightly different. Each claimant had suffered a fire which severely damaged their property, and each alleged that the damage was the result of the relevant fire brigade's negligence. In **Capital & Counties**, the negligence was said to be that fire officers had turned off the building's sprinkler system when they arrived, allowing the fire to get out of control; in **John Munroe**, the claimant's building was set alight by smouldering debris from a fire in a nearby building; the negligence was alleged to be that after examining the adjacent building and deciding the fire there was out, the fire officers had neglected to check the claimant's building, where they would have found the debris; in **Church of Jesus Christ**, the fire brigade had been unable to fight a fire because the water supply from nearby hydrants was inadequate, and the negligence was alleged to arise from the brigade's failure to inspect these hydrants regularly, which they had a statutory duty to do.

The first issue the Court of Appeal looked at was whether the fire services owed a duty of care to members of the public who had called them out to fires, to turn up to those fires, or at least to take reasonable care to do so. Purely on the authority of **Alexandrou** *v* **Oxford** (1993) (see p. 64), they held that there was no such duty; if the police were not liable for failing to turn up in response to an emergency call, there was no reason to make the fire services subject to a different rule. This may sound odd, but remember that the Court of Appeal was not considering whether the fire services have a moral or social duty to attend fires when called, nor even a duty under their employment contracts; what they were considering was whether they owed a duty of care to the victims of fires that would enable those victims to sue if the duty was breached. The court found it quite easy to conclude that no such duty existed.

Bearing this in mind, the court went on to consider whether, assuming they had turned up and begun to deal with the fire, the fire services owed a duty of care regarding the way in which a fire was fought; if they did so negligently, were they liable to those who suffered damage as a result? In the first case, **Capital & Counties**, it was argued that turning the sprinkler system off was a positive act which made the fire spread further than it otherwise would have done, and so actually caused harm to the claimant's property over and above that which the fire would otherwise have caused. The Court of Appeal agreed that there was a duty of care not to cause or increase harm in this way.

In the other two cases, it was argued that by turning up at the fires, the fire services had assumed responsibility for fighting the fires and the claimants had relied on this assumption, thus creating the necessary relationship of proximity between them and imposing a duty of care. The Court of Appeal disagreed, for three reasons. First, that the fire service's primary duty was to the public at large, and imposing a duty to individual property owners might conflict with this. Secondly, it was difficult to see precisely who such a duty would actually be owed to. If it were only the owner of the building on fire, this would leave the owners of adjacent buildings unprotected, and suggest that the burning building should be saved at the expense of those around it, but if the owners of adjacent buildings were also owed a duty, then a duty might as well be owed to everyone in the vicinity, since they would all be potentially at risk (remember again that the point under consideration is not whose property should actually be protected by the fire services, but who should be entitled to sue if they fail to protect it). Thirdly, it would be irrational to impose a duty of care regarding the way in which a fire was fought, when it had been established that there was no duty to turn up and fight it at all. It would mean that fire brigades would be better off in terms of legal protection from negligence suits if they simply refused ever to attend fires! For these reasons, the Court of Appeal held that apart from situations where the fire services' actions positively increased the damage done to the claimant, there was not a sufficient relationship of proximity between fire services and members of the public who suffered fires to give rise to a duty of care.

The Court of Appeal then considered public policy, and pointed out that in order for public policy reasons to prevent a duty of care arising, it was necessary to establish that such a duty would clash with 'some wider object of the law or interest of the particular parties'. In cases like that of **Capital & Counties**, where the fire services had increased the harm done, they concluded that there was no policy argument to prevent the imposition of a duty of care. In the other two cases, they had already established that no duty existed because there was no relationship of proximity, but they nevertheless considered what the public policy position would have been if a relationship of proximity had been found. The main public policy arguments against such liability were the usual floodgates issue, plus the fact that damages would ultimately have to be paid by the taxpayer, thus diverting taxes from more socially useful purposes. The court rejected these arguments on the grounds that they were equally applicable to other public services, such as the National Health Service, and these bodies were not immune from negligence actions.

This reasoning leaves aside a rather stronger public policy argument, namely the existence and widespread use of a simpler method of compensation for fire damage: insurance. Most owners of property are likely to have such insurance, and in practice, claims brought against fire brigades are likely to stem not from the owners of property themselves, but from their insurers, who bring such cases because they hope to avoid paying out the benefits they have been paid to provide and instead to shunt the financial responsibility onto the taxpayer.

A similar approach was followed when the courts looked at the liability of coastguard services in **OLL Ltd *v* Secretary of State for Transport** (1997). Here, it was held that the coastguards do not owe a duty of care to people in trouble at sea, except – as in **Capital & Counties** – where their behaviour at the scene actually causes harm.

However, when the courts looked at the position of the ambulance services, they took a different view. The issue was examined in **Kent *v* Griffiths and Others** (2000), which concerned the London Ambulance Service's failure to respond promptly to a call from the claimant's doctor. The claimant was a pregnant woman who had asthma. Having been called in to see her during a bad attack, her GP rang for an ambulance, and was told one was on its way; however it took 38 minutes to arrive, despite two further calls from the GP. As a result of the delay, she temporarily stopped breathing, which caused her to lose her baby, and to suffer long-term memory problems and personality changes.

The ambulance service argued that, on the authority of **Capital & Counties**, they owed the claimant no duty of care, but the Court of Appeal disagreed. It said that the nature of the service provided by the ambulance service was not comparable with that provided by fire brigades or police, but was more like that provided by National Health Service hospitals, which are accepted to have duties of care towards individual patients. Whereas the fire brigades and the police tended to provide services to the public at large, the ambulance service, once called to the assistance of an individual, was providing a service to that individual, and that individual would be the only person who could be caused damage by their failure to provide the service properly. Therefore, the Court of Appeal held, the ambulance service did owe a duty of care to the claimant.

The Court of Appeal did, however, stress that the distinction between operational and policy matters (see p. 63) would still apply, as it did in other cases involving emergency services. This meant that where there was a question of ambulances being delayed because of lack of resources, or because of demand elsewhere which the Ambulance Service had decided to give priority to, the duty of care question might be decided differently. What was important in this case was that these issues did not arise; the resources had been available, and what was alleged was a careless failure to use them.

The armed forces

In **Mulcahy** *v* **Ministry of Defence** (1996), the Court of Appeal considered whether a member of the armed forces, injured by the negligent behaviour of a colleague during battle conditions, could sue for that injury. The reason why this – presumably fairly common – situation had never come before the courts before was that until 1987 the situation was covered by a statutory immunity, but this was removed in the Crown Proceedings (Armed Forces) Act 1987. The Act provides that the immunity can be restored by the Secretary of State for Defence in respect of any particular 'warlike operations' outside the UK, but no such order was made regarding the Gulf War, in which the claimant met his injury when a fellow soldier negligently discharged a gun beside him, damaging his hearing.

The Court of Appeal held that there was no duty of care between fellow soldiers engaged in battle conditions. Following the **Caparo** approach (see p. 18 above), the court found that there was foreseeability and proximity, but that it was not just and reasonable to impose a duty in the circumstances, because military operations would be adversely affected if every soldier had to be conscious even in the heat of battle that their actions could result in being sued by a comrade.

However, the armed forces can be sued by their members for damage occurring outside battle conditions: **Barrett** *v* **Ministry of Defence** (see p. 59) is an example of this.

Local authorities and public bodies

Local authorities and other public bodies pose special problems regarding negligence actions, for two main reasons. The first is that even where foreseeability and proximity can be established, there will very often be reasons why imposing a duty of care may not be just and reasonable: in particular, the problem of damages ultimately being paid by taxpayers, and the danger of employees being distracted from their main task, and possibly changing their working practices, in order to avoid being sued. In these respects the dilemma is similar to that regarding public services such as the police and fire brigades. But there is a further problem with many cases involving public bodies, and in particular, democratically elected ones. This is the question of 'justiciability', which simply means suitability for examination by a court.

The justiciability issue arises because in many cases, the actions and decisions of public bodies can only be properly examined by reference to factors which the court process is not equipped to assess. Public bodies are frequently given powers to act, but allowed a discretion as to how, when and even whether they exercise those powers. The exercise of such discretion may depend on many different factors: the availability of re-sources and the other demands on those resources; the weight given to competing aims and objectives; the preference given to different methods of solving a problem or meeting a need. As an example, take the facts of **Stovin** *v* **Wise** (1996). Here the claimant had been injured when the motorbike he was riding was hit by a car driven by the defendant. The defendant claimed that the accident was partly due to the negligence of the local authority, which he therefore joined to the action. The basis for his claim was that he had been unable to see the claimant because an overhanging bank of earth was obstructing his view; the authority had a statutory power to order the removal of such obstructions, and had failed to do so. We will discuss the decision in the case further on in this section, but for our purposes here it illustrates very well the problem of justiciability. The council did know about the obstruction (in fact the council had asked the landowner to remove the obstruction, but had not followed up when this was not done), and it knew that previous accidents had happened in the same spot. But there were even worse accident black spots in other areas of the county; there were calls other than accident black spots on the authority's road maintenance budget; and this budget was limited. On what basis should a court decide whether the authority should have spent its money and manpower on removing this particular obstruction?

Up until recently, these problems were generally taken by the courts to mean that it was desirable to protect local authorities and other public bodies from actions for negligence, for the reasons explained. The bench-mark case establishing this approach was **X** *v* **Bedfordshire County Coun-cil** (1995), in which the House of Lords grouped together five separate cases which all raised the issue of local authority liability in negligence; in each case the local authorities had applied to have the actions struck out, arguing that there was no cause of action. Two of the cases were brought by claimants who alleged that their local authorities had acted negligently regarding their powers to prevent child abuse; the other three cases concerned local authorities' powers with regard to providing education for children with special needs.

The House of Lords held that it was not just and reasonable to impose a duty with regard to protection from child abuse, on the grounds that this was an area where a degree of discretion had to be exercised and there might well be different views as to the wisdom of any decision taken. Imposing a duty of care would mean local authority employees making such decisions with one eye on whether they might be sued, and would also divert public money and manpower away from child protection. In addition, private citizens had other means of challenging decisions made in this area, including statutory appeals procedures and the right to petition the local authority ombudsman.

In the education cases, however, the House of Lords found that it was arguable that a duty of care might arise, because here there was not the same danger of defensive practices, and because advice was being given directly to and relied upon by parents.

A similarly restrictive approach was taken in **Stovin** *v* **Wise**, the facts of which are set out above. The defendant argued that the existence of a statutory power to remove the obstruction was sufficient to create a relationship of proximity between the council and users of the road, which would not otherwise exist. The House of Lords compared the position regarding a statutory power to that regarding a statutory duty (see Chapter 6), and said the position was similar. Therefore in order to discover whether a statutory power was intended to give rise to an individual right to sue in negligence, it was necessary to look at the statute itself, and decide whether in making it, Parliament intended to create a private right to compensation. On this point, the very fact that Parliament had granted a power to act, rather than a duty to do so, suggested it did not intend to create such a right.

This did not mean that a statutory power could never give rise to a right to compensation if the power was not exercised, but in order to do so, two fairly strict requirements would have to be satisfied. First, the non-exercise of the power must have been irrational in the circumstances. This term (sometimes known as 'Wednesbury unreasonableness' after the case in which it was first described) is borrowed from public law, and essentially applies when a public body or official makes a decision that is so unreasonable that no reasonable public body or official could have made it.

Secondly, there must be 'exceptional grounds' for imposing an obligation to pay compensation. This will only be the case if, as Lord Hoffmann explained, there is 'general reliance' on the power being exercised, to the extent that 'the general pattern of social and economic behaviour' is affected by this reliance (an example of this might be the setting of insurance premiums). Lord Hoffmann stressed that the doctrine was concerned with the general expectations of the community at large, not those of the defendant; defendants would not have to prove that they had relied on the exercise of the power, but equally, the fact that they did so rely would be irrelevant unless shared by the general public. Lord Hoffmann also pointed out that general reliance could only exist where the benefit provided if and when the statutory power was exercised was of 'uniform and routine' nature, so that it is clear exactly what the defendant was expected to do.

Similar issues have arisen in cases involving public bodies other than local authorities. In **Harris** *v* **Evans** (1998), Harris ran bungee jumps using a mobile crane, which was checked by an inspector from the Health and Safety Executive (HSE). Sections 2 and 3 of the Health and Safety at Work Act 1974 impose a duty to ensure that, as far as practicable, neither employees working on or near the crane, nor members of the public, were exposed to risks affecting their safety. The inspector found (wrongly) that Harris was in breach of these requirements, and on the inspector's advice, the local council served improvement notices on Harris, as a result of which he suffered some financial loss.

By looking at the legislation which gives Health and Safety inspectors their powers, the House of Lords held that no duty of care was owed by such inspectors to the owners of businesses they inspected. The legislation was intended to protect health and safety, and the very fact that it gave powers to close businesses down if they were in breach of its requirements implied that economic loss to business owners was a possibility which Parliament accepted as necessary in the cause of improving health and safety. This being the case, clearly it was not intended that business owners should have the right to sue for such losses. In addition, there were other remedies for errors made by inspectors, including an appeal process.

These cases seemed to establish that the courts intended strictly to limit the liability of public bodies for negligence. But in **W** *v* **Essex County Council** (1998), a shift of approach began to appear. The claimants were foster parents for the council. They had children of their own, and before accepting their first foster-child, they had told the council that they could not foster any child who was a known or suspected child abuser; the council had agreed to this condition. The council then placed a 15-year-old boy with them, who the council knew had indecently assaulted his sister, and during his stay, he sexually abused the claimants' children. They sued the council for negligence on their children's behalf. The Court of Appeal was asked to decide whether the case could go ahead. It pointed out that there were good policy reasons why a duty of care should not be imposed on the council: the task of dealing with children at risk was a difficult and delicate one, and a duty of care might lead councils to protect themselves from liability, at the expense of their duties towards children needing fostering. However, it stated that in this case, it was arguable that the policy reasons should not apply, since the children who had been abused were not actually subject to the council's powers under statute, but were living at home with their parents, and in addition, the council had given express assurances which it had broken. For these reasons the case was allowed to go ahead.

Since the decision in **W**, there has been a decisive move away from the restrictive approach of **X** *v* **Bedfordshire**. In **Barrett** *v* **Enfield London Borough Council** (1999), it was argued that the local authority owed a duty to a child who it has placed in care. The claimant was taken into care by the local authority when he was 10 months old. He remained there until he was 17, and had had a thoroughly unpleasant and difficult childhood. He alleged that the authority had a duty to place him for adoption, locate suitable foster homes and oversee his re-introduction to his birth mother; the fact that none of this had been done, he claimed, had led to him suffering psychiatric damage. The case was initially struck out on the grounds that, following **X** *v* **Bedfordshire**, there were sound policy reasons why it was not fair, just and reasonable to impose a duty of care. The striking out decision was eventually appealed to the House of Lords, who held that the action should not be struck out, because without a proper examination of the facts, it was not possible to determine whether the decisions taken with regard to the claimant's upbringing were policy ones, which would not be justiciable and so could not give rise to a duty of care, or operational ones, which could.

More recently, in four cases which ultimately ended up being considered together by the House of Lords, the courts looked again at the issue of the duties owed by local educational authorities to children using their educational services, which you will remember was one of the issues raised in **X** itself. The first case was **Phelps** *v* **Hillingdon London Borough** (1998), in which the claimant – now grown-up – had had problems with learning as a child and was referred to an educational psychologist employed by the local authority, who said her difficulties were the result of emotional and behavioural problems. In fact it was later discovered that the claimant was dyslexic. She claimed that the psychologist's failure to diagnose this had prevented her getting the educational help she needed, help which would have improved her employment prospects.

The second of the four cases, **Jarvis** *v* **Hampshire County Council** (1999) also concerned a claimant with dyslexia, though in this case it had been diagnosed correctly; the alleged negligence concerned the education authority's failure to give appropriate advice on the right kind of school for him.

In the third case, **G (a child)** *v* **Bromley London Borough Council** (1999), the claimant had a progressive muscle disease which meant he needed special equipment in order to be able to communicate; this was not provided and he alleged that his education had suffered as a result, causing psychological damage.

The fourth case concerned a claimant, Anderton, who was seeking access to her educational records in order to prove that she had been damaged by inadequate education. **Phelps** was the only case of the four which had been tried; in the other three, the House of Lords was only required to decide whether there was a potentially arguable case. It found in favour of all four claimants, holding that a local education authority has a duty of care to provide an education appropriate to a child's needs, and where this does not happen as a result of the negligent actions of a teacher or educational psychologist, the council may be liable.

The House of Lords stressed that although there was a duty of care, liability for negligence would not be imposed merely because a child had done badly at school – a teacher or educational psychologist would have to fall below the standards expected of a reasonable body of similarly professional people for negligence to be found. They argued that this requirement would ensure that the decision did not result in a flood of claims.

In **S** *v* **Gloucestershire County Council**, **L** *v* **Tower Hamlets** (2000), the Court of Appeal held that there should be no blanket immunity with regard to the second kind of claim examined in **X** *v* **Bedfordshire**, namely child abuse claims against local authorities. As with the education services claims, the court stated that it was essential to look at the whole context of the case, and that strike-out applications would succeed only in the very clearest of cases.

Why have we seen such a change in approach in the five years since **X** *v* **Bedfordshire**? While there may be a genuine change of view on the part of the courts as to the proper legal liabilities of public bodies, a more likely explanation is the effect of the decision of the European Court of Human Rights in **Osman** *v* **UK**, where it took a very dim view of the use of blanket immunities from suit – the case and its implications in this area are discussed at p. 77.

It is worth noting that the issue of immunity from suit for public bodies and local authorities only arises in cases where a local authority or public body is claimed to be negligent with regard to something they have done or failed to do in their specific role as a public body – usually this will concern a statutory power or duty. If a local authority or public body is alleged to be negligent because they have done something which would amount to negligence if it was done by a private individual or organization, the normal rules apply and the fact that the defendant is a public body is not an issue. An example of this is **Beasley** *v* **Buckinghamshire County Council** (1997). Here the claimant was a paid foster parent to a handicapped teenager. The child was heavy and so badly handicapped that she needed a lot of help, and as a result of the work, the claimant was injured. She claimed that the council had been negligent in failing to give her the necessary equipment and training to protect herself from injury. The council sought to have the case struck out, relying on **X** *v* **Bedfordshire** to argue that on public policy grounds no duty of care should exist; they argued that their decision to use the claimant's services had been one of policy, and within the discretion allowed them by statute. The court disagreed: the alleged negligence arose not from the decision to use the claimant's services, but from the way the council acted once it had taken that decision, namely the refusal to provide proper training and equipment. The case was not comparable with **X**, but was more like a case involving an employer's duty of care to provide a safe working environment. The court therefore refused to strike the case out.

Lawyers

Until July 2000, there was a further group which was subject to special rules on liability for negligence: lawyers. The case of **Rondel** *v* **Worsley** (1969) had established that barristers could not be sued for negligently conducting a client's case in court, nor for any work that was closely linked to the conduct of the case in court. This immunity was widened under the Courts and Legal Services Act 1991, which increased the range of professionals who could advocate in the higher courts, to include for example solicitors, and at the same time allowed them all to be covered by the immunity.

In **Rondel**, the court gave three main reasons for the immunity. First, that advocates owe a duty to the court; they must cite all relevant points of law, including those which support their opponent's case rather than their own; they may not mislead the court or allow the judge to take what they know to be a bad point in their favour; and they should not waste court time on irrelevant issues, even if the client thinks that they are important. Clearly, there will be times when this duty is in conflict with the advocate's duty to their client, and, it was argued, if an advocate had to worry about being sued for breach of duty to the client, it might discourage them from properly fulfilling the duty to the court.

Secondly, considering that a client who sues their advocate is likely to be one who has lost their case, it is thought that allowing a negligence action would amount to re-trying the case – since the claim would be alleging that had the advocate not acted negligently, the client would have won, or at least that the remedy ordered would have been less. If the negligence suit was successful, it would be unfair to the losing party in the original case to let the decision stand, but perhaps equally unfair to the original winning party to set it aside – not to mention the added delay, uncertainty and cost.

Over the years, the immunity has been much criticized and seen as an example of lawyers making law for the benefit of lawyers. As consumer awareness increased over the past two decades, it looked more and more odd that other professionals should be required to answer for their mistakes in court, but not lawyers, and both the scope and the very existence of the immunity was challenged in a number of cases. Finally, in **Hall** *v* **Simons** (2000), a seven-judge House of Lords reconsidered the matter and decided that the advocate's immunity was simply no longer justified. Although the case actually concerned solicitors, the court explicitly included barristers within it.

Their Lordships pointed out that the world had changed since **Rondel**, and an increasingly consumer-focused society expected that where a person relies on a member of a profession to give advice or otherwise to exercise professional skills on that person's behalf, the professional should carry out that task with reasonable care; anyone who fails to do so and causes loss as a result should be liable to compensate for that loss. The arguments made in **Rondel** were easily dealt with. On the point of re-litigating previous cases, the Lords pointed out that new procedures already gave the courts considerable powers to strike out cases which have no real chance of succeeding, or are an abuse of process, and attempts to re-open cases by suing lawyers would fall within these categories. As for the issue of balancing the duty to the court against the duty to the client, the House of Lords pointed out that other professionals, such as doctors, also had to balance a duty to the individual client against a general code of ethics, and seemed able to do this. In any case, they stated, a lawyer would not be considered negligent if they caused damage to a client's interests through performing their duty to the court. The House of Lords therefore found that the immunity should be abolished.

However, it is important to realize that, as the House of Lords pointed out, there are still important hurdles in the way of anyone who wants to sue a lawyer for negligent work in court. First, a defendant in a criminal case who attempts to sue a lawyer on the basis that but for their negligence, he or she would not have been convicted, is likely to find the claim struck out as being an abuse of process, because it questions the decision of the court in the criminal case, a role which is supposed to be played by the appeal process (such a case is called a collateral attack, and the rule against it arises from the case of **Hunter** *v* **Chief Constable of West Midlands** (1980)). The House of Lords suggested that this principle would rarely apply to negligence alleged with regard to civil cases.

The second hurdle, which applies to claims arising from either civil or criminal cases, is that proving that a lawyer's negligence in court actually caused damage will be very difficult. As Lord Steyn pointed out in **Hall**, to succeed in such a claim, a claimant will need to prove that a better standard of work from the lawyer would have resulted in a different outcome, which involves one court essentially guessing how another might have reacted. How keen the courts will be to find that better advocacy would have resulted in a different result is impossible to predict.

The future for special group immunities

As we have seen, the long-standing immunity from negligence suits of lawyers has now been killed off by the House of Lords, and a recent decision from the European Court of Human Rights suggests that the future for the other immunities discussed above may be questionable. The case, which has been referred to previously in this section, is **Osman *v* UK** (1998). It concerned a family who had suffered a tragedy at the hands of a criminal, and sought to sue the police for negligence in failing to prevent it.

The story began when the family's son, Ahmet, was a teenager. A teacher at his school, Paul Paget-Lewis, became obsessed with Ahmet, following him home, taking pictures of him and (allegedly) painting graffiti of a sexual nature about him in the local area. The parents complained to the police, who visited the school but took no further action. Over a period of months, the Osman's home and car were damaged, and a friend of Ahmet's was attacked by Mr Paget-Lewis. The family complained to the police after each incident, and Mr Paget-Lewis was interviewed by the police several times. They were also informed after Mr Paget-Lewis told employees of the education authority that he 'felt like doing a Hungerford', a reference to an indiscriminate mass killing carried out in the town of Hungerford, and made threats against the deputy headmaster of the school.

At one point the police decided to arrest Mr Paget-Lewis on suspicion of causing criminal damage to the Osmans' property, but he was not at home. Some months after that, he stole a gun, went to the Osmans' house and shot both Ahmet and his father. Mr Osman was killed and Ahmet badly injured. He then drove to the home of the deputy headmaster, whom he shot and injured. He shot and killed the deputy headmaster's son.

Paget-Lewis was convicted of charges of manslaughter, and sentenced to be detained in a secure mental hospital. The Osmans sought to sue the police for negligence, but the police made an application to strike out their claim, on the ground that **Hill** established that the police could not be sued for negligence concerning the investigation and suppression of crime.

The Osmans then brought a case against the British government before the European Court of Human Rights (ECHR). They made a number of different allegations, but as far as our discussion here is concerned, the important one was that the striking out of their case was in breach of Art 6.1 of the European Convention on Human Rights, which provides a right to a fair trial. The argument was that the decision in **Hill** gave the police a blanket immunity from negligence suits in cases which involved the investigation and suppression of crime, and that this meant that the English courts would not even look at the merits of a such a case, and that therefore people in the position of the Osmans would be denied a fair trial of their claim.

The British government argued that the rule established in **Hill** did not confer a blanket immunity; it did not mean that an action against the police on the issue of their work against crime was always doomed to fail. However, the ECHR found that the way in which the rule had been used did confer a blanket immunity. The courts had not looked at the merits of the Osmans' claim, nor the facts on which it was based; their case was simply rejected by the Court of Appeal since it was found to fall squarely within the scope of the exclusionary rule formulated by the House of Lords in the **Hill** case, and the Court of Appeal had assumed that this provided the police with a watertight defence.

The ECHR pointed out that the aim of the **Hill** rule – to promote the effectiveness of the police service and so prevent crime – might well be legitimate within the terms of the Convention, but its scope and the way it had been used in this case were problematic. In particular, in dealing with the case on the basis of a striking out application, the Court of Appeal had denied itself the chance to consider whether there were competing public interest issues which would outweigh the public interest argument for the **Hill** rule. The ECHR suggested that clearly there were competing public interest issues: the applicants' case had involved the alleged failure to protect the life of a child; they alleged that that failure was the result of a catalogue of acts and omissions which amounted to grave negligence as opposed to minor acts of incompetence; and the harm sustained was of the most serious nature. The ECHR held that these were considerations which should have been examined on their merits and not automatically excluded by the application of a rule which amounted to the grant of an immunity to the police.

The Government argued that the Osmans had available to them alternative routes for securing compensation, such as a civil action against Paget-Lewis or the psychiatrist who had examined him during the period before the killing and concluded that he was not mentally ill. However the ECHR argued that these remedies would not have met the Osmans' aim in bringing the action against the police, namely to secure answers to the question of why the police failed to take action against Paget-Lewis soon enough to protect his victims. While the Osmans might or might not have succeeded in proving that the police were negligent, they were at least entitled to have the police account for their actions and omissions in a court hearing which would examine the facts and merits of the case.

For these reasons, the Court concluded unanimously that the application of the **Hill** rule in the Osmans' case was a restriction on the applicants' right of access to a court and therefore a violation of Art 6.1 of the Convention.

Where does this leave negligence actions against the police and other public bodies? One thing that seems clear is that whatever implications the case has will apply equally to cases against bodies other than the police – the argument that public policy arguments in favour of immunity must be balanced with public policy arguments against immunity is equally applicable to any of the special groups discussed above.

Perhaps the clearest implication is a procedural one: the use of striking out applications to decide whether it is fair, just and reasonable to impose a duty of care now seems permissible in only the clearest cases, where all the considerations can be weighed in the pre-trial examination; it may even not be permissible at all. The English courts have already shown them-selves much more reluctant to grant striking out applications in cases concerning immunity for special groups, and in **Barrett** and **Phelps** they made specific reference to the **Osman** decision in explaining this. Lord Browne-Wilkinson criticized the decision, but stated that 'in the present very unsatisfactory state of affairs' it was sensible not to allow use of the striking-out procedure except in very clear cases; he also noted that once the Human Rights Act came into force in October 2000, the Convention, and therefore the right to a fair trial, would become part of British law.

However, the decision in **Kinsella** *v* **Chief Constable of Nottingham-shire** (1999) suggests that use of public body immunities as a pre-trial filter is not dead. Ms Kinsella brought an action in negligence against the police on the ground that they had negligently damaged her property while carrying out a search of her house. The case was struck out, and the claimant appealed. The Queen's Bench Division dismissed her appeal, stating that **Osman** did not rule out use of a striking out action to decide whether an immunity applied. The decision on whether the matter could be decided in a striking out application had to be made on a case-by-case basis, and where, as here, there was sufficient information in the plead-ings to allow the court to examine the question, the question of immunity could be decided pre-trial. In this case the court held that as the police had been acting in the course of a criminal investigation, and there were no public policy reasons in favour of lifting the immunity, the striking out application should succeed.

The other important implication of **Osman** concerns substantive negli-gence law. As we have seen, the approach of English tort law to the duty of care issue is to lay down general rules regarding policy questions, and using these to decide whether a particular individual's case gives rise to a duty of care – the implication being that if the rules say there is no duty of care in a particular type of situation, then nothing about the individu-al's case can affect that. The **Osman** decision takes a different view, suggesting that it is important to balance the policy considerations behind general rules against the circumstances of the individual case – so that, for example, the seriousness of the harm done to the victim and the degree of carelessness alleged against the police might outweigh the policy considerations behind the immunity. This could have very impor-tant implications for the development of duties of care.

BREACH OF A DUTY OF CARE

At the very beginning of this chapter, we explained that negligence has three elements: a duty of care; breach of that duty; and damage caused by the breach. Now that we have looked at the various tests for establishing whether a duty exists between the claimant and the defendant, we can move on to consider what, assuming a duty has been found in any particular circumstances, will constitute a breach of that duty.

Breach of a duty of care essentially means that the defendant has fallen below the standard of behaviour expected in someone undertaking the activity concerned, so, for example, driving carelessly is a breach of the duty owed to other road users, while bad medical treatment may be a breach of the duty owed by doctors to patients. In each case, the standard of care is an objective one: the defendant's conduct is tested against the standard of care which could be expected from a reasonable person. This means that it is irrelevant that the defendant's conduct seemed fine to them; it must meet a general standard of reasonableness.

This principle was established in **Vaughan *v* Menlove** (1837). The defendant built a haystack on land adjoining the claimant's cottages, and because the haystack was poorly ventilated, it caught alight, causing damage to the cottages. The state of the haystack, and the almost inevitable result of leaving it like that, had been pointed out to the defendant, but he refused to do anything about it, and simply answered that he would 'chance it', apparently because the haystack was insured, so he stood to lose nothing if it caught fire. The defendant argued that he had genuinely acted honestly and in accordance with his own best judgment of the risk, but it was held that this was not enough; in such a situation, a reasonable person would have taken precautions.

As the test is objective, the particular defendant's own characteristics are usually ignored. A striking example of this is that the standard of care required of a driver is that of a reasonable driver with no account taken of whether the driver has been driving for 20 years or 20 minutes, or even is a learner driver. In **Nettleship *v* Weston** (1971) the claimant was a driving instructor, and the defendant his pupil. On her third lesson, she drove into a lamp post and the claimant was injured. The court held that she was required to come up to the standard of the average competent driver, and anything less amounted to negligence: 'The learner driver may be doing his best, but his incompetent best is not good enough. He must drive in as good a manner as a driver of skill, experience and care.' However, there are a limited number of situations in which special characteristics of the defendant will be taken into account (see below).

▶ The standard of reasonableness

It is important to realize that the standard of care in negligence never amounts to an absolute duty to prevent harm to others. Instead, it sets a standard of reasonableness: if a duty of care exists between two parties, the duty is to do whatever a reasonable person would do to prevent harm occurring, not to do absolutely anything and everything possible to prevent harm. We can see this principle in operation in **Etheridge *v* East Sussex County Council** (1999). The claimant here was a teacher who was injured in an accident at school: she had been coming up the stairs when a pupil threw a heavy basketball down them, hitting her on the head. She sued the County Council, who ran the school, alleging that they were negligent in allowing such an accident to happen. However, the court found that the council had taken all reasonable steps to prevent accidents: the school was well run, with no evidence of behavioural problems, and there were rules in place designed to help prevent accidents and systems for enforcing them. The school was not required to guarantee the safety of every person in the school against every possible way that an accident could happen; its duty was to make the premises reasonably safe and it had done that, so there was no negligence.

In deciding what behaviour would be expected of the reasonable person in the circumstances of a case, the courts consider a number of factors, balancing them against each other. These include special characteristics of the defendant; special characteristics of the claimant; the magnitude of the risk; how far it was practicable to prevent the risk; and any benefits that might be gained from taking the risk. None of the factors is conclusive by itself; they interact with each other. For example, if a type of damage is not very serious nor very likely to occur, the precautions required may be quite slight, but the requirements would be stricter if the damage, though not serious, was very likely to occur. Equally, a risk of very serious damage will require relatively careful precautions even if it is not very likely to occur.

Special characteristics of the defendant

Children

Where the defendant is a child, the standard of care is that of an ordinarily careful and reasonable child of the same age. In **Mullin *v* Richards** (1998), the defendant and claimant were 15-year-old schoolgirls. They were fencing with plastic rulers during a lesson, when one of the rulers snapped and a piece of plastic flew into the claimant's eye, causing her to lose all useful sight in it. The Court of Appeal held that the correct test was whether an ordinarily careful and reasonable 15-year-old would have foreseen that the game carried a risk of injury. On the facts, the practice was common and was not banned in the school, and the girls had never been warned that it could be dangerous, so the injury was not foreseeable.

Illness

A difficult issue is what standard should be applied when a defendant's conduct is affected by some kind of infirmity beyond their control. In **Roberts v Ramsbottom** (1980), the defendant had suffered a stroke while driving and, as a result, lost control of the car and hit the claimant. The court held that he should nevertheless be judged according to the standards of a reasonably competent driver. This may seem extremely unjust, but remember that motorists are covered by insurance; the question in the case was not whether the driver himself would have to compensate the claimant, but whether his insurance company could avoid doing so by establishing that he had not been negligent. This is also one explanation for the apparently impossible standard imposed in **Nettleship** (above).

Even so, in a more recent case, **Mansfield v Weetabix Ltd** (1997), the Court of Appeal took a different approach. Here the driver of a lorry was suffering from a disease which on the day in question caused a hypoglycaemic state (a condition in which the blood sugar falls so low that the brain's efficiency becomes temporarily impaired). This affected his driving, with the result that he crashed into the defendant's shop. The driver did not know that his ability to drive was impaired, and there was evidence that he would not have continued to drive if he had known. The Court of Appeal said that the standard by which he should be measured was that of a reasonably competent driver who was unaware that he suffered from a condition which impaired his ability to drive; on this basis he was found not to be negligent.

Professionals and special skills

Account will also be taken of the fact that a particular defendant has a professional skill, where the case involves the exercise of that skill. In such a case, the law will expect the defendant to show the degree of competence usually to be expected of an ordinary skilled member of that profession, when doing their duties properly. A defendant who falls short of that level of competence, with the result that damage is done, is likely to be held negligent. It would be ridiculous to demand of a surgeon, for example, no more than the skill of the untrained person in the street when carrying out an operation.

So, for example, in **Gates v McKenna** (1998), a stage hypnotist was expected to take the precautions that a 'reasonably careful exponent of stage hypnotism' would take to prevent psychiatric injury to members of his audience, while in **Watson v Gray** (1998), a defendant professional footballer could only be liable for negligently injuring another player if a reasonable professional footballer would have known that what the defendant did carried a significant risk of serious injury.

In assessing the standard of care to be expected in areas where the defendant is exercising special skill or knowledge, the courts have accepted that within a profession or trade, there may be differences of opinion as to the best techniques and procedures in any situation. This issue was addressed in **Bolam** *v* **Friern Barnet Hospital Management Committee** (1957), a case brought by a patient who had had electric shock treatment for psychiatric problems and had suffered broken bones as a result of the relaxant drugs given before the treatment. These drugs were not always given to patients undergoing electric shock treatment; some doctors felt they should not be given because of the risk of fractures; others, including the defendant, believed their use was desirable. How was the court then to decide whether in using them, the defendant had fallen below the standard of a reasonable doctor?

Their answer was a formula which has been taken as allowing the medical profession (and to a certain extent other professions, as the test has been adopted in other types of case too) to fix their own standards. According to McNair J:

> A doctor is not guilty of negligence if he has acted in accordance with a practice accepted as proper by a responsible body of medical men skilled in that particular art.

Providing this was the case, the fact that other doctors might disagree could not make the conduct negligent. The practical effect of this decision (which was only given in a High Court case, but was adopted in several later House of Lords' cases) was that so long as a doctor could find a medical expert prepared to state that the actions complained of were in keeping with a responsible body of medical opinion, it would be impossible to find him or her negligent.

The House of Lords has, however, now modified this much-criticized decision in **Bolitho** *v* **City & Hackney Health Authority** (1997). This case involved a two-year-old boy, who was admitted to hospital suffering breathing difficulties. He was not seen by a doctor. Shortly after his second attack of breathing problems, his breathing failed completely, he suffered a heart attack and died. His mother sued the health authority on his behalf, arguing that he should have been seen by a doctor, who should have intubated him (inserted a tube into his throat to help him breathe), and that it was the failure to do this which caused his death. The doctor maintained that even if she had seen the boy, she would not have intubated him, which meant that the court had to decide whether she would have been negligent in not doing so. The doctor was able to produce an expert witness to say that intubation would not have been the correct treatment, and the claimant was able to produce one who said it would.

In this situation, the **Bolam** principle had always been taken as suggesting that the doctor was therefore not negligent – other medical opinion might disagree with what she did, but she could produce evidence that it was a practice accepted by a responsible body of medical opinion. Lord Browne-Wilkinson, delivering the leading judgment with which the others agreed, thought differently. While agreeing that the **Bolam** test was still the correct one to apply, he said that the court was not obliged to hold that a doctor was not liable for negligence simply because some medical experts had testified that the doctor's actions were in line with accepted practice. The court had to satisfy itself that the medical experts' opinion was reasonable, in that they had weighed up the risks and benefits, and had a logical basis for their conclusion. He then went on, however, to water down this statement by suggesting that in most cases the fact that medical experts held a particular view would in itself demonstrate its reasonableness, and that it would only be in very rare cases that a court would reject such a view as unreasonable. The case before the House of Lords, he concluded, was not one of those rare situations, and so the claimant's claim was rejected.

Bolitho was applied in **Wisniewski *v* Central Manchester Health Authority** (1998). Here the claimant had cerebral palsy, caused by complications at his birth. A cardiotachograph trace during labour had shown that there were problems with his heart rate, but the midwife had negligently failed to show this to the doctor. The claimant sued the health authority as vicariously liable for the midwife's negligence. The basis of the claim was that any reasonable doctor who had been shown the trace would have done an examination and as a result, delivered the baby by Ceasarean section; if this had happened, the damage which caused the condition would not have occurred. The health authority submitted expert evidence that a reasonable doctor might well have delayed the examination anyway, so that the midwife's failure to show the trace could not be said to have caused the damage. However, the judge was swayed by the fact that the doctor who was on duty on the night of the birth did not attend the trial and merely submitted a statement saying he had no recollection of the case. The judge held that, provided the claimant had submitted a substantial case to answer, adverse inferences could be drawn from the fact that someone who would normally be expected to give evidence had declined to do so, and these inferences might well strengthen the value of the claimant's evidence and weaken the case for the defence. As a result, he upheld the claimant's expert evidence that no reasonable doctor would have delayed examining the patient, against the defendant's expert evidence to the contrary, following **Bolitho**. The health authority appealed, and the Court of Appeal held that this was not the kind of case envisaged in **Bolitho** as allowing the judge to hold that the defendant's expert evidence could not logically be supported (although the appeal was dismissed on other grounds, so the claimant still won the case).

However, there are some signs that **Bolitho** is now being used more forcefully, to hold medical opinion to a proper standard of reasonableness.

In **Marriott** *v* **West Midlands Regional Health Authority** (1999), the claimant had suffered a head injury after a fall at home; he spent the night in hospital but was discharged the next day after tests. After continuing to feel ill for a week, he called his GP, who could find nothing wrong but told Mrs Marriott to call him again if her husband's condition got any worse. Four days later, Mr Marriott became partially paralysed, and this was later discovered to be a result of the original injury. He claimed that the GP had been negligent in not referring him back to the hospital, given that the GP did not have the resources to test for the condition which he was eventually found to have. At trial, Mr Marriott's expert witness claimed that, given the symptoms Mr Marriott had shown, the GP should have sent him back to the hospital for more tests; however the GP brought expert evidence to suggest that although this would have been a reasonable course of action, keeping a patient at home for review was equally reasonable in the circumstances.

The old **Bolam** approach would have required the judge to find for the GP, given that he could prove that a reasonable body of medical opinion supported his actions, but, following **Bolitho**, the trial judge looked at the reasonableness of this opinion, given the risk to Mr Marriott, and concluded that, in the circumstances, deciding to review his case at home, without asking for further tests, was not a reasonable use of a GP's discretion. He therefore found the GP negligent. The Court of Appeal upheld his approach: a trial judge was entitled to carry out his own assessment of the risk in the circumstances, and was not bound to follow the opinion of a body of experts.

The use of the **Bolam** test has been extended to cover not just other professionals, but also defendants who do not have the skills of a particular profession, but have made a decision or taken an action which professionals in the relevant area might disagree about. In **Adams and Another** *v* **Rhymney Valley District Council** (2000), the claimants were a family whose children had died when fire broke out in the house they rented from the defendant council. The house had double-glazed windows which could only be opened with a key, and the claimants had been unable to smash the glass quickly enough to save the children. They argued that the council had been negligent in providing this type of window, and the issue arose of whether it was correct to decide this by applying the **Bolam** test, given that the council were not window designers. The court held that it was. They pointed out that in deciding on the window design, the council had to balance the risk of fire against the risk of children falling out of a more easily opened window, and professional opinions varied on how this balance should be struck. If a reasonable body of experts in the field would consider that the council's window design struck this balance in an acceptable way, and the court accepted this view as reasonable, there was no negligence, even though other experts might disagree, and even though the council had neither consulted experts, nor gone through the same processes when choosing the design as an expert would have done.

It was also established in **Bolam** (and **Bolitho** does not affect this point) that where a defendant is exercising a particular skill, he or she is expected to do so to the standard of a reasonable person at the same level within that profession or trade. No account is taken of the defendant's actual experience, so that a junior doctor is not expected to have the same level of skill as a consultant, but is expected to be as competent as an average junior doctor, whether he or she has been one for a year or a week. This principle was upheld in **Djemal** *v* **Bexley Heath Health Authority** (1995) where the standard required was held to be that of a reasonably senior houseman acting as a casualty officer (which was the defendant's position at the time), regardless of how long the defendant had actually been doing that job at that level.

The standard of care imposed is only that of a reasonably skilled member of the profession; the defendant is not required to be a genius, or possess skills way beyond those normally to be expected. In **Wells** *v* **Cooper** (1958) the defendant, a carpenter, fixed a door handle on to a door. Later the handle came away in the claimant's hand, causing him injury. It was held that the carpenter had done the work as well as any ordinary carpenter would, and therefore had exercised such care as was required of him; he was not liable for the claimant's injury.

In **Balamoan** *v* **Holden & Co** (1999) the defendant was a solicitor who ran a small town practice, in which he was the only qualified lawyer. The claimant consulted him over a claim for nuisance. During the following two years, he had two 30-minute interviews with non-qualified members of the solicitor's staff, but no contact with the defendant himself. At the end of that time, he was advised that his claim was worth no more than £3,000, and when he refused to accept that advice, his legal aid certificate was discharged and he stopped using the firm. He went on to conduct the nuisance case himself, and won a settlement of £25,000. He then sued the solicitor, arguing that, but for the solicitor's negligence in, for example, failing to gather all the available evidence at the time, he could have won £1 million in damages. The Court of Appeal held that the solicitor was only to be judged by the standard to be expected of a solicitor in a small country town (rather than, for example, a specialist firm which might have expert knowledge of big claims). However, if such a solicitor delegated the conduct of claims to unqualified staff who could not come up to that standard, they could be held negligent.

In areas such as medicine and technology, the state of knowledge about a particular subject may change rapidly, so that procedures and techniques which are approved as safe and effective may very quickly become outdated, and even be discovered to be dangerous. The case of **Roe** *v* **Minister of Health** (1954) established that where this happens, a defendant is entitled to be judged according to the standards that were accepted at the time when they acted.

The claimant in the case was left paralysed after surgery, because a disinfectant, in which ampoules of anaesthetic were kept, leaked into the ampoules through microscopic cracks in the glass, invisible to the naked eye. Medical witnesses in the case said that until the man's accident occurred, keeping the ampoules in disinfectant was a standard procedure, and there was no way of knowing that it was dangerous; it was only the injuries to the claimant that had revealed the risk. Therefore the defendant was held not to be liable.

However, once a risk is suspected, the position may change. In **N *v* UK Medical Research Council** (1996), the Queen's Bench Division looked at this issue. In 1959, the Medical Research Council (MRC) started a medical trial of human growth hormone, which involved giving the hormone to children with growth problems. The children were each given the hormone by one of four different methods. In 1976, the MRC were warned that the hormone could cause Creutzfeld Jakob Disease (CJD, which most readers will know is the human form of BSE, the fatal brain disease generally known as Mad Cow Disease – though this litigation has no connection with the controversy over BSE-infected beef). A year later, the MRC were told that two of the four methods of giving the hormone carried a particular risk of transmitting CJD. Ultimately, several of the children who received the hormone died from CJD, and their parents alleged that the MRC had been negligent in not investigating the risk when it was first suggested in 1976, and suspending the programme until it was proved safe.

The court held that the failure to look into the risk was negligent, and if the MRC had looked into it then, failure to suspend the trial programme would also have been negligent.

Special characteristics of the claimant

A reasonable person would have due regard to the fact that a claimant has some characteristic or incapacity which increases the risk of harm. In **Paris *v* Stepney Borough Council** (1951), the claimant was employed by the defendants in a garage. As a result of a previous injury at work, he could only see with one eye. His job included welding, and while doing this one day, a piece of metal flew into his good eye and damaged it. No goggles had been provided by the defendant. Although the House of Lords accepted that failing to provide goggles would not have made the defendants liable to a worker with no previous sight problems, in this case they held that the defendants were liable. The risk of injury was small, but the potential consequences to this particular employee if such injury did occur were extremely serious, as he could easily end up completely blind; moreover, the provision of goggles was not difficult or expensive.

In a number of recent cases the courts have looked at the issue of claimants who are drunk, and whether this amounts to a characteristic which in some way increases a defendant's duty towards them. In **Barrett v Ministry of Defence**, the case of the drunken airman discussed on p. 59, the Court of Appeal took the view that there is no duty to stop someone else from getting drunk, but once the claimant was drunk, it accepted that the defendant had assumed some responsibility for protecting him from the consequences of his intoxication, by virtue of the relationship between them and the fact that the defendant had ordered the claimant to be taken to lie down.

However, without such a relationship, it seems there is no general duty to give extra protection to a drunken claimant. In **Griffiths v Brown** (1998), the claimant had got drunk and asked a taxi driver to take him to a particular cashpoint machine. The driver dropped him off on the opposite side of the road from the machine, and he was injured while crossing. He argued that the driver, knowing he was drunk, had a duty not to expose him to the danger of crossing a road. The court rejected this argument: the duty of a taxi driver was to carry a passenger safely during the journey, and then stop at a place where they can get out of the car safely; that duty should not be increased by the fact that the claimant was drunk. However, he accepted that the duty might be extended if, for example, a passenger who intended to spend the evening drinking, arranged for a taxi driver to collect them and see them home safely; this clearly accords with the **Barrett** approach that there may be a duty to protect a claimant from the effects of drunkenness where the defendant has actually done something which amounts to assuming responsibility for such protection.

The courts are likely to be more severe on defendants who have actively encouraged the claimant to get drunk, rather than merely failing to stop them. The claimant in **Brannon v Airtours Plc** (1999), had been on an Airtours holiday, and joined in an evening excursion organized by them, which offered dinner, dancing and unlimited free wine. Above the table where he was sitting was a revolving electric fan seven feet from the floor; the party guests had been warned not to climb onto the tables because of the danger from these fans if they did. The claimant did climb on the table, in order to get out of his seat without people nearby having to move, and he was injured. The Court of Appeal held that the fact that the holiday company had actively created an atmosphere where people would drink too much, lose their inhibitions and have less than usual regard for their personal safety was relevant to assessing whether they had been negligent.

Magnitude of the risk

This includes both the chances of damage occurring, and the seriousness of that damage. In **Bolton v Stone** (1951), the claimant was standing outside her house in a quiet street, when she was hit by a cricket ball from a nearby ground. It was clear that the cricketers could have foreseen that a ball would be hit out of the ground, and this had happened before, but only six times in the previous 30 years. Taking into consideration the presence of a 17-foot fence, the distance from the pitch to the edge of the ground, and the fact that the ground sloped upwards in the direction in which the ball was struck, the House of Lords considered that the chances of injury to someone standing where the claimant was were so slight that the cricket club was not negligent in allowing cricket to be played without having taken any other precautions against such an event. The only way to ensure that such an injury could not occur would be to erect an extremely high fence, or possibly even a dome over the whole ground, and the trouble and expense in such precautions were completely out of proportion to the degree of risk.

A case in which the potential seriousness of an injury was decisive is **Paris** *v* **Stepney Borough Council** (above).

Practicality of protection

The magnitude of the risk must be balanced against the cost and trouble to the defendant of taking the measures necessary to eliminate it. The more serious the risk (in terms of both foreseeability and degree of potential harm), the more the defendant is expected to do to protect against it. Conversely, as **Bolton** *v* **Stone** shows, defendants are not expected to take extreme precaution against very slight risks. This was also the case in **Latimer** *v* **AEC Ltd** (1952). Flooding had occurred in a factory owned by the defendants following an unusually heavy spell of rain. This had left patches of the floor very slippery. The defendants had covered some of the wet areas with sawdust, but had not had enough to cover all of them. The claimant, a factory employee, was injured after slipping on an uncovered area, and sued, alleging that the defendants had not taken sufficient precautions; in view of the danger, they should have closed the factory. The House of Lords agreed that the only way to eradicate the danger was to close the factory, but held that given the level of risk, particularly bearing in mind that the slippery patches were clearly visible, such an onerous precaution would be out of proportion. The defendants were held not liable.

Where the defendant is reacting to an emergency, they are then judged according to what a reasonable person could be expected to do in such a position and with the time available to decide on an action, and this will clearly allow for a lesser standard of conduct than that expected where the situation allows time for careful thought.

Common practice

In deciding whether the precautions taken by the defendant (if any) are reasonable, the courts may look at the general practice in the relevant field. In **Wilson *v* Governors of Sacred Heart Roman Catholic Primary School, Carlton** (1997), the claimant, a nine-year-old boy, was hit in the eye with a coat by a fellow pupil as he crossed the playground to go home at the end of the day. The trial judge had looked at the fact that attendants were provided to supervise the children during the lunch break, and inferred from this that such supervision should also have been provided at the end of the school day. The Court of Appeal, however, noted that most primary schools did not supervise children at this time; they also pointed out that the incident could just as easily have happened outside the school gates anyway. Consequently the school had not fallen below the standard of care required.

In **Thompson *v* Smith Shiprepairers (North Shields) Ltd** (1984), it was made clear that companies whose industrial practices showed serious disregard for workers' health and safety would not evade liability simply by showing that their approach was common practice in the relevant industry. The case involved a claimant who suffered deafness as a result of working in the defendant's shipyard, and the defendants argued that the conditions in which he worked were common across the industry and therefore did not fall below the required standard of care. Mustill J disagreed, stating that they could not evade liability simply by proving that all the other employers were just as bad. He pointed out that their whole industry seemed to be characterized by indifference to the problem, and held that there were some circumstances in which an employer had a duty to take the initiative to look at the risks and seek out precautions which could be taken to protect workers. He pointed out, however, that this approach must still be balanced against the practicalities; employers were not expected to have standards way above the rest of their industry, though they were expected to keep their knowledge and practices in the field of safety up to date.

Potential benefits of the risk

Some risks have potential benefits for society, and these must be weighed against the possible damage if the risk is taken.

This principle was applied in **Watt *v* Hertfordshire County Council** (1954). The claimant was a firefighter. He was among others called to the scene of an accident where a woman was trapped under a car; a heavy jack was needed to rescue her. The vehicle in which the fire officers travelled to the scene was not designed to carry the jack, and the claimant was injured when it slipped. He sued his employers, but the court held that the risk taken in transporting the jack was outweighed by the need to get there quickly in order to save the woman's life. However, the court stated that if the same accident had occurred in a commercial situation, where the risk was taken in order to get a job done for profit, the claimant would have been able to recover.

DAMAGE

The negligence must cause damage; if no damage is caused, there is no claim in negligence, no matter how careless the defendant's conduct. In the vast majority of cases this is not an issue: there will be obvious personal injury, damage to property or economic loss. However, there are cases where the claimant perceives that the defendant's negligence has caused damage, yet the law does not recognize the results of that negligence as damage. The cases discussed in this section give an insight into how the law decides what is damage and what is not.

The issue of damage to property was the subject of **Hunter** *v* **Canary Wharf Ltd and London Docklands Development Corporation** (1997). The case arose from the construction of the big tower block known as Canary Wharf in East London. An action concerning the effects of the construction work was brought by local residents, and one of the issues that arose from the case was whether excessive dust could be sufficient to constitute damage to property for the purposes of negligence. The Court of Appeal concluded that the mere deposit of dust was not in itself sufficient because dust was an inevitable incident of urban life. In order to bring an action for negligence, there had to be damage in the sense of a physical change in property, which rendered the property less useful or less valuable. Examples given by the court included excessive dust being trodden into the fabric of a carpet by householders in such a way as to lessen the value of the fabric, or excessive dust causing damage to electrical equipment.

A very different issue was examined in **R** *v* **Croydon Health Authority** (1997) and **McFarlane** *v* **Tayside Health Board** (1999); could the birth of a child be considered damage? In **R** *v* **Croydon Health Authority**, an employee of the defendant had routinely examined the claimant, a woman of childbearing age, and found that she was suffering from a life-threatening heart condition, which could be made worse by pregnancy. The claimant was not told this, and went on to become pregnant and have a child. Although she did want a child, the claimant claimed she would not have become pregnant if she had known of the danger to herself in doing so. In addition to claiming for the fact that her heart condition was made worse by the pregnancy, she claimed for the expenses of pregnancy and the cost of bringing up the child, and was successful at first instance. The defendant appealed against the award of damages for the costs of pregnancy and bringing up the child. The Court of Appeal supported its view: where a mother wanted a healthy child and a healthy child was what she got, there was no loss. The court emphasized that a key factor in this case was that the claimant had wanted a child; the decision might be different, it was suggested, when a child was not wanted.

However, when this issue was addressed in **McFarlane** *v* **Tayside Health Board**, the House of Lords found it impossible to view as damage the birth of a healthy child, even to parents who had expressly decided that they did not want more children (the case is a Scottish one, but thought likely to be treated as representing English law too). The claimants were a couple who had four children, and decided that they did not want any more, so Mr McFarlane had a vasectomy. After he was wrongly advised that the operation had been successful, Mrs McFarlane became pregnant again, and gave birth to a healthy daughter. The couple sought to sue the health authority, with Mrs McFarlane claiming damages for the pain and discomfort of pregnancy and birth, and both claimants claiming for the costs of bringing up the child.

The House of Lords allowed the claim for pain and discomfort, pointing out that tort law regularly compensated for pain arising from personal injury, and there was no reason to treat pregnancy as involving a less serious form of pain. But they refused to allow the claim for the costs of bringing up the child, though there was some difference of opinion as to why. Lords Slynn and Hope simply argued that this was pure economic loss and it was not fair, just and reasonable to impose a duty on the health board to prevent such loss. Lords Steyn and Millett based their decision more on policy grounds, stating that the birth of a normal, healthy baby was universally regarded as a blessing, not a detriment, and therefore could not be viewed as damage. Lord Millett pointed out that although there were disadvantages involved in parenthood (cost being one), they were inextricably linked with the advantages, and so parents could not justifiably seek to transfer the disadvantages to others while themselves having the benefit of the advantages.

Both cases focused on the fact that the baby was healthy, and in **McFarlane** the House of Lords specifically declined to consider what the position is when a baby is born handicapped, who would not have been born at all if it were not for a defendant's negligence. Can that now be considered damage for the purpose of a negligence action? On the basis of Lord Millett's analysis it would appear not: handicapped children, just like healthy ones, bring benefits to a family as well as problems, and the Court seemed to consider this an all-or-nothing situation, in which the existence of benefits meant there could not be damage. While this would be a welcome recognition of the dignity of the disabled (judges in other cases have been known to speak of parents being 'afflicted' with a handicapped child), its practical implication for families in this situation may not be so welcome.

CAUSATION

In order to establish negligence, it must be proved that the defendant's breach of duty actually caused the damage suffered by the claimant, and that the damage caused was not too 'remote' from the breach (a legal test which is covered at pp. 99–104 below). The rules on causation covered in this section also apply to every other tort where proof of damage is required. In practice, the rules are also applied in torts which are actionable *per se* (merely because they have been committed, whether or not damage is caused) because where no damage is caused, compensation is usually a token amount, known as nominal damages, so most cases are likely to involve damage of some kind and to require proof of it. We discuss the issue here in the chapter on negligence so that you can get a complete overview of the first tort you study (and also because most of the cases on causation are in negligence), but remember when you look at the other torts that these rules apply there too.

The 'but for' test

Causation is established by proving that the defendant's breach of duty was, as a matter of fact, a cause of the damage. To decide this issue the first question to be asked is whether the damage would not have occurred but for the breach of duty; this is known as the 'but for' test.

The operation of the test can be seen in **Barnett *v* Chelsea and Kensington Hospital Management Committee** (1968). A night-watchman arrived early in the morning at the defendants' hospital, suffering from nausea after having a cup of tea at work. The nurse on duty telephoned the casualty doctor, who refused to examine the man, and simply advised that he should go home, and consult his GP if he still felt unwell in the morning. The man died five hours later, of arsenic poisoning: he had been murdered. The hospital was sued for negligence, but the action failed. The court accepted that the defendants owed the deceased a duty of care, and that they had breached that duty by failing to examine him. However, the breach did not cause his death. There was evidence that even if he had been examined, it was too late for any treatment to save him, and therefore it could not be said that but for the hospital's negligence, he would not have died.

A similar result was reached in **Brooks *v* Home Office** (1999). The claimant was a woman in prison, who was pregnant with twins. Her pregnancy had been classified as high risk, so she needed regular ultrasound scans. One of these scans showed that one of the twins was not developing properly, but the prison doctor, who had little experience in this area of medicine, waited five days before seeking specialist advice. It was then discovered that the affected twin had died two days after the scan. Ms Brooks sued the Home Office (which is responsible for the prison service), arguing that she was entitled to receive that same standard of health care as a woman outside prison, and that the prison doctor's five-day delay in seeking expert advice fell below this standard. The court agreed with these two points, but it was found that a wait of two days before getting expert advice would have been reasonable, and as the baby had actually died within this time, the doctor's negligence could not be said to have caused its death.

Of course it is not always clear what would have happened but for the defendant's negligence. In **Mount** *v* **Barker Austin** (1998), a complex chain of alleged negligence was involved. The claimant had entered a business deal in which a bank was involved. He alleged that the bank had acted in breach of their duty to him, and instructed his solicitors to sue the bank. The solicitors failed to pursue the action against the bank in time, and so the claimant instructed another firm of solicitors to sue the first firm. The second firm then failed to do so in time, and so he sued them, seeking damages to compensate for what he claimed he would have won in the original case against the bank. The trial judge found that the case against the bank would have failed anyway, and awarded only the wasted costs in that action and in the action against the first solicitors. The Court of Appeal upheld the judgment. It said that the defendants had to bring evidence to show that the action against the bank was bound to fail, with the result that their negligence had not caused the claimant any loss, but they had fulfilled this requirement. It was then up to the claimant to disprove this evidence by showing that the action against the bank had a realistic prospect of success; a negligible chance of success was not enough. The claimant had not been able to prove this.

Multiple causes

In some cases there may be more than one cause of damage, with the defendant's conduct one among them. This has proved a difficult area for the courts, and the cases are contradictory. One approach can be seen in **McGhee** *v* **National Coal Board** (1972). Here the claimant suffered from dermatitis through exposure to brick dust at work. It was known that the type of work he did carried a risk of dermatitis, but this risk could have been lessened if his employers had installed showers, as this would mean the brick dust remaining in contact with workers' skin for less time. The problem for the court was that although the Coal Board's negligence had increased the risk to Mr McGhee, he might have got dermatitis even if showers had been installed – they would have lessened the risk, not taken it away. Could his employers' negligence therefore be said to have caused his condition? The House of Lords said that it could: where a defendant's negligence made a substantial contribution to the injury they could be liable, and it was not necessary to prove that their negligence was the sole cause.

A different approach was taken in **Wilsher** *v* **Essex Area Health Authority** (1988). The claimant, Martin Wilsher, was born three months prematurely, and suffered from a variety of problems associated with being born too early. He was put on an oxygen supply and, as a result of a doctor's admitted negligence, was twice given too much oxygen. He eventually suffered permanent blindness, and the hospital was sued.

However, medical evidence suggested that although the overdoses of oxygen could have caused Martin's blindness, it could also have been caused by any one of five separate medical conditions which he suffered from. The House of Lords held that the claimant had to prove, on a balance of probabilities, that the defendant's breach of duty was a material cause of the injury; it was not enough to prove that the defendant had increased the risk that the damage might occur, or had added another possible cause of it. On the facts of the case, the defendant's negligence was only one of the possible causes of the damage, and this was not sufficient to prove causation.

Yet another approach was taken in **Hotson** *v* **East Berkshire Health Authority** (1987). Here the claimant, a young boy, had gone to hospital after falling from a rope and injuring his knee. An X-ray showed no apparent injury, so he was sent home. Five days later, the boy was still in pain, and when he was taken back to the hospital, a hip injury was diagnosed and treated. He went on to develop a condition known as avascular necrosis, which is caused when the blood supply to the site of an injury is restricted, and eventually results in pain and deformity. This condition could have arisen as a result of the injury anyway, but medical evidence showed that there was a 25 per cent chance that if he had been diagnosed and treated properly on his first visit to the hospital, the injury would have healed and the avascular necrosis would not have developed. The Court of Appeal treated this evidence as relevant to the issue of damages, holding that it meant his action could succeed but he should receive only 25 per cent of the damages he would have got if the condition was wholly due to the defendant's negligence.

The House of Lords, however, ruled that this was the wrong approach; what was really in issue was whether the claimant had proved that the defendant's negligence caused his condition. The House held that he had not: the law required that he should prove causation on a balance of probabilities, which means proving that it was more likely that they had caused his condition than that they had not. What the medical evidence showed was that there was a 75 per cent chance of him developing the condition even if the negligence had not occurred; proving causation on a balance of probabilities required at least a 51 per cent chance that the negligence caused the damage.

Recent cases show that no consensus has been reached on which of these approaches – if any – is correct. In **Stovold** *v* **Barlows** (1995), the claimant claimed that the defendant's negligence had caused him to lose the sale of his house. The Court of Appeal decided that there was a 50 per cent chance that the sale would have gone ahead had the defendant not been negligent, and on this basis they upheld the claimant's claim, but awarded him 50 per cent of the damages that he would normally have won (thus following the approach it had taken in **Hotson**, and not that taken by the House of Lords in that case).

In **Allied Maples Group** *v* **Simmons & Simmons** (1995), the claimants hoped to make a particular business deal, but were prevented from doing so by the defendant's negligence; it was possible that the deal might not have gone ahead for other reasons even if the negligence had not happened. The Court of Appeal held that where the damage alleged depends on the possible action of a third party (in this case the other party to the deal), the claimant must prove that the chance was a substantial one, as opposed to pure speculation on what might have happened. If so, the action can succeed on causation, and the evaluation of the chance will be taken into account when calculating damages.

In **Page** *v* **Smith (No 2)** (1996), the Court of Appeal referred back to the **McGhee** test. The case arose from the action originally discussed in the section on psychiatric shock (see p. 41 above), where the claimant argued that his physical condition, ME, was reactivated and made worse by the mental shock of the car crash caused by the defendant. In this case, the defendant appealed on the issue of causation, arguing that the trial judge had been wrong in applying a test of causation derived from **McGhee**:

> . . . did the accident, on the balance of probabilities, cause or materially contribute to or materially increase the risk of development or prolongation of the symptoms which [the defendant] currently suffers?

The Court of Appeal held that this was the correct test and dismissed the appeal.

The **McGhee** approach also found favour in **Athey v Leonati** (1999). The claimant, who had a history of minor back problems, was injured in two successive car crashes. Some months afterwards, he suffered severe back pain while exercising, and was diagnosed as having a back condition called a disc herniation. This resulted in him having to leave his job and take lower-paid work. He sued the drivers involved in the accident, who admitted liability for his original injuries, but disputed the claim that these had caused the disc herniation, suggesting that it could have been caused by his previous back problems, in which case they were not liable for it; or by a combination of these and the car accident injuries, in which case their liability would only be partial.

The Court of Appeal held that while it would generally need to be shown that 'but for' the defendants' negligence the condition would not have happened, where that test was unworkable, it was enough to show that the defendant materially contributed to the injury; it did not have to be the sole cause. They were fully liable for the injury, since there was no evidence that the disc herniation would have happened as a result of the defendant's previous back problems if the car accidents had not taken place.

However, the **McGhee** approach works slightly differently where all the possible causes of the damage are the result of negligence (as opposed to

McGhee and **Athey**, where the other possible causes were not the result of anyone's negligence). In **Holtby** *v* **Brigham & Cowan** (2000), the claimant suffered asbestosis as a result of breathing asbestos dust at work over a long period. He had been employed by the defendants for approximately half that time, and by other firms doing similar work for the rest; for reasons which are not important here, he was only sueing the defendants. The Court of Appeal stated that the defendants were liable if it was proved that their negligence had made a material contribution to the claimant's disability; their negligence did not have to be the sole cause of it. However, if the injury had also been partially caused by the negligence of others, the defendants would only be liable for the proportion they had caused. In deciding how big this proportion was, the judge followed the practice of insurance companies and related it to the amount of time the claimant had been exposed to the defendants' negligence and, erring on the side of the claimant, set the proportion of liability at 75 per cent.

An interesting new development in the area of causation can be seen in **Bolitho** *v* **City & Hackney Health Authority** (1997), the case discussed earlier concerning the little boy brought to hospital with breathing difficulties (see p. 83). The doctor in the case had argued that even if she had attended the little boy, she would not have intubated him, so that her failure to attend could not therefore be a cause of his death. Had this argument been allowed to succeed, it would mean that a patient who could prove that a doctor was negligent in not attending could lose the action on the basis that even if the doctor had attended, she would have behaved negligently. The House of Lords rightly refused to accept this, and stated that causation could be established if the claimant proved either that the doctor would have intubated if she had attended; or that she *should* have intubated if she had attended, because it would be a breach of duty not to have done so.

The case of **Pickford** *v* **Imperial Chemical Industries** (1998) stresses that the onus is always on the claimant to prove causation. In that case the claimant was a secretary who had suffered severe pains in her hands after her employers greatly increased the amount of typing she had to do, a condition usually known as Repetitive Strain Injury (RSI). Evidence was presented that the condition could be caused by physical or psychological factors or a combination of the two, and the defendants suggested that the cause in this case was psychological. The Court of Appeal held that the claimant had to prove that her condition was caused by the typing and not merely associated with it, and she had not done that. The defendants were not required to prove that the cause was psychological.

Intervening events

In some cases, an intervening event may occur after the breach of duty, and contribute to the claimant's damage. Where such an event is said to break the chain of causation, the defendant will only be liable for such damage as occurred up to the intervening event. In such cases the intervening event is called a *novus actus interveniens*.

Where there is an intervening event but the original tort is still a cause of the damage, the defendant remains liable. In **Baker** *v* **Willoughby** (1969) the claimant injured his left leg in a road accident as a result of the defendant's negligence. After the accident he was shot in the left leg by an armed robber, and ended up having his leg amputated. The robber was not caught and so could not be sued for the incident.

The defendant argued that his liability only extended to the point at which the armed robbery occurred, when the effects of his negligence were overtaken by the robber's shooting. However, in this context the 'but for' test is not strictly applied: it would be inaccurate to suggest that the damage would not have occurred but for the breach of duty, for the claimant's leg would have been damaged later anyway, as a result of the robbery. However, the House of Lords took the approach that tort law compensates as much for the inability to lead a full life as for the specific injury itself. This inability continues even where the original injury had been superseded by a later one.

However, **Baker** *v* **Willoughby** was not followed in the decision of **Jobling** *v* **Associated Dairies** (1982). As a result of the defendant's breach of duty, the claimant hurt his back at work in 1973, which rendered him disabled and reduced his earning capacity by 50 per cent. In 1976, the claimant was diagnosed as suffering from a back condition, known as myelopathy, which had no connection with the accident. By the end of that year he was unable to work. The defendants argued that they should only be liable for the effects of the back injury up to the point at which the myelopathy occurred, to which the claimant responded that the case of **Baker** *v* **Willoughby** should apply. The House of Lords found unanimously in favour of the defendants' argument, applying the 'but for' test strictly. The risk of unrelated medical conditions occurring was habitually taken into account when calculating damages for future loss of earnings. It could therefore not be ignored when it had already developed.

In **Thompson** *v* **Blake-James** (1998), the defendant was a doctor, who was sued by the parents of a child on the basis that he had been negligent in advising them not to have the child immunized against measles. The child had caught measles and as a result developed a rare condition which caused brain damage. The defendant had given the advice because the child's medical history made her more likely than most to suffer damage as a result of the immunization. She was six months old at the time, and the decision not to immunize her was not taken until a year later, after the parents had talked to other doctors. The Court of Appeal held that the advice given by the other doctors was an intervening event which broke the chain of causation because it showed that the parents were not relying on the defendant's advice.

The issue of intervening acts was raised recently in **Reeves *v* Commissioner of Police for the Metropolis** (1999), which we have already looked at in the context of liability for omissions (p. 58). This was the case where the police were successfully sued by the wife of a man who had committed suicide while in police custody. The police argued that Reeves' action in deliberately killing himself broke the chain of causation between their negligence in not preventing him from attempting to kill himself and his death. The House of Lords rejected this approach, and said it was absurd to suggest that the very act which the police had a duty to prevent could be an intervening act and prevent liability.

REMOTENESS OF DAMAGE

As well as proving that the defendant's breach of duty factually caused the damage suffered by the claimant, the claimant must prove that the damage was not too remote from the defendant's breach. Like the issue of duty of care, the remoteness test is a legal test (rather than a factual one) which forms one of the ways in which the law draws the line between damage which can be compensated in law, and that which cannot. This means that there are some circumstances where the defendant will undoubtedly have caused damage in fact, but in law, it is considered that they should not have to compensate the claimant for it (remoteness of damage also arises in other torts, but as the rules sometimes differ from those in negligence, the issue is also considered in the relevant chapters).

▶ The test of remoteness

The traditional test of whether damage was too remote was laid down in **Re Polemis** (1921), and essentially imposed liability for all direct physical consequences of a defendant's negligence; it became known as the direct consequence test. The case concerned the renting of a ship, an arrangement known as a charter. The people renting the ship, called the charterers, had loaded it with tins of petrol, and during the voyage these leaked, releasing large amounts of petrol vapour into the hold. The ship docked at Casablanca, and was unloaded. The workers unloading it had positioned some heavy planks as a platform over the hold, and as a result of their negligence, one of the planks fell into the hold. It caused a spark, which ignited the petrol vapour, and ultimately the ship was completely burnt, causing the owners a loss of almost £200,000. They sued the charterers.

The trial judge had found as a fact that the charterers could not reasonably have foreseen that the fire was likely to occur as a result of the plank falling into the hold, though they might reasonably have foreseen that some damage to the ship might result from that incident. However, the Court of Appeal held that this was irrelevant; the charterers were liable for any consequence that was a direct result of their breach of duty, even if such consequences might be different and much more serious from those which they might reasonably have foreseen. A consequence would only be too remote if it was 'due to the operation of independent causes having no connection with the negligent act, except that they could not avoid its results'.

As time went on and the tort of negligence grew, the direct consequence test came to be seen as rather hard on defendants. As a result, a new test was laid down in **Overseas Tankship (UK) v Morts Dock & Engineering Co (The Wagon Mound)** (1961), which is usually referred to as **Wagon Mound No 1** (a second case, **Wagon Mound No 2**, arose from the same incident, but raised different issues; it is discussed later). The incident which gave rise to the litigation was an accident which occurred in Sydney Harbour, Australia. In **Wagon Mound No 1**, the defendants were the owners of a ship which was loading oil there, and owing to the negligence of their employees, some of it leaked into the water and spread, forming a thin film on the surface. Within hours, the oil had spread to a neighbouring wharf, owned by the claimants, where another ship was being repaired by welders. It caused some damage to the slipway, but then a few days later, further and much more serious damage was caused when the oil was ignited by sparks from the welding operations.

The trial judge found that the damage to the slipway was reasonably foreseeable, but given that the evidence showed that the oil needed to be raised to a very high temperature before it would catch fire, the fire damage was not reasonably foreseeable. Nevertheless, as the Australian courts were also following **Re Polemis**, he found the defendants liable for both types of damage.

The Privy Council, however, took a different view, stating that **Re Polemis** was no longer good law. The new test of remoteness was the foresight of the reasonable person: was the kind of damage suffered by the claimant reasonably foreseeable at the time of the breach of duty? Under this test, the defendants in **Wagon Mound No 1** were only liable for the damage to the slipway, and not for the fire damage. The reasonable foreseeability test as set down in **Wagon Mound No 1** is now the standard test for remoteness of damage in negligence.

Type of damage

Under the remoteness of damage test, a defendant will only be liable if it was reasonable to foresee the type of damage that in fact happened – in **Wagon Mound No 1**, it was clear that this covered the damage to the slipway, but not the fire damage. However, this has led to some difficult distinctions in other cases, as the contrasting decisions in **Doughty** *v* **Turner Manufacturing Co** (1964) and **Hughes** *v* **Lord Advocate** (1963) show.

In **Doughty**, the claimant was an employee who was injured when an asbestos cover was knocked into a vat of hot liquid. A chemical reaction between the asbestos and the liquid caused the liquid to bubble up and erupt over the edge of the vat, burning the claimant. The chemical reaction was not foreseeable, but the claimant argued that it was foreseeable that the lid falling in would cause some liquid to splash out, and the result of this was likely to be burning, the same injury as resulted from the liquid erupting. The court disagreed, holding that an eruption was different in kind to a splash.

In **Hughes**, Post Office employees had opened a manhole in the street, and left it open when they finished work for the day, covering it with a canvas shelter and surrounding it with paraffin lamps. The claimant, an eight-year-old boy, picked up one of the lamps and took it into the shelter. While playing there, he knocked the lamp into the manhole, and paraffin vapour from the lamp ignited, causing an explosion in which the claimant fell into the hole and was badly burnt. The defendants claimed that although they could have foreseen a risk that someone might be burnt, they could not have foreseen injuries caused by an explosion, and so the damage was too remote. The House of Lords rejected this view: if it was reasonably foreseeable that the damage would be burning, it did not matter that the burns were produced in an unforeseeable way.

Recent cases seem to suggest that the less narrow **Hughes** approach is gaining favour. In **Page** *v* **Smith (No 2)** (1996) (see p. 96), it was argued that where some form of personal injury was foreseeable, the fact that the damage suffered was psychiatric rather than physical did not make it too remote; they were both types of personal injury and that was foreseeable. Similarly, in **Margereson** *v* **J W Roberts Ltd** (1996), the Court of Appeal considered the case of claimants who had contracted the lung disease mesothelioma as a result of playing near the defendant's asbestos factory as children. The court held that it was not necessary for mesothelioma to be a reasonably foreseeable result of exposure to the asbestos dust, it was sufficient that some form of lung damage was reasonably foreseeable.

However, the case of **Brown** *v* **Lewisham and North Southwark Health Authority** (1999) makes it clear that the courts can still manipulate the foreseeability concept as a potential restriction on liability. The case involved a complicated medical negligence claim. The claimant had had heart surgery at Guy's, a London hospital, after which he was given a blood-thinning drug called Heparin and discharged to travel by train and taxi to his local hospital in Blackpool; at the time of his discharge, he was suffering from a chest infection. A few days later he was diagnosed as having a deep vein thrombosis (a potentially fatal blood clot) in his leg, and was given Heparin again. In rare cases, patients can develop a reaction, called HITT, to a first dose of Heparin, which results in later doses causing or worsening a thrombosis rather than treating it; this happened to Mr Brown. The hospital failed to recognize it, and gave him another course of Heparin, and eventually the worsening thrombosis meant that he had to have his leg amputated.

The claimant sued the health authority which ran Guy's Hospital, on the basis that if he had stayed there, the HITT would have been diagnosed, and he would not have had to undertake the journey to Blackpool and the later courses of Heparin, both of which, it was claimed, had materially contributed to the thrombosis and loss of his leg. However, it was acknowledged that if he had not had the chest infection, it would not have been negligent for the hospital to discharge him when it did, and the chest infection had had nothing to do with his subsequent problems. The Court of Appeal held that causation had not been proved, but Beldam LJ also considered the issue of the type of damage suffered by the claimant. He argued that it was not fair to hold a doctor liable for failing to diagnose the HITT, simply because that doctor was at fault in his treatment of the chest infection:

> . . . it must be shown that the injury suffered by the patient is within the risk from which it was the doctor's duty to protect him. If it is not, the breach is not a relevant breach of duty.

This view would seem to go against the **Page** principle that where some kind of personal injury is foreseeable, any kind of personal injury is sufficient. It is worth noting that although a series of apparently conflicting cases like these can seem confusing, as a student you are not expected to know which path a court would take when faced with this issue; what you have to do is show that you are aware that the cases illustrate different approaches. You can do this by stating that there are conflicting cases, and describing how the decision on the facts before you might go if the courts took, for example, the **Page** approach, and how this might differ if the view expressed in **Brown** was preferred. It is also important to point out any differences in the authority of apparently clashing cases, such as whether one was a House of Lords case and the other from the Court of Appeal, or whether, as in **Brown**, the issue was not decisive because other factors played a part in the judgment.

Extent of damage

So long as the type of damage sustained is reasonably foreseeable, it does not matter that it is in fact more serious than could reasonably have been foreseen. The extreme application of this principle is the gruesome-sounding 'eggshell-skull' rule, which essentially establishes that defendants will be liable even if the reason why the damage is more serious than could be expected is due to some weakness or infirmity in the claimant. In **Smith *v* Leech Brain & Co Ltd** (1962), the claimant was burnt on the lip as a result of the defendant's negligence. He had a pre-cancerous condition, which became cancerous as a result of the burn, and the defendant was held liable for the full result of the negligence.

It is not clear whether a version of the 'eggshell-skull' rule applies in economic loss cases, where the claimant's lack of funds results in the financial loss being greater than it might otherwise have been. An example of this occurred in **Liesbosch Dredger** *v* **SS Edison** (1933). The defendants negligently sank the claimants' ship, and because the claimants had already made contracts which required the use of the ship, they had to hire another vessel to do the work. It would have been cheaper overall to buy another ship, but the claimants' funds at the time did not allow them to do this. They therefore claimed for the cost of a new ship, plus the expenses of hiring the one they had used to fulfil their contractual obligations. The House of Lords refused to compensate them for the cost of the hired ship, on the ground that this loss was caused by their own financial circumstances, and was not foreseeable by the defendants.

More recent cases however take a more generous view. In **Dodd Properties (Kent)** *v* **Canterbury City Council** (1980), the defendants caused damage to the claimants' property, and did not admit liability until just before the case came to court. The claimants did not carry out repairs until liability was admitted, because they were worried that if they lost the case, they would not be able to afford to pay for them; this increased the amount of their claim because the cost of the repairs had risen in the meantime. The Court of Appeal awarded them the full cost of the repairs.

A similar view was taken in **Alcoa Minerals of Jamaica** *v* **Broderick** (2000). The case concerned damage done to a building owned by the claimants, which was caused by fumes from the defendant's smelting plant. The claimants sued, and at the time they began the action, submitted a claim for what the repairs would cost. However, they did not actually have the repairs done because they were unable to pay for them. By the time the case came to court, there had been extremely high inflation, and the cost of doing the repairs was by then much higher. The court allowed the claimants to claim the higher figure.

Risk of damage

The case of **Overseas Tankship (UK)** *v* **Miller Steamship Co (The Wagon Mound No 2)** (1967) establishes that so long as a type of damage is foreseeable, it will not be too remote, even if the chances of it happening were slim. The case arose from the accident in Sydney Harbour discussed at p. 100 when we looked at **Wagon Mound No 1**; the defendants were the same, but in this case the claimants were the owners of some ships which were also damaged in the fire. When this case was heard, different evidence was brought which led the trial judge to conclude that it was foreseeable that the oil on the water would ignite, and when the case was appealed to the Privy Council, it held that on the evidence before that judge, he was entitled to reach this conclusion. The risk was small but it clearly existed, and therefore the damage was not too remote.

Intervening events

An intervening event will only make damage too remote if the event itself was unforeseeable. The old case of **Scott** *v* **Shepherd** (1773) is still one of the best illustrations of this. The defendant threw a lighted firework into a market hall while a fair was being held there. It landed on a stall, and the stall owner picked it up and tossed it away from his stall; it landed on another, whose owner did the same, and after the firework had done a lively tour of the market, it eventually exploded in the claimant's face, blinding him in one eye. The court held that the defendant was liable; the actions of the stallholders were a foreseeable result of throwing the firework and therefore could not be considered intervening events.

In **Humber Oil Terminal Trustee Ltd** *v* **Owners of the ship Sivand** (1998), the defendants' ship had damaged the claimants' wharf as a result of negligent navigation. The claimants engaged contractors to repair the wharf, and their agreement with the contractors included a clause that obliged the claimants to pay any extra repair costs which might be necessary if the repairers encountered physical conditions which could not have been foreseen. This in fact happened, as the seabed proved unable to take the weight of the jack-up barge the repairers used, and so the barge sank. The claimants were claiming against the defendants for damage caused to the wharf by their negligence, and they sought to add this increased cost to their claim. The defendants argued that the loss of the barge was not foreseeable, and was an intervening act which broke the chain of causation. The Court of Appeal disagreed: although the precise circumstances were not reasonably foreseeable, it was the kind of circumstance envisaged by the contract, and the loss of the barge was not caused by an intervening event, but an existing state of affairs, namely the condition of the seabed, and it did not break the chain of causation.

▶ Proving negligence

The claimant normally has the burden of proof in relation to proving negligence, which can be a considerable obstacle. However, there are two exceptions to this rule: where the defendant has a criminal conviction related to the incident in question, and where the principle of *res ipsa loquitur* (see below) applies.

Criminal convictions

Under s. 11 of the Civil Evidence Act 1968, a defendant's criminal conviction is admissible evidence in a subsequent civil case based on the same facts. This means that if a defendant whose conduct is alleged to have been negligent has already been convicted of a crime for that conduct, that is evidence of negligence, and it is for the defendant to disprove it if they can. A common example is where a defendant in a motor accident case has already been convicted of dangerous driving as a result of the accident.

Res ipsa loquitur

There are circumstances in which the facts of the case are such that the injury complained of could not have happened unless there had been negligence, and in such cases, the maxim *res ipsa loquitur*, which means 'the facts speak for themselves', may apply. One example is the case of **Scott v London and St Katherine's Docks** (1865), where the claimant was injured by some bags of sugar which fell from the open door of the defendant's warehouse above. There was no actual evidence of negligence, but the Court of Appeal held that negligence could be inferred from what had happened, since the bags of sugar could not have fallen out of the door all by themselves. Similarly in **Mahon v Osborne** (1939), it was held that a swab left inside the claimant after a stomach operation could not have got there unless someone had been negligent. In such circumstances, the courts may treat the facts themselves as evidence of negligence (but only evidence, which may be rebutted), provided that two other conditions are satisfied: the events are under the control of the defendant or the defendant's employees, and there is no direct evidence of negligence.

Under the control of the defendant

This point is illustrated by two contrasting cases. In **Gee v Metropolitan Railway** (1873), the claimant fell out of a train just after it left a station, when the door he was leaning against flew open. The railway staff clearly had a duty to ensure that the door was properly shut, and since the train had so recently left the station, it could be inferred from the fact of what happened that they had not shut it properly. However, in a similar case, **Easson v LNE Railway** (1944), the train was seven miles past the last station when the door flew open. In this case it was held that the fact that the door had opened in this way did not necessarily mean that railway staff had been negligent, because the situation was not under their exclusive control; any passenger could have interfered with the door during the time since the train had left the station. The staff might have been negligent, but the facts alone were not enough to act as reasonable evidence to that effect.

No direct evidence of negligence

If there is direct evidence of what caused the damage, the courts will examine that, rather than inferring it from the facts alone. In **Barkway** *v* **South Wales Transport Co Ltd** (1950), the claimant was injured when the bus he was travelling in burst a tyre and crashed. The tyre burst because of a defect that could not have been discovered beforehand, but there was evidence that the bus company should have told drivers to report any blows to their tyres, which could weaken them, and they had not done so. The court held that it should examine this evidence rather than rely on *res ipsa loquitur*.

Using res ipsa loquitur

The operation of *res ipsa loquitur* was explained by the Court of Appeal in **Ratcliffe** *v* **Plymouth and Torbay Health Authority** (1998). Here the claimant had gone into hospital for an ankle operation, and had ended up with a serious neurological condition which it was agreed had been triggered by the injection of a spinal anaesthetic. He argued that this was a case of *res ipsa loquitur*; the injection must have been given negligently, or it could not have caused the problem. The health authority produced expert evidence which stated that the condition might be due to the claimant already having a susceptibility to spinal cord damage, and the injection triggering such damage even though it was not given negligently. The Court of Appeal, referring back to **Scott**, stated that where there was no direct evidence of negligence, but a situation was under the management of the defendant and/or the defendant's employees, and the damaging event was such that in the ordinary course of things would not happen if proper care was taken, that in itself could be taken as evidence of negligence, and in the absence of any other explanation, a judge would be entitled to infer that negligence had taken place.

However, the defendant could prevent the judge from inferring negligence by either showing that he or she took reasonable care, or by supplying another explanation for the events. The court stressed that nothing in the application of *res ipsa* changed the rule that the burden of proof was on the claimant. The defendant's alternative explanation would have to be plausible, and not merely theoretically possible, but the defendant is not required to prove that it was more likely to be correct than any other. In this case the defendant had provided a plausible explanation and it was up to the claimant to prove that negligence, rather than the claimant's explanation, had caused his injury, which he could not do.

By contrast, a claimant's case succeeded on the basis of *res ipsa* in **Widdowson** *v* **Newgate Meat Corporation** (1997). Here the claimant, who suffered from a serious mental disorder, was knocked down by the defendant's van while he was walking along the side of a dual carriageway at night. Because of his disorder, the claimant was not considered a reliable witness and was not called at the trial; the defendant pleaded that there was no case to answer and offered no evidence. The trial judge declined to apply *res ipsa loquitur* on the grounds of lack of evidence regarding the events leading up to the trial. The Court of Appeal disagreed with this approach: case law had established that where it was impossible to pinpoint an exact act or omission that was negligent, but the circumstances were such that it was more likely than not that the damage was caused by the defendant's negligence, it was up to the defendant to rebut this inference. In this case, the road was deserted and the defendant would have had a clear view of the claimant, so it was more likely than not that his negligence caused the action. The defendant driver had failed to rebut the inference by providing a credible explanation of what happened.

Rebutting the inference of negligence

An inference of negligence under the doctrine of *res ipsa loquitur* can be rebutted by the defendant. In **Ngu Chun Piu** *v* **Lee Chuen Tat** (1988), a coach driver swerved while travelling along a dual carriageway, and crossed the central reservation, hitting a bus that was moving in the opposite direction. A passenger on the bus was killed, and his personal representatives sued the driver and owner of the coach. The Privy Council ruled that on the facts negligence could be inferred, but the coach driver was able to rebut this inference by explaining that he had had to swerve to avoid a car which had cut in front of him. Therefore the claimant had to provide actual evidence to prove negligence.

In **Ward** *v* **Tesco Stores Ltd** (1976), the claimant slipped on some yogurt which had been spilt on the floor of the defendant's supermarket. She put forward evidence that three weeks later, another spill, this time of orange juice, was left on the supermarket's floor for 15 minutes, though she had no evidence of the circumstances leading up to her own accident. The defendant gave evidence that the floor was swept five or six times a day, and that staff were instructed that if they saw a spillage, they should stay by it and call someone to clean it up. Nevertheless, the Court of Appeal relied on the doctrine of *res ipsa loquitur* to find that negligence could be inferred, and this inference was not rebutted by the defendant's evidence.

The Highway Code

Following the Road Traffic Act 1988, s. 38(7), where a road user fails to comply with any provision of the Highway Code, that fact may be submitted as evidence of negligence.

DEFENCES

The defences described in this section are often called the general defences, because they apply to a range of different torts, as opposed to specific defences which are only applicable to particular torts. In this chapter we discuss their application to negligence. Not all of them can in fact be used in negligence cases; we have included some inapplicable defences which students commonly imagine might apply in negligence, and explained why they do not.

Where the defences described in this chapter are used in other torts, the rules detailed here will usually apply in the same way. Where there are differences, this information can be found in the relevant chapters, along with discussion of defences which are specific to torts other than negligence.

▶ Contributory negligence

Common law traditionally provided that anyone who was partly responsible for the harm done to them could not recover in tort. Not surprisingly, this caused considerable injustice in some cases, and the Law Reform (Contributory Negligence) Act 1945 now provides that in such cases, the claim need not fail, but the defence of contributory negligence may apply. Where this defence applies, damages can be reduced to take account of the fact that the fault was not entirely the defendant's.

An example of the application of this defence can be seen in **Baker** *v* **Willoughby** (1969), the case discussed earlier, in which the claimant was run over by the defendant and then in a separate incident, shot by a robber. In the first incident he was crossing the road; the defendant was driving carelessly, but the claimant had had a clear view of the road for the last 200 yards travelled by the car, and had taken no evasive action. The Court of Appeal found that he was 50 per cent contributorily negligent – in other words, that both parties were equally to blame. The result was that the claimant received 50 per cent of the damages he would have got if there had been no contributory negligence.

In much of the following discussion, we talk about the claimant taking care for their own safety, because many of the cases on contributory negligence in negligence actions concern accidents. However, contributory negligence can equally well be raised in an economic loss case, where the claimant has failed to take reasonable care of their own economic interests.

It is important to realize that a finding of contributory negligence cannot be made unless it is first clear that the defendant was negligent. Although obviously the defendant must have a duty of care towards the claimant before this can happen, the claimant does not need to have a duty of care towards the defendant; all that is necessary is that they failed to take reasonable care for their own safety, and by that lack of care, contributed to the harm suffered.

In many cases, the claimant's negligent behaviour will contribute to causing the accident which results in damage. An obvious example would be a pedestrian who walks out into the path of a car without looking. However, contributory negligence can also apply where the claimant's behaviour does not cause the accident itself, but contributes to the amount of damage done. For this reason, damages to drivers or passengers in road accidents are always reduced if seatbelts have not been worn, since this negligence would usually increase the injuries suffered.

This principle can be seen clearly in economic loss cases, such as **Cavendish Funding Ltd** *v* **Henry Spencer & Sons Ltd** (1998). Here the claimants had lent money for the purchase of a property which had been negligently valued by the defendants. The defendants had valued the building at over £1½ million, and the claimants had also had a valuation from another company, at around £1 million. The property was actually worth around £250,000. The claimants based their loan on the defendants' valuation and lost money as a result; they sued the defendants for the loss. The Court of Appeal held that the claimants had been contributorily negligent: the discrepancy between the two valuations should have made it clear that something might be wrong, and they should have checked; had they done so the valuation would have been reduced and they would not have lost so much. The court deducted 25 per cent from their damages for contributory negligence.

The damage to which the claimant's negligence has contributed must fall within the general scope of the risk they were taking, but the courts have been willing to give this a fairly wide interpretation. In **Jones** *v* **Livox Quarries** (1952), the claimant was riding on the back of a vehicle called a traxcavator at the quarry where he worked. The vehicle was not designed to carry passengers in this way. The claimant was injured when another vehicle drove into the back of the traxcavator. He argued that his contributory negligence amounted only to taking the risk that he might fall off the back of the traxcavator, but the court held that being hit from behind by another vehicle was also within the range of possible risks arising from riding on the traxcavator, and the claimant's negligence in doing so had contributed to his injury.

The standard of care

The standard of care which the claimant must show for their own safety in order to avoid being found contributorily negligent is essentially the same as the standard of care required of a defendant in negligence: that of the reasonable person involved in the relevant activity. Like the standard of care in negligence, it is usually objective, but allowance is made for children, and probably for people with some type of disability which makes it impossible for them to reach the required standard.

A claimant will not be contributorily negligent where they have only fallen below the standard of care as a result of an error of judgment: the courts have pointed out that reasonable people do make errors of judgment from time to time, and especially in emergency situations. In **Jones v Boyce** (1816), the claimant was riding on top of the defendant's coach when one of the horses' reins broke, and it looked as though the coach might topple over. The claimant jumped from the coach, breaking his leg. As it turned out, the coach was kept on the road, so if the claimant had kept his seat, he would not have been injured. Clearly he had contributed to his own injury, but the court held that this did not amount to contributory negligence; he had acted reasonably in the face of what appeared to be a dangerous situation.

In **Brannon v Airtours Plc** (1999), the Court of Appeal dealt with a case where the defendant's conduct had made the claimant's error of judgment more likely. This is the case discussed at p. 88, concerning the claimant injured at a drunken party organized by the defendant holiday company. The holiday company was found to be negligent, but the court reduced the damages by 75 per cent on the basis that the claimant had been contributorily negligent in ignoring warnings given to holidaymakers about the risk of injury if they climbed on tables. However, the Court of Appeal thought differently; they agreed that there had been some contributory negligence, but stated that the trial judge should have considered the fact that the holiday company had actively created an atmosphere where people would drink a lot and so lose their inhibitions and be less cautious. They reduced the assessment of contributory negligence to 50 per cent. This part of the judgment is an interesting contrast to the views expressed in **Barrett v Ministry of Defence** (1995), to the effect that adults should take responsibility for their own alcohol consumption and not expect others to prevent them getting drunk (see p. 88).

In **Revill v Newberry** (1996), the claimant had entered the defendant's land intending to steal from his shed, but was shot by the defendant, who had taken to sleeping in his shed because he was concerned, rightly as it turned out, about the risk of theft and vandalism. He was sued for negligence by the would-be burglar, and successfully raised the defence of contributory negligence.

The case of **Reeves v Metropolitan Commissioner** (1999) makes it clear that intentionally harming yourself can be contributory negligence. This, you may remember, is the case where police were found negligent in allowing a prisoner to commit suicide. The court found that the claimant's death was caused equally by two factors: the police negligence in allowing him to take his own life; and his action in doing so. Therefore he was 50 per cent contributorily negligent.

Children

Where the claimant is a child, the standard of care is that which could reasonably be expected, taking into account the child's age and development. In **Gough v Thorne** (1966) a 13-year-old girl was injured crossing the road. A lorry driver had stopped to let her cross, and signalled to her that she should cross, so the girl did so, without checking to see whether there was any other vehicle coming up from behind to overtake the lorry. In fact there was a lorry approaching, and it hit and killed her. The court held that taking into account her age, she had not fallen below the expected standard of care and so was not contributorily negligent.

In **Yachuk** *v* **Oliver Blais Co Ltd** (1949), a nine-year-old boy bought some gasoline, a highly inflammable fuel, from the defendants, saying his mother needed it for her car. He took it away and played with it, and ended up being seriously burnt. The company was found to be negligent in supplying the gasoline to a child of that age, but the boy was not found contributorily negligent on the grounds that at his age he could not be expected to know the dangers of gasoline. By contrast, in **Evans** *v* **Souls Garage** (2000), the plaintiff was one of two 13-year-old boys who bought petrol from the defendant, intending to inhale the fumes. Spilled petrol caught light, burning the plaintiff badly. He successfully sued the defendant for negligence in selling the petrol to children, but damages were reduced by a third for his contributory negligence in playing with petrol which he knew to be dangerous.

Very young children are unlikely ever to be found contributorily negligent, since they cannot be expected to have enough awareness and experience to guard their own safety at all.

Reduction of damages

Where contributory negligence is proved, the claimant's damages will be reduced 'to such extent as the court thinks just and equitable having regard to the claimant's share in the responsibility for the damage' (Law Reform (Contributory Negligence) Act 1945, s. 1(1)).

The exact calculations are at the discretion of the court and will vary according to the facts. However, in one of the most common examples of contributory negligence, failure to wear a seatbelt in road accident cases, the courts have laid down a standard set of reductions. In **Froom** *v* **Butcher** (1976), it was stated that in cases where using a seatbelt would have prevented the claimant's injuries from happening at all, damages should be reduced by 25 per cent. Where the injuries would have happened anyway, but wearing a seatbelt would have made them less serious, damages should be reduced by 15 per cent.

▶ *Volenti non fit injuria*

This Latin phrase means 'no injury can be done to a willing person', and describes a defence which applies where the claimant has in some way consented to what was done by the defendant, on the basis that in giving consent the claimant was voluntarily taking the risk of harm. An obvious example is that of a boxer, who by entering a boxing match consents to being hit by an opponent. Unlike contributory negligence, it is a complete defence, rather than a means of reducing damages: if the claimant consented, the defendant is not liable at all.

The test of consent is objective: clearly it is impossible for the courts to see inside the minds of claimants, and so they judge whether there was consent on the basis of the claimant's behaviour. What they are therefore asking is not so much whether the claimant actually consented, but whether their behaviour was such that it was reasonable for the defendant to think that there was consent. As our boxer example shows, consent is easily signified by conduct: the boxer may not say 'I agree that you can hit me', but by stepping into the ring at the start of the match, he makes it reasonable for his opponent to assume he has consented to being hit.

What will amount to consent?

As we have said, the courts are unable to look into the minds of claimants to see whether they consented, so they look to the claimant's outward behaviour as evidence of whether consent was given. Where a claimant clearly knew of a risk, this may be evidence that they consented to it, but it is not in itself conclusive proof. In addition, consent will only amount to a defence if it is freely given; consent given under pressure is not satisfactory.

Both these principles can be seen in the decision in **Smith** *v* **Baker** (1891). The claimant worked in the defendant's quarry. The defendant was negligently using a crane, so that stones swung above the claimant's head while he was drilling in the quarry. The claimant was aware of this happening, and of the risk that a stone could fall, and had complained about it to his employer, but with no success. Sure enough (you will have recognized by now that the stories leading up to tort cases tend not to have happy endings), one did fall, and seriously injured him. When he sued, his employers argued *volenti*, claiming that in continuing to work when he knew of the risk, he was accepting it. The House of Lords said no: taking on work that was intrinsically dangerous might be acceptance of a risk, but continuing to do work that was not in itself dangerous, but was made so by the employer's negligence did not qualify as consent merely because the claimant had known of the risk. They also recognized that the claimant in fact had little practical choice in the matter.

A contrasting case is that of **Imperial Chemical Industries** *v* **Shatwell** (1965). Here the claimant and his brother, James, were employed in the defendants' quarry. They needed to test some detonators, and had been told by the defendants to take certain precautions when doing so. However, they decided to do the test without taking these precautions, and as a result, there was an explosion which injured the claimant. He sued the defendants on the basis of their vicarious liability for James' negligence and for breach of their statutory duty regarding health and safety. The claim failed because James would have been able to rely on the defence of *volenti*: the claimant was fully aware of the risk he was taking, and had clearly consented to it.

The claimant must be mentally capable of giving consent. In **Kirkham v Chief Constable of Greater Manchester** (1990), the police were sued on behalf of a man who had committed suicide while in police custody; the police had known he was a suicide risk and failed to prevent him taking his own life. They tried to raise the defence of *volenti*, but the court said this could not apply where the claimant had not been of sound mind.

The case of **Reeves v Commissioner of Police for the Metropolis** (1999) in fact seems to suggest that *volenti* can never be a defence to a negligent failure to prevent suicide; in that case the facts were similar to **Kirkham**, but the dead man was found to have been of sound mind. Nevertheless, the Court of Appeal said *volenti* was not an applicable defence, given that the act the police were basing the defence on – the suicide – was the exact act they had a duty to prevent.

In a number of recent cases, claimants who were drunk at the time of the relevant incident have tried to argue that this meant *volenti* could not apply, because they could not be considered to be making a conscious decision. However, the courts take a very dim view of this argument, and have generally held that drunkenness will only prevent a claim of *volenti* if the claimant was so drunk that they really did not know what they were doing; moreover, the cases show that they are very unwilling to find that any claimant has actually been sufficiently drunk for that to be the case. In **Sacco v Chief Constable of South Wales Constabulary** (1998), the 17-year-old claimant had been arrested during a drunken brawl, and was being taken to the police station in a van. While it was travelling at about 25 miles per hour, he kicked the door open and jumped out, hitting his head on the road. The police put forward the defence of *volenti*, and the claimant claimed it could not apply because he was drunk; the Court of Appeal rejected this argument, saying that even a child would have recognized the risk. The same approach has been taken to a claimant injured after spending the afternoon drinking with a friend and then going up in a plane piloted by the same friend (**Morris v Murray** (1990)), and to another injured by jumping into a swimming pool at night (**Ratcliff v McConnell** (1999), discussed at p. 154).

Disclaimers and exclusions

Where harm has come from an activity which arises from a contract between claimant and defendant, the defendant may try to use the existence of exclusion clauses in the contract to raise the defence of *volenti*. A common example might be that car parks frequently display notices disclaiming liability for negligence regarding any damage to cars parked there, and they may argue that any motorist who uses the car park is voluntarily assuming the risk that if their car is damaged, they will have no claim on the car park owners. Under common law, so long as the claimant was given sufficient notice of the relevant term of the contract (in our car park scenario, for example, this would require that the notices were clearly displayed and visible before the motorist was committed to parking there), the term would apply as a complete defence.

However, the use of exclusion clauses to avoid liability is now restricted by the Unfair Contract Terms Act 1977. This provides that 'where a contract term or a notice purports to exclude or restrict liability for negligence, a person's agreement to or awareness of it is not of itself to be taken as indicating his voluntary acceptance of any risk'. In addition, the 1977 Act states that a defendant who is acting in the course of a business, or who occupies premises for business purposes, cannot use a contract term to avoid or restrict their liability for death or personal injury resulting from negligence. In the same circumstances, liability for other types of damage can only be avoided or restricted if it is reasonable to do so. The test of reasonableness is whether the term is 'a fair and reasonable one to be included having regard to the circumstances which were, or ought reasonably to have been, known to or in the contemplation of the parties when the contract was made'.

Special cases

Passengers in road accidents

The Road Traffic Act 1988, as interpreted by the courts, effectively excludes the use of *volenti* to allow drivers to avoid liability to passengers. Before the Act was passed, drivers who had not taken out insurance sometimes tried to exclude liability to passengers in the event of a crash by placing notices in their cars stating that they would not accept liability for injury to passengers. The Road Traffic Act 1988 makes insurance compulsory for motorists, and s. 149 further provides that any attempt to avoid liability to passengers will be ineffective.

Section 149 has been given a fairly broad interpretation by the courts, and held to prevent motorists relying on any form of *volenti* defence with regard to passengers. In **Pitts** *v* **Hunt** (1991), the claimant was a passenger on a motorbike being driven by the defendant. He knew that the defendant was uninsured and had been drinking, but encouraged him to drive in a dangerous way. The bike crashed, seriously injuring the claimant, who therefore sued the defendant. The Court of Appeal held that the defendant could not rely on the defence of *volenti* because of the

Road Traffic Act (in fact the defence of illegality, discussed below, was successfully pleaded, so the defendant was not liable).

Sports

Where an injury is received by a player during a lawful game or sport, played according to the rules, the defence of *volenti* can apply, because players are deemed to have taken the risk of such injury voluntarily. In **Simms** *v* **Leigh Rugby Football Club** (1969), the claimant broke his leg when he was tackled and thrown against a wall. The court held that because the injury occurred during the course of the tackle, which was within the rules of the game, the defence of *volenti* applied and the defendants were not liable. Similarly, in **Wooldridge** *v* **Sumner** (1963), it was held that spectators at sporting events have voluntarily assumed the risk of any harm caused by the players, providing it does not result from intentional or reckless behaviour.

Where the game has not been played according to the rules, the defence is much less likely to apply. In **Smoldon** *v* **Whitworth** (1996), the claimant was a player in a rugby match. The match involved young players (under-19s) and the rules for this age group included a provision that there should be no collapsed scrums, as these could cause injury. However, the referee failed to prevent a collapsed scrum and the claimant was seriously injured as a result. He sued the referee, who claimed the defence of *volenti*, on the basis that the claimant had voluntarily participated in the scrum. The Court of Appeal refused to accept this: the player might have consented to the ordinary rules of the game, but that did not mean he had agreed to the defendant's breach of duty in failing to apply anti-injury rules.

Rescuers

Where a defendant's negligence causes an emergency, and as a result the claimant consciously and deliberately takes a risk in order to rescue someone in imminent danger, the defence of *volenti* will not apply. This is because a rescuer is deemed to be acting instinctively due to their moral or social conscience, and therefore not exercising genuine freedom of choice. In addition, in a rescue case, the defendant's negligence will have happened before the rescuer took a risk, and so they cannot really be said to have consented to what the defendant did; in fact they may not even know about it.

In **Haynes** *v* **Harwood** (1935), the defendant's employee left his van and horses unattended in a busy street and the horses bolted when a child threw a stone at them. The claimant was a police officer, on duty inside the nearby police station. Hearing the commotion, he ran out and managed to stop both runaway horses, but in the process, one of them fell on him, causing him serious injury. The defendant pleaded *volenti*, but the Court of Appeal said the defence could not apply, because the police officer was acting under a duty to protect the public.

Volenti was also put forward as a defence in the case of **Chadwick v British Railways Board** (1967), where the claimant suffered psychiatric injury as a result of the many hours he spent helping the injured victims of a terrible train crash near his home. The defendants argued that since he was not related to any of the victims, or involved in the crash himself, he could be said to be exercising a voluntary choice, but once again, the court rejected the defence. On policy grounds alone, both decisions are clearly sensible: any other approach would effectively mean penalizing those who risk their own safety to help others.

However, the defence may apply where the risk taken was actually unnecessary in the circumstances. In **Cutler v United Dairies (London) Ltd** (1933), a cab driver's horses bolted and ran into a field, and the claimant was injured when he went in to try to recapture them. The horses were in fact creating no risk to people or even property where they were, and so the claimant could not be said to be acting in an emergency. The court held that in this case *volenti* could apply.

Illegality

Where the claimant's case is connected with the fact that they have committed a criminal act, the defence of illegality (sometimes known as *ex turpi causa*) may apply. The basic reason for this defence is public policy: many people would find it offensive that a person committing a crime could sue for damages if they were injured as a result of doing so. An example of the defence in use is **Ashton v Turner** (1981), where both claimant and defendant had taken part in a burglary. The defendant had the job of driving the getaway car, but did it so badly that the claimant was injured. The claimant attempted to sue his co-burglar for the injury, but the court held that the defence of illegality could apply to prevent the claim. Similarly, in **Pitts v Hunt** (1991) (see p. 114), the claimant was prevented from claiming for injuries caused when the defendant's drunken driving caused an accident, because he had encouraged the defendant to drive dangerously.

There must be a causal link between the illegal act and the tort. This was explained in **National Coal Board v England** (1954):

> If two burglars, A and B, agree to open a safe by means
> of explosives, and A so negligently handles the explosive charge as to
> injure B, B might find some difficulty in maintaining an action for
> negligence against A. But if A and B are proceeding to the premises
> which they intend burglariously to enter, and before they enter
> them, B picks A's pocket and steals A's watch, I cannot prevail upon
> myself to believe that A could not sue in tort.

The defence has been tested in three recent cases. In **Revill** *v* **Newbury** (1996), the case discussed at p. 110 above, concerning an occupier who shot a burglar. The defendant put forward *ex turpi causa* as a defence, but the Court of Appeal held that it was not applicable, because the Occupiers' Liability Act 1984 had created a duty of care from occupiers to trespassers. This leaves us with the bizarre situation that a fellow burglar cannot be sued for injuries they cause during the process of the burglary, but their victim can.

In **Clunis** *v* **Camden and Islington Health Authority** (1998), the case resulted from the murder of a young man, Jonathon Zito, by Christopher Clunis, who was mentally ill. Clunis, the claimant in this case, was supposed to have had psychiatric care from the health authority, and claimed that the authority had been negligent in not providing this, the implication being that he would not have killed if he had been receiving the proper treatment. The Court of Appeal said he could not use his own illegal act to form the basis of a claim.

In **Cross** *v* **Kirby** (2000) the defendant had been hit with a baseball bat by the claimant, a hunt saboteur; he then grabbed the bat and hit the claimant, fracturing his skull. The Court of Appeal refused the claimant's claim on the grounds that his injury arose from his own unlawful act.

▶ Statutory authority

If a statute entitles a person or body to do something which would normally be considered a tort, the person committing the act cannot be sued, and anyone who suffers damage as a result will be unable to get compensation unless the statute provides that they should. The defence is most commonly used in nuisance, but it can apply in negligence too. In **X** *v* **Bedfordshire County Council** (1995) (see p. 70), the House of Lords stated that where a public body is given a discretion to act, they will have the defence of statutory authority when exercising that discretion, unless the choice they make is completely unreasonable. The House explained:

> Most statutes which impose a statutory duty on local authorities confer on the authority a discretion as to the extent to which, and the methods by which, such statutory duty is to be performed. It is clear both in principle and from the decided cases that the local authority cannot be liable in damages for doing that which Parliament has authorised. Therefore if the decisions complained of fall within the ambit of such statutory discretion they cannot be actionable in common law. However, if the decision complained of is so unreasonable that it falls outside the ambit of the discretion conferred upon the local authority, there is no *a priori* reason for excluding all common law liability.

The House stated that the reason for the defence is that in reaching such decisions the public body would take into account policy issues such as the allocation of resources and the best balance between competing social aims, and it was not appropriate for the courts to second-guess such decisions.

The defence only applies to the use of discretion; it will not excuse negligent carrying out of a decision once made. For example, a council which has discretion over the issue of how to provide special teaching help for dyslexic students is protected by the defence when it decides whether to provide special classes once a week rather than every day, and unless it makes a completely unreasonable decision, the courts will not allow a claimant to sue in negligence on the basis that the wrong option was chosen. However once the council has settled on, for example, one class a week, the defence of statutory authority would not protect it if it is then negligent in providing that service.

Equally, the defence will not apply if the decision made goes outside the discretion permitted by the statute. In the previous example, if the statute had allowed a discretion on the number and timing of classes, but stipulated that they must be held in schools, the council could not rely on statutory authority as a defence if it was sued because it held the classes somewhere else.

Necessity

This is a defence which applies where a defendant intentionally causes damage in the course of preventing some other, worse, damage. An example might be a motorist knocking down a wall at the side of a road while swerving to avoid a head-on collision with another car. Because it only applies to intentional damage, it is not used in negligence cases (**Rigby** *v* **Chief Constable of Northamptonshire** (1985)).

Mistake

Mistake is generally not a defence in negligence, because of the emphasis on the standards of the reasonable person. For example, if a doctor says that their incorrect diagnosis or treatment was the result of a mistake, there are two possible outcomes. First, the mistake might be one which the court believes a reasonable doctor could make; in that case, the defendant has not fallen below the required standard of care, and so needs no defence because they have not been negligent. An example would be **Roe** *v* **Minister of Health** (1954) (see p. 86), where storing the ampoules of anaesthetic in disinfectant was, with hindsight, a mistake, but given the state of knowledge at the time, it was a reasonable one. Or alternatively, the mistake might be one which no reasonable doctor could make, in which case the doctor has fallen below the standard of care and the mistake, far from offering a defence, is the thing which makes them negligent.

▶ Inevitable accident

An inevitable accident is one which the defendant did not cause, and could not possibly have avoided, no matter how much care they took. Like mistake, it has no real application in negligence, because if the claimant fails to prove that the defendant caused the accident and could have avoided it if they had taken more care, there is no negligence anyway so no defence is needed.

▶ Time limits

The law recognizes that it would be unfair to defendants if claimants could bring an action against them at any time in the years after a wrong has taken place. The courts were always able to hold that a particular claimant had delayed too long in bringing an action, but in 1980 the Limitation Act for the first time laid down specific time limits for different types of court case.

The general limitation period for an action in tort is six years, which means that an action must be begun within six years of the date on which the cause of action came into existence (different rules apply to defamation, discussed in Chapter 8, product liability, discussed in Chapter 5, and personal injury cases, which are discussed below). For torts which are actionable *per se* (without proof of damage), the cause of action comes into existence when the defendant commits the tort; for torts where damage must be proved, including negligence, the cause of action comes into existence when the claimant suffers the damage. This can be very difficult to pinpoint: damage may not occur until some time after the event which caused it, and may not be discovered until some time after that.

The difficulties this can cause can be seen in **Pirelli General Cable Works** *v* **Oscar Faber & Partners** (1983). The defendant in the case had designed a chimney for the claimants in 1969. By April 1977, cracks could be seen around the top of the chimney, and in 1978, the claimants began an action against the defendant for negligence, but technical evidence revealed that the cracks had actually begun forming in 1970, even though they were not visible from the ground until later. The House of Lords held that the case was outside the six-year time limit, which began to run when the cracks occurred, and not when they were discovered.

In recognition of problems like these, the Latent Damage Act 1986 was passed. It provides that where damage is not apparent when it first occurs, the time limit is either six years from the time when the damage occurred, or three years from the time when the claimant knew, or ought to have known, of the damage (whichever is the later) up to a final limit of 15 years from the time the damage occurred. A claimant who ought to have known of damage is said to have 'constructive knowledge': even if the claimant does not actually know of the damage, the limitation period will begin to run when they are in possession of such facts as would enable a reasonable person to realize there might be damage (see **Forbes** *v* **Wandsworth Health Authority** (1996) below). The Limitation Act 1980 also allows the courts some discretion to extend time limits in exceptional circumstances.

Personal injury cases

The problems time limits may cause can be even more serious in personal injury cases, as the example of **Cartledge** *v* **Jopling** (1963) shows. The claimant's husband had died from a lung disease caused by the defendant's negligence, but the nature of the illness was such that it did not show symptoms until decades after the damage was done. As a result, his widow was unable to claim damages from those responsible for his illness and premature death.

In recognition of the specific problems faced by personal injury claimants, the Limitation Act 1980 lays down a time limit of three years for personal injury cases, but states that this limit begins to run either from when the damage was done, or from the point at which the claimant first had knowledge of the following facts, whichever is the later:

- that the injury was significant;
- that it was wholly or partly caused by the act or omission which is alleged to constitute negligence, nuisance or breach of statutory duty;
- the identity of the defendant;
- where the allegation is that someone other than the defendant committed the relevant act or omission, the identity of that person, and the additional facts which suggest that the defendant should be held liable.

A claimant can be deemed to have 'knowledge' of the above issues where they might reasonably be expected to have acquired it from facts which could be seen, or which could have been found out, with or without the help of medical or other experts. In **Forbes** *v* **Wandsworth Health Authority** (1996) the claimant had had an operation on his leg in 1982; it was unsuccessful, as was a second operation the next day, and in order to save his life, the leg was amputated. Nine years later, the claimant consulted a solicitor and a year after that medical evidence was found to show that the need for the amputation had been caused by the failure to perform the first operation properly. The trial judge held that the limitation period should run from the time when the claimant was made aware of the alleged negligence, 10 years after it happened.

The defendant appealed, and the Court of Appeal held that although the claimant had no actual knowledge of the alleged negligence until he received the medical evidence, he had always known that the amputation must be significant, since it was not the inevitable consequence of the operations he had had. The court said that a reasonable man who had suffered a major injury as a result of an unsuccessful operation would take advice reasonably promptly, and even allowing time to get over the shock of what had happened, that would be within 12 to 18 months of the amputation. Therefore he would be taken to have had constructive knowledge of the possible negligence at that time, and the limitation period would run from then, which meant it had run out by the time his action was brought.

Section 33 of the Limitation Act 1980 gives the courts a wide discretion to extend the limitation period in personal injury cases. In deciding whether to do so, the court should look at all the circumstances of the case, and in particular, the following issues:

- the length of the delay and the reason for it;
- the effect of this delay on the evidence;
- the conduct of the defendant after the cause of action arose;
- how long the claimant's disability has lasted;
- whether the claimant acted reasonably once they knew that they might have a claim;
- the steps taken by the claimant to get expert advice, and the nature of that advice.

In **Forbes**, the claimant attempted to have this discretion exercised in his favour, but the court refused on the grounds that the claimant had not acted reasonably, and that the delay was so long that it would cause serious prejudice to the defendant.

An example of a case where the discretion was exercised is **Das** *v* **Ganju** (1999). The claimant had a child who, it was claimed, was injured as a result of medical negligence. She was told by her lawyers that if she did not sue on her daughter's behalf, her daughter could bring an action herself when she was grown up, for which she could claim legal aid. This was incorrect, but the claimant did not discover that until five years after her 'date of knowledge', and so outside the statutory time limit. The court held that it could exercise its discretion under s. 33, because the delay was not the claimant's fault, and she should not be prejudiced because of her lawyer's negligence.

Where negligent personal injury results in a death within three years of the date on which the cause of action came into existence, a fresh

limitation period of three years begins to run for the personal representatives or dependants of the dead person.

CRITICISMS OF NEGLIGENCE LAW

In order to highlight the general problems with the law of negligence, we
need to look first at what the aims of this area of the law are, in order to
provide a gauge by which its success can be measured. The law of negligence has several aims, not all of which are necessarily consistent with
each other: to compensate victims of harm caused by others; to mark the
fault of those who cause harm; to deter carelessness; to spread the financial costs of harm caused by carelessness; and to do all these things
quickly and fairly. To judge how well it achieves these aims, we need to
look at both the law itself, and the context in which it operates.

Compensating victims of harm

Considering that compensation is generally seen to be its most important
function, the law of negligence is remarkably inefficient in this area and,
in practice, only a small proportion of victims of harm get compensation
through it.

The first reason for this is that, if we take a wide view of harm, many
people are caused harm by circumstances in which nobody can be blamed,
for example those with genetic illnesses or those who suffer damage of
any kind in accidents which are genuinely nobody's fault. You might well
ask why they should be compensated, but the wider picture is that, as we
shall see, society as a whole spends a lot of money on negligence cases,
yet the result is that a few people get large amounts of money in damages, while many other people whose needs are the same, but result from
different causes, do not. The question is therefore whether the system we
currently have gives good value for our money.

Added to those people who cannot prove fault in anyone are those
who possibly could, but who the law of negligence will not compensate:
those victims of psychiatric injury and economic loss who fall outside the
rules on compensating these types of damage; and those whose damage is
the result of carelessness by categories of defendant to whom the law
gives special protection in certain circumstances, such as the police and
local authorities.

Even among those who have suffered damage in circumstances where
someone else might be liable, only a small proportion take legal action;
the 1984 study *Compensation and Support for Injury and Illness*, by Harris et
al. (Clarendon Press) found that just 12 per cent of seriously injured
accident victims made a legal claim. The reasons for this will be well

known to those of you who have studied access to justice on English Legal System courses: people are often unaware of the possibility of legal action, or are put off by the inaccessible image of the legal world, and the cost of legal action is extremely expensive.

Among those who do bring cases, the chances of success are sometimes slim. This is particularly the case in medical negligence, where the **Bolam** ruling has essentially meant that if doctors stick together, it is extremely difficult to prove them negligent. How far this will change in the light of **Bolitho** (see p. 83 above) still remains to be seen; certainly the judgment in **Bolitho** leaves plenty of room to keep the old standard in all but exceptional cases. Yet there seems no compelling reason why medical negligence should be treated so differently from other areas of negligence, and English law is alone among the major common law jurisdictions in giving doctors this privileged status.

In practice the vast majority of negligence cases are settled without going to court – sometimes early on, often almost literally at the door of the court. This saves a lot of money for the side which would have lost the case, since a trial can drastically raise the costs, and the loser must pay those of the winner as well as their own. From the point of view of adequately compensating those injured though, out of court settlements can be problematic. Hazel Genn's 1984 study, *Hard Bargaining*, showed that in cases where the defendant is an insurance company (which is the case in the vast majority of accident and professional negligence claims, for example) and the claimant an ordinary member of the public, the insurance companies, with their vast experience of these cases, are able to manipulate the pre-trial process in order to achieve not a fair settlement but the lowest offer they can get away with. What seems to happen is that small claims are over-compensated because it is not cost-effective for insurance companies to fight them, while very big claims (such as, for example, those brought by parents of children damaged by negligence at birth, who will need care throughout their lives) are often under-compensated because the claimants need compensation quickly, and so can effectively be forced to accept a lower settlement than they might get if they went to court.

Because the law on negligence is complicated, cases can be long and involved. Specialist legal representation is usually required, and the expert witnesses often needed to prove fault add to the cost. The result in practice is that only a fraction of the money spent on negligence cases goes to the victims of harm.

Marking fault

The original basis of the law of negligence was claimed to be essentially moral: those who carelessly cause harm to others should bear the responsibility for that harm. In fact this was always debatable; for example, the direct consequence test for remoteness of damage, laid down in **Re Polemis** (1921), created cases where the damage the defendant was required to compensate could be violently out of proportion to their fault, and even though this test has been superseded, the 'eggshell-skull' rule can have a similar effect.

What makes the shift away from a moral basis much clearer though are the cases on economic loss and psychiatric injury. They show that where new sources of potential liability arise, what the courts look at now is not the rights and wrongs of the situation, but what the economic effects of such liability would be. In **Alcock** *v* **Chief Constable of South Yorkshire** (1992), the lines drawn with regard to closeness of relationship take no account of the degree of carelessness involved in the police decision that caused the tragedy: the decision was no more or less careless because the relationship between some of the deceased victims and their relatives was or was not factually close. What the court was looking for was a way to limit liability, and it based its decision not on degree of fault, but essentially on the effect it would have on insurance premiums for the police and the workloads of the courts.

The very existence of insurance is a double-edged sword for the law of negligence. Without it, far fewer claims would be brought, because the majority of defendants would not have the money to pay damages, and in terms of compensation, this would make the law even more inadequate. But in terms of fault, insurance causes a problem, because the damages are usually paid by insurance companies, and not by the party whose carelessness has caused harm. Insurance premiums may rise slightly as a result of a claim, but not usually by anything like the cost of that claim, and in many cases, premiums are indirectly paid for by all of us, rather than the individual policyholder anyway: companies' insurance is paid for in higher prices to customers, for example; insurance for health authorities is paid for by our taxes; and the damages paid out by motor insurance companies are funded by all of us who have motor insurance, whether we claim or not.

Deterring carelessness

The argument here seems obvious: the tort system means that people and organizations know they are liable to be sued if their carelessness causes damage, and therefore its existence should mean that they are more likely to take care to avoid causing harm. In practice, however, the deterrence issue is not so straightforward. First, as we have seen, the problems of access to justice mean that in some types of case there is relatively little risk of being sued.

The impact of insurance is relevant here too; if insurance means that even if you are sued, your carelessness is not going to cost anything, there is little incentive to be careful. Furthermore, the market system on which our society is run actually makes it much more difficult for businesses to take sufficient care, where such care costs (and it usually does). This is because in a market system, companies have to keep their costs in line with those of other competing companies. Any company which went out on a limb and spent a lot more money on safety precautions than its competitors were spending would soon be put out of business (a fact which was implicitly acknowledged by the courts in **Thompson** *v* **Smith Shiprepairers (North Shields)**, see p. 190 above). Therefore the possibility of being sued for negligence can only really work as a deterrent if it is clear that everyone who suffers damage through negligence will sue, and as we have seen, this is not the case.

The objective approach can mean that it is actually impossible for the tortfeasor to reach the required standard; in **Nettleship** *v* **Weston** (1971), and **Djemal** *v* **Bexley Heath Health Authority** (1995) (see pp. 80 and 86 above), the defendants were judged by standards that in reality they could not have been expected to attain. The decisions may have been right, given that both defendants would have been protected by insurance, but as far as deterrence is concerned, they were meaningless.

Another practical problem is that in many cases the standard of care imposed is too vague to be of much use in deterring careless behaviour. In practice, most tortfeasors do not sit and balance the magnitude of the risk against its seriousness, while taking into account their own special characteristics and those of the potential claimant, and contemplating the possible benefits to society of what they are about to do. In an ideal world they should, but in practice they do not. What the law of negligence really does is not so much deter carelessness, as attempt to mop up the mess that carelessness leaves behind.

Spreading risk

This is one area where the law of negligence can be seen to work very well at times; rather than leaving loss to lie where it falls, it can pass it on to those most able to bear it financially. The fine judgments needed to do this are not always easy, but there are many cases where the courts have shown obvious good sense in this area. An example is the case of **Smith** *v* **Eric Bush** (1990) (see p. 30 above), where the courts explicitly considered who was best able to bear the loss, and concluded that it was the surveyors, since they were insured, and their liability was in any case limited to the value of the house.

Having said that, it is worth bearing in mind that, as we have explained, when loss is shifted to insurers, in practice it is actually shifted from them to all of us. This is not necessarily a bad thing, since it spreads the costs of harm thinly – but if this is what society wants to do, it might be more efficiently done by compensating all victims of harm, however caused, through welfare systems based on need and paid for by taxes. In this way much more of the money spent would go to victims of harm, because there would be no need to take out the element of profit for insurance companies, nor the costs of legal actions.

Individualism and negligence

Supporters of the school of thought known as critical legal theory criticize negligence law for the way it focuses almost exclusively on individual fault, when in fact there may be wider issues involved. For example, many of the activities which crop up in negligence cases – transport, industry and medicine, for example – are activities which benefit society as a whole, but also necessarily carry risks. As the judge in **Duborn *v* Bath Tramways** (1946) put it:

> If all the trains in this country were restricted to a speed of five miles per hour, there would be fewer accidents, but our national life would be intolerably slowed down.

It can be argued then that those people who are injured as a result of such risks bear the brunt of the convenience and other benefits which the relevant activities provide for all members of society, and that it might therefore be appropriate for society to compensate such victims automatically, rather than making them jump through the hoops of negligence law.

This argument becomes even stronger when the harm suffered by the claimant actually results in a benefit to society, through better knowledge of possible risks. For example, in **Roe *v* Minister of Health** (1954) (see p. 86), it was only the injury caused to the claimant that revealed the danger of keeping ampoules of anaesthetic in disinfectant. Because the hospital could not have known of the risk beforehand, they were not liable. As a direct result of what happened, they had changed their procedures so that it could not happen to any future patients, but the patient whose suffering had caused this progress went uncompensated.

Critical theorists argue that since society benefits in all these cases, society should pay; this would require an acceptance that we have social, as well as individual responsibilities.

An economic solution?

It has been suggested that negligence should be assessed on the basis of an economic formula: if the likelihood of the injury, multiplied by its seriousness, exceeds the cost to the defendant of taking adequate precautions, they would be liable. The rationale behind this approach is that finding negligence effectively transfers the loss from the claimant to the defendant, and for economic reasons, this should only happen where the cost of avoiding the accident is less than paying compensation for it.

While this approach may have practical attractions, it lacks any concept of disapproving the wrongdoer's conduct, and could also raise difficulties when it came to calculating (or guessing) the cost of preventing an accident.

ANSWERING QUESTIONS

1 **To what extent, if any, is there a duty not to cause economic loss?** *OCR*
This essay question offers plenty of opportunity to use the information in the sections on economic loss. You should begin by talking about the nature of economic loss, and distinguishing between economic loss caused by physical injury or damage to property, and pure economic loss, perhaps using the case of **Spartan Steel** v **Martin** to illustrate the difference.

You can then go on to explain that as far as economic loss caused by personal injury or property damage is concerned, the existence of a duty of care is not problematic; if negligence causing these types of damage is proved, then the defendant will also be liable to compensate the claimant for resulting economic loss, within the rules of causation and remoteness. Then you can get into the real point of the essay: the issue of pure economic loss.

It would be useful to begin your discussion with a summary of the historical development of the law in this area, as discussed in this chapter, but do not get too bogged down: a simple recital of what happened first and what happened next and what happened after that will not earn you too many marks. Outline the development, but in doing so, make it clear that you know not just what happened, but why, by discussing the reasons why the courts pulled back after **Junior Books** v **Veitchi**.

The biggest part of your essay should be a discussion of what the law on pure economic loss is now. Talk about those situations in which a duty of care will exist, looking in detail at the **Hedley Byrne** principles, as extended by **Henderson** v **Merrett Syndicates** and the 'wills cases'. You should also discuss the situations where a duty of care with regard to pure economic loss will not exist, namely defective products (see Chapter 5) and negligent acts other than provision of services.

The question asks how far there *is* a duty not to cause economic loss, but to win yourself some more marks, finish your essay with a discussion of how far there *should* be such a duty. The material on problems with the law on economic loss will be useful here.

2 **In relation to the concept of nervous shock, Lord Justice Oliver has stated that he could not 'regard the present state of the law as entirely satisfactory or as logically defensible' and concluded that only 'considerations of policy' made it explicable.**
Is Lord Oliver's view justified? *OCR*

You could start this essay by briefly explaining what nervous shock is, and pointing out that it is an area in which the law of tort has seen much activity in recent years. You should then go on to show that you know what the current law is, discussing the different categories of claimant and explaining the rules applicable to each. As always, you should make sure that this statement of the law does not dominate your essay, so do not spend too much time on it: the question asks for an assessment of the present law, so a pure description of it, while necessary, will not get all the marks you need. Be sure to mention the key cases and the principles they establish, but avoid long descriptions of the facts.

The main part of your essay should look at the problems associated with the law on nervous shock, which are described in this chapter, and then talk about why these problems have arisen. As the quote from Lord Oliver in the question suggests, policy has very clearly played a role in the development of the law, and you need to talk about issues such as the 'floodgates' problem and the implications for insurance. You should then consider whether in the light of all you have said, Lord Oliver's view seems justified, but you will get more marks if you can go further than that. Even if these considerations of policy *explain* the current state of the law, do you consider that such considerations *justify* the law as it stands – in other words, have the courts been right in taking these considerations into account, and have they done so in the right way?

3 **Critically evaluate the system of 'fault based' liability for personal injuries and consider whether there are any reasonable alternatives.** *OCR*
A good way to begin this essay would be to explain briefly what fault-based liability is, mentioning how compensation through a fault-based system differs from non-fault-based sources of compensation such as social security.

Then you need to look at the main part of the question, which essentially requires an assessment of how well the tort system does its job with regard to victims of personal injury. As we explain in the section on Criticisms of negligence law (at pp. 122–7) (where you will find much of the relevant information for this essay), in order to evaluate the system, you need to consider first what its aims are, and then to look at how far, if at all, the system meets those aims. To keep your structure clear, it would be a good idea to list the aims, and then look at how the system meets – or does not meet – each one in turn.

Finally, you should look at possible alternatives, such as specific no-fault schemes, greater use of social security and the 'economic solution' described on p. 126. In each case you should highlight the pros and cons of these alternatives, and show whether you think any of them would work better than the current system, and why.

4 **'One of the purposes of the law of torts is said to be to encourage people to take care in what they do and to discourage activities that are dangerous to others.'**

Do the rules that courts apply in determining the standard of care in negligence achieve this aim? *OCR*

The first thing to notice here is that you are specifically asked to talk about the rules concerning the standard of care, so even though there is a lot of material on duty of care and the operation of negligence law in practice that is relevant to the issue of whether the law encourages care for the safety of others, in this essay you must stick to discussing the rules on the standard of care.

A good way to start would be to outline the basis of these rules: the standard of reasonableness; the objective approach; and the factors which the courts will weigh against each other to assess reasonableness. You can then go on to discuss each of these areas in more detail, stating how they operate to discourage dangerous behaviour, and highlighting any ways in which they fail to do this. As regards the objective standard, you could point to the fact that it can be vague, and in some cases unachievable. The case of **Nettleship v Weston** is relevant here, and in discussing it, you should talk about the implications of insurance in negligence cases: the standard of driving imposed in **Nettleship** may not discourage unsafe driving, since a learner driver is unlikely to be able to reach that standard, however hard they try, but what it does is to ensure that the financial risk is borne by the party who is insured and therefore able to pay. Similar comments apply to the rules on defendants whose conduct is affected by an infirmity over which they have no control, as in **Roberts v Ramsbottom**. You could contrast this with **Mansfield v Weetabix**, where the standard imposed seems more in keeping with the aim of promoting care, and yet its practical effect was to leave the injured claimant uncompensated, even though the defendant was insured.

In discussing the rules on special characteristics of the defendant, you should talk about the special rules for professionals, and in particular doctors. Discuss the criticisms made of **Bolam v Friern Barnet Hospital Management Committee**, and the idea that doctors are in effect allowed to set their own standard of care; how far can such rules effectively discourage medical negligence? Consider whether **Bolitho v City & Hackney Hospital Authority** has made a difference.

You should also point out that the rules on practicality of protection mean that defendants are not required to eliminate risk, only to take reasonable precautions. The cases of **Latimer v AEC** and **Bolton v Stone** are relevant here.

To extend the coverage of your essay, you could discuss the fact that in some cases, the law's emphasis on promoting care in individuals ignores the wider picture and can result in injustice to claimants. On the issue of risks unknown at the time when the defendant acted, you can point out that there is no liability for damage caused as a result of such risks, and this can be justified by the argument that defendants cannot be expected to take care to avoid risks which are not known by anyone to exist. You can then go on to explain that this approach can be unfair to the claimant, whose injury will often result in some advance in knowledge that benefits others (as in **Roe v Minister of Health**) yet remains uncompensated because of the law's focus on individual fault.

5

To what extent do the rules relating to causation and remoteness of damage achieve the aim of compensating the claimant for loss and injury? *OCR*

A good way to begin this essay would be to explain that in tort, not every injury or loss that is factually caused by someone else will result in that person being required to pay compensation. The law aims to strike a balance between ensuring fair compensation for claimants, and not imposing too harsh a burden on defendants, and the rules on causation and remoteness of damage are part of the legal framework which helps the courts to strike this balance. Note that the question does not specifically ask about negligence: as you know, the rules of causation and remoteness of damage apply to all torts, though the test for remoteness of damage varies. You should show that you know this, but so long as you do that, it is permissible to state that you are going to show how the rules work with regard to one tort, that of negligence, and how far in that tort the rules achieve the aim of compensating the claimant (you do not have to take this approach, but since most of the cases you will know will have come from negligence, concentrating on this area will make your essay clearer, and if you state that that is what you are going to do, you show that you are aware of the bigger picture even though your focus in this essay is on negligence).

The clearest structure then is to take the rules on causation first, moving on to remoteness of damage when you have finished causation. Explain that the basic rule is that claimants must satisfy the 'but for' test, and then go on to talk about the difficulties that cases involving multiple causes have created for the courts, and the variety of approaches taken to them. In discussing these approaches, you need to highlight which of them best fulfil the aim of compensating the claimant, and which have weaknesses in this area.

Go on to discuss the rules on intervening events, again looking at the different approaches, and which seem to serve the claimant's need for compensation best. You could also mention the issue of causation in product liability, and how well the rules work here to compensate victims.

You can then turn to remoteness of damage. Talk about the original direct consequence test from **Re Polemis**, describing how this was thought to cause injustice to defendants, but was obviously useful to claimants, and then explain the current reasonable foreseeability test from **Wagon Mound 1** (you should point out that the direct consequence test still applies in some torts, and say which they are). You can consider how far the current test achieves the aim of compensating claimants. You might highlight the strange distinctions made using this test, comparing cases such as **Doughty** v **Turner** and **Hughes** v **Lord Advocate**; does the unpredictability such cases cause help claimants seeking compensation? You should also talk about the eggshell-skull rule in personal injury and the apparently similar approach in economic loss cases, and the rule arising from **Wagon Mound 2**; how far do these rules promote the aim of compensation for the claimant?

6 Mr King and his son Augustus are both injured when their car is involved in a collision with a bus. The collision is caused by the bus driver's negligence. Augustus's hip is badly jarred. Mr King suffers severe spinal injuries. Both are rushed to St Crisp's Hospital where Mr King is left unattended for many hours. The staff X-ray Augustus's head but fail to examine his hip. As a result, Augustus is in much pain for several days, before his hip is finally X-rayed and a fracture identified. Subsequently Augustus develops a weakness in his hip. The medical evidence indicates that such a weakness would occur in 80 per cent of patients injured in this way, but that the delay in treatment for the fracture made it virtually certain that the weakness would develop. As a result of the accident Mr King is paralysed from the waist down. The medical evidence indicates that this would have occurred even if he had been treated immediately for the injuries which he had sustained. When Mrs King is told by a consultant at St Crisp's Hospital of the permanent injuries to her husband and son she suffers from severe depression.

Advise Mr King, Augustus and Mrs King as to any potential claims they may have. *OCR*

In problem questions concerning negligence, you should always remember the three elements of the tort: there must be a duty of care between claimant and defendant; breach of that duty of care; and damage to the claimant, which is caused by the defendant and within the rules on remoteness. Although questions rarely require you to look in detail at all these elements, keeping them in mind will help you structure your thoughts and make sure you leave nothing out.

Take the claim of each claimant in turn, dealing completely with each one's claim or claims before starting on the next. Starting with Mr King, there are two possible claims: against the bus driver and against the hospital staff (you should point out that in practice the parties sued would probably be the bus company and the hospital, since they are likely to have vicarious liability for their staff).

As regards the claim against the bus company, we know that drivers owe a duty of care to other road users, and we are told that his driving was negligent so we know he has fallen below the standard of care; therefore the issue here seems to be causation and remoteness of damage. Which aspects of the damage caused to Mr King will the bus company be liable for? Clearly personal injury is a foreseeable result of such a crash, so the company will be liable for Mr King's spinal injury. Are they also liable for the paralysis? Here you have to consider whether the failure to treat him immediately is an intervening act, breaking the chain of causation: the medical evidence that the paralysis would have happened anyway shows that the chain of causation was not broken, and so the bus company will be liable for the paralysis too.

As regards the hospital's liability to Mr King, we know that hospital staff have a duty of care towards patients, but we do not know whether the time taken to treat his injuries would fall below the standard of care. Where you are not given enough information to judge a particular issue, it is perfectly reasonable to say so, and you can earn yourself marks if you say what information would help you come to a decision: in this case, you can point to the rule in **Bolam** (and the modification in **Bolitho**) and say that Mr King would have to show that what happened was not in line with the practice followed by a responsible body of doctors. However, you should point out that in fact we do not need this information, since the claim would clearly fail on causation: it cannot be said that but for the hospital's failure to treat him quickly the paralysis would not have happened, so they will have no liability towards him.

Augustus's situation is more complicated, and again, the best way to treat it is by taking each possible claim in turn. Starting with the bus company, we have already dealt with duty of care and breach of duty; once again, the issue is causation and remoteness of damage. Clearly the bus company is liable for Augustus's fractured hip, because personal injury was reasonably foreseeable; are they also liable for the weakness he later develops, or was this caused by the delay in treatment? You should point out that the courts have taken a variety of approaches to this issue; where this is the case, it is a good idea to explore each of the possible approaches and say how each would apply to the facts of the problem. If we take the approach in **Hotson v East Berkshire Health Authority**, the question to be asked is whether there was at least a 51 per cent chance of developing the weakness as a result of the accident, and we are told that there was an 80 per cent chance. Under the **Hotson** principle therefore, the bus company would be liable to Augustus for all his injuries. If we look at the test laid down in **McGhee v National Coal Board**, the result is the same: clearly the accident did make a substantial contribution to the injury, even though the hospital's failure to give the right treatment increased it. The situation also satisfies the test in **Wilsher v Essex Area Health Authority**, so it seems fairly clear that the bus company is liable for both the hip fracture and the weakness. (You might wonder at this stage why we are looking at the cases on multiple causes, rather than treating the hospital's lack of care as an intervening event. The distinction can be difficult, but where as here, the hospital has increased the risk, their conduct merely increases the risk of the same injury which the original accident caused; an intervening event usually introduces a new risk or injury. If, for example, Augustus had been given the wrong drugs in hospital and suffered a heart attack, the correct cases to consider would be those on intervening events.)

We know then that Augustus has a claim against the bus company for all his injuries, but it is still worth considering whether the hospital has any liability towards him; as you will read in Chapter 12, it is possible for two or more parties to be liable for the same injury or damage, and in that case, the claimant can sue either of them, though they cannot get damages twice for the same injury (this would probably not be necessary here, but might be useful if, for example, the accident had been caused by a hit and run driver, who could not be found and sued). The hospital are clearly not liable for the hip fracture, but do they have any liability for the hip weakness? Clearly we cannot say that but for their lack of care the weakness would not have happened, so we have to look at the cases on multiple causes again. Here Augustus's best argument would be **McGhee**, because he could argue that increasing the risk from 80 per cent to virtually certain amounts to making a substantial contribution to the injury; without the hospital's negligence, he had a 20 per cent chance of not developing hip weakness, but after their negligence he had almost no chance. By contrast, **Wilsher** offers little hope for Augustus, because it says that the fact that a defendant's negligence has increased the risk of damage is not sufficient. Nor is **Hotson** helpful to Augustus, because we know there is a less than 51 per cent chance that the hospital's negligence caused the damage. In cases like this, where different authorities suggest different answers to the problem, it is worth mentioning any aspects of the problem that lead you to think a court would prefer one approach over another, but you are not required to *know* which view they would take; all you have to do is show you know what cases they could follow, and how the principles in those cases apply to the facts before you.

Finally, we have Mrs King's potential claim on the hospital. The first thing to point out is that her claim would be against whichever party was found to be liable for the injuries to her husband and son, and not necessarily to the hospital merely because it was the consultant who told her of their injuries. Her claim, if she has one, will be for psychiatric injury, and in most problem questions where this arises, the issue you will need to spend most time on will be that of whether the defendant owes the claimant a duty of care. You should point out that claimants for psychiatric injury fall into different groups, with different rules for whether a duty of care will arise. Mrs King clearly falls into the category of witnesses/secondary victims, so you need to go through the requirements set down in **Alcock**, covering the nature of the injury, the class of person into which Mrs King falls, and her proximity to the accident. She clearly falls within the 'class of person' requirements, but there are problems with the other two requirements.

On the nature of her injury, she needs to show that her depression is a recognized psychiatric illness, and would have to produce medical evidence to that effect, and that it was caused by a sudden and unexpected shock; you could point out that Lord Keith in **Alcock** seems to think that this can only be the case where the claimant is 'within sight or hearing of the event in question', which Mrs King, as far as we know, was not. Proximity is also a problem, since **Alcock** makes it clear that merely being informed of a shocking incident by a third party is not sufficient to meet the proximity requirement. The result would seem to be that Mrs King has no claim.

Questions set by the Associated Examining Board usually combine issues of negligence with nuisance. Sample questions and guidelines on answering them can be found at the end of the chapter on nuisance.

3 Employers' liability

In addition to the general common law rules of negligence, there are some areas where the law has created special rules – including statutory ones – about the way in which carelessness that damages others should be treated. This chapter deals with the duty of care owed by employers to their employees: other examples of special liability regimes are occupiers' liability, discussed in the following chapter; and liability for harm caused by defective products, considered in Chapter 5.

As far as employers are concerned there are three main ways in which they can incur liability for harm done to an employee. The first is vicarious liability, which can arise when one employee injures another and the law requires the employer to take responsibility; this is the subject of Chapter 13. The second arises where an employer has a statutory duty to protect the safety of employees, as a result of legislation such as the Health and Safety at Work Act 1974; the rules concerning breach of a statutory duty are examined in Chapter 6. The third type of liability comes from the common law rules which impose on employers a personal duty to take reasonable care of their employees' safety with regard to work. This type of liability is the subject of this chapter.

▶ The employer's personal duty

An employer has a duty in law to see that reasonable care is taken to ensure the safety of employees; the duty is essentially the same as the usual duty of care in negligence. In **Wilsons and Clyde Coal Co Ltd** *v* **English** (1938) Lord Wright stated that the duty required 'the provision of a competent staff of men, adequate material, and a proper system and effective supervision'. Later cases have included a requirement to provide a safe place of work.

Competent staff

Where an employer takes on someone without sufficient experience or training for a particular job, and as a result a worker is injured, the employer may be in breach of their personal duty of care towards employees. The practical importance of this principle is limited by the fact that in most such cases, the injured employee will be able to sue the employer vicariously for the wrongdoing of their colleague, but it is still valuable in situations where vicarious liability does not apply, such as where the injury was not caused by any specific employee, or where the employee causing the injury was acting outside the course of employment (this concept is explained in Chapter 13). An example of such liability occurred in **Hudson** *v* **Ridge Manufacturing Co Ltd** (1957), where injury was caused by an employee playing a practical joke. While playing jokes was obviously not within the course of his employment, making the imposition of vicarious liability impossible, the employee concerned had a reputation for persistently engaging in practical jokes, and his employers were held liable for not taking any steps to curb this habit.

An employer's duty also includes protecting employees from harassment, bullying or victimization by other employees. In **Waters** *v* **Commissioner of Police of the Metropolis** (2000), the claimant was a police officer who claimed that the police force were negligent in failing to protect her from harassment by her colleagues, after she alleged that one of them had raped her (strictly speaking, a police officer is not an 'employee' of the police force, for historical reasons that are not important here, but in such cases the courts will often assume that the relationship is one of employer–employee). The House of Lords confirmed that an employer who knows, or can foresee, that acts done to an employee by their colleagues may cause physical or mental harm, and does nothing to prevent such harm, may be in breach of their duty to the injured employee. A breach can also arise when harm was not foreseeable from the start, but becomes foreseeable while the harassment is going on, and the employer fails to take steps to prevent it. In this case the court held that harassment was a foreseeable result of the claimant's complaint about a fellow officer, and that therefore she had an arguable case.

Adequate equipment

Employers have a duty to take reasonable care to provide their workers with adequate equipment, including protective devices and clothing, and to maintain it all properly. In some cases, this duty will include a responsibility to warn employees that such equipment should be used. In **Bux** *v* **Slough Metals** (1973), the claimant was a foundry worker, who was splashed with molten metal and lost the sight of one eye. His employer was bound by statute to provide protective goggles, and had complied with this duty, but the court held that his personal duty at common law went further than the statutory duty, and required him to encourage or even insist on the use of protective equipment. Having failed to do so, he was in breach of his duty towards the injured employee.

This common law liability will not apply if an injury is caused by some latent defect in equipment, which could not have been discovered by the employee concerned using reasonable care. However, under the Employers' Liability (Defective Equipment) Act 1969, s. 1(1), if employees are injured in the course of their employment as a result of defective equipment provided by their employer, and the defect is due to the fault of a third party, the employer may be held liable, even if they are in no way to blame. This means that if an employee injured by a defective tool or other equipment can show that, on a balance of probabilities, the defect resulted from negligence or other fault in the tool's manufacture, and that the injury was caused by that defect, then both the employer and the manufacturer will be liable. The main advantage of this for employees is that they do not need to track down the manufacturer of the defective equipment, which may prove difficult, while employers are entitled to an indemnity from the manufacturer. In practice, however, employers are rarely found liable under the Act due to the problems of proving third-party fault and causation.

A safe place of work

Employers must take reasonable steps to ensure a safe place of work; but this does not mean that every foreseeable risk must be eliminated, if doing so would be unreasonably onerous. This principle can be seen in the case of **Latimer** *v* **AEC**, discussed at p. 89.

Where a place of work is in the occupation or control of the employer, this poses no major problems, but in some cases, employees may be working on premises controlled by a third party – an obvious example would be a painter sent out to a private house. At one time it was thought that an employer owed no duty to provide a safe place of work in such cases, but in the case of **Wilson** *v* **Tyneside Window Cleaning Co** (1958), it was established that the duty of care remains, though the standard of care required may be lower where the place of work is not under the employer's control:

> The master's own premises are under his control: if they are dangerously in need of repair he can and must rectify the fault at once if he is to escape the censure of negligence. But if a master sends his plumber to mend a leak in a private house, no one could hold him negligent for not visiting the house himself to see if the carpet in the hall creates a trap.

The nature of the duty was further explained in **Cook** *v* **Square D Ltd** (1992), which concerned an employee sent to Saudi Arabia on a two-month contract. The court said that as the employers had satisfied themselves that the site occupiers and the general contractors were both reliable companies and aware of their responsibility for the safety of workers on the site, they could not be expected to be held responsible for daily events on the site; however, if several employees had been sent out there, or if one or two had been sent for a considerable period of time, the employer's duty might include a responsibility to inspect the site and ensure that the occupiers were conscious of their safety obligations. What the courts seem to be suggesting is that the possible risks must be balanced against the onerousness of the employer's task.

A safe system of working

This duty includes such matters as organization of work, the manner and order in which it is to be carried out, the number of employees needed for specific tasks and what each person is actually to do, safety precautions and special instructions, warnings and notices, particularly to inexperienced employees. In **Johnstone** *v* **Bloomsbury Health Authority** (1991), for example, it was held that a breach of duty might occur if the claimant was obliged to work such long hours as might foreseeably injure his health.

As with safety equipment, it is not necessarily enough simply to tell employees what the safety procedures are; employers may be required to make sure they are followed. In **Pape** *v* **Cumbria County Council** (1992), the claimant developed dermatitis as a result of contact with cleaning products. His employers had provided protective gloves, but were nevertheless held liable for breach of their duty towards the employee because they had failed to warn cleaning staff about the dangers of exposing the skin to chemicals, or to tell them to wear protective gloves at all times. The degree of care required will vary in different circumstances; where a worker is skilled and experienced, for example, it may be reasonable to expect them to guard against obvious dangers which a less experienced worker might not recognize.

In **Fraser** *v* **Winchester Health Authority** (1999), the claimant was a 21-year-old support worker employed by the health authority, who was sent on a camping trip with a patient. She was burnt when she attempted to change a gas cylinder near a lit candle; she had not been given any training in using the camping equipment, nor instructions on how to use it. The health authority argued that they were not negligent, because the risks involved in what the claimant had done were so obvious that she must have seen them, and therefore there was no need for them to have given any warnings or instruction. The Court of Appeal disagreed: the claimant's inexperience and the importance of her responsibilities meant that she should have been given some instruction. They agreed that she must have seen the risk, but held that this amounted to contributory negligence rather than to a complete lack of liability on the health

authority's part; they were held to be negligent but damages were reduced by one-third for the contributory negligence.

The duty to organize a safe system of work applies most obviously to
work done regularly – the operation of a production line, for example,
or the routine for loading or unloading a lorry. If such systems are in
place, the employer may leave it to employees to decide how smaller,
one-off tasks should be done, and it seems, may not be liable if they are
injured as a result. In **Chalk** *v* **Devizes Reclamation Co Ltd** (1999), the
claimant injured his back when bending down to pick up a large piece
of lead that had fallen from a pallet being unloaded from a lorry. He
claimed that his employers had been negligent in not providing training
in safe lifting techniques. The Court of Appeal refused this claim, on the
ground that the lifting had been a one-off incident; it was not part of his
usual duties, and so could not be considered part of a system of work.
The Court said that the claimant was an experienced labourer, who was
acting on his own initiative and using his own common sense; they could
not see what instructions could have been provided that would have
prevented the accident from happening.

Where an employer's practice is in line with that generally followed
in their trade or industry, the claimant is unlikely to succeed in a claim
that such a practice is negligent unless it displays serious lack of concern
for employees' health and safety (see **Thompson** *v* **Smiths Shiprepairers**
(North Shields) (1984) on p. 90).

The type of harm

The vast majority of employers' liability cases concern physical injury, but
two other important types of harm have also been the subject of litigation. The first is psychiatric injury. The case of **Walker** *v* **Northumberland
County Council** (1995) established that the employers' duty to take reasonable steps to ensure employees' safety could include a duty not to
cause psychiatric damage. The claimant was employed by the council to
manage four teams of social workers in an area with a high proportion
of children at risk, which created a huge caseload for his department. In
1986, due to the stress and pressure of work, he had a nervous breakdown and was off sick for three months. When he went back to work, the
council agreed to provide assistance to reduce his workload, but this was
never properly done, and six months later, he had another breakdown
and was unable to carry on working. He sued for negligence and it was
held that the council were liable for the second breakdown; once the first
breakdown had happened, it was foreseeable that a continuation of the
stress he was under would damage his mental health, and they were
negligent in failing to take reasonable steps to prevent that.

However, the case of **White and Others** *v* **Chief Constable of South
Yorkshire** (1998) makes it plain that this duty is subject to the normal
rules of negligence. In that case this meant that the claimants could not

claim compensation for their psychiatric shock because they were considered 'secondary victims', whereas Mr Walker came within the category of 'primary victims' (see p. 50).

The courts have also stated that in exceptional cases, employers may have a duty not to cause economic loss to employees. This was the case in **Spring** *v* **Guardian Assurance Plc** (1995), where an employer was successfully sued for negligence after giving a bad reference, and in **Scally** *v* **Southern Health and Social Services Board** (1992), where the employer was found negligent in failing to advise the employee that he was entitled to exercise valuable pension options. However, it was stressed in **White** that just as the employers' duty with regard to psychiatric shock is subject to the normal rules of negligence, so is the duty for employers to protect employees from economic loss; there is no blanket duty on employers not to cause economic loss to employees by, for example, reducing opportunities to earn bonuses.

The scope of the employer's duty

An employer's personal duty to employees, under any of the above heads, can be discharged by taking reasonable care; it is not an absolute duty to eliminate all risks. This is highlighted by the case of **Withers** *v* **Perry Chain** (1961). The claimant had in the past suffered from dermatitis due to contact with grease while at work, so her employers gave her the driest work that they could offer. However, she developed dermatitis once more, and sued her employers on the basis that, while aware that she was susceptible to the illness, they ought not to have allowed her to do work involving any risk of activating it. The Court of Appeal rejected her claim: the employers had done everything reasonable for her protection.

This approach was confirmed in **Henderson** *v* **Wakefield Shirt Co Ltd** (1997). Here the employee's job was to press garments, but she had a back condition which made such work painful. She claimed that her employers' failure to take steps to alleviate this problem – by altering the equipment she used or her work routine – was in breach of their duty regarding her safety at work. The Court of Appeal disagreed, finding that as the work conditions and equipment were not actually unsafe, the employers were not in breach of their duty.

The employer's personal duty to employees cannot be delegated. Performance of the obligations may be delegated to someone else, but if this performance is deficient, the employer still bears full liability. In **Wilsons and Clyde Coal Co Ltd** *v* **English** (1938), the defendant employers were held liable when a miner was injured because the system of working was not reasonably safe. The system had been worked out by the mine manager, who was also an employee of the claimant. Statute allowed such a delegation, but although the employers had taken reasonable steps in the sense that the mine manager was suitably qualified and experienced, they were still liable for breach of their personal duty to the employee.

The personal duty discussed here only arises in an employer–employee relationship, so the owner of a company owes no such duty to independent contractors who come to work on the premises, nor to any visitors to the premises (though other duties may be owed by virtue of occupiers' liability, discussed in Chapter 4). The personal duty is owed individually to each employee, so any characteristics of the particular worker which are known or which ought to be known to the employer will affect the precautions which the employer must take in order to fulfil the duty. In **Paris** *v* **Stepney Borough Council** (1951), the claimant, who worked in a garage, had only one eye; his employer was aware of this. The claimant did work which involved a risk of injury to his remaining eye, and his eye was in fact injured. It was held that although the risk was not so great as to require protective goggles to be issued to other workers doing the same job, the fact that if the claimant's eye was injured he might lose his sight completely meant that better precautions should have been taken, and the employers' failure to issue goggles was a breach of their duty to him.

▶ Defences

The general defences of contributory negligence and *volenti non fit injuria* are available in actions for breach of the employer's duty, but you can see from the case of **Smith** *v* **Baker** (1891), described at p. 112, that the courts are aware that in many employment cases, what looks like a voluntary choice may in reality be nothing of the kind, and they will bear this in mind when considering such cases.

ANSWERING QUESTIONS

Employer's liability most often appears on exam papers as part of a problem question, often combined with other torts, as below, where the question also raises issues of nuisance, occupiers' liability, breach of statutory duty and negligence; these are discussed in later chapters and the text below assumes knowledge of them.

Nathan and his very large number of friends are all addicted to watching sport on television. He frequently invites them to his house where they tend to stay until the early hours of the morning. There is always a lot of shouting and cheering and they often drink and talk in the garden, and sometimes take a television out there. People in neighbouring houses are disturbed by this noise and the noise when they leave. Also, there are frequent arguments over car parking and access.

To make it more convenient to watch programmes in the garden, Nathan installed a supply of electricity to an outbuilding by running a cable to it

from the house. Though he buried the cable in the ground, he did not use the materials or method required by law and he did not have the installation properly checked. Subsequently, he engaged Owen, a gardener, to install some fencing. While drilling holes for fence posts, Owen cut through the cable and was electrocuted and seriously injured. This incident was witnessed by Nathan's neighbour, Richard, who collapsed with shock.

Though he was using the supply to the outbuilding to power his machinery, Owen had not asked Nathan about the electricity cable, and Nathan had not attempted to mention it to him.

(a) Discuss what legal action Nathan's neighbours might pursue in respect of the noise and inconvenience, and consider how effective any remedies might be. *(10 marks)*

(b) Consider whether Owen may be able to recover compensation from Nathan for his injuries. *(15 marks)*

(c) Assuming that Owen were able to do so, explain whether Richard could also recover compensation from Nathan. *(10 marks)*

(d) Assuming that Owen has little money, how might he be able to pay for legal advice about his case? *(5 marks)*

(e) To what extent is the influence of policy considerations evident in the rules of law which you have discussed in examining the cases of Owen and Richard? *(10 marks)* AQA (AEB)

(a) Nathan's neighbours could sue him in nuisance (see Chapter 9). Looking first at private nuisance, three things need to be proved: an indirect interference with enjoyment of land, damage to the claimant, and that the interference was unreasonable. You should consider each in turn. Points to consider are whether Nathan's right to enjoy his land as he pleases should give way to his neighbours' right to do the same, and as regards unreasonableness, one of the factors taken into account will be the nature of the locality, which appears to be residential, the duration of the nuisance and the presence or otherwise of malice. Note **Hunter** v **Canary Wharf** now confirms that private nuisance is an action available only to those who have an interest in land, so it may not apply to the problems with car parking and access.

Moving on to public nuisance, as far as the problems caused are concerned, the definition of public nuisance would seem to cover both the noise and the problems with access and parking. You need to consider whether the neighbours can constitute a class of people; the leading case of **Attorney-General** v **PYA Quarries** (1957) concerned neighbours of the quarry causing the nuisance (see p. 234 below), so there seems to be no problem with this, but remember that an action will only be available if the nuisance has caused special damage to one of the neighbours, and we are not told whether this is the case.

You then need to look at possible remedies in either case. The neighbours are most likely to want an injunction, so you should consider this, but damages or abatement are also possibilities. You should mention that the latter are not necessarily very helpful – to use abatement for example, the neighbours would have to enter the land and switch off the television, which is hardly an appealing option.

(b) To recover compensation, Owen would need to sue Nathan. If Owen can prove that he is an employee (not an independent contractor), Nathan has an employer's duty to provide a safe place of work. Note that this duty does not require Nathan to eliminate every risk, but the fact that he has not even met the legal standard for installation of the cable, nor had it checked, would suggest that he has not taken reasonable steps to ensure the place is safe. This duty is non-delegable, so Nathan cannot suggest that it was Owen's responsibility to check where the cable was. You also need to discuss Nathan's duty of care as an occupier of land (see Chapter 4). Finally, you should consider whether Nathan may be in breach of a statutory duty, as we are told that he did not use the method or material specified by law. The issue for the court to decide here will be whether the relevant statute was intended to create individual liability; we are not given sufficient facts to decide this.

(c) The issue here is whether compensation can be claimed for negligence causing psychiatric damage, otherwise known as nervous shock. You need to explain that claimants making claims for psychiatric injury fall into various categories, and the rules differ between them. Richard clearly falls into the category of witnesses/secondary victims, so you need to go through the requirements set down in **Alcock** *v* **Chief Constable of South Yorkshire Police**, covering the nature of the injury, the class of person into which Richard falls, and his proximity to the accident. Clearly there is no problem with proximity, as Richard directly witnesses the accident. He also needs to show that he has developed a recognized psychiatric illness as a result of the shock of seeing the accident; we do not have enough evidence to decide whether this is the case. Where his claim seems likely to fail however, is on the 'class of person' requirement, since as far as we know, he has no particular relationship with Owen.

(d) This part of the question raises issues which are outside the scope of this book, which you will study as part of an English Legal System course. A textbook by the same authors on the English Legal System is available.

(e) As far as Owen's case is concerned, policy issues concerning negligence in general are discussed in the introduction to this book. Policy issues with regard to nervous shock, and therefore Richard's case, are discussed in the chapter on negligence.

4 Occupiers' liability

For well over a century, the law has recognized that people who occupy land (including buildings on land) have a duty towards the safety of others who come onto the land. This duty developed through the common law, but in 1957 it began to be regulated by statute with the introduction of the Occupiers' Liability Act, which laid down rules about the duty of occupiers towards people who come onto their land with permission. This was followed by the Occupiers' Liability Act 1984, which set out the duty owed by occupiers towards those who enter their land without permission, known as trespassers. The modern duty of occupiers of land is now contained in these two pieces of legislation; both of them incorporated some concepts from the previous common law, which is why this chapter refers to some pre-1957 cases which remain good law.

Who is an occupier?

Neither of the Acts define 'occupier'; they state that an occupier is a person who would be treated as such under common law. Under common law an occupier is the person who controls the premises. They do not have to be the physical occupier, nor the owner; the critical issue is whether they exercise a sufficient degree of control to allow or prevent other people entering. In each case, whether this level of control is exercised will be a question of fact.

In **Harris** *v* **Birkenhead Corporation** (1976) a compulsory purchase order had been served on a house by a local council, with a notice of entry which allowed the council to take over the premises 14 days later. After the residents had moved out, the council failed to board up the house. The claimant, a four-year-old child, got into the house through an unsecured door, and ended up falling from a second-floor window. The Court of Appeal held that the fact that the local authority had the legal right to control the premises made them the occupiers, and excluded the previous owners from any liability; the local authority was in the best position to prevent any accidents.

In some situations, there may be more than one occupier, in which case both or all can be liable in respect of the same damage. For example, if a landlord rents a whole building to one tenant, the tenant is the occupier, not the landlord. However, if the landlord retains possession of part of the building, such as a common staircase, or has a right to enter the premises to do repairs, both the tenant and the landlord will be occupiers at the same time.

In **Wheat** *v* **E Lacon & Co** (1966) the defendants owned a public house. It was run by a manager and his wife, who lived on the first floor, and were allowed to take in paying guests. The manager lived on the first floor because of his status as an employee, not as a tenant. A paying guest was killed when he fell on the emergency staircase, while trying to get to the bar on the first floor. The House of Lords held that both the manager and the owners were occupiers but on the facts, neither was held to be in breach of duty. The bad lighting on the staircase was caused by a stranger removing the bulb, and they were not responsible for the stranger's actions.

In **Bailey** *v* **Armes** (1999), the defendants were a couple who lived in a flat above a supermarket, where the husband worked. From one of their windows, it was possible to gain access to a flat roof; they allowed their son to play there, but had forbidden him to take any other children onto it. The supermarket owners owned the roof, but knew nothing of the fact that the child was allowed to play there. One day, he disobeyed his parents and persuaded the eight-year-old claimant, who was a friend of his, to climb up onto the roof from the garden. The claimant fell from the roof and was injured. He sued both the couple and the supermarket owners, but the Court of Appeal said that none of the defendants could be considered occupiers, because they did not have a sufficient degree of control over the roof area.

In **Revill** *v* **Newberry** (1996) it was made clear that the legislation does not apply to every situation where the defendant happens to be an occupier of the land in which the incident complained of occurred. The claimant and an accomplice had sneaked onto the defendant's land, intending to steal from his shed. The defendant, an elderly man, had taken to sleeping in his shed with a shotgun, as his property had frequently suffered the attentions of vandals and thieves. Hearing movement outside, he poked his gun through a little hole in the shed door, and fired, hitting the claimant in the arm. The Court of Appeal held that the situation was covered by the general law of negligence, and not statutory occupiers' liability, because the fact that he was the occupier of the land was not relevant to his liability – he was liable in just the same way as he would have been if he had been, for example, a friend of the occupier staying in the shed.

This seems to suggest that the Acts will only be applied to situations where harm is caused by dangerous conditions on land, or dangerous conduct which resembles a dangerous condition in that it is a continuing source of danger on the land. It seems not to be applicable where the harm arises from an isolated action of the occupier which could equally have been the action of someone who was not the occupier.

What must they occupy?

The Acts impose liability on 'occupiers of premises', and premises are defined in s. 1(3) of the 1957 Act as including land, buildings and 'any fixed or movable structure, including any vessel, vehicle or aircraft'.

▶ Liability to visitors: Occupiers' Liability Act 1957

The central provision of the 1957 Act is s. 2(1), which provides that an occupier of premises owes a common duty of care to visitors to those premises.

Who is a visitor?

A visitor is someone who has express or implied permission from the occupier to enter the premises. Anyone who enters the property without such permission is a trespasser, whose rights are governed not by the Act of 1957 but by the Occupiers' Liability Act 1984 (discussed at p. 152).

Where permission to enter has been given but is then withdrawn while the entrant is still on the property, they are allowed a reasonable time in which to leave; once that expires, the person becomes a trespasser.

Implied permission

Permission can be implied from conduct or circumstances. Occupiers are treated as having given implied permission to people such as meter readers, police officers with search warrants, and even door-to-door salespeople, and all of these will be legally classed as visitors.

There must be a genuine permission, and not just toleration of the person's entry, but in some cases the courts have gone to surprising lengths to imply permission when the facts seem to suggest otherwise. An example is **Lowery** *v* **Walker** (1911). The defendant was a farmer, and for 35 years people had walked through his unfenced field as a short cut to the railway station. He had frequently asked them not to do this, but had stopped short of taking legal action because he was anxious not to lose customers for his milk. He then put a wild horse on the land to graze, which attacked and injured the claimant. Despite the fact that the farmer clearly did not want people walking through the land and had told them not to, the House of Lords held that the claimant (who had taken the short cut as usual and been attacked by the horse) had implied permission to be on the land, and was therefore owed a duty of care. It is possible that the decision can be explained by the law's dislike of 'self-help' measures such as leaving a wild horse to deal with trespassers.

Similarly, the courts have been known to conclude that having on the premises an object likely to attract a child (sometimes called an allurement) amounts to giving a child implied permission to enter. In **Cooke** *v* **Midland Great Western Railway of Ireland** (1909) the claimant was a young child, who was injured while playing with others on a railway turntable on the defendant's premises. The turntable was close to a public road and was usually left unlocked. Though aware that children often got on to the premises from the road and played on the turntable, the company took no precautions to prevent this. The House of Lords held that there was evidence of negligence on the part of the railway company. Although they had no duty of care towards trespassing children, the fact that they knew the children were coming on to the premises because of the allurement of the turntable and did nothing to stop them meant that there was sufficient evidence to suggest that the claimant was not a trespasser, but was on the railway premises with the company's implied permission.

A contrasting case is that of **Edwards** *v* **Railway Executive** (1952). Here the claimant was a nine-year-old boy, who, chasing a ball which had been thrown over the railway line, climbed through a fence separating a playground from the railway, went up the embankment and was injured by a train. The Railway Executive knew that for a very long time children had been breaking through the fence and getting on to the embankment, but as soon as they saw any damage in the fence, they repaired it immediately. On these facts the court found that there were no grounds for finding an implied permission to enter the railway property.

In many early cases the reason for the courts' keenness to find implied permission was that the law gave trespassers very few rights, and while this may have been appropriate for trespassers such as burglars, it could operate very harshly where the trespasser was, for example, a child. The position of a trespasser has now been improved by the 1984 Act, so there is less need for this approach.

Legal rights of entry
The 1957 Act includes in the definition of a visitor anyone who enters premises under a right conferred by law (s. 2(6)) with or without the occupier's express permission. Examples would be police officers and firefighters carrying out their legal duties.

Rights of way
A person using a public right of way (walking down an ordinary street for example) is not considered to be a visitor, and is therefore not owed a duty of care under the 1957 Act by the people over whose land the right of way passes. This rule was laid down in the old case of **Gautret** *v* **Egerton** (1867) but was recently confirmed by the House of Lords in **McGeown** *v* **Northern Ireland Housing Executive** (1994). The appellant was walking along a public footpath which ran over the defendant's land.

She tripped in a hole and was injured and sued the defendants. Her case was rejected. The House of Lords confirmed that people who used rights of way were neither visitors nor trespassers and were therefore owed no duty. Lord Keith justified this conclusion on the basis that:

> Rights of way pass over many different types of terrain, and it would place an impossible burden on landowners if they not only had to submit to the passage over them of anyone who might choose to exercise them but also were under a duty to maintain them in a safe condition. Persons using rights of way do so not with the permission of the owner . . . but in the exercise of a right.

This exception can be criticized, particularly in the light of the greater protection now afforded trespassers.

The common duty of care

Section 2(2) of the 1957 Act provides that 'The common duty of care is a duty to take such care as in all the circumstances of the case is reasonable to see that the visitor will be reasonably safe in using the premises for the purposes for which he is invited or permitted to be there.' The premises do not therefore have to be safe providing the visitor is made safe, for example, by being given a sufficient warning of the existence of a danger.

Two recent cases provide useful discussions of the standard of care required. In **Horton** *v* **Jackson** (1996), the claimant was a golfer who had lost the sight in one eye after being hit by a ball. He successfully sued the golfer who had hit the ball, who then claimed that the accident was partly the fault of the golf club where they were playing. He argued that the club was in breach of its duty under the 1957 Act, because they should have erected a screen between two particular tees to prevent balls hit at one from hitting people playing at the other; there was a sign asking players at the second tee to wait until those at the first had moved on, but he argued that this rule was not enforced. The Court of Appeal disagreed: there was expert evidence that a screen would not have prevented the accident, and the fact that in 800,000 rounds of golf played at the club only two accidents had ever occurred in that spot entitled the judge to conclude that the existing precautions were reasonable and there was no breach of duty.

Darby *v* **National Trust** (2001) concerned a man who drowned while swimming in a pond at a National Trust property. His widow sued under the 1957 Act, claiming that as there had been no warnings about the danger of drowning, the National Trust had not taken reasonable care. The Court of Appeal disagreed: drowning was an obvious risk, even if a small one, so there was no need to warn against it.

The Act gives specific guidance on particular issues concerning the statutory common duty of care.

Children

Section 2(3)(a) of the 1957 Act states: 'An occupier must be prepared for children to be less careful than adults. If the occupier allows a child to enter the premises then the premises must be reasonably safe for a child of that age.'

In **Perry** *v* **Butlins Holiday World** (1997), the claimant was a three-year-old who badly cut his ear when he fell onto a brick wall at the defendants' holiday camp. The wall was a low one built of very sharp bricks, and was near an open area where children's shows were regularly performed. The Court of Appeal held that the case was borderline, but the design of the wall, coupled with its position where children were obviously likely to be, meant that the defendants had breached their duty under the Act.

In the tragic case of **Jolley** *v* **London Borough of Sutton** (2000), the claimant was a 14-year-old boy. He and a friend had found an old boat abandoned on the council estate where they lived, and had decided to try to repair it. They had propped it up with a car jack, but this collapsed; the boat fell on the claimant, injuring him so badly that he was left paralysed. The council admitted that they should have moved the boat, because it was reasonably foreseeable that children would be attracted to it; however, they argued, what was foreseeable was that children would get into it to play, and possibly fall through the rotten floor. They claimed that what the claimant and his friend had done was an unusual use of the boat and so the accident he had was not foreseeable. The Court of Appeal had agreed with that view, but the House of Lords held that this approach was too narrow. What was foreseeable was that children would meddle with the boat; it was not necessary for the council to be able to foresee exactly what they would do with it. The Lords made the point that children typically show considerable ingenuity in finding ways to put themselves in danger, and said that this needed to be taken into account when assessing the precautions needed to keep them safe. They also pointed out that the council had admitted that the risk of children playing in the boat was foreseeable, and that they should therefore have removed the boat; preventing the wider risk would have involved exactly the same action, and would therefore not have involved any more effort or expense.

In **Glasgow Corporation** *v* **Taylor** (1922), a seven-year-old child had died from eating poisonous berries that he had picked from a bush in a park, which was under the control of the corporation. The corporation knew the berries were poisonous, but had neither fenced off the shrub, nor put up any warning notice. They were held liable. It was accepted that the child had no right to take the berries and that an adult doing the same thing might well have been considered a trespasser. However, the berries, which looked like cherries, were obviously tempting to children, and the court held that that constituted an 'allurement' to the child.

Simply by leaving the berries there the corporation had breached their duty of care to the child, though this would not have been the case if the victim had been an adult. This case was obviously decided well before either of the Occupiers' Liability Acts existed; were the same circumstances to arise today, it would probably be decided on the basis of the 1984 Act, though the result might well be the same given the allowances made for children in the legislation.

An occupier is entitled to assume that very young children will be accompanied by someone looking after them, and a duty of care in that case may amount to no more than giving a warning which is sufficiently clear to be understood by somebody competent to look after such children. In **Phipps** *v* **Rochester Corporation** (1955) the claimant was a boy aged five, who was picking blackberries with his seven-year-old sister. They crossed some open land where the defendants were building houses. The land was commonly used by local children as a play area, and although the defendants knew this, they made no attempt to keep the children out.

In the centre of the land, the defendants had dug a long, deep trench, and the claimant fell into this, breaking his leg. An adult would have seen the danger immediately. The defendants were held not liable, because they could presume that no sensible parent would allow such young children to enter the area in question alone, without at least checking first for danger themselves. Although the defendants' failure to try to keep children out meant that the claimant had implied permission to be on the land, giving rise to a duty of care, the defendants were not in breach of that duty.

Persons exercising a calling

Section 2(3)(b) of the 1957 Act states: 'An occupier may expect that a person, in the exercise of his calling, will appreciate and guard against any special risks ordinarily incident to it, so far as the occupier leaves him free to do so.' This means that where a risk normally arises in the course of a person's work, the occupier need not take special precautions to protect that person against such a risk, so long as they allow the person to take their own precautions.

In **Roles** *v* **Nathan** (1963) two chimney sweeps were killed by carbon monoxide gas while working on the chimney of a coke-fired boiler, which was alight at the time. The occupiers were held not liable, because they could expect sweeps to be aware of this particular danger and these sweeps had in fact also been warned of the danger. As Lord Denning pointed out, the result would have been different if the sweeps had been killed because the stairs leading to the basement had given way; only a risk relevant to the trade in question can allow the occupier to escape liability.

This section does not mean that the occupier owes no duty to the skilled professional. In **Ogwo** *v* **Taylor** (1988) the defendant negligently set fire to his house. The claimant was a firefighter who was called to the house to put out the fire and he was injured while doing so. The blaze was such that no amount of care by the claimant could have protected him so the defendant could not rely on s. 2(3)(b) to avoid liability.

Independent contractors

Section 2(4)(b) of the 1957 Act provides that:

> Where damage is caused to a visitor by a danger due to the faulty execution of any work of construction, maintenance or repair by an independent contractor employed by the occupier, the occupier is not to be treated without more as answerable for the danger if in all the circumstances he had acted reasonably in entrusting the work to an independent contractor and had taken such steps (if any) as he reasonably ought in order to satisfy himself that the contractor was competent and that the work had been properly done.

This essentially means that occupiers employing independent contractors will be found liable when their independent contractor's activities fall below the common duty of care, unless they take reasonable steps to satisfy themselves that the contractor is competent; and, if the nature of the work allows, to make sure that the work has been properly done. What amounts to reasonable steps will depend on the nature of the work; in a large-scale, complex project such as the construction of a large building, it may involve employing an architect or other expert to supervise the work, whereas in a small job such as installing a central heating system in a house, the occupier is entitled to rely solely on the contractor.

In **Haseldine** *v* **Daw** (1941), the claimant was killed when a lift plunged to the bottom of its shaft. It was held that the building's occupiers were not liable for the death; they had fulfilled their duty of care by appointing an apparently competent firm to maintain the lift, and the highly technical nature of the work meant that they could not be expected to check whether it had been done properly.

In **Woodward** *v* **Mayor of Hastings** (1945), the claimant, a child, slipped at school on a step covered in snow. The step had been negligently cleaned, and although there was some doubt as to whether the cleaner was an employee, the occupiers were held liable for failing to take reasonable steps to check that the work had been done properly, because the nature of the work was such that this could be easily checked.

The contractor will often also be liable to the claimant, either by being regarded as an occupier, or under the general principles of negligence.

Contractual rights of entry

A person entering premises under a contractual right is in the same position as any other visitor, unless the contract expressly provides for a higher standard of care than the statutory common duty of care – s. 5(1).

▶ Defences under the 1957 Act

The two general defences of contributory negligence and *volenti* are available for actions concerning breach of the 1957 Act; in addition, occupiers can protect themselves from liability by the use of warnings and exclusion notices, subject to the rules explained below.

Contributory negligence

Section 2(3) of the 1957 Act specifies that in considering whether an occupier has breached the common duty of care, the courts may take into account the degree of care a reasonable visitor can be expected to show for their own safety.

Volenti

Section 2(5) of the 1957 Act states that 'The common duty of care does not impose on an occupier any obligation willingly accepted as his by the visitor', thus allowing for the application of *volenti*. However, a visitor will not be deemed to have accepted a risk merely because the occupier displays a notice to that effect (see below).

Warnings

Under s. 2(4)(a) of the 1957 Act if an occupier gives a visitor sufficient warning of a danger to render a visitor reasonably safe, the occupier will not be liable for any damage suffered by the visitor as a result of that danger. Lord Denning gave an illustration of such a situation in **Roles** *v* **Nathan** (1963). If a house has a river in front of it, and the sole means of access to the house is by crossing a dangerous bridge, the occupier will not secure a defence by simply affixing a sign stating that the bridge is dangerous. The sign would not make visitors safe, since they would have to use the bridge anyway. If, however, there were two bridges and a notice on the dangerous one warned visitors to use the other, the occupier would bear no liability for injury caused to a visitor who was injured through ignoring the warning and using the dangerous bridge.

Exclusion of the common duty of care

Section 2(1) of the 1957 Act states that 'An occupier of premises owes the same duty, the "common duty of care", to all his visitors, except in so far as he is free to and does extend, restrict, modify or exclude his duty to any visitor or visitors by agreement or otherwise.'

This means that an exclusion notice or clause may be used to impose a lesser duty of care, or even none at all. However, this provision is subject to the Unfair Contract Terms Act 1977 (UCTA). Section 2(1) of UCTA prevents an occupier from excluding liability for death or personal injuries caused by negligence (defined as including the common duty of care). Where an occupier is acting in the course of a business, or from premises used for business purposes, liability for damage to property can only be excluded if it is reasonable to do so (1957 Act, s. 2(2)).

Section 3(1) of UCTA states that an occupier cannot use a contract to reduce their obligations to less than those required by the common duty of care, for visitors who are not parties to the contract.

These provisions of UCTA do not apply where visitors enter premises for recreational or educational purposes, unless that access is itself allowed for business purposes (Occupiers' Liability Act 1984, s. 2). So a church which allows the local badminton club to play in its hall may exclude all liability as an occupier, but a leisure centre doing the same could not.

Section 2(3) of the 1957 Act provides that a visitor will not be considered to have voluntarily accepted a risk just because the occupier has displayed a notice excluding liability for that risk, and the visitor is aware of that. There must be evidence of voluntary acceptance of the risk.

▶ Damage under the 1957 Act

Section 1(3) of the 1957 Act provides that a claim can be made for personal injuries and damage to property, including subsequent financial loss that is not too remote, but not for pure economic loss.

▶ Liability to trespassers: Occupiers' Liability Act 1984

The 1984 Act provides that an occupier has a duty to persons other than visitors to take such care as is reasonable in the circumstances to see that they do not suffer injury on the premises. However the duty only exists if the following conditions, stated in s. 1(3), are met:

(a) [the occupier] is aware of the danger or has reasonable grounds to believe that it exists;

(b) he knows or has reasonable grounds to believe that the other [i.e. the trespasser] is in the vicinity of the danger concerned or that he may come into the vicinity of the danger . . . ; and

(c) the risk is one which in all the circumstances of the case, [the occupier] may reasonably be expected to offer the other some protection from.

Where a defendant actually knows of a risk, or actually knows that trespassers are or may come within the vicinity of it, there is little problem; what tends to arise in the cases are the issues of what will amount to 'reasonable grounds to believe' that a risk exists and 'reasonable grounds to believe' that a trespasser will or may be in the vicinity.

In **Swain** *v* **Natui Ram Puri** (1996), the claimant was a nine-year-old boy who was injured when he fell from the defendant's factory roof, where he was trespassing. His case was that there was reason to believe that children would climb the roof, and the defendants were therefore in breach of their duty because they had not made sufficient efforts to keep children away. The Court of Appeal disagreed; there was no evidence of previous trespass, and while the factory fences were not completely in-truder-proof, they were substantial, so there were no reasonable grounds to suspect that trespassers might enter and try to scale the roof. The court held that the phrase 'reasonable grounds to believe' in s. 1(3) meant that it was necessary to show that the defendants had actual knowledge of relevant facts which provided grounds for such a belief; it did not mean 'ought to have known'.

An example of a case where this requirement was satisfied is **Scott** *v* **Associated British Ports** (1999). The defendants owned land on which there was a railway line. In separate accidents, four years apart, two boys had lost limbs when they had played on the land and attempted to get on to moving trains. The court held that the defendants owed no duty under the 1984 Act for the first accident, because they had been unaware of the risk. However, their knowledge of the first accident, along with newspa-per coverage and complaints made to them later, meant that they did owe a duty under the Act with regard to the second accident (they were, however, not liable because the court held that the claimant was old enough to be aware of the risk he was taking).

Who is a trespasser?

A trespasser is someone who goes on to land without any kind of permis-sion, and whose presence there is either not known to the occupier, or if known, is objected to. This means that trespassers can include not only burglars and squatters, but also anyone who, for example, innocently wanders on to land because the boundaries are not marked, or because they are lost.

The duty of care

In practice, the appropriate precautions for avoiding injury to trespassers are often obvious, and the presence of trespassers not significantly less foreseeable than that of lawful visitors, so that there is little effective difference between when a duty is owed to lawful visitors under the 1957 Act and when it is owed to trespassers under the 1984 Act (but see the section on 'Damage' below).

According to the Lord Chancellor of the time, the standard of the duty of care imposed by the 1984 Act was intended to be pitched at a similar level to that which had previously existed under the old common law in **British Rail Board** *v* **Herrington** (1972), so while the old common law has been specifically abolished by the 1984 Act it can still be of assistance in understanding the duty imposed under the Act. The case involved a six-year-old claimant who passed through a gap in a fence and was electrocuted on the defendant's railway line. The fence had been in need of repair for some time but the stationmaster had done nothing about it, despite the fact that he was both aware that it needed repair and that children had the habit of passing through it. The House of Lords found on these facts that the defendants were in breach of the duty they owed to a trespasser, known as the duty of 'common humanity'. This duty was less demanding than that owed to a legitimate visitor.

The Act was applied in **White** *v* **St Albans City** (1990). The claimant was taking a short cut across the council's land to a car park, when he fell down a 12-foot trench and injured himself. The land was clearly private, and surrounded by a fence, and there was no evidence that the council were aware of it being used as a short cut to the car park. The Court of Appeal concluded that this made the claimant a trespasser. According to the provisions of the 1984 Act, the council had taken reasonable care in the circumstances and so were not liable for his injury. The common duty of humanity was less onerous than the usual duty of care owed to visitors as opposed to trespassers.

In **Platt** *v* **Liverpool City Council** (1997), a group of boys had entered derelict buildings, which collapsed, killing one boy and injuring another. The buildings were owned by the council, who had secured them against intruders using metal sheets over the windows and doors, and regularly checked that these were still in place. The day before the accident, an employee had checked and found the building so badly vandalized that it would have to be demolished; that could not be done for a week, so the council erected an eight-foot high metal fence around the building, secured by wooden posts embedded in concrete. The building could only be entered by climbing the fence or wriggling under it. The Court of Appeal held that the council had done all that was reasonable in the circumstances to prevent injury and was not liable.

In **Ratcliff** *v* **McConnell and Another** (1998), the claimant was a student who, after going out drinking at night with some friends, decided to take a swim in the college pool. The pool, which was enclosed by high walls, was closed for the winter, and the water level was low. The gate to it was locked, and there were signs prohibiting its use at night, and warning of the depth at the shallow end. The claimant and his friends climbed the gate and he dived in, probably at the shallow end, and hit his head on the bottom of the pool, causing injuries which left him paralysed. He sued under the 1984 Act, but the Court of Appeal held that the college was not in breach of its duty under that Act. The danger that someone diving into the shallow end might hit their head was common to all swimming pools and obvious to any adult; it was not a hidden risk, but one which the claimant was fully aware of.

▶ Defences under the 1984 Act

The general defences of contributory negligence and *volenti* are available for actions under the 1984 Act, and occupiers may also protect themselves from liability by using warnings and (probably) exclusion notices.

Contributory negligence

The case of **Revill** *v* **Newberry** (1996), which is discussed at p. 110, suggests that contributory negligence is also a defence to actions against trespassers. However, in that case, coming onto someone's land in the middle of the night and acting in a manner that was likely to make the occupier suspect wrongdoing was not considered contributorily negligent, so it is difficult to see what might be sufficient to activate the defence (you may recall that in **Revill** the Court of Appeal decided the case on the basis of general negligence, rather than statutory occupiers' liability; however, they used the 1984 Act to determine the scope of the duty owed, and so their findings on defences are likely to be relevant to cases of true occupiers' liability).

Volenti

Section 1(6) of the 1984 Act provides that 'No duty is owed by virtue of this section to any person in respect of risks willingly accepted as his by that person (the question of whether a risk was so accepted to be decided on the same principles as in other cases in which one person owes a duty of care to another).'

Where trespassers were concerned, before the 1984 Act was passed, the courts adopted an objective rather than a subjective test of acceptance of risk. In **Titchener** *v* **British Railways Board** (1983), it was stated that adult claimants are regarded as accepting any risk which they knew about when entering the land. Should this principle apply to the 1984 Act, the defence of *volenti* provides greater protection for occupiers with regard to trespassers than it does with regard to visitors, where the defence only applies if the visitor knows enough to be reasonably safe.

Warnings

Section 1(5) of the 1984 Act provides that an occupier of premises discharges their duty to a trespasser 'by taking such steps as are reasonable in all the circumstances of the case to give warning of the danger concerned or to discourage persons from incurring the risk'. As a general rule, the existence of a warning sign is not enough; it must be sufficiently clear to ensure that the risk is obvious.

Exclusion

The 1984 Act does not state whether the duty under it can be excluded by the occupier. It is sometimes suggested that this implies exclusion is possible, since it is not forbidden nor made subject to any special rules under the Act. If exclusion is possible, then such exclusions would not be subject to the Unfair Contract Terms Act 1977, which is stated to apply only to the old common law and the 1957 Act; the result would be that occupiers would have a wide opportunity to exclude their liability, thus weakening the Act considerably.

An alternative view is that the duty imposed by the 1984 Act cannot be excluded, because it was designed to uphold the old common law 'duty of humanity', which was unexcludable because it was a minimum standard below which the law would not allow occupiers to fall, no matter how unwelcome the visitor. Unfortunately there is no authority on the point; should it come up in an exam problem question, you will need to explain this, and examine what the implications in the situation described would be if the duty is excludable, and then what they would be if it is not.

Damage under the 1984 Act

One major difference between the 1957 and 1984 Acts is that the latter only allows claims for death or personal injury; unlike visitors, trespassers cannot claim for damage to property. Take, for example, a situation where A has gone out for a drive in the country in her brand-new car. She becomes lost and accidentally ends up on B's land, where there is a dangerous bridge. She drives across the bridge, which collapses, depositing her and the car in the river. She may be able to claim for her own injuries, but not for the damage to her car.

ANSWERING QUESTIONS

1 Ken and Mavis live next door to Jean, a 55-year-old widow, who suffers from a bad back. Ken and Mavis look after Jean, doing her cooking and cleaning. Ken and Mavis hold the keys to Jean's house, and make use of Jean's washing machine for their own purposes. While Jean is in hospital,

Mavis enters Jean's house to make a telephone call, but on her way out Mavis slips on the crumbling concrete step by the back door and breaks her leg.

On a subsequent occasion Ken is in Jean's kitchen, cooking her dinner, when the central heating boiler explodes. Ken is injured. The explosion shatters the glass in the kitchen window. Pat, the postman, is walking along the pavement outside Jean's bungalow and is hit by a piece of this glass. The central heating boiler has recently been serviced by All Gas Appliances.

Advise Jean and All Gas Appliances as to their liabilities. *OCR*

Consider each of the possible liabilities in turn; a sensible structure would be to consider all Jean's possible liabilities first, and then all those of All Gas.

Jean may be liable to Mavis, Ken and/or Pat, and in each case, the possible source of liability will be the Occupiers' Liability Acts, because the house clearly qualifies as premises and Jean has control of it. Taking Mavis first, it is not clear whether she is a visitor or a trespasser. She clearly has some degree of permission to enter the house, given that she has the keys and the suggestion seems to be that Jean allows use of the washing machine, but she may not have permission to go in and use the phone, in which case doing so would render her a trespasser. The best approach here is to consider the implications if she is a visitor, and those if she is a trespasser, explaining what would make the difference (in this case, permission from Jean to enter the house to use the telephone). If she has permission to go in and use the phone and is therefore a visitor, Jean's liability is covered by the 1957 Act, which requires her to take reasonable care to ensure that Mavis is reasonably safe for the purposes for which she is permitted to be there. Point out that to decide whether this is the case, the courts will look at the same kinds of issues which are discussed in connection with the standard of care in negligence, such as the magnitude of the risk and the practicality of protection. We do not have enough information to know whether Jean has breached this standard, but this does not matter as long as you know what issues the court will take into account. The court will also want to know whether the risk was clearly visible (**Staples v West Dorset District Council**) and whether Jean had ever warned Mavis about it; again, we have no information either way. What you need to say is that if, having considered all these aspects, the court finds that Jean has breached the duty of care under the 1957 Act, she will be liable for Mavis's broken leg.

If Mavis does not have permission to enter and use the phone and is therefore a trespasser, Jean's liability is covered by the 1984 Act. This imposes a duty to take reasonable care to see that trespassers do not suffer injury, but only where the conditions in s. 1(3) (set out at p. 152) are met. Clearly Jean knew that Mavis was likely to be crossing the step; what we do not know is whether Jean knew that the step was dangerous, or whether the circumstances were such that it would be reasonable to expect her to protect people from being injured on it. Only if the answer to these two questions is yes can she have any liability to a trespasser. If she does, Mavis will have to prove that Jean did not take such care as was reasonable in the circumstances to prevent her injury.

As regards Jean's possible liability to Ken, this would appear to be covered by the 1957 Act, as we can assume that if Ken is cooking Jean's dinner, he has permission to be there. The question therefore is whether the explosion was caused by something Jean has done or failed to do. If so, and if her conduct is deemed to fall below the reasonable standard of care, she will be liable to Ken. However, it looks more likely that the explosion was a result of negligent servicing by All Gas, who are presumably independent contractors. If this is the case, Jean will still be liable if she failed to take reasonable steps to make sure All Gas were competent; if she did take such steps however, she will not be liable. In some cases there is also a duty to ensure that the work is done properly, but this is unlikely to be imposed where the work is technical in nature (**Haseldine v Daw**).

Jean's last possible liability is to Pat, the postman. The 1957 Act states that there is no duty owed to those who are merely exercising a right of way, so Pat has no claim on Jean arising from the Occupiers' Liability Acts. If the explosion is caused by negligence on Jean's part, it is possible that Pat has a case in negligence, depending on whether the injury to him was considered to fall within the rules on remoteness of damage (see p. 99).

Turning to the possible liabilities of All Gas, their case is covered not by occupiers' liability legislation, but by the ordinary rules of negligence. As the damage caused is personal injury, the standard test for a duty of care applies in both Ken and Pat's cases (see p. 19). You will also need to discuss the issues of causation and remoteness of damage here.

5

Product liability

In the first chapter, you will have read the story of the unfortunate Mrs Donoghue, whose encounter with a decomposing snail not only spoilt what she thought was going to be a quiet drink with a friend, but went on to form the basis of the case which is credited with giving birth to the modern law of negligence, **Donoghue** *v* **Stevenson** (1932). One of the reasons why the case was such a landmark is that before it, the remedies available to a consumer who was injured by a product were very limited. Today, however, the picture is very different, and there are a range of remedies available for the users of defective products, coming from the common law of both contract and tort, and from statutory provisions, again both in contract and tort. Which actions are available in a particular case will depend on whether the claimant is the person who bought the product or not, whether the product is defective in the sense of not doing its job properly, or actually dangerous, and what type of damage is caused as a result of the product's defects; the three types of action interlock, each more or less restrictive in these different areas.

In this chapter we look at all the main ways in which a claimant can claim for loss or injury caused by defective products, beginning with the earliest, contract, and ending with the newest, product liability legislation as represented by the Consumer Protection Act 1987.

▶ Product liability in contract

Before Mrs Donaghue's snail popped out of her ginger beer bottle and started a legal revolution, the only real remedy for users of defective goods was the law of contract. This provided that someone who bought a product that was defective could sue the person they bought it from for breach of contract. The protection that this offered was increased by a line of statutes, beginning with the Sale of Goods Act 1893, which stated that certain terms regarding the quality of the goods sold should be implied into sales contracts, even though the parties themselves had not specifically mentioned them, and therefore giving the buyer a remedy if the goods were not up to the standard implied by the Act. Since 1893, the

159

Sale of Goods Act has been regularly updated and extended by further statutes (see below).

Today, contract law is still a very important source of claims for defective products, and has both advantages and disadvantages over other types of claim, in terms of who can sue and be sued, what type of damage can be the subject of a claim, and what must be proved.

Who can sue?

Until very recently, with very few exceptions, only the person who actually bought the defective product could bring an action for breach of contract. This rule is known as the doctrine of privity, and meant that there was no contract claim available, for example, to anyone who received a defective product as a gift, or who used something belonging to another member of the family or an employer. This is why Mrs Donoghue could not have brought a claim in contract, as it was not her but a friend who had bought the drink.

The Contracts (Rights of Third Parties) Act 1999 has now changed this position. It states that a third party can enforce a contractual term where the contract either expressly states that that term (or the whole contract) should give rights to a third party, or where the particular term purports to confer a benefit on the third party. For example, a shopper buying a gift for someone else can write on the receipt that the recipient should have rights under the contract of sale, and get the retailer to sign it. If the product then turns out to be defective, the recipient can sue in their own right. Where a contract does not state whether it should give rights to third parties, a court will look at whether there is other evidence that suggests the relevant term purports to confer a benefit on a third party.

Who can be sued?

The other side of the privity rule is that only the person (or company) who actually sold the product can be sued, and this part of the rule remains. If the seller cannot be traced, is bankrupt or otherwise unable to pay damages, the consumer has no claim in contract against anyone else involved in the product's supply.

This rule can also cause hardship to the seller, since it applies even if it was not the seller but the manufacturer who caused the defect. To make a manufacturer responsible for a defective product in contract, the consumer must sue the seller, who in turn sues their supplier, and so on back up the chain to the manufacturer. If at any point the next person in line turns out to be bankrupt, to have disappeared or to be insufficiently well-off or insured to be worth sueing, there is no way for the last party sued to leap-frog over them to their supplier, and so the chain breaks and the loss lies with the last party sued.

Types of product covered

A breach of contract action can be brought regarding the sale of any type of product or commodity.

Defects and damage

As we suggested above, there are two ways in which a product can be considered defective: first, it may simply fail to perform as expected, or to be of adequate quality; secondly, it may be dangerous, which includes having the potential to damage other property as well as to injure people. Either (or both) of these types of defect can give rise to a claim for breach of contract.

Of the three main types of product liability claim, contract is the least restrictive in terms of the type of damage that can be compensated: damages for breach of contract can cover personal injury, damage to property, pure economic loss and even, in limited cases, anxiety, distress and loss of recreational enjoyment.

What must be proved?

A claimant claiming breach of contract does not need to prove that the product was defective because of something that the seller did or failed to do; in other words, there is no need to prove fault. What has to be proved is that there was a term in the contract which stated that the product would be of a certain quality, and that the defect concerned means that this term has not been fulfilled. The term may be something agreed specifically between buyer and seller, but more commonly in consumer disputes, it will be one of the terms implied into contracts by the Sale of Goods Act 1979. The main terms implied by the Act are that goods sold are 'of satisfactory quality' and reasonably fit for their purpose.

Defences

There are a number of defences available to a breach of contract action; these are outside the scope of this book as they are usually taught on a contract law course.

Evaluating product liability in contract

In many ways, contract offers a very effective method of compensation for defective products. It covers all kinds of defects, not just those which make a product dangerous, and a claimant need only prove that a term of the contract has been breached; there is no need to prove fault, which, as we shall see when we look at negligence claims for product liability, can be a huge hurdle, especially for an individual claimant sueing a big manufacturer.

In the past, the major drawback to contract as a cause of action for product liability claims was the privity rule, because it severely limited the class of people who could sue in contract. The Contracts (Rights of Third Parties) Act was designed to address this problem, and while it is too early to assess its effects, it should in principle increase the chances of compensation for defective products considerably. However, one possible threat to this is that it is easy for sellers to exclude their contracts from the Act; they need only include an express term to this effect. Top law firms are advising clients to do so as routine when they issue a contract. Of course in principle a buyer can refuse to agree to the exclusion term – but given that in many consumer transactions, the consumer simply accepts the terms offered by the seller, this could seriously restrict the practical value of the Act, so that many third parties will still be unable to sue in contract.

▶ Product liability in tort

As we have seen, **Donoghue *v* Stevenson** established for the first time that the producers of defective products can owe a duty to the end consumer of that product. Over the (almost) 70 years since it was decided, the tort of negligence has played an extremely important role in consumer protection, and remains important even since the passing of consumer protection legislation.

Who can sue?

Anyone injured by a defective product can bring an action in negligence. Unlike contract, this allows a remedy for people given a defective product and for users of something belonging to someone else. It also applies to someone who, while not actually using the product, is injured as a result of the defect in it. Two examples of this are **Brown *v* Cotterill** (1934), where a tombstone fell on a child, and **Stennett *v* Hancock** (1939), where a pedestrian was hit by part of a defective wheel on a passing lorry.

Who can be sued?

In **Donoghue**, Lord Atkin spoke of a duty owed by manufacturers to the end consumers of their products. This duty was very quickly widened; in less than 10 years after **Donoghue**, it had come to include repairers (**Stennett *v* Hancock**, above); erectors (**Brown *v* Cotterill**, above); assemblers (**Howard *v* Furness, Houlder Ltd** (1936)); and distributors (**Watson *v* Buckley, Osborne, Garrett & Co** (1940)).

It now seems that anyone involved in the supply chain of a defective product can potentially be sued in negligence, including sellers. In **Andrews *v* Hopkinson** (1957), the defendant, a second-hand car dealer, sold an 18-year-old car to the claimant without checking whether it was in a roadworthy condition. In fact the car had a dangerous steering defect; a week after buying it, the steering failed and the claimant was injured. Expert evidence suggested that the steering mechanism is a well-known danger spot in very old cars, and that the defect could quite easily have been discovered by a competent mechanic. The court held that, given the serious risk involved, the supplier owed a duty to have the car examined, or at least to have warned the buyer if no examination had been made.

Whether a seller will be found negligent will, however, depend on the circumstances of the case. In **Andrews**, it was emphasized that the defect posed a very great danger, and also that it would have been very easy to discover it. By contrast, in **Fisher *v* Harrods** (1966), it was held that a retailer of tinned foods could not be expected to examine the goods, though they did have a duty to make sure the supplier was reputable and follow proper hygiene processes in storing goods.

Types of product covered

Donoghue could have been read as applying a duty only to manufacturers of food and drink, but the courts soon extended it beyond this, and decided cases have covered products ranging from underpants to tombstones, and also packaging (**Barnes *v* Irwell Valley Water Board** (1938)), and labels or instructions for use (**Watson *v* Buckley** (1940)).

Defects and damage

A product liability action in negligence can only be brought in respect of products which are dangerous; defects which make a product work less well, or products which are simply low-quality, are not covered. As you will remember from the first chapter, an action for negligence requires proof of damage, so the product must not only be dangerous, but must actually have caused some harm as a result; a claimant cannot bring a negligence claim on the basis that a product could cause harm, if that harm has not actually happened. This was confirmed in **D & F Estates *v* Church Commissioners** (1998).

In terms of the type of damage which a negligence claim will compensate, it is clear that both personal injury and damage to other property is covered. However, damage to the defective product itself is classified as pure economic loss, and is not recoverable in negligence. This means that if, for example, a defective television blows up and causes a fire in the claimant's living room, they can sue for the value of all the property damaged by the fire, but not for the cost of the television itself (a claim for the cost of the television can only be made in contract, by the person who bought it, provided that is the same person who has been caused loss by it blowing up).

Difficulties arise where the defect is in a component part of a bigger product – the tyres of a car, for example, or the heating system of a house. Where the defective component is a replacement for an earlier component (such as a new tyre on a car when an old one has worn out), any damage which it causes to the bigger product (the car) can be compensated. Take, for example, a claimant who buys a car, and three years later, has new tyres fitted. If the tyres prove to be defective and cause an accident which damages the car, the claimant can claim for the damage to the car (though not the tyres themselves). The same is likely to apply if the tyres are the original ones fitted by the manufacturer, but supplied by another firm.

At the other end of the spectrum, where a component is made and assembled by the same firm as that which makes the rest of the car, the component will probably not be treated as a separate product – so, for example, a claimant who buys a Ford car, with an engine made and fitted by Ford, will not be able to claim for damage to either the car or the engine if that engine proves defective (though they would be able to claim for any damage caused to other property, such as nearby property burnt if the car caught fire, and of course for personal injury). As you can imagine, between these two situations lie a mass of grey areas, given that complex products can contain components from many different manufacturers. For example, if one company produces a car with an engine component manufactured by another firm, and a defect in that component leads to a fire that destroys the car, can the claimant claim for damage to the engine, to the rest of the car, or to neither?

Similar issues arise when a defect in packaging causes damage to the contents of that packaging. In **M/S Aswan Engineering Establishment Co v Lupdine Ltd** (1987), the claimants, a building company, bought some waterproofing compound, called Lupguard, from the first defendants. The Lupguard was packed in strong plastic buckets, which were made by the second defendants. The claimants had ordered the Lupguard for use on a project in Kuwait, and when the consignment arrived there by ship and was unloaded and stacked on the quayside, the extremely high temperatures there melted the plastic buckets and the Lupguard spilled away. The action in tort failed because the damage was held not to be reasonably foreseeable, but the court also discussed the issue of whether, if there had been liability, the Lupguard should be considered a separate product from the buckets; if it could, the loss of it would be considered damage to property; if it could not, the damage would be pure economic loss and so not recoverable in tort. The majority held that it was 'other property' and therefore a recoverable loss.

What must be proved?

Product liability cases in tort are subject to the ordinary rules of negligence. As you will remember from the first chapter, negligence requires proof of fault, and of causation; the claimant must prove that the defendant's failure to take reasonable care caused the defect that made the product dangerous. We also saw in Chapter 2 (p. 81) that in deciding whether a defendant has taken reasonable care, the court will seek to balance a variety of factors, including the seriousness of the danger, and how practical it would have been for the defendant to prevent it – as the leading tort academics Winfield and Jolowicz put it, 'the law expects a great deal more care in the handling of a pound of dynamite than a pound of butter' (*Winfield and Jolowicz on Tort*, fifteenth edn by WVH Rogers, Sweet & Maxwell 1998, p. 328).

Although a claimant must prove that the defect was due to the defendant's lack of reasonable care, they need not show exactly what it was that the defendant did wrong. In **Mason** *v* **Williams & Williams Ltd** (1955), the claimant was injured through using a chisel that was too hard for its purpose. He could not point to anything that was done wrong in its manufacture, but he could prove that nothing had happened to it since it left the defendant's factory that could have caused the excessive hardness. The court held that this was enough to establish that the defendant had been negligent.

This approach was challenged in **Carroll** *v* **Fearon** (1998), but the courts stood firmly behind it. The case concerned a car crash in which a little girl was killed, a woman blinded and six other people seriously injured. The crash was caused by faulty tyres, made by Dunlop, and there was overwhelming evidence that the manufacturing process had been defective (in fact it was stated that the company had already known that there was a problem with the tyres, but had decided to conceal the risk rather than alert the public and recall the tyres). The trial judge found that Dunlop had been negligent, and Dunlop appealed, on the ground that the judge had not been able to identify any particular negligent act or omission by anyone involved in their manufacturing process. The Court of Appeal held that it was not necessary to do so: it had been established overwhelmingly that the tyres were defective because of a fault in the manufacturing process, and since the manufacturer could not explain how the defects could have been caused without negligence, it was open to the judge to conclude that, on the facts, there was negligence.

In some cases this approach can look very like strict liability. In the famous case of **Grant** *v* **Australian Knitting Mills** (1936), the claimant suffered a painful skin condition after wearing some new underpants. Tests showed that the fabric of the pants contained high residues of a chemical which was used in the manufacturing process, and that this had caused the problem. The claimant could not point to a specific defect in the manufacturing process, and the manufacturers argued that they had taken reasonable care to prevent the risk, by putting in place a quality control system which complied with industry standards. However the court held that this was not only insufficient to prove reasonable care had been taken, but in fact could be taken as evidence of negligence – in that if there was such a system in place, the problem could only have arisen if one of the company's employees had been careless and prevented the quality control system from operating properly. The manufacturers were vicariously liable for the acts of their employees, and therefore the claimant won his case.

However, other cases make it clear that this approach cannot always be relied on. In **Daniels** *v* **R White & Son** (1938), a lemonade bottle shattered when the claimant did nothing more than pick it up, yet the court held that there was insufficient evidence of negligence.

One factor that will make a difference is whether there is sufficient evidence that the defect existed when the product left the defendant's hands. In **Evans** *v* **Triplex Safety Glass Co Ltd** (1936), the claimant bought a car with a windscreen made of what was described as 'toughened safety glass', manufactured by Triplex. A year later, he was driving along in the car when the windscreen suddenly shattered, for no apparent reason, injuring the claimant and his wife and son. He sued Triplex, but the court held that the defect could have been caused after the glass left the defendant's factory; there had been a long period of time between the sale and the accident, and it was known that the glass could be strained during installation.

An important factor in the **Triplex** decision was that it was possible to examine the glass for defects in the time between it leaving the manufacturer and the car journey during which it shattered. This factor was emphasized by Lord Atkin in **Donoghue**, and is taken into account in deciding whether the damage to the ultimate consumer was foreseeable – if goods are likely to be examined by someone other than the defendant before they reach the ultimate consumer, there is obviously reason to believe that any defects will be spotted, preventing the product from reaching the consumer and injuring them.

However, the possibility of intermediate examination will only affect foreseeability if it gives the defendant reason to expect that it would reveal the defect and that, as a result, the product will be made safe or not allowed to reach an ultimate consumer, or the consumer would be warned about it in such a way as to allow them to avoid the danger. In **Griffiths** *v* **Arch Engineering Co** (1968), the claimant borrowed a tool from the first defendants, which had been lent to them by the second defendants. The tool was dangerous because the second defendants had repaired it badly, and the claimant was injured as a result. The second defendants claimed that they were not liable, because the first defendants had had time to examine the tool before they lent it out, but the court disagreed; although it was true that the first defendants had the chance to look at the tool and spot the danger, there was no evidence that the second defendants had any reason to think that such an examination would be carried out. Both sets of defendants were held liable, and damages apportioned between them (this is a case of several liability – see Chapter 12).

Similarly, a defendant can in some cases avoid liability by warning of a risk. This was the case in **Kubach** *v* **Hollands** (1937). In this case a schoolgirl was injured when chemicals used in a science lesson exploded. The manufacturer had sold the chemicals to a retailer, with a warning that they should be tested before resale; the retailers ignored the warning and sold the chemicals to the school without testing them, and without passing on any warnings. The court held that the retailers were liable, but the manufacturers were not.

Defences

The usual defences to negligence apply (see p. 107), the most important in practice being *volenti* and contributory negligence.

Evaluating product liability in tort

Types of defect

Tortious liability does not cover defects which are not dangerous; in the past, the privity rule in contract meant that those who received defective but not dangerous products as gifts, or in some other non-contractual way, had no claim. The Contracts (Rights of Third Parties) Act 1999 goes some way to dealing with this problem, though, as we have seen, how useful it turns out to be depends on sellers' use of exclusion terms.

The need to prove fault

The main drawback with negligence as a means of compensating users of dangerous products is the need to prove fault; unless the claimant proves that a defendant has failed to take reasonable care, the defendant will not be liable for any risks caused by their products. To many people, all this will seem perfectly reasonable: why should a producer be sued when they have not done anything wrong? Accidents happen, after all.

The first point to bear in mind in response to this argument is that tort law does not just require that the defendant was at fault, but that the claimant can prove it. You will remember from the chapter on negligence that this can be a difficult process in any negligence action; given that in many product liability cases, the claimant will be an individual consumer and the defendant a large and wealthy company, with access to the very best legal advice, you can see that already the chances may be tipped in favour of the defendant. Add to that the fact that the most convincing evidence of negligence in a manufacturing or quality control process is likely to come from someone involved in that process, and the problems increase: employees are unlikely to be keen to testify against their employer. In addition, in many cases processes will be highly specialized and technical, so that only those with a detailed knowledge of them would be able to spot a problem. Of course claimants can use expert witnesses, but this all adds to the expense of a case and makes the prospect of litigation more off-putting. What this all adds up to is that it may be all too easy for manufacturers to get away with negligence in relation to their products.

The courts have made some attempts to address this problem in the approach they have adopted in cases such as **Mason** *v* **Williams & Williams Ltd**, **Carroll** *v* **Fearon** and **Grant** *v* **Australian Knitting Mills**, where they have tended to infer negligence from the mere existence of a dangerous defect that must have happened during manufacture – but as **Daniels** *v* **R White** shows, this approach cannot be relied upon.

Over and above the problems of proving negligence where it exists, there is an argument that product liability should not even depend on the existence of negligence, and that instead, manufacturers should be liable for any injury caused by their products, whether or not they were to blame for it. The reasons why this should be the case are well expressed in the US case of **Escola** *v* **Coca-Cola Bottling Co of Fresno** (1944). The judge, Traynor J, argued that the manufacturer of a dangerous product should be held liable, regardless of whether they were negligent or not, because:

> public policy demands that responsibility be fixed wherever it will most effectively reduce the hazards to life and health inherent in defective products that reach the market. It is evident that the manufacturer can anticipate some hazards and guard against the recurrence of others, as the public cannot. Those who suffer injury from defective products are unprepared to meet its consequences. The cost of injury and the loss of time and health may be an overwhelming misfortune to the person injured, and a needless one, for the risk of injury can be insured by the manufacturer and distributed among the public as the cost of doing business. It is to the public interest to discourage the marketing of products having defects that are a menace to the public. If such products nevertheless reach the market, it is to the public interest to place the responsibility for whatever injury they may cause upon the manufacturer, who, even if he is not negligent in the manufacture of the product, is responsible for its reaching the market.

Another reason for strict liability is that manufacturers stand to benefit financially from launching products on to the market, so they should bear the cost of any injury caused by those products.

There are, however, other arguments against the imposition of strict liability; these are discussed at p. 177.

Are decisions suitable for the courts?

As we saw in the negligence chapter, deciding whether a defendant has taken reasonable care involves balancing up a number of different factors, including the usefulness of the activity which caused the damage, the practicality of preventing the damage, and the seriousness of the risk, in terms of both the likelihood of causing harm, and the seriousness of the harm if it happens. These are often difficult choices, but in product liability cases they can very easily involve choices that the courts are ill-equipped to make. Take, for example, the situation where a company discovers a cure for heart disease, but subsequently the drug is found to cause side-effects which can kill some patients, though it cures the majority. Is a tort action really the place to decide whether that drug should have been put on the market? Are judges qualified to decide whether the risk to some people outweighs that chance of life to the others? Or should this kind of decision be made somewhere else, where it is not linked to individuals' claims for compensation, and where the whole social context can be examined?

▶ The Consumer Protection Act 1987

The Consumer Protection Act was passed against a background of concern about the inability of the law of negligence to protect consumers against dangerous products, and in particular, the Thalidomide scandal, which arose when it was discovered that Thalidomide, a drug widely given to pregnant women during the 1960s (for morning sickness), had caused severe damage to their babies during pregnancy. The parents, and later the children themselves, had to fight for years to prove that the drug had caused their injuries and receive compensation. However, the actual trigger for the new law was the drive towards establishing a single market across the countries of the EEC (for those who have not studied European Law, this was the original name for the community which evolved into what we now call the European Union, or EU). To make this possible, it was necessary to harmonize laws affecting trade in the different countries, so that firms in one country would not have an advantage over those in another – as would be the case if, for example, manufacturers in one country faced strict liability for dangerous products, while in another, consumers had to prove negligence.

In 1985, the EEC issued a Directive laying down its requirements; the Consumer Protection Act 1987 was passed to give effect to these requirements. The Directive, and the Act, are often described as imposing strict liability, but there is considerable debate whether this has been the result. There is also some debate about what exactly some of the provisions mean, because so far very few cases under the Act have been brought to court, so there has been little opportunity to clarify the terms.

Who can sue?

Anyone who suffers personal injury or property damage caused by a defective product can sue under the Act; as with a claim in tort, this includes bystanders as well as actual users of the product.

Who can be sued?

The Act imposes liability on the 'producer' of the defective product, and gives this term a wide definition. It is stated to include the manufacturer of the product and the person who 'wins or abstracts' it (this applies to, for example, products that are mined or excavated). It also applies to anyone who is responsible for a process which adds 'essential characteristics' to the product; this might include, for example, cleaning, peeling and slicing vegetables to be sold in ready-to-cook packs.

Retailers can also be liable for products made by other companies which are sold under the retailer's 'own brand'. This is an important provision when you realize that it applies not only to the 'own brand' goods sold by supermarkets alongside other brands, but, for example, to most, if not all, of the products sold by chain stores such as Marks & Spencer, BhS and Next, which tend not to manufacture goods themselves, but nevertheless sell everything under their own labels. However, a retailer will only be liable for defects in 'own brand' goods where it can be said that they 'hold themselves out' as being the producer, so a retailer who uses a label clearly stating that a product is made *for* the store, rather than *by* it, will almost certainly escape liability. In theory it could even be found that a retailer such as Marks & Spencer is not 'holding themselves out' to be the producer simply by attaching their branding to a product, since they make no secret of the fact that they use outside suppliers, but this question has not been tested so far.

Where goods originate outside the EU, a further category imposes liability on the person who first imported the goods into the EU, but not on anyone who imports it from one European country to another (unless they fall within one of the other categories of liability, by, for example, being responsible for a process which adds essential characteristics, or selling it under an 'own brand'). So if, for example, a toy made in China was imported into Britain by firm A, and then exported by firm B to Sweden, firm A could be liable but not firm B.

Someone who merely supplies the goods is generally not liable under the Act. However, they may become liable if a claimant uses s. 2(3). This states that a claimant who does not know who the 'producer' is can ask the supplier of the goods to identify the producer. If the supplier fails to identify either the producer or their own supplier within a reasonable time, they will be liable as if they were the producer. The idea of this provision is to enable the claimant to trace goods back along the supply chain to the actual producer, with the risk of being sued themselves acting as an encouragement for suppliers to keep accurate records of their suppliers, and to divulge that information when required. Whoever breaks the chain by failing to identify their own supplier can be liable.

Types of product covered

A 'product' is defined in s. 2(1) of the Act as 'any goods or electricity', and 'goods' is further explained as including 'substances, growing crops, and things comprised in land by virtue of being attached to it, and any ship, aircraft or vehicle' (the reference to electricity applies only to defects in the generation of electricity, and not breaks in the supply of it). The term 'product' also includes 'a product which is comprised in other products, whether by virtue of being a component part, raw material or otherwise'.

The Act lists a number of types of item which do not fall within the term 'product'. 'Immovables', which essentially means buildings, are not covered by the Act, but building materials are. This means that a house which was dangerous through defects in construction or design would not be covered, but one made dangerous through defects in the materials used to build it could be.

Unprocessed agricultural produce and game are specifically excluded; however, once agricultural produce undergoes some kind of industrial process, it then comes within the Act. This is a difficult factor to define: clearly a whole cow sold by a farmer is unprocessed agricultural produce that does not come within the Act, and a tin of beef stroganoff has undergone an industrial process and is a product covered by the Act. But what about the stages in between? Does butchering and packaging meat for sale count as an industrial process? Or freezing it? Again, this has not yet been tested by the courts. However, the distinction is set to become less important; a new European Directive, Directive 99/34, has now extended the Products Liability Directive to primary agricultural products, and the change was implemented in the UK in December 2000.

Another grey area is whether information can count as a product. If, for example, you buy a book on DIY which gives you incorrect instructions on how to wire a plug, can you sue the publisher if the plug blows up and injures you? Common sense would suggest the answer should be yes, since the book is clearly a product and a defect in it has caused you injury, but again, the issue is untested.

Defects and damage

The Act only covers defects which are dangerous, and not those which merely make the product perform less well or become less valuable. Section 3 states that a product will be held to be defective under the Act if 'the safety of the product is not such as persons generally are entitled to expect'. It is important to note the word 'entitled'; essentially, this means that the courts can set the standard according to what it is reasonable to expect from a particular type of product; the fact that the claimant personally might have expected a higher standard is not relevant.

In assessing the standard of safety, the Act directs the courts to take into account 'all the circumstances', and it mentions three different types of factor which are considered relevant. The first is the way the product is marketed, including any advertising claims, instructions or warnings that come with the product. Clearly, the way a product is advertised can affect the standard of safety which people are entitled to expect from it: a skin cream marketed as hypo-allergenic, for example, might legitimately be expected to be less likely than other skin creams to cause a rash. Similarly, products which are inherently dangerous can be brought within the standard of safety by their instructions or warnings; an obvious example is a medicine which would be dangerous if taken in large amounts but is safe when taken at the dosage recommended on the labels, and is also clearly labelled with warnings of the risk of overdosing.

The second set of factors concerns 'what might reasonably be expected to be done with or in relation to the product'. For example, a bed should to be safe to sleep on, and possibly for children to jump up and down on, but would probably not be expected to protect from injury a consumer who chooses to hide under it during a hurricane. The provision is not restricted to the way a product is actually used, however, but also covers, for example, whether it might be expected to fall into the hands of children. This could mean that the packaging of drugs or dangerous household chemicals could be considered defective if not made child-proof.

The third set of factors relates to the time when the product was supplied by the producer to another. Essentially, this provision refers to the fact that as manufacturers develop their products, they often add new safety features; the section goes on to explain that the mere fact that products supplied after the one in question are safer than it does not establish that the product is defective.

The Act only covers personal injury and damage to property worth more than £275; property damage worth less is not covered, and nor is economic loss, including damage to the defective product itself. There is also another important restriction in that the Act does not cover damage to business property, which is defined as property which is not ordinarily intended for private use, occupation or consumption, and not intended by the person who suffers the loss for their own private use, occupation or consumption. This means that, for example, if a computer which was used purely for private purposes, in a private house, blew up and burnt the house down, the house owner could claim under the Act, but the Act would not apply if the computer was in a commercial office.

What must be proved

The key difference between a claim under the Act and a product liability claim in negligence is that the Act is said to impose strict liability. All a claimant has to prove is that the product is defective under the terms of the Act, and that this defect caused them personal injury or damaged property worth more than £275. However, it is important to note that liability may be strict, but it is not absolute: there are a number of defences, discussed below, that can place considerable hurdles in the way of claimants. Moreover, it can be argued that the assessment which the court is required to make in deciding whether a product is defective under the terms of the Act can come very close to a requirement for negligence; we will look at this issue towards the end of this chapter when we examine the problems with the Act.

Defences

The ordinary defence of contributory negligence applies under the Act, and can be applied where the claimant has been caused damage partly as a result of a defective product, and partly by their own fault (for example, by using the product in an unsafe way).

Section 4 of the Act also sets down the following six specific defences, which a defendant can put forward to avoid liability once the claimant has established that they have been caused damage by a defect in a product for which the defendant is responsible under the Act.

Compliance with the law

A defendant can avoid liability by proving that the defect is 'attributable to compliance with any requirement imposed by law'. If, for example, the law required that bread had to contain a certain type of preservative, and this preservative was later found to be harmful – either to people generally, or to a particular claimant – the producer of the bread would have a defence.

This defence can only apply where the law actually requires whatever caused the defect, and not where it merely permits it. So in the bread example above, there would be no defence if the law merely allowed manufacturers to add the preservative, but did not insist on it. In such a case, the fact that the ingredient is legally permitted will be relevant to the question of whether the product should be considered defective, but it is not a complete defence.

Product not supplied

Where a supplier is sued under the Act, they will have a defence if they can prove that they did not actually supply the product. Supply is widely defined and includes hiring out and lending as well as selling goods, but it would not apply where a product is simply given to someone to use – for example, if an employer gives an employee a tool to use at work (though obviously in this case there would be other remedies for the employee to use – see Chapter 3).

Non-commercial supply

The Consumer Protection Act was designed to impose liability on businesses rather than individuals, so it does not apply to goods which have not been supplied in the course of business, or with a view to making a profit. Examples would be home-made products sold at village fairs, or cakes sold at a school fete.

Defects arising later

Producers will not be liable for defects that arise after they release a product. This defence applies to cases where a product has been interfered with or misused after it leaves the producer, or where the defect is the result of wear and tear. It can also be of use where goods are perishable, or need regular servicing, and a chain of suppliers is involved; anyone in the chain who can prove that the defect did not exist when the product left their hands will have a defence. The product must have left the hands of the relevant defendant when the defect occurs, so there is no defence where, for example, a product is deliberately sabotaged before it leaves the factory or warehouse, whether by an employee of the producer or someone else; in that case strict liability still applies.

It is for the defendant to prove that a defect occurred after the product had left their control; where it is not clear whether the defect existed before the producers released it or happened later, the defence will fail and the claimant should win their case.

The development risks defence

This is the most controversial part of the Act. It is similar to the 'state of the art' defence developed in negligence from the case of **Roe *v* Minister of Health** (see p. 86), and allows a defence where:

> . . . the state of scientific and technical knowledge at the relevant
> time was not such that a producer of products of the same
> description as the product in question might be expected to have
> discovered the defect if it had existed in his products while they were
> under his control.

This defence can apply where, for example, a drug turns out to have harmful side-effects, but at the time when it was launched, no-one in the drug industry would have been able to spot the risk, or where, for example, a car is fitted with a faulty brake system, but at the time when it was launched, no car manufacturer's quality control system would have been able to spot it.

The wording of the development risks defence in the Act differs from that used in the Directive, which states that the defence will only allow a producer to avoid liability where 'the state of scientific and technical knowledge at the time when he put the product into circulation was not such as to enable the existence of the defect to be discovered'. The difference here is that the Directive refers to the general state of scientific and technical knowledge, whereas the Act appears to narrow the standard to what the members of a particular industry could be expected to know. Take, for example, a situation where, at the time a product was put into circulation, the possibility of a risk had been suggested in a handful of scientific journals, but had not filtered down to become known in the relevant industry. The wording of the defence in the Act seems to suggest that the producer could avoid liability, but the wording of the Directive would seem to suggest that the development risks defence should not apply, because the state of scientific knowledge was such that the existence could have been discovered.

As students of EU law will know, the European Commission can bring a case before the European Court of Justice (ECJ) against any EU country which it claims has failed to apply EU law properly, and in **European Commission** *v* **United Kingdom** (1997), it challenged the part of the Act which contains the defence, s. 4(1)(e), on the grounds described above. In its judgment, the ECJ clarified how the development risks defence should apply. It acknowledged that the 'state of scientific and technical knowledge' could be a fairly fluid concept; for example, when a risk was first suggested, the idea might be criticized and rejected by other experts, but then over time, as evidence built up, could come to be accepted. The issue for the application of the development risks defence was at what point in that process it could be said that the state of knowledge was such that the risk could be discovered.

The court said that it was not acceptable to wait until a risk was widely recognized: the standard was that of the most advanced research, and once even one isolated opinion suggests there may be a risk, the risk cannot be said to be unforeseeable. However, the ECJ acknowledged that the availability of information could be taken into account. It gave the example of two pieces of research, one undertaken by a researcher at an American university and published in an English language journal, and the other carried out by an academic in Manchuria and published in Chinese in a local scientific journal. Clearly it would be more reasonable to expect a producer to know about the former than the latter, and the ECJ stated that a producer should not be held liable on the ground that when the product was put into circulation, one brilliant researcher in Manchuria had spotted a problem with it. Therefore, the ECJ concluded:

> . . . the state of knowledge must be construed so as to include all data in the information circuit of the scientific community as a

whole, bearing in mind, however, on the basis of a reasonableness test, the actual opportunities for the information to circulate.

Interestingly, the ECJ found that the Act did not fail to achieve the effects laid down in the Directive. It acknowledged that there was a potential ambiguity, and that the narrow interpretation of the defence described earlier in this section would not properly put into effect the aims of the Directive. But, it said, the words of the Act were also open to an interpretation which did fulfil the requirements of the Directive, and there was no evidence that the English courts would interpret the Act in a way that would not do so. The effect of this judgment is that the English courts are now likely to interpret the defence in line with the guidance offered by the ECJ, rather than in the narrower way.

Component products not defective

The Act also allows a defence where the defendant has supplied a component which is made up into a product (referred to as the 'subsequent product'), and they can prove that the defect complained of is in the subsequent product rather than the component, and is completely due to the design of the subsequent product, or to the producer of the component complying with instructions given by the producer of the subsequent product. This would apply where, for example, a tyre manufacturer sells ordinary tyres to a car manufacturer, who fits them to a racing car; if the tyres exploded, the tyre manufacturers could use the defence to argue that the defect was in the car, not the tyres.

Limitation periods

Cases brought under the Consumer Protection Act are subject to a special limitation period, which states that the right to bring a case is lost after 10 years from the date on which the defendant supplied the product. Subject to this, claimants must begin proceedings within three years of discovering the defect, the damage, or the identity of the defendant, or if the damage is latent, within three years of the date of knowledge (see p. 120). Where the case concerns personal injury, the courts have a discretion to override the three-year rule, but not the 10-year limitation.

Evaluating the Consumer Protection Act

Is liability really strict?

As we have seen, there are powerful arguments for the imposition of strict liability in the area of product liability, and the Consumer Protection Act is generally described as imposing such liability. Looked at closely, however, clearly it falls short of strict liability, and some academics have suggested that it actually offers little more than a standard of negligence, with the burden of proof reversed. Take, for example, the issues which a court will take into account when deciding whether a product should be considered defective under the Act. As we have seen, s. 3 states that a product will be held to be defective under the Act if 'the safety of the product is not such as persons generally are entitled to expect', and this means that the courts can set the standard according to what it is reasonable to expect from a particular type of product. In deciding this, the courts can look at all the circumstances, and in practice these are likely to include many of the same factors that they would look at in a negligence claim when deciding whether reasonable care was taken. What is being judged is still a standard of reasonableness, albeit looked at from a slightly different angle.

A further consideration is that of causation. The Act states that a causal link between the defect and the damage must be established, apparently by the claimant, but does not give explicit rules on what will and will not amount to causation. The courts are therefore likely to apply the rules of causation used in negligence, and as we have seen in cases such as the chapter on negligence, this can be a formidable hurdle for the claimant, and could considerably weaken the concept of strict liability. However, s. 2 does provide that where damage is caused partly by the defective product and partly by something else, the producer will still be liable.

Should liability be strict?

In contrast to the argument above, some believe that strict liability for defective products is not a good idea. This has not just been an academic debate; fuelled by bizarre-sounding cases (usually from the USA) the British press have criticized the willingness to sue over injuries caused by defective products. The main argument used is that the threat of strict liability strangles innovation and enterprise; manufacturers, it is argued, will be less likely to launch ground-breaking new products if they are afraid of being sued if those products turn out to be dangerous, through no fault of the manufacturer, or that the threat of strict liability might lead to manufacturers taking excessive care, so that the costs of the product are pushed up so high that they are priced out of the market. A study reported in the *Financial Times* (9 February 1993) suggested that this was already happening, just six years after the introduction of the Act. That may be a shame, but it hardly compares with the risk of people being killed or injured.

A further argument refutes the suggestion that producers are in the best position to insure against injury from defective products. As far as injury to property is concerned, that may be true – since many people have insurance for cars and household contents, strict liability for damage to such property may be nothing more than double insurance. However, the argument is much weaker when it comes to personal injury. It can be argued that since the risks of product innovation come with the potential for huge social benefits, society, rather than individual producers, should pay when the risks cause harm, in the form of welfare benefits rather than tort damages. The argument for this as a reason for abolishing personal injury actions in negligence is a strong one, and we discuss it on p. 122, but it would require much better welfare provision than we have today; the suggestion that within the current system, product liability actions should be scrapped because people can claim benefits as a result of their injuries would be a recipe for lowering safety standards.

The apparent watering-down of liability would appear to be the result of massive lobbying by industry during the passing of both the Directive and the Act. Farmers were successful in removing agricultural products from their scope (though these have since been added), while the development risks defence was demanded largely by drugs companies, and backed up by a Conservative government which was keen to make sure that British industry was not weakened by higher costs.

The development risks defence

This is perhaps the most criticized part of the Act. Many of the earlier criticisms of the defence centred around the accusation that its expression in the Act was weaker than that intended by the Directive. However, as we saw earlier, the ECJ has clarified that the words of the Act can, and should, be read in a way that is in line with the intention of the Directive. Even so, some critics have argued that the whole idea of the defence is mistaken, and too serious a compromise of the idea of strict liability – it is argued that in practice it is really no more than an application of the foreseeability rule from negligence, and that essentially it means that a supplier that can prove that their lack of knowledge was not negligent can escape liability. In recognition of these concerns, several EU states do not include the defence in the legislation they put in place to enact the Directive.

However, the development risks defence does compare favourably with its counterpart in negligence, the 'state of the art' defence laid down in **Roe** *v* **Minister of Health** (1954). Whereas **Roe** seems to set a minimal standard, in that the defendant's practices must be no worse than what another person in the same field would do, but need not be as good as the best, the development risks defence, as explained by the ECJ, imposes a much higher standard, requiring producers to be aware of the latest knowledge, provided it is accessible.

The Act in practice

Since the Act was passed, there have been only a handful of reported judgments under it – approximately 10 cases throughout the whole of the EU, with its population of 750 million people. Some critics have seen this as a criticism of the Act, suggesting that it adds little to the remedies previously available, but this may be misleading. In the first place, a reported case frequently suggests a problem with a statute, in that the parties disagree over its interpretation or application; a lack of such disputes can be a sign that a statute is clear and well expressed.

Secondly, many cases are settled out of court, and we have no way of knowing how many of these have been successfully settled because of the Act; it may be that the threat of strict liability (even if not as strict as it could be) encourages suppliers to settle. Nor do we know how far the existence of the Act has encouraged manufacturers and suppliers to take more care, though it should probably be assumed to have had at least some threatening effect, given the degree to which industry lobbied against it being passed in the first place.

▶ Other remedies for defective products

The Consumer Credit Act 1974

This is an important, though surprisingly little-known, remedy available to consumers of defective products. The Consumer Credit Act 1974 states that if goods are bought using a credit card and prove to be defective, the buyer can sue the credit card company. The action applies to any goods which cost more than £100 and less than £30,000, and covers defects in quality or performance as well as dangerous defects. It can provide a useful remedy where the seller is bankrupt or impossible to find.

Safety regulations

The Consumer Protection Act 1961 gave the Secretary of State powers to make regulations which impose safety requirements on particular types of product, and to make orders prohibiting the supply of goods which are not safe. These powers are now contained in Part II of the Consumer Protection Act 1987, and anyone affected by breach of such regulations can sue as a breach of statutory duty. Part II also allows the enforcement of safety rules by criminal sanctions.

ANSWERING QUESTIONS

1 Frida is out shopping for a birthday present for her husband Benny. He wants an electric drill, and she sees one at what she thinks is a bargain price. The shop assistant explains that the drill is cheap because the manufacturer has gone bankrupt and all their stock has to be sold off

as quickly as possible. Frida buys it and, pleased at having saved money, she buys him a little radio as well. Later, she calls in at their daughter's school, where the parent teacher association is running a fair, and she buys some cakes.

Benny is delighted with his present, but when he switches on the radio, he finds that it does not work. He decides to try out his drill, but within a couple of minutes, it gets very hot, and then explodes, injuring him and burning a section of the wall. When they eventually get back from the local casualty department, Benny and Frida settle down in front of the TV with their cakes. Unfortunately, when Frida takes a bite of one of them, she cracks a tooth on a stone.

Four weeks later, they read a newspaper report which says that the drill manufacturers are recalling the model of drill that Frida bought because of a scientific report stating that the material that the casing is made from is potentially dangerous. The newspaper story says that the manufacturers had no idea of this before the report was published.

Advise Benny and Frida.

The clearest way to answer this question is to take the potential claims raised by each product in turn, and look at whether a claim might lie in contract, in negligence, or under the Consumer Protection Act; important issues in deciding this will be who bought the product and what type of damage it causes.

Beginning with the radio, the important issue here is that the product is defective, but as far as we know, not dangerous. As a result, the only claim is in contract. Benny has no contract with the retailer, since Frida bought the radio, so you will need to look at whether he can claim as a result of the Contracts (Rights of Third Parties) Act 1999.

The drill offers more possibilities because it has caused physical harm to Benny, as well as damage to property. He may therefore be able to claim under both the common law of negligence and the Consumer Protection Act, but you will need to consider who he can sue, given that the manufacturer has apparently gone bankrupt. One possibility is the manufacturer of the casing material; this is possible in negligence and under the Act, but in an action under the Act, they may argue that the drill manufacturer caused the danger by the way they used it. An alternative is sueing the retailer, and again, you should discuss what would need to be proved in each type of case. You should take into account the potential effect of the information contained in the newspaper report, if it is true – the case of **Roe** will be relevant in an action for negligence, and the development risks defence for an action under the Consumer Protection Act. You should be in a position to say which action gives Benny the best chance of success, although he can of course bring both.

It is also worth pointing out that he may also be able to bring an action in contract, if the Contracts (Rights of Third Parties) Act 1999 applies, and this may be advantageous since it does not require proof of fault. Note that if you discussed what would decide whether the 1999 Act applies when looking at the issue of the radio, you should not repeat the same material again: it is quite sufficient to say that if, on the rules you have discussed previously, the Act does apply, Benny will have a claim, and if it does not apply, he will not.

Finally, consider Frida's potential claim with regard to the cakes, and here you should discuss both contract and negligence. Note that the Consumer Protection Act is unlikely to apply, because the cakes were not sold in the course of a business.

2 How far has the Consumer Protection Act 1987 improved the law on defective products?

For this essay, you need to begin by looking at what actions were available for defective products before the 1987 Act was passed. Discuss contract and tort in turn, highlighting any problems and gaps: these will include the doctrine of privity for contract, and for tort, the need to prove fault and the lack of cover for non-dangerous defects. You should discuss the issue of whether liability for defective products should be strict.

You can go on to outline what the 1987 Act brings to the law, and then to look at the problems with it. You need to discuss the issue of how far the Act really introduces strict liability, and how it compares to negligence, and also look at the suggestion that it has stifled manufacturing innovation, and whether you feel this is a valid criticism.

You could also briefly mention that the situation has also been improved by other measures, notably the Contracts (Rights of Third Parties) Act 1999, and the Consumer Credit Act.

6

Breach of statutory duty

Among the many statutes enacted by Parliament, a high proportion will impose duties – some on public bodies, some on companies or private individuals. The issue discussed in this chapter concerns what happens when those duties are not performed (or not performed properly): namely, can those affected by the non-performance sue those who should be performing the duty? The answer, unfortunately for students but fortunately for lawyers, is that sometimes they can, and sometimes not.

Some statutes expressly state that failure to perform a specified duty will give rise to a right to sue, and some expressly state that it will not; the Race Relations Act 1976 and the Sex Discrimination Act 1975 are examples of statutes that make it plain that they do give rise to liability in tort, while the Health and Safety at Work etc Act 1974 and the Safety of Sports Grounds Act 1975 are among those which state that they do not. However, the reason why this chapter exists is that a great many statutes simply say nothing on the subject, leaving the courts to decide whether a right to sue should exist, and it is the rules they have developed to do this which are discussed here.

It might be thought that, in a modern, sophisticated democracy, where statute is the highest form of domestic law, that Parliament would make a point of deciding this important issue during the passage of a piece of legislation. The fact that there are so many statutes where this is not done suggests it may be more than the result of an oversight or lack of time; in **M** *v* **Newham Borough Council**, Staughton LJ suggested that in some cases the reason may be that it is politically embarrassing to state specifically that people will not be entitled to a common law remedy where a public authority fails in its duty.

▶ Scope of the tort

The general rule, confirmed in the most important recent House of Lords judgment in this area, **X** *v* **Bedfordshire County Council** (1995) is that breach of a statutory duty does not give rise to a right to sue in tort, unless the statute concerned makes it clear that Parliament intended to create such a right. In order to decide whether this is the case, the courts look at the words of the relevant statute, and consider a number of factors, including who the statute was intended to benefit, whether any other remedies for breach are available and the degree of detail with which the duty is set out. No single one will be treated as conclusive proof that tortious liability was intended; the courts tend to use them as starting points for their reasoning, but may include other factors as well.

Who is the statute intended to benefit?

The courts will consider whether the Act was aimed merely to confer a general public benefit, or whether it was actually designed to create individual rights against the party supposed to provide the benefit. Only in the latter case will any tortious liability arise. **X *v* Bedfordshire County Council** was concerned with legislation instructing local authorities to provide protection for children at risk of abuse and to provide education services for children with special needs. Lord Browne-Wilkinson said:

> Although regulatory or welfare legislation affecting a particular area of activity does in fact provide protection to those individuals particularly affected by that activity, the legislation is not to be treated as being passed for the benefit of those individuals but for the benefit of society in general.

The House of Lords concluded that the relevant statutes did not create liability in tort if the statutory duty was breached.

The approach taken in **X *v* Bedfordshire County Council** confirms the earlier case of **Lonrho *v* Shell Petroleum (No 2)** (1982). Shell had contracted to use Lonrho's pipeline for transporting their petroleum products into Rhodesia, but when Rhodesia unilaterally declared independence, exporting oil to it became illegal under the Southern Rhodesia (Petroleum) Order 1965, part of legislation designed to undermine the illegal government by means of economic sanctions. Shell in fact continued to supply oil by different means, in contravention of the Order, and Lonrho sued for the loss this caused them by prolonging the illegal government. The House of Lords held that they had no right of action; the clear intention of the legislation was to undermine the Rhodesian government, and not to create individual legal rights for those caused loss by its continuance.

In **Atkinson *v* Newcastle and Gateshead Waterworks Co** (1877) the water company was under a statutory duty to maintain a specified water pressure, and as a result of their failure to do so, the claimant's house could not be saved when it caught fire. The courts held that to interpret the statute as allowing a civil right of action would effectively be to expect the water company to act as fire insurers for the whole district, and this could not have been the intention of the legislature.

The courts are more likely to allow tortious liability where a statute is aimed at protecting a particular class of individuals. In **Ex parte Island Records Ltd** (1978), the statute in question provided that it was an offence to record a live musical performance without the performers' consent. The Court of Appeal found that such a provision was clearly for the benefit of a specific class of individuals, namely musicians, and that they should have a right of action under it, in addition to the imposition of criminal sanctions.

Availability of alternative remedies

Where a statute provides for some other way to penalize breach of the duty, the courts will generally presume that Parliament meant this to be the only way, and will not impose liability in tort as well.

In **Atkinson** *v* **Newcastle and Gateshead Waterworks Co** (above) the statute provided that breach of the duty was a criminal offence, punishable by a fine of £10. The court concluded that the legislature had considered this a sufficient burden for the party in breach, and had intended no civil liability.

In **Olotu** *v* **Home Office** (1997), the claimant had been charged with various criminal offences and detained in custody awaiting trial. Under statute, there was a limit on the length of time she could lawfully be detained in such circumstances, and regulations made under the Prosecution of Offences Act 1985 imposed a duty on the Crown Prosecution Service (CPS) to ensure that accused persons did not spend longer than the lawful period in custody. The claimant brought an action against the CPS for breach of this statutory duty. In the Court of Appeal, Lord Bingham CJ explained that the approach laid down in **X** *v* **Bedfordshire County Council** required them to discern the attention of Parliament by looking at 'the object and scope of the provisions, the class (if any) intended to be protected by them, and the means of redress open to such a class if the statutory duty is not performed'. In this case, the court held that no tortious liability was incurred: there were several other remedies available to people in the claimant's situation, including an application of bail and certain public law actions. In addition, there was no sign in the words of the 1985 Act that the Secretary of State, who made the regulations, had power to confer a private right of action in such cases, and in policy terms, the existence of a private right to sue might adversely influence the way prosecutors conducted their work, and could open the floodgates to a vast amount of litigation.

The fact that the common law provides sufficient remedies for the individual may be taken to suggest that the legislature did not intend to provide a further cause of action when passing a relevant statute. In **McCall** *v* **Abelesz** (1976) the Court of Appeal was asked to consider whether the criminal offence of harassment of tenants in s. 30 of the Rent Act 1965 gave rise to civil liability. In deciding that it did not, the court stressed that most such acts of harassment by a landlord would involve trespass or breach of contract, and these would be the appropriate causes of action.

However, there are a handful of cases where the courts have not treated the existence of an alternative remedy as decisive, and they give an interesting insight into the way policy, and the judges' view of the justice of a particular case, have affected the law in this area. In **Groves** *v* **Wimbourne** (1898) a 15-year-old factory employee had to have his arm amputated after catching his hand in an unfenced machine. A statute provided that such machines should be fenced, that factory owners who failed to do this could be fined £100, and that all or part of that fine could be used for the benefit of someone injured by the breach, at the Secretary of State's discretion. Following the general presumption, this provision should have meant that this was the only penalty for the breach, and no tortious liability existed. However, the courts interpreted the provision as suggesting that there should be tortious liability by arguing that it clearly intended that compensation to the victim should be possible, and since there was no certainty that all or any of the fine would go to the victim, and even if it did, £100 would be insufficient compensation for a serious injury, they must have meant further compensation to be possible. Therefore the court allowed the boy to sue in tort.

It is not hard to see that the convoluted reasoning which allowed the claim actually owes very little to the provisions of the statute; the case took place at a time when there was increasing concern about the danger to employees from industrial work, and a growing amount of legislation on the subject, and against this background, the courts seem to have consulted their own sense of justice first, and constructed support from the statute afterwards.

A similar approach can be seen in **Monk** *v* **Warbey** (1935). The claimant was injured when riding in a car owned by the defendant; the driver was a third party who had borrowed the car. The driver was not covered by insurance, and the Road Traffic Act 1930 made it a criminal offence for an owner to allow an uninsured person to drive their car. However, the Court of Appeal held that the existence of criminal penalties did not mean that there could not be civil liability; the provision was clearly there for the very purpose of making sure that people injured in such circumstances could be compensated, yet without the possibility of civil liability, it could not offer them that protection as the imposition of criminal sanctions would not compensate the claimant.

The Court of Appeal recently declined to apply **Monk** *v* **Warbey** in the case of **Richardson** *v* **Pitt-Stanley** (1995), which involved an employer who was in breach of a statutory requirement to have insurance cover for the possibility of injury to employees, but it remains to be seen whether the courts will accept the presumption next time they are faced with a case where it would offend their sense of justice.

Degree of detail

The more detailed and specific the statutory provisions concerning a duty, the more likely it is that the courts will find civil liability in respect of that duty. In **X v Bedfordshire County Council**, discussed above, Lord Browne-Wilkinson said:

> The cases where a private right of action for breach of statutory duty have been held to arise are all cases in which the statutory duty has been very limited and specific as opposed to a general administrative function imposed on public bodies and involving the exercise of administrative discretion.

In that case the House of Lords concluded that Parliament was unlikely to have intended to create a private right of action under the relevant statutes because of the very general nature of the duties imposed on the authorities (such as to 'safeguard and protect the welfare of the children within [the area] who are in need') and the wide discretion granted to the authorities in carrying out these duties.

In **Danns v Department of Health** (1998), the relevant statute was the Ministry of Health Act 1919, which provides that the Minister of Health has a duty, among other things, to give out such information as is desirable for the health of people in the country. The claimant alleged that this duty had been breached, because the department had not warned the public after a medical research paper suggested that in men who had had a vasectomy, there remained a 1 in 2,000 chance that the operation might reverse itself, and where this happened, the man would no longer be sterile. The claimant had had exactly this experience, with the result that his wife had become pregnant. The Court of Appeal rejected his claim, stating that the statute clearly gave the ministry a wide discretion as to how it performed the duty, and warning the public was not the only reasonable way to act.

▶ Elements of the tort

Once the court has decided that breach of a particular statutory provision does give rise to liability in tort, it must then decide whether, in the case before it, there has actually been a breach, and whether the damage suffered by the claimant is of a kind that falls within the tortious liability arising from that statute.

Breach of duty

In order to decide whether there has been a breach, the court must decide precisely what the duty imposed by the statute consists of, and whether the situation complained of conforms with it or not. This is done by looking closely at the words of the statute. In **R** *v* **East Sussex County Council, ex parte T** (1998), the council had been supplying five hours a week of home tuition to a child who was unable to attend school through illness. When it reduced those hours in order to save money, it was sued on the grounds that the reduction was in breach of the statutory duty under the Education Act 1993 to provide suitable education for children who could not attend school due to illness.

The House of Lords held that the statute imposed a duty on the council to decide what was suitable education, and to do so on educational grounds, not financial ones. It came to this conclusion on the basis that other parts of the Act made reference to taking into account financial considerations, but the section in question did not; if Parliament had intended finance to be an issue in the decision it would have said so, as it had elsewhere. Therefore Parliament could not have intended that such considerations should affect the council's assessment of what was suitable education for the claimant, and the council were in breach of their duty.

As well as looking at precisely what the statute requires the defendant to do, the courts have to look at the degree of fault required to constitute a breach of duty. Some statutes impose absolute duties, which means that where a court finds that tortious liability can be imposed, that liability will be strict, and a defendant may be in breach even if they could not have prevented the harm. Such cases are rare, but one example is **Galashiels Gas Co Ltd** *v* **Millar** (1949). Here the relevant statute was the Factories Act 1937, which provided that 'every hoist or lift shall be properly maintained'. The House of Lords held that this could only be read as imposing an absolute duty to maintain a lift in perfect working order; not a duty to do so where it was reasonably practical, or to take reasonable steps to do so. Therefore any failure in a lift mechanism meant there had been a breach of the duty, regardless of whether the failure or the harm caused by it was foreseeable, or could have been prevented.

The majority of statutes, however, impose qualified duties, which create a fault requirement similar to that of negligence, in that it is based on a standard of reasonableness. In these cases the courts apply the same balancing exercise as they would in a negligence case. An example of this is **McCarthy** *v* **Coldair Ltd** (1951), where the relevant statute stated that 'there shall, as far as is reasonably practicable, be provided and maintained safe means of access to every place at which any person has at any time to work'. The claimant in the case had been injured when he fell from a short ladder, which slipped on a shiny floor that had been splashed with paint. He alleged that his employer was in breach of the duty imposed by the Act, because it would have been 'reasonably practicable' to have another employee standing by to keep the ladder in place, but the employer had not done this. The court said that the risk of harm from falling from a ladder of this length was not great and, ordinarily, placing an extra employee at the foot of the ladder would be a dispro- portionately expensive way to avoiding a small risk; however, the slipperi- ness of the floor increased the risk, and so meant that the precaution suggested would have been reasonably practicable, and by not taking it, the employer was in breach. Had the floor not been slippery, there would have been no breach.

Damage

The claimant can only recover for damage which is of the kind that the statutory provision is intended to prevent. Again, in deciding this, the courts will look closely at the words of the statute, and its purpose. The leading case on this issue is **Gorris** *v* **Scott** (1874). The defendant was a ship owner, who was transporting some of the claimant's sheep. The Contagious Diseases (Animals) Act 1869 required that cattle or sheep being transported by ship to Great Britain from abroad had to be kept in special pens on board. The defendant failed to do this, and the claimant's sheep were washed overboard. However, the court held that he could not succeed in his action for breach of the duty, because the statute had been passed to prevent disease spreading between different groups of animals on the ship, and not to prevent the animals from being washed over- board and drowning. The defendant had been in breach of the duty, but the damage caused as a result was not the kind for which the statute could allow a remedy.

A more difficult issue is what happens when the damage caused by the breach is the kind that the statute aims to prevent, but it happens in a different way to that referred to in the statute. In **Donaghey** *v* **Bolton & Paul** (1968), regulations made under a statute required that special safety equipment should be used where employees had to climb on 'roofs . . . covered with fragile materials through which a person is likely to fall a distance of more than ten feet'. The claimant was injured by falling through a hole in a roof, rather than through fragile material, but the House of Lords held that he could recover compensation under the statute: the damage caused to him by failure to provide the safety equip- ment was exactly the kind which the statute sought to prevent, and it did not matter that it had happened in a way that the makers of the regula- tion had not considered.

However, in other cases, the House of Lords has taken a more restric- tive approach. **Close** *v* **Steel Co of Wales** (1962) is one of a number of 'flying part' cases, where the courts have held that legislation imposing a duty on factory owners to fence off the moving parts of dangerous machinery was intended to prevent employees being injured by being caught in the machines; employees who had been injured when parts of the machine came loose and flew out could not recover compensation for breach of such provisions.

▶ Defences

Contributory negligence is available as a defence to breach of statutory duty. This was stated to be the case in **ICI** *v* **Shatwell** (1965), discussed on p. 112. The defence of *volenti* may be available, but its use is limited by the need to prove genuine consent; where the claimant has had no real choice in the matter, as in many cases where the statutory duty is one imposed on employers for the benefit of employees, for example, *volenti* will not apply.

▶ Problems with statutory torts

As we have seen, there is a lot of uncertainty in this area of law and the courts' view that the existence or not of tortious liability is merely a question of statutory interpretation conceals (as emphasis on statutory interpretation normally does) the exercise of some discretion, as the contrast between, for example, **Atkinson** *v* **Newcastle and Gateshead Waterworks Co** and **Groves** *v* **Wimbourne** shows.

It has been suggested that Parliament's intentions would be better known if statutes expressly stated whether or not civil liability should be incurred for breach, and moves towards this are visible in modern legislation. The Sex Discrimination Act 1975, s. 66(1) and the Race Relations Act 1976, s. 57(1), for example, provide that discriminatory acts 'may be made the subject of civil proceedings in like manner as any other claim in tort . . . for breach of statutory duty'.

ANSWERING QUESTIONS

The issue of breach of statutory duty rarely arises as the sole topic of an exam question; it forms part of the question on employers' liability answered in Chapter 3.

7 Deceit

The tort of deceit is also known as fraud and as the two names suggest, it essentially concerns behaviour which tricks someone, usually with the result that they lose money.

▶ The elements of deceit

There are six elements which must be satisfied in order for the tort to be committed.

- The defendant must have made a false representation to the claimant – in other words, the defendant must have lied.
- The representation must be one of fact.
- The defendant must know that the representation is false, or be reckless about whether it is false.
- The claimant must have acted on the false representation.
- The defendant must have intended that the representation should be acted on.
- The claimant must have suffered damage as a result of acting on the representation.

The false representation

Words or conduct
A false representation can be made by spoken or written words, or by conduct. An example of a false representation by conduct is the case of **R *v* Barnard** (1837), where the defendant wore an academic cap and gown when trying to obtain goods on credit in Oxford, in order to give the (false) impression that he was a student at the University.

Silence
Mere silence cannot usually amount to a false representation, but there are four qualifications to this principle.

- A statement which tells only part of the truth may be rendered false by what is left out.
- Actively concealing a particular fact amounts to making a representation that that fact does not exist. So, for example, if, when selling something, you actively conceal its defects with the aim of preventing the buyer from seeing them, you are effectively making a false representation that those defects are not there.
- If the defendant makes a representation, believing at the time that it was true, but discovering before the claimant acts on it that it is not, failing to disclose the truth amounts to a false representation.
- Where there is a statutory duty to disclose certain information, failing to do so will amount to a false representation. For example, under the Companies Act 1985 certain information must be provided in a company prospectus; failure to disclose that information could give rise to liability in deceit.

Representation of fact

The misrepresentation must be a false statement of fact, rather than a promise or a mere opinion. However, an expression of opinion which concerns a present or future event can be a representation of fact if it implies that it is an opinion held at the time. As Bowen LJ put it in **Edgington** *v* **Fitzmaurice** (1885), 'There must be a misstatement of an existing fact: but the state of a man's mind is as much a fact as the state of his digestion.' In that case, the directors of a company were held liable for deceit when they tried to secure investment in their company by publishing a prospectus claiming that the investment was to be used for finishing off company buildings, buying horses and vans, and generally developing the company's business. In fact, the directors intended to use any money they raised to pay off debts.

However, the courts are flexible when it comes to 'sales talk', and merely exaggerating the qualities of an item for sale is not usually a false representation, though this will depend on how precise the claims made are.

Knowledge or recklessness

It was established in **Derry** *v* **Peek** (1889) that to be liable for deceit, the defendant must know that the statement is false, or be reckless about whether it is false. In this context, recklessness means that the defendant must have been consciously indifferent as to whether the statement was true or not. Mere negligence, as in failing to make sure it was true, for example, is not enough.

Derry *v* **Peek** concerned the directors of a tram company who issued a prospectus which stated, among other things, that they had the necessary permission to run steam-driven trams. In fact they had not yet obtained this permission, which had to be given by the Board of Trade, but the directors honestly, though mistakenly, believed that getting it was a mere formality. Unfortunately it was refused. As a result, the company was wound up, and the directors were sued by the claimant, who had purchased shares in the company relying on the information in the prospectus. The Court of Appeal found for the claimant, but the House of Lords reversed that decision, on the ground that a false statement which was merely made carelessly and without reasonable grounds for believing it to be true did not amount to fraud, though in some cases it might be evidence of it. Their Lordships held that the tort of fraud applied to dishonest behaviour, and mere carelessness was not sufficient.

Reliance

It must be proved that the claimant acted on the statement, though the statement need not be the only or even the decisive reason for acting, so long as it was a material reason.

Intention

The defendant must intend the statement to be acted on by the claimant, though they need not necessarily intend the resulting damage. In **Langridge** *v* **Levy** (1837), the claimant's father bought a gun from the defendant, saying that he was going to give it to his son. The defendant said that the gun was sound, though he knew it was not. In the event, the son was injured by a fault in the gun, and the defendant was held liable in deceit, because he knew that the father was going to give the gun to his son.

Damage

The claimant must prove that they suffered damage as a result of acting on the defendant's false representation. Damage will usually be financial, but other types, such as physical injury or property damage, are also covered. The test of remoteness of damage is directness, and not reasonable foresight. Therefore the defendant is liable for all losses flowing directly from the claimant acting on the false representation.

In **Smith New Court Securities Ltd** *v* **Scrimgeour Vickers (Asset Management) Ltd** (1996), the defendants falsely told the claimants that they were competing with two other bidders for some shares they wanted to buy; this encouraged them to offer a higher price that they otherwise would have done. When the value of the shares fell, the claimants successfully sued in deceit. The Court of Appeal held that the damages should be the difference between the price the claimants paid per share (82.5p) and the price which they would have paid had they not been given the false information (78p). The House of Lords disagreed, confirming that in cases of deceit, the measure of damages was all the loss directly caused by the false representation, whether it was foreseeable or not. The claimants had not been able to mitigate their losses by selling the shares, and therefore the damages would be the difference between the true value of the shares (by this time 44p) and the price paid.

Deceit and negligent misstatement

The tort of deceit is related to the action for negligent misstatement under **Hedley Byrne** (see p. 24). The difference between them is that negligent misstatement arises from negligence, and covers statements of fact and opinion, whereas deceit is based on an intentional or reckless misrepresentation and covers only statements of fact.

ANSWERING QUESTIONS

1 **Discuss the current law on the torts of deceit and negligent misstatement.** Your introduction could explain that these torts deal with similar types of behaviour, but that there are important differences between them. You can then discuss each in turn, explaining the elements of the tort, and highlighting areas of difference. As always, it is useful to discuss any problems with the law, such as those on compensation for pure economic loss and overlap with contract, and suggested reforms.

8 Defamation

The right of free speech has long been considered an important one in democratic societies, but equally, most democratic societies accept some degree of legal restriction on it, in order that the right to free speech is balanced against, for example, rights to privacy or reputation, or to the need to protect national security or commercial information. Defamation is one of those restrictions, and in this country its main function is to protect reputation.

Defamation has been succinctly defined by the leading tort expert Professor Winfield:

> Defamation is the publication of a statement which tends to lower a person in the estimation of right-thinking members of society generally, or which tends to make them shun or avoid that person.

There are two types of defamation, libel and slander. Libel covers statements made in some permanent form: this usually means printed or written words, but also covers film, pictures, statues and effigies. By statute it includes radio broadcasts (the Defamation Act 1952) and the performance of plays (Theatres Act 1968). Slander applies to defamation made in a transitory form, such as spoken words, or gestures. The English law on defamation has been the subject of criticism from both academics and the media for many years. As a result, several important changes have been made in the Defamation Act 1996, though these by no means solve all the problems in this important area of the law.

▶ Elements of defamation

The tort of defamation is committed when the defendant publishes an untrue statement referring to the claimant and affecting their reputation, and no defence is available. In the case of libel, merely committing the tort without a defence is sufficient for liability, but with slander, a defendant will usually only be liable if the defamation has caused the claimant special damage, usually in the form of financial loss, over and above the injury to the claimant's reputation (there are some exceptions to this rule, discussed below).

An untrue statement affecting the claimant's reputation

A statement which can be proved to be true cannot be defamatory, no matter how damaging to the claimant's reputation. A defendant who maintains that a statement is true pleads the defence of justification, which is discussed at p. 201. In addition to being untrue, in order to be defamatory, a statement must lower the claimant in the eyes of right-thinking members of society; in other words, it must affect the claimant's reputation among others. That it causes them distress, anger or embarrassment is not by itself sufficient.

The requirement that the claimant be 'lowered in the estimation of right-thinking members of society generally' is illustrated by **Byrne** *v* **Deane** (1937). After the police raided a golf club and removed an illegal gambling machine, a verse appeared on the club notice board, which included the words, 'but he who gave the game away may he byrne in hell and rue the day', thereby hinting that Mr Byrne was the person who had informed the police about the existence of the machines. The claimant sued the club, alleging that the statement was defamatory. It was held that although the statement might lower him in the estimation of the club members, it would not do so in the estimation of right-thinking members of society, who would not disapprove of conduct designed to prevent crime. The action failed.

In **Berkoff** *v* **Burchill** (1996), the claimant, the actor Stephen Berkoff, sued the journalist Julie Burchill for describing him as hideously ugly. Burchill claimed that her words were not defamatory, since they did not injure his reputation: the fact that they would make him angry and upset was not sufficient. The Court of Appeal agreed that merely causing anger or upset was not enough to amount to defamation, but pointed out that as the claimant earned his living as an actor, the words were likely to lower him in the estimation of the public and make him an object of ridicule, and were therefore capable of being defamatory.

In **Mitchell** *v* **Faber & Faber** (1998), the claimant was a musician who had worked with the black guitarist Jimi Hendrix during the 1960s. The defendant published a book about Hendrix, in which he stated that the claimant had 'a strange contempt' for Hendrix, and routinely used words such as 'nigger' and 'coon' in everyday conversation with other members of the band. The book further stated that the claimant had no idea about what might offend black Americans, and did not intend 'any real harm' by the comments he made. The claimant claimed that these comments would make readers think that he was a racist who held Hendrix in contempt because of his colour.

The defendant applied to have the case struck out on the basis that the words were not capable of carrying this defamatory meaning, and the judge on the application agreed, pointing out that the book made it plain that the claimant did not intend to offend Hendrix, that his attitude was merely typical of many people in the UK at the time, and that if he had realized his words were offensive, he would not have used them. However the claimant successfully appealed against the striking out. The Court of Appeal stated that in deciding whether or not words could be defamatory, it was necessary to consider the reaction of a reader who was neither unduly suspicious nor unduly naive, who was capable of reading between the lines and detecting implications, but not avid for scandal, and who was not prone to assume a derogatory meaning where an innocent one could apply. In this case, the court said, it was important to bear in mind that although the attitudes described were those of 30 years ago, the question to ask was what effect the allegation that someone had held those attitudes at that time would have on a reader in the 1990s.

A statement need not directly criticize the claimant; it may do so by implication, known as an 'innuendo'. In **Tolley** *v* **J S Fry & Sons Ltd** (1931) the claimant was an amateur golfer, and his amateur status meant that he was not allowed to accept money to advertise products. Without his knowledge the defendants published an advertisement containing a cartoon of him, with a rhyme praising the chocolate. He succeeded in proving that the advertisement amounted to a defamatory statement by way of innuendo, because readers seeing the advertisement were likely to assume that Tolley had been paid to lend his name to it and therefore compromised his amateur status (it is interesting to note that in the USA, unauthorized use of someone's likeness or name can be a tort in itself; English law however makes no such provision, and had Tolley been a professional golfer, so that no defamatory innuendo occurred, he would not have been able to succeed in his claim).

In **Dwek** *v* **Macmillan Publishers** (1999), the 'statement' complained of arose from a picture and its caption, which did not even name the claimant. The picture, taken 20 years earlier, appeared in a book and showed the claimant, who was not the subject of the book, and was not named anywhere in it, sitting next to a woman who was (correctly) identified as a prostitute. The claimant argued that readers would understand the words and photograph as suggesting that he was a client of the prostitute. The defendant applied to have the action struck out, claiming that the words and picture were not capable of bearing this defamatory meaning because they made no reference to the claimant, there was nothing in the picture or anywhere else in the book to suggest that he even knew the woman was a prostitute, and he had not produced any readers who had recognized him in the photo.

The Court of Appeal said that the action should not be struck out; taken together, the words and photo were capable of carrying the alleged meaning, and it should therefore be left to a jury to decide whether they were actually defamatory. The claimant was not required to prove that identified individuals had recognized him in the photograph.

In assessing whether a statement is defamatory, a court will look at the whole context in which it was made. In **Norman** *v* **Future Publishing** (1998), the claimant was the famous opera singer, Jessie Norman. She was interviewed by a classical music magazine, and in the article was quoted as saying, with apparent reference to her size, that she never went through doorways sideways because 'Honey, I ain't got no sideways'. Ms Norman denied making the remark, and claimed that it suggested she was vulgar and undignified, and 'conformed to a degrading racist stereotype of a person of African-American heritage'. The Court of Appeal dismissed her appeal against a strike-out application, on the ground that the words had to be read within the context of the article as a whole, which portrayed her as a person of high standing and impeccable dignity. The case also makes the point that the fact that Ms Norman claimed she had never made the remarks was irrelevant if the remark itself was not defamatory; there is no liability in defamation simply for making up a quote from someone and publishing it, unless the alleged quote is defamatory.

Whether a statement is capable of carrying a defamatory meaning is a matter of law, but whether it actually is defamatory in the circumstances of the case is a matter of fact, to be decided by the jury if there is one. This was reiterated in **Mitchell**, discussed above, where the court held that the words complained of were capable of having both a defamatory and a non-defamatory meaning, and it was for the jury to decide which applied. It was not for the judge in a striking out application to decide that the context of the words took away any defamatory meaning; however, where the defamatory meaning could only be found in a strained or utterly unreasonable interpretation of the words, the courts were entitled to reject it.

Statements must refer to the claimant

Where the claimant is named (or, as in **Dwek**, pictured) in the statement, this is not a problem, but there are cases where the person referred to in a defamatory statement is not named. This can still be defamatory if a reasonable person knowing the claimant would have thought the claimant was referred to. For example, in **J'Anson** *v* **Stuart** (1787) a newspaper referred to 'a swindler', describing the person meant in the words 'his diabolical character, like Polyphemus the man-eater, has but one eye, and is well known to all persons acquainted with the name of a certain noble circumnavigator'. The claimant had only one eye, and his name was very similar to the name of a famous admiral; he was able to prove that the statement referred to him, even though his name was never mentioned.

It is not usually possible to defame a class of people, so, for example, if a newspaper said that all politicians were useless, no individual politician could sue (in that case, some might also have trouble with the requirement that the statement was false). However, where the class mentioned is very small, the statement may be taken to refer to each and every member of it, and any or all of them may sue. If, for example, a defamatory statement was applied to 'all female football managers', when in fact there were only three or four in the country, any of them could sue. A remark about football managers in general would not usually allow any of them to sue because the class referred to would be too big. This rule was laid down in **Knupffer *v* London Express Newspapers Ltd** (1944). The defendants had published an article stating that an émigré Russian group was a Fascist organization. The group had approximately 2,000 members, of whom 24 were based in the UK. The claimant was a Russian immigrant living in London and he brought an action for defamation. His action was rejected by the House of Lords on the basis that the accusation of fascism was aimed at the class of people and there was nothing that singled him out.

Where a defamatory statement was intended to refer to a fictitious character, or to someone other than the claimant, the defendant will be liable for defamation of the claimant if a reasonable person would think the statement referred to the claimant. An example of a case where the defamatory statement referred to a fictitious character is **Hulton *v* Jones** (1910). The defendants published a humorous story of the discreditable behaviour in Dieppe of a fictitious character called Artemus Jones in a newspaper. He was said to be a churchwarden in Peckham. Unknown to the author or editor, the claimant was also known as Artemus Jones, though he had actually been baptized Thomas Jones. He was a barrister not a churchwarden, did not live in Peckham and had never visited Dieppe. But he had contributed articles to the newspaper in the past and some of his friends thought that the article referred to him. He sued the owners of the newspaper for libel and was awarded £1,750, a decision that was upheld by the House of Lords. It did not matter that the defendants did not intend to defame him, all that mattered was what a reasonable person would understand the words to mean.

A case where the defamatory statement was intended to refer to someone other than the claimant is **Newstead *v* London Express Newspapers Ltd** (1940). The newspaper had printed a story saying that a Harold Newstead, described as a 30-year-old Camberwell man, had been convicted of bigamy. This was in fact true of the Harold Newstead the paper was talking about, but there was also another Harold Newstead living in Camberwell, who was not a bigamist. In fact the newspaper had been given the bigamist's exact address and occupation, which would have distinguished him from the innocent Harold Newstead, but this was left out of the published report due to lack of space. The defendants were held liable. However, in such cases of unintentional defamation, a special defence of offer of amends may be available under the Defamation Act 1996 (see p. 208).

The statement must be published

Most high-profile defamation cases involve publication of untrue statements in newspapers, magazines or books, or sometimes on radio or television. However, the law covers much more than this. For the purposes of establishing a case for defamation, a statement is considered to have been published when the defendant communicates it to anyone other than the claimant, or the defendant's husband or wife.

A defendant may escape liability if they can prove that it was not possible to foresee that publication would occur. In **Huth** *v* **Huth** (1915), a letter was sent in an unsealed envelope by the defendant to the claimant. The butler secretly read the letter without the claimant's permission. This was not treated as a publication, as the defendant could not have foreseen the butler's behaviour, so he was not liable for defamation.

By contrast, in **Theaker** *v* **Richardson** (1962), communication to a third party was foreseen by the defendant and therefore amounted to publication. The defendant had written a letter stating that the claimant was 'a lying, low down brothel keeping whore and thief'. He put the letter in a sealed envelope and posted it through the claimant's door. The claimant's husband opened the envelope and the defendant was held liable for defamation as he had foreseen that the letter might be opened by some person other than the claimant.

Where an allegation is published in print, it is not just the writer who can be liable; booksellers, publishers and lending libraries have all been held to have published libels contained in books, newspapers and magazines. In **Godfrey** *v* **Demon Internet** (1999), it was stated that an Internet service provider could be said to have 'published' messages posted on its server by users.

Every repetition of a defamation (by the original publisher or anyone else) amounts to a fresh cause of action.

Proof of damage

In a libel action, commission of the tort is enough; it is not necessary to prove damage. To succeed in an action for slander, the claimant must usually prove that the slander has caused some actual damage, generally financial loss (sometimes known as 'special damage') over and above their loss of reputation. However, there are a few exceptions where the slander will be actionable *per se* (i.e. without the need to prove damage). These exceptions are where the slander suggests any of the following:

- That the claimant has committed an imprisonable offence.
- That the claimant has a contagious disease of a kind which might lead to their exclusion from society – AIDS would be an obvious example, but any venereal disease might be judged to have this effect.
- That a female claimant is not chaste. This exception is provided for in the Slander of Women Act 1891, s. 1. Rather oddly, this has been held to include suggesting that she is a lesbian – **Kerr** *v* **Kennedy** (1942).
- That the claimant is unfit for their trade, profession or business, or any appointment they hold: the Defamation Act 1952, s. 2. Examples would be saying that a particular cook could not boil an egg, or that the local mayor was corrupt.

▶ Parties to a defamation action

Who can be sued?

Where a libel is printed, liability extends not only to the writer and the owner of the publication, but also to the printer and anyone involved in distributing the publication. So, for example, a newsagent who sold a magazine containing a defamatory statement could be sued along with the author and the publisher. There is however a defence of innocent dissemination which may cover printers and distributors in such situations (see p. 209).

Who can sue?

Only living persons can sue for defamation – it is not generally possible to sue for damage to the reputation of a dead relative, for example, unless the claimant can prove that the alleged defamation of their relative affected the claimant's own reputation.

As stated earlier, the law of defamation is a curb on the general right of free speech, and in an attempt to preserve a balance between free speech and the protection of reputation that is in the public interest, the courts have developed some limitations on libel actions brought by certain types of public body. In **Derbyshire County Council** *v* **Times Newspapers** (1992), the Court of Appeal held that local authorities may not sue for libel; to allow such actions to be brought by democratically elected bodies, or any government body, would be against the public interest in free debate about the actions of elected authorities. Individual members of a council may still sue for libels against them personally. In **Goldsmith** *v* **Bhoyrul** (1998), Buckley J built on the **Derbyshire** decision in holding that political parties were unable to sue for libel because of the public interest in free speech concerning those who put themselves forward for public office.

Commercial companies can – and frequently do – sue for libel. In the long-running and much-publicized litigation popularly known as the McLibel case, the defendants attempted to argue that there was a public interest in free speech concerning the activities of huge multi-national corporations such as McDonalds, and that therefore such companies should be unable to sue for libel, but the argument was unsuccessful (**Steel *v* McDonalds Corp (Locus Standi)** (1999)).

Defences

The general defences described in Chapter 2 technically apply here, though in practice only *volenti* is likely to be of much practical use; it applies where the claimant has consented to the information being published. The following defences, which are specific to defamation, are of more importance.

Justification

If a defamatory statement is true, the defendant will have a defence, so long as they can prove it. It is not necessary to prove that every single detail of the statement is true, so long as, taken as a whole, it is accurate. In **Alexander *v* North Eastern Railway Co** (1865), the defendants had said that the claimant, when convicted of a criminal offence, had been offered alternative sentences of a fine or three weeks' imprisonment. In fact he was offered a fine or two weeks' imprisonment, but the defendants successfully pleaded justification.

Under s. 5 of the Defamation Act 1952, where a statement comprises two or more different charges against the claimant, it is not necessary to prove that each charge is true, as long as the words which are not proved to be true do not materially injure the claimant's reputation having regard to the truth of the remaining charges. This provision is of considerable potential advantage to defendants, but in practice, justification is rarely pleaded, because if it fails, damages may be higher than they would otherwise have been, to mark the fact that the defamer has persisted in the untruth.

Fair comment

A defendant will have a defence if it can be proved that the statement made was fair comment on a matter of public interest. The key difference between the defence of justification and the defence of fair comment is that the former is concerned with whether the facts on which the statement was based are true, whereas the latter looks at whether the opinion expressed was fair. For the defence of fair comment to succeed the defendant must prove the following.

- The subject was of public interest. This is for the judge to decide in each case, but areas which generally fall into this category include local and national government, the behaviour and remarks of people involved in public affairs, trade unions, the police, and comments on works of art, including books, plays and broadcasts. The personal lives of people such as actors or authors do not amount to matters of public interest.
- The words must be a comment and not a statement of fact.
- Any facts which form part of the comment must be true, or if untrue, subject to privilege (see below). Following s. 6 of the Defamation Act 1952 not all the facts need to be proved to be true, only those facts on which the comment is based.
- The comment must be an honest and relevant expression of the defendant's opinion.
- It must be made without malice. Malice has the same meaning here as in the case of qualified privilege (see p. 203), that is, bad motive. In **Thomas *v* Bradbury, Agnew and Co Ltd** (1906) the defendant had written a very unfavourable review of the claimant's book in the magazine *Punch*. It became apparent that he had acted out of personal dislike for the writer and so his comment could not be viewed as fair. He was liable for defamation.

Absolute privilege

This defence protects the makers of certain defamatory statements because the law considers that in the circumstances covered by the defence, free expression is more important than protection of reputation. The defence covers the following:

- Any statement made in Parliament by a member of either House, or in any report published by either House (such as Hansard). This privilege is founded on Art. 9 of the Bill of Rights of 1689 which states:

  That the freedome of speech and debates or proceedings in Parlyament ought not to be impeached or questioned in any court or place out of Parlyament.

- Any report published by either House (such as Hansard), or such a report when republished in full by someone else (Parliamentary Papers Act 1840, s. 1).
- Any statement made by one officer of state to another in the course of the officers' duty. Secretaries of State and Ministers are officers of state, but it is not clear how far below that rank absolute privilege extends.

- Any statement made by one spouse to another.
- Statements made in the course of judicial proceedings, by judge, jury, witnesses, lawyers or the parties themselves.
- Fair and accurate media reports of public judicial proceedings (Defamation Act 1996, s. 14).
- Statements made by officials and other servants of the EU in the exercise of their functions.

Qualified privilege

Qualified privilege is another defence based on public interest. It applies to a broader range of statements than absolute privilege, but is subject to one restriction: it is not available if the statement complained of was made with malice, which can mean with a bad motive, or simply without an honest belief that the statement was true (see p. 207). The defence can arise under statute, and at common law.

Qualified privilege under statute

The statutory provisions are now contained in s. 15 of the Defamation Act 1996, which provides that certain types of statement listed in the Act are subject to qualified privilege. These types of statement fall into two groups. The first group, listed in Sch I to the Act, are statements which the Act describes as having 'qualified privilege without explanation or contradiction'. The most important ones are:

- Fair and accurate reports of the proceedings of legislatures, courts, governmental inquiries and international organizations held in public anywhere in the world.
- Fair and accurate copies of, or extracts from, material published by or on the authority of any government, legislature, international organization or international conference, anywhere in the world.

Schedule II lists the second group, which the Act describes as 'privileged subject to explanation or contradiction'. Publication of statements in this group is covered by the privilege, but that protection will be lost if the person claiming defamation has supplied a reasonable explanation or contradiction of the statement, and requested its publication, but the defendant has failed to publish it, or to publish it in 'a reasonable manner'. The most important types of statement listed in Sch II are fair and accurate reports of the following:

- Proceedings of public meetings held in any EU state. (In **Turkington** *v* **Times Newspapers** (2000) the House of Lords said a press conference could be regarded as a 'public meeting', although not open to the general public, because its purpose was to convey information to the public.)

- General meetings of any UK public companies.
- Public sittings of tribunals, boards and committees acting under statutory powers.
- Decisions by associations in the fields of the arts, sciences, religion, charity, trade, industry and sports.

The Act provides that s. 15 does not apply 'to the publication to the public, or a section of the public, of matter which is not of public concern and the publication of which is not for the public benefit'.

Qualified privilege under common law

At common law, the traditional definition of where qualified privilege will apply comes from **Adam** *v* **Ward** (1917), in which Lord Atkinson explained that:

> a privileged occasion is . . . an occasion where the person who makes a communication has an interest or a duty, legal, social or moral, to make it to the person to whom it is made, and the person to whom it is so made has a corresponding interest or duty to receive it. This reciprocity is essential.

Cases have established a number of categories in which these mutual duties and/or interests can be found, among them the following:

- Protection of an interest. In **Bryanston Finance** *v* **De Vries** (1975), the defendant was found to be covered by qualified privilege when he made defamatory statements which were concerned with protecting his business interests in a memo to a secretary. Similarly in **Adam** *v* **Ward**, the claimant had severely criticized an army general. These criticisms were protected by absolute privilege because they were made within Parliament, but after the army investigated his allegations and announced that they were totally unfounded, the claimant wrote to a newspaper defending his position, and again criticizing the general. The House of Lords held that the letter was covered by qualified privilege as the claimant was protecting his own reputation.
- Communications between officers of a company. In **Watt** *v* **Longsdon** (1930), the claimant was working abroad for the company of which the defendant was director. While the claimant was away, the defendant received a letter saying that the claimant was, among other things, 'a blackguard, a thief and a liar' who 'lived exclusively to satisfy his own passions and lust'. None of this was true. The defendant showed the letter to the chairman of the board of directors, and also to the claimant's wife, who decided to get a divorce as a result. When the claimant sued for defamation, it was held that showing the letter to the board was covered by qualified privilege, because they had an interest in seeing it, and as a fellow officer of the company, the claimant had a duty to show it

to them. However, showing the letter to the claimant's wife was not covered by the privilege; although she had an interest in receiving the information, he had no duty to give it to her.

- Information given to the police where a crime is suspected. In **Croucher *v* Inglis** (1889), it was stated that 'when a person suspects that a crime has been committed, it is his right and his duty to inform the police'.

The defence is not restricted to these categories; the courts have frequently stated that this is an area of the law that must adapt to changing social conditions, and that in each case, a court must look at all the circumstances surrounding publication of the statement. The recent high-profile case of **Reynolds *v* Times Newspapers** (1999) gives the latest House of Lords view on the application of the defence. The case arose from a news story published by The Times about the former Irish Taoiseach (Prime Minister), Albert Reynolds. Mr Reynolds claimed that the article suggested that he had deliberately misled the Irish parliament, and sued for libel. The newspaper put forward the defence of qualified privilege, claiming that this should cover all discussion of political information, but this was rejected by the judge. Mr Reynolds won his case, but the jury awarded only nominal damages. Mr Reynolds then appealed, on the basis that the judge had misdirected the jury. The newspaper also appealed, on the issue of whether qualified privilege should apply. The Court of Appeal allowed Mr Reynolds' appeal and ordered a re-trial, but rejected the defence of qualified privilege for the newspaper, and this aspect of the case was then appealed to the House of Lords. They too rejected it, and in the process of doing so, took the opportunity to examine the principles behind the defence, and to make a detailed statement on the factors to be taken into consideration when deciding whether it applies in any particular situation.

The House reiterated the definition stated in **Adam *v* Ward**, and explained that the essence of the defence 'lies in the law's recognition of the need, in the public interest, for a particular recipient to receive frank and uninhibited communication of particular information from a particular source'. They acknowledged that this concept included not only communications between particular individuals, but also, in some cases, publications made to the world at large by, for example, newspapers. However, they refused to accept the argument made by *The Times* that it was in the public interest that all discussion of political information should be covered by qualified privilege. They agreed that it was important that information on political matters should be freely available, so that people could make informed choices between politicians and policies when exercising their democratic rights. However, they pointed out, it was also in the public interest that politicians who were the subject of false allegations should be able to defend themselves:

. . . it should not be supposed that protection of reputation is a matter of importance only to the individual and his family . . . It is in the public interest that the reputation of public figures should not be debated falsely. In the political field, in order to make an informed choice, the electorate needs to be able to identify the good as well as the bad.

Therefore, they concluded, there was no reason to create a special category of protection for political information; instead the courts should continue to take the type of information into account as part of the overall examination of the circumstances surrounding publication. It went on to specify some of the important factors that should be taken into consideration:

- the seriousness of the allegation;
- the nature of the information and the extent to which it is the subject of public concern;
- the source of the information – important issues here included whether the informants had direct knowledge of the events, whether they were being paid for their stories, or whether they had 'their own axes to grind';
- the steps taken to verify the information;
- the status of the information – for example, an allegation which has already been the subject of an authoritative investigation would be more highly regarded;
- the urgency of the matter;
- whether comment was sought from the claimant;
- whether the article contained the claimant's side of the story, at least in general terms;
- the tone of the article – a story raising queries or suggesting an investigation might, it was implied, be more likely to be protected than one presenting allegations as matters of fact;
- the circumstances of publication, including the timing.

The court stated that these were not necessarily the only issues to be taken into consideration, and that their weight would vary from case to case – but in weighing them up, courts should always have particular regard to the importance of free expression, and therefore should be slow to conclude that a publication was not in the public interest and that the public had no right to know, especially when the information is in the field of public discussion. Any lingering doubts should be resolved in favour of publication.

With reference to the facts of the **Reynolds** case, the House of Lords agreed that the subject matter of the story was clearly of public concern. However, they said, the fact that the allegation made was a serious one, yet the newspaper made no reference to Mr Reynolds' explanation for the events concerned even though this was available to them (and had in fact been mentioned in Irish editions of the paper), meant it was not in the public interest that the story itself should be covered by privilege.

Reynolds was applied in **Irving *v* Associated Newspapers** (1999). The claimants were a firm of solicitors who had encouraged residents housed in substandard properties to sue the local council; the defendant was a newspaper which had written about the profits the solicitors were making from these actions. The claimants argued that the newspaper articles had suggested that their main motivation was profit, and their conduct dishonest. The newspaper tried to claim qualified privilege, but the court held that this could not apply; there was no legal, moral or social duty to publish the material, and the public had no legitimate interest in reading it.

Malice

Where a statement is made with malice, the defence of qualified privilege cannot apply (and nor can that of fair comment). In everyday language, malice means spite or ill-will, and in some cases it will be precisely this that deprives the defendant of qualified privilege. This was the situation in **Angel *v* H H Bushell & Co** (1968). The claimant and defendant had started to do business together, but relations between them soured, and the defendant wrote a letter to the mutual friend who had introduced them saying that the claimant 'did not know normal business ethics'. He claimed qualified privilege, but the court held that it did not apply because the letter had clearly been motivated by anger, rather than any duty to inform the friend of what had happened.

However, the legal definition also goes wider than this. In **Halpin *v* Oxford Brookes University** (1995), the claimant was a lecturer who had been the subject of a number of memos stating untrue allegations about him, which were circulated to other members of staff. The Court of Appeal stated that malice could be proved if it could be shown that the writer knew what he was publishing was untrue, or was reckless as to whether it was accurate or not.

What happens when a defendant is motivated by ill-will, but nevertheless honestly believes that what they are saying is true? This was the case in **Horrocks *v* Lowe** (1975). The claimant and the defendant were both local councillors in Bolton. The claimant had interests in a large amount of property in the town, and it was accepted that the defendant felt this made him unsuitable to sit on the council because of the potential for conflicts of interest. During a council meeting, the defendant accused the claimant of misleading the council over a property-related dispute, and the claimant sued for slander. It was accepted that the council meeting was a privileged occasion, but the claimant held that the defendant's personal prejudice against him amounted to malice and should prevent the defendant being protected by privilege. The trial judge had found that, on the evidence, the defendant believed that what he had said was true, but his motivation in saying it was his prejudice against the claimant, and so qualified privilege could not apply. The House of Lords disagreed, and held that on these facts, the defence could apply; if a defendant, however prejudiced, honestly believed in the truth of the allegations made, there was no malice.

Apology

Apology is not a true defence, but it can be used to reduce the damages payable. Under s. 2 of the Libel Act 1843 (sometimes known as Lord Campbell's Act), as amended by the Libel Act 1845, a defendant newspaper may plead that the libel was published in the newspaper without malice or gross negligence, and that before the legal action was brought, or as soon as possible after it, a full apology was published in the newspaper. If the newspaper is published less frequently than weekly, the defendant must have offered to publish the apology in any newspaper of the claimant's choice. The plea must be accompanied by payment of money into court by way of amends.

Section 1 of the 1843 Act, which is not limited to newspapers, provides that if the defendant gives notice to the claimant at the time they serve their defence, they can offer evidence that an apology was offered before the action began, or as soon as possible afterwards, and this evidence may reduce the damages awarded. In this case there need be no payment into court.

Offer of amends

To cover situations where words have been published quite innocently, the Defamation Act 1952, s. 4 established the defence of offer of amends. The original defence has now been amended and replaced by ss. 2–4 of the Defamation Act 1996. It applies only where the defendant has published a false and defamatory statement without knowing that it might be taken to refer to the claimant, and the defendant bears the responsibility for proving this. In order to be covered by the defence, defendants must offer to publish a suitable correction and apology and to pay compensation. If the offer is accepted, the proceedings for defamation come to an end. If the parties cannot agree on the appropriate compensation, the court may decide the question for them.

If an offer of amends is refused, the claimant can use the fact that the offer was made as a defence.

In **Ross** *v* **Hopkinson** (1956) the defendant was a novelist, a character in her novel was an actress and she had accidentally given that character the same name as a real actress. Her defence under s. 4 of the 1952 Act failed as she had not taken all reasonable care; she could have checked whether there was an actress currently using that name without too much difficulty.

Innocent dissemination

This defence is designed to protect printers and distributors from unfair libel actions. It was first laid down in **Vizetelly** *v* **Mudie's Select Library** (1900), where the owners of a circulating library were sued for a libel that was contained in a book that they had loaned out. They had had nothing to do with publishing the book, but the publisher, on realizing that the book contained a libel, had written to them asking for the book to be withdrawn from circulation. They ignored the letter and were therefore held liable, but the court held that where distributors did not know of a libel, had no reason to suspect one, and were not negligent in failing to discover it, they would escape liability.

This defence is now contained in s. 1 of the Defamation Act 1996. It is available to parties who are not the author, editor or publisher of the statement complained of, and the list of those who are considered to fall within this group makes it clear that it is intended to cover those who do not have any editorial control over the material they handle – from the printers who simply reproduce the material given to them by magazines and newspapers, to broadcasters of live programmes in circumstances where they have no control over remarks made by those appearing on them.

The defence was tested in **Godfrey** *v* **Demon Internet** (1999). Here the defendant was an Internet service provider, and the statement complained of was part of a message posted to an Internet newsgroup by an unknown person. The message made an untrue allegation about the claimant, who asked the defendant to remove it; they failed to do so and the claimant sued for libel. The defendants claimed that they were covered by the defence of innocent dissemination, because they were not the publisher of the statement, and they had no reason to believe that they had contributed to the publication of a defamatory statement. The court agreed that for the purposes of the defence, they were not the author, editor or publisher of the statement, but said that they could not meet the requirement of taking reasonable care with regard to its publication, because they failed to remove it once they knew it was there.

It is important to realize that the fact that an organization is considered not to be a publisher for the purposes of this defence does not mean that information transmitted through them is not published by them. You will remember from the beginning of this chapter that one of the requirements of an action for defamation is that the statement must have been published by the defendant. As well as claiming the defence of innocent dissemination, the defendants in **Godfrey** made an alternative argument, to the effect that they could not be liable for defamation because storing the message on their server was not publishing it. The court rejected this view, pointing out that booksellers and libraries had been held to have published defamatory material contained in the books and magazines they stocked, and by analogy, an Internet service provider which stores a posting on its server can be said to publish it whenever it is called up and read by a user. For that purpose, they were the publisher, but for the purposes of the defence of innocent dissemination, they were not.

▶ Procedural issues

There are a number of unusual features concerning the way in which defamation cases are actually tried. First, defamation is one of the few civil actions which can still be tried by a jury, and usually is (in some cases one or other side may argue that the issues involved are too complex to be suitable for jury trial, in which case the judge can decide to try the case without a jury). The jury also decides the amount of damages (see below).

Secondly, legal aid is not available for any kind of action for defamation. Because they are usually heard by juries, and because lawyers regard them as a difficult and complex area of work, defamation cases can be very expensive to bring (or defend), which means that in practice only the wealthy can afford to sue for defamation; for example, in the much-publicized case involving the Sun newspaper and the former *EastEnders* actress Gillian Taylforth, Ms Taylforth was left with a bill for around half a million pounds, following an 11-day hearing.

Possibly the most important provision in the Defamation Act 1996 is the introduction of a new summary procedure for defamation actions. Under this procedure, cases where the claim is less than £10,000 may be heard by a judge alone, with the aim of getting such cases heard quickly, so that costs are kept down. The Defamation Act 1996 also reduces the limitation period within which defamation actions must be brought to one year; it was previously three.

▶ Remedies for defamation

Damages

Damages for defamation may simply compensate for the claimant's loss, or may be exemplary, designed to punish the publisher. In mitigation of damages, the court may take into account the following.

- Whether the defendant apologized as quickly as possible.
- Whether the claimant already had a bad reputation.
- Whether there was provocation by counter-libels.

- Whether the claimant has already received damages for the publication of approximately the same defamation.
- The remoteness of damage done to the claimant.

In the past there has been much concern at the size of the awards of damages in defamation cases. The level of damages has been essentially an issue for the jury and in a string of high-profile cases, juries awarded what appeared to be excessively high damages (see p. 213). The Court of Appeal has attempted to tackle this problem head on in an appeal against an award of damages to the famous pop star Elton John in **John** *v* **Mirror Group Newspapers** (1996). He had initially been awarded £350,000, comprising £275,000 exemplary damages and £75,000 compensation. The award related to an untrue story that the singer-songwriter was hooked on a bizarre diet which was a form of the eating disorder bulimia nervosa.

The initial award was slashed to £75,000, which comprised £50,000 exemplary damages and £25,000 compensation. The Court of Appeal stated that under the old system, juries were like 'sheep loosed on an unfenced common with no shepherd' and commented that it was clearly undesirable for higher compensation to be given for loss of reputation than for many cases of severe mental or physical injury. The court considered that in future judges and lawyers could give clear guidance to juries in valuing damaged reputations, by citing typical awards for victims suffering personal injury and inviting juries to compare the damage a libel claimant has suffered. They might point out, for example, that a paraplegic gets a maximum of £125,000 compensation for the injury, while a lost arm is 'worth' £45,000 and a lost eye £20,000. The Court of Appeal even went as far as suggesting that there should be a £125,000 limit on defamation awards.

Since **John**, the Court of Appeal has continued to be active in levelling down what it considers to be excessive damages. In **McCartan Turkington Breen** *v* **The Times Newspaper** (1998), it reduced an award of £145,000 to £75,000.

Injunction

A claimant may also seek an injunction, either where a defamatory statement has already been published, to prevent it being published again, or where the claimant knows that the defendant plans to publish a defamatory statement, to prevent this happening. Where the claimant is seeking to prevent initial publication, they will be asking for an interlocutory injunction, which means one that is granted without the issue actually being tried by a court. This clearly has important implications for free speech; it is not difficult to see how wealthy and powerful claimants could effectively freeze all criticism of their activities if these types of injunction were freely granted. For this reason, the courts will only rarely grant interlocutory injunctions in defamation cases; in **Bonnard** *v* **Perryman** (1891), it was stated that they should only do so in the clearest cases, where it was obvious that any reasonable jury would say the statement concerned was libellous.

The courts are particularly unlikely to grant an interlocutory injunction where the defendant states that they would be able to plead justification if sued for defamation. In **Holley** *v* **Smyth** (1998), the defendant and the claimants had been involved in a financial transaction, in which the defendant claimed that the claimants had acted disreputably. He prepared a press release stating his allegations, and informed the claimants that he would send it to the press if they failed to put matters right. The claimants attempted to get an interlocutory injunction to prevent him sending the material to the press, but it was refused by the Court of Appeal because the defendant stated that if he was allowed to publish and then was then sued for defamation, he intended to prove at trial that the allegations were true. The Court of Appeal said they would only grant the injunction if, on the material before them, it was clear that the statement was untrue; as this was not the case, the injunction would not be available.

Time limits

The limitation period for defamation actions is one year, although the courts have a discretion to extend this in some circumstances.

▶ Problems with defamation

The distinction between libel and slander

The distinction has been justified on the grounds that libel is more likely to be premeditated and is likely to cause greater harm. However, it can cause apparent injustice; a person deliberately making a false and malicious public speech will not be liable for slander if no damage results, but a journalist who honestly reports the speech may be liable for libel. In reviewing this area of the law, in 1975 the Faulks Committee recommended that the distinction should be abolished. Some fear that if the distinction were abolished there would be a rise in petty actions for defamation by words as damage would no longer have to be proved. However, in countries where the distinction does not exist this does not appear to be a problem; the high cost of defamation actions also makes it unlikely.

Remedies

Neither of the remedies for defamation is entirely satisfactory. Damages cannot always buy back a reputation; by the time they are awarded, the defamation has not only been published in the first place, but in high-profile cases, will also have received a huge amount of media attention during the case. This can mean that even if the claimant succeeds, doubts may linger in the public's mind, which is after all exactly the effect the claimant is seeking to avoid.

The use of juries to decide the level of damages is also a problem: while jury trial of defamation cases can be defended on the simple grounds that the best way to tell if a statement would make right-thinking members of society think less of the claimant is simply to ask that question of a cross-section of such people, it is less easy to defend the rule that juries decide not only the verdict, but the damages. In several high-profile cases over the past few years, juries have awarded quite irrational damages, apparently as a mark of their disapproval of certain newspapers or publishers. For example, in 1989 Lord Aldington was awarded £1.5 million against Count Nikolai Tolstoy and his publisher. Some of this criticism has now been side-stepped by the Elton John case (see p. 211). The Law Commission gave its approval to the approach of this case, with its comparisons to awards for non-pecuniary loss in personal injury cases, in a consultation paper published in January 1996. The Law Commission wrote: 'We accept the force of [public] criticism that it is wrong for the law to appear to convey the impression that reputations are valued more highly than lives and limbs.' In addition there is provision for jury awards to be reduced on appeal.

There is some support for the idea that assessing the amount of damages should be left to the judge. The Faulks Committee concluded, after hearing much evidence, that the role of the jury should be curtailed, so that its role would be to state whether the damages should be substantial, moderate, nominal or contemptuous and the judge would then state the precise figure.

Even though damages can be extremely high, newspapers in particular are often very rich, and a high damages award may simply be set against the increased sales achieved by publishing the libel in the first place and the publicity arising from the court case. Where large and powerful publishing organizations are concerned, alternative (or additional) sanctions, such as being prohibited from publishing at all for a certain period of time, might be more effective. Even losing publication for a day would have a deterrent effect, given the enormous competition between rival publications. After his award of damages was drastically cut in 1995, Elton John said that the result left him £85,000 out of pocket after paying legal fees, and declared that the decision 'has given the press carte blanche to print and be damned, and confirmed to the press that it makes commercial sense to print whatever lies they want and, if sued, just pay what to them is a small fine'.

By contrast, an interim injunction does what the claimant really needs, by preventing the defamation from being published in the first place. However, it amounts to censorship without a jury trial and may therefore be seen as unfair to the defendant and a serious restriction on freedom of the press.

Access

Defamation cases can be long and expensive, and legal aid is not available for them. This suggests that the law believes a poor person's reputation is not worth defending. Perhaps more seriously, it means that unscrupulous newspapers know very well that they can write what they like about most ordinary people, with no fear of being sued. For example, in 1997, the *Daily Mail* published pictures of five youths who it accused of the murder of the London teenager, Stephen Lawrence, with the words 'let them sue us if we are wrong'. While this was presented as the newspaper making a bold gesture in the interests of finding the perpetrators of Stephen's murder, in practice the *Daily Mail* (which like much of the media had taken relatively little interest in the case initially) knew perfectly well that the youths were extremely unlikely to be able to afford to sue, regardless of whether the accusation was true. Had the alleged killers been the sons of wealthy businessmen, the gesture might well have been a brave one (though the question of whether it was wise or likely to help achieve justice is less clear), but as things stood, the paper took no real risk at all.

The summary procedure laid down under the Defamation Act 1996 was intended to make defamation actions quicker and therefore cheaper, but without legal aid, such actions are still out of reach of most ordinary people. Of potentially more use is the availability of no win, no fee agreements. The first recorded libel action taken on this basis was announced in December 1998, in **Luisa Morelli** *v* **Sunday Times**, **Vincent Coyle** *v* **Sunday Times**, where the claimants won £30,000 and £15,000 respectively over a newspaper story suggesting that they had exaggerated complaints made about a holiday they had taken.

Extension of liability

Where small publishers are concerned, the rule that liability can extend to printers and distributors can be used as a severe restriction on freedom of the press. In **Goldsmith** *v* **Pressdram** (1987) the businessman James Goldsmith was able to use threats that distributors would be sued to secure the removal of copies of the satirical magazine *Private Eye* from many newsagents. Such threats work because newsagents and distributors clearly do not have the same interest in publishing as writers and editors, and they are unwilling to take the risk of being sued, knowing that the fact that the threat has been made will make the defence of innocent dissemination unavailable to them. The reason why this approach hits smaller publications is that the vast majority of outlets for newspapers and magazines are under the control of a handful of companies; small publishers have little influence with such firms, and need outlets more than the distribution companies need their publications (by contrast, large publishers with many profitable titles have more influence over distribution networks so are more difficult to control in this way).

A Periodical Publishers Association conference on libel actions in 1993 was told of several occasions when small magazines had been forced to remove critical (but allegedly true) articles after the subjects of those articles threatened to sue the major newsagent chains if the stories were published; as a result the newsagents refused to stock the magazines unless the offending articles were removed. Even leaving aside the fact that there is little point publishing the stories if few outlets would sell them, the loss of even a week's normal sales could do severe financial damage to a small publisher, and possibly even put it out of business, so that magazines are forced to comply. The result is that wealthy and powerful complainants can use economic muscle to secure the practical effect of an injunction, without subjecting the allegations to the scrutiny of a court.

Restrictions on press freedom

Perhaps the most serious criticism of English defamation law is that it fails to strike anything like an adequate balance between freedom of the press and the protection of reputation. In most other jurisdictions, a greater distinction is made between issues of public interest, for example, alleged wrongdoing by government bodies, or corruption within the police force, and issues which merely happen to interest the public, such as the sexual antics of TV stars and the eating habits of pop singers. In the USA, for example, much greater protection is given to freedom of speech concerning matters of public interest. As we have seen, the English law on defamation does contain some concessions in this direction (the defences of privilege and fair comment, and principles laid down in **Derbyshire County Council** *v* **Times Newspapers** and **Goldsmith** *v* **Bhoyrul**) but it is still widely criticized as stifling free debate on matters of public interest.

ANSWERING QUESTIONS

1 Yesterday Mr Cook was told by his wife that a person called Letitia, who lives in the same village, had a baby when she was only 13 years old. Letitia has always kept this secret and has referred to the child as her own younger sister. 'She's no better than a prostitute,' said Mrs Cook, 'and when you think of all the lies she must have told, she's the last person you'd trust to be honest.'

Today while Mr Cook is at work he is telephoned by the personnel officer who has received a job application from Letitia Smith. As she lives in the same village as Mr Cook, the personnel officer wonders whether Mr Cook knows if she is reliable and honest. Remembering what his wife told him last night, Mr Cook tells the personnel officer that he believes Letitia Smith to be immoral and dishonest.

Letitia Smith eventually finds out why she did not get the job. She is very angry as she is not the person referred to by Mrs Cook and she has now demanded an apology and compensation from both Mr and Mrs Cook.

Advise Mr and Mrs Cook as to their liability, if any, in tort. *OCR*

With problems on defamation, it is useful to remember the definition of the tort, and use it as a framework to work through the elements of liability. What has to be established is that the defendant published an untrue statement referring to the claimant, which lowers the claimant in the eyes of right-thinking people (and that there was no defence). The first point to make here is that in both cases, the alleged defamations were made in speech, and so the form of defamation we are concerned with is slander. This imposes a further requirement, in that the claimant must prove damage, unless the case falls within the Slander of Women Act 1891, s. 1.

Looking first at Mrs Cook's possible liability, work through the elements of the tort, relating them to her statement. Clearly the statement was defamatory, and was untrue of the claimant. Mrs Cook did not intend it to refer to the claimant, but to another woman, but this may not help her given that the test laid down in **Newstead** v **London Express Newspapers Ltd** was whether a reasonable person would think it referred to the claimant. The requirement for damage may be satisfied by the fact that as a result of the remark, the claimant failed to get a job, but in any case, the remark clearly falls within the requirements of the Slander of Women Act 1891. However, despite all this, Mrs Cook is not liable, because telling her husband does not amount to publication.

Turning to Mr Cook, once again, he has clearly made a defamatory statement, and in this case he actually intends to refer to the claimant. As we have said, the issue of damage is not a problem, and in this case, the statement is published (remember that this does not only cover activities like printing in a newspaper or broadcasting on the radio; for the purposes of libel, publication has a much wider meaning). However, Mr Cook could try to argue that he has the defence of qualified privilege. To succeed with this defence, he must establish that he made the remark without malice, that he honestly believed it was true (which as far as we know is the case), and that he had a legal or moral duty to pass it on to the personnel officer, who had a legal or moral duty to receive it. The case of **Watt** v **Longsdon** suggests that there may be such duties in Mr Cook's situation.

2 **'The tort of defamation protects interests in reputation' (Hepple & Matthews). Does the tort of defamation operate in a logical and effective way?** *OCR*

As usual there is no single right answer to this question; the goal is an essay which shows a knowledge of the law while evaluating whether that law 'protects interests in reputation'. To achieve this you can use the material under the heading 'Problems with defamation' but do not limit yourself to this as this does not contain the detailed legal rules which the examiner will be impressed to see that you know. Illustrate some of the points by detailed examples from the law; you can also look at some of the detailed case law such as **Newstead** v **London Express Newspapers Ltd** and consider whether the law currently reaches a fair balance between the interests of the public and the defendant and the interests of the claimant. Do you consider that we need the broad defences of absolute and qualified privilege? How does this fit with issues of freedom of speech? Do we need a tort protecting people's privacy? All these issues are relevant, but in discussing them, you should aim to highlight your knowledge of the law as it is, and its problems, as well as discussing what the law on protecting interests in reputation should be.

9 Nuisance

The tort of nuisance sets out to protect the right to use and enjoy land, without interference from others. There are actually three types of nuisance: private, public and statutory, but this chapter (and this book) deals only with the first two. Private nuisance is a common law tort, and the main subject of this chapter. Public nuisance is a crime, and therefore dealt with through prosecution under the criminal law, but it also comes into the study of tort because there are some cases where parties who have suffered as a result of a public nuisance can sue in tort.

Statutory nuisance is the name given to offences created under various statutes concerning public health and environmental issues – for example, creating excessive noise can be a statutory nuisance under the Control of Pollution Act 1974, and emission of smoke may amount to a statutory nuisance under the Clean Air Act 1956. Statutory nuisances are dealt with by local authorities, who can issue orders to stop the harmful activity. In many cases statutes have given them responsibility for harmful activities that would once have been tackled by tort actions brought by affected individuals, the idea being that these are problems that affect the community as a whole and so should be dealt with by public bodies. Statutory nuisance is not generally considered as part of a tort course and so is not discussed further in this book.

PRIVATE NUISANCE

The tort of private nuisance essentially arises from the fact that, whether we are out in the countryside or in the middle of a city, we all have neighbours – and the way they behave on their land may affect us on ours. The essence of liability for private nuisance is an unreasonable interference with another's use or enjoyment of land, and in assessing what is reasonable, the courts will try to balance each party's right to use the land as they wish.

Elements of the tort

The claimant must prove three elements: an indirect interference with the enjoyment of the land; that this interference caused damage to the claimant; and that the interference was unreasonable. In addition, there are rules about the parties' relationship to the land, which determine who can sue and who can be sued.

Interference

The claimant must prove that the defendant has caused an interference with the claimant's use or enjoyment of their land. There are many ways that such interference can be caused, but what they have in common is that they must be indirect, and that they will usually (though not always) be the result of a continuing state of affairs, rather than a one-off incident. In some cases there will be a physical invasion of the claimant's land, such as the roots of a neighbour's tree spreading into the claimant's land (**Davey *v* Harrow Corporation** (1958)) or water flooding onto land as a result of something done by a neighbour (**Sedleigh-Denfield *v* O'Callaghan** (1940)), but often the nuisance is caused by something intangible, such as noise (**Christie *v* Davey** (1893)), or smells (**Wheeler *v* J J Saunders** (1995)).

An occupier of land can also be liable for nuisance caused by naturally arising hazards, providing they are aware of their existence and fail to take reasonable precautions. This was the case in **Leakey *v* National Trust** (1980). The defendants occupied land on which there was a large, naturally occurring mound known as Barrow Mump. After one very hot summer, they were aware that the area could be affected by landslides, due to the earth drying out, but they took no precautions against this. A landslide did occur, casting earth and tree roots onto neighbouring land, and the defendants refused to remove the debris. The courts held that they were liable for the nuisance, even though they had not actually done anything to cause it, but had merely failed to prevent it. This principle was taken further in **Holbeck Hall Hotel *v* Scarborough Borough Council** (2000); **Leakey** involved things falling onto a neighbour's land, but in **Holbeck** the issue was whether allowing physical support for a neighbour's land to fall away could give rise to an action for nuisance. The claimants were the owners of a hotel which collapsed as a result of a landslip on neighbouring land owned by the council. The council had done nothing to cause the landslip, but knew that there was a risk of it happening. However, they had not realized how badly the problem could affect the land where the hotel stood, and could not have known this without ordering very expensive investigations. The Court of Appeal held that a landowner who knows or ought to have known that there is a risk that their property will cease to support a neighbour's may be liable in nuisance if they do not take precautions (though such precautions might be as little as informing the neighbour; it was not necessary to remove the risk of withdrawing the support). However, the council were not liable since they could not have foreseen the damage without an expensive survey.

The situation complained of must be sufficient to interfere with the claimant's use and enjoyment of their land. Anything which causes actual physical damage to the land fits this requirement, and it is established that things like fumes, noise or smells which make it physically unpleasant to be on the land can be included. The courts have also allowed actions for nuisance caused by situations which cause emotional distress; in **Thompson-Schwab** *v* **Costaki** (1956), the Court of Appeal held that running a brothel in an otherwise respectable residential street could be considered a nuisance.

However, the courts have not allowed the tort to protect what they consider to be recreational facilities, or as Wray CJ put it in **Bland** *v* **Moseley** (1587), 'things of delight'. That case established that blocking a neighbour's pleasant view could not be considered a nuisance, while the issue was brought right up to date in **Hunter** *v* **Canary Wharf** (1997). Here the claimants were people living in the area near the huge tower known as Canary Wharf, which was causing interference with their television reception. The Court of Appeal decided that loss of this kind of recreational facility was not sufficient interference to give rise to an action in nuisance.

Interference may apply directly to the claimant's land, or to a right in land known as a servitude. Examples of servitudes include private rights of way, a right to light through a particular window, or a right to have one's land held in place by adjoining land (called a right of support).

Unreasonableness

The interference must have been unreasonable. The basic premise is that if we are all to live together, there must be give and take, but interference which goes beyond the normal bounds of acceptable behaviour will be unreasonable. This principle can be seen in **Southwark London Borough Council** *v* **Mills** (1999). Here the council had converted a house into flats and the claimant lived in one of them. She sued the council, claiming that the building was poorly sound-proofed and she was troubled by the everyday noise generated by the occupants of other flats. The House of Lords held that the ordinary use of residential premises could not amount to a nuisance; there was nothing unusual about the way the building had been converted and the noise was normal for such a residential building.

In deciding whether an interference is unreasonable, the courts will take into account all the circumstances, and in particular, the following factors.

Sensitivity

A defendant is not responsible for damage which occurs solely because the claimant, or the claimant's situation, is abnormally sensitive. In **Robinson** *v* **Kilvert** (1889) the claimant occupied the ground floor of the defendant's premises, using it to store brown paper. The defendant's business, carried on in the basement of the same building, involved making paper boxes. This needed a hot, dry atmosphere. The heating used by the defendant in the cellar made the claimant's floor hot too, which dried out the brown paper, reducing its value. The claimant sued in nuisance, but the court found that brown paper was exceptionally delicate. As the heat was not sufficient to damage paper generally and it had not inconvenienced the claimant's workmen, the damage was due more to the sensitivity of the paper than to the defendant's activities, so there was no nuisance.

On the other hand, as soon as the claimant has proved that the defendant has infringed the claimant's right to ordinary enjoyment, they can also claim protection from damage due to unusual sensitivity. In **McKinnon Industries** *v* **Walker** (1951), the claimant's orchids were damaged and his enjoyment of his land generally affected by fumes and sulphur dioxide gas from the defendant's factory. The defendant claimed that, even if he were liable for the general interference, he should not incur responsibility for the orchids, since growing these was a difficult and delicate operation, and the plants could therefore be considered abnormally sensitive. The Privy Council rejected this argument, stating that as the right to ordinary enjoyment had been infringed the claimant could also claim protection for his more unusual and sensitive activities.

Locality

Where the interference takes place will have an important bearing on whether it is reasonable; a landowner in the centre of London cannot reasonably expect the same level of peace and quiet as one in the depths of the country. This point was made in **St Helens Smelting Co** *v* **Tipping Ltd** (1865). The claimant's estate was situated in an industrial area, and in deciding whether the fumes from the copper works amounted to nuisance, the House of Lords distinguished between nuisances causing actual injury to property, as in this case, and nuisances causing personal discomfort. In the latter case, claimants should be prepared to put up with the level of discomfort common to the area in which they are situated. However, claimants were not expected to put up with actual damage to their land resulting from the normal activities of the locality, and so an injunction was granted.

The result is that interference which would be reasonable in one area may be unreasonable in another. In **Sturges** *v* **Bridgman** (1879), the claimant was a doctor, who sued a confectioner for the noise caused by his industrial equipment. The court took into account the fact that the area in which they both worked consisted mainly of doctors' consulting rooms and concluded that there was a nuisance, explaining that that which would be a nuisance in a quiet residential area would not necessarily be so in a busy industrialized one.

In **Murdoch** *v* **Glacier Metal Co Ltd** (1998) the claimant lived near to the defendant's factory. She complained that a low droning noise which came from the factory at night was preventing her from sleeping. Her evidence included a report from the World Health Organization stating that this type of noise had been proved to disturb sleep if it went above a particular level, and the noise from the factory was measured and found to be at or above this level. The Court of Appeal held that the trial judge was right in holding that this did not constitute an actionable nuisance considering the area in which the claimant's house was situated, which was among other things close to a busy bypass, and considering the fact that no other local residents had complained about the noise.

The character of a locality can be changed by decisions on planning permission. In **Gillingham Borough Council** *v* **Medway (Chatham) Dock Co** (1993), the dock company had been granted planning permission for the operation of a commercial port. Access to it was only possible via residential roads, which caused a lot of traffic noise, and so the council sued in nuisance to try to get traffic limited at night. The court held that the fact that planning permission had been granted for a particular activity did not mean that that activity could not give rise to liability in nuisance; however, the existence of planning permission could mean that the character of the neighbourhood had changed (for example from primarily residential to commercial) which could mean that what might have amounted to a nuisance before the change could now be considered reasonable. It held that that had happened in this case and so the dock authority were not liable in nuisance.

However, planning permission will not, by itself, provide immunity from a nuisance action. In **Wheeler** *v* **J J Saunders** (1995), the defendants had obtained planning permission to build two pig houses close to the claimant's land, resulting in strong smells drifting across the claimant's property. The Court of Appeal confirmed that planning permission could only be taken as authorization of nuisance if its effect was to alter the character of the neighbourhood so that the nuisance could not be considered unreasonable. The planning permission in this case did not have that effect.

Duration

The longer the interference goes on, the more likely it is to be considered unreasonable. However, a nuisance need not necessarily last long. In **Crown River Cruises Ltd** *v* **Kimbolton Fireworks Ltd** (1996), it was held that a 20-minute firework display could amount to nuisance.

Malice

Malice here means a bad motive. A defendant need not act with malice, but where malice is present, that may be relevant to the question of reasonableness, in that it may make what would have been reasonable conduct unreasonable.

The case of **Christie *v* Davey** (1893) illustrates this point. The claimant was a music teacher, and held musical parties in his house. The defendant, his next-door neighbour, deliberately tried to disturb both lessons and parties by blowing whistles, banging trays, shrieking and hammering on the wall. The court held that this malicious motive made the defendant's conduct unreasonable and a nuisance. Had he not been trying to disturb the lessons, he might have had the right to make a noise, just as the claimant did with his lessons and parties.

Another example is **Hollywood Silver Fox Farm Ltd *v* Emmett** (1936). The claimant bred foxes on his land. The defendant was a neighbour and after a disagreement with the claimant, told his son to shoot his gun in the air while standing close to the claimant's land in order to frighten the vixens so that they would not breed. The claimant's action succeeded, for while the claimant was entitled to go shooting for the purposes of hunting game, his malicious motive rendered his activity an unreasonable interference with his neighbour's enjoyment of his land.

Damage

The interference must have caused some sort of damage to the claimant. This can mean physical damage to their land, as in **St Helens Smelting Co *v* Tipping** (1865), where the fumes from the copper-smelting works actually damaged trees and shrubs growing on the claimant's neighbouring land. However, physical damage is not essential; discomfort and inconvenience may be enough. In practice the courts tend to treat the type of damage caused as part of the examination of whether the interference was reasonable; interference which causes actual physical damage is more likely to be seen as unreasonable than that which causes mere discomfort or inconvenience.

The claimant must prove that the interference actually caused the damage complained of, under the rules of causation described on p. 92. The case of **Cambridge Water Co *v* Eastern Counties Leather** (1994) establishes that the test for remoteness of damage in nuisance is reasonable foreseeability (see p. 99).

Nuisance and fault

Nuisance was originally a tort of strict liability, in the sense that a defendant who was found to have committed an unreasonable interference with the claimant's land would be liable, regardless of whether they had done so deliberately, carelessly or quite unknowingly. In cases where the claimant is seeking an injunction (an order to stop the defendant from continuing the alleged nuisance), it can be said that strict liability still applies, because, as the House of Lords pointed out in **Cambridge Water Co** *v* **Eastern Counties Leather** (1994), the very fact that the case is being brought means that the defendant knows that their behaviour is alleged to be causing interference with the claimant's enjoyment of land, and is refusing to stop it. If that behaviour is found to amount to nuisance, there is no further fault requirement to be satisfied.

However, where a claimant is seeking damages, and therefore compensation for a past wrong rather than the prevention of a current one, the issue is rather more cloudy. Recent cases have established that strict liability no longer applies, but quite what the fault requirement is has not been made as clear as we, and probably you, would like. The latest House of Lords case on the issue is **Cambridge Water**, which involved the pollution of a water supply by chemicals from a tannery (the full facts are explained at p. 241). The claimants sued in negligence, nuisance and under **Rylands** *v* **Fletcher** (see the following chapter). All three claims failed, and as far as nuisance was concerned, this was because the fault element was not satisfied. Lord Goff explained that if a defendant's use of their land was reasonable, they would not be liable for any damage caused to the claimant's use and enjoyment of their own land. However, if the use was not reasonable, the defendant will be liable, even if they have used reasonable care to avoid damaging the claimant's enjoyment of their land. At this stage of the explanation, what Lord Goff seems to be putting forward is the traditional strict liability view of nuisance. However, he went on to say that '. . . it by no means follows that the defendant should be liable for damage of a type which he could not reasonably foresee'. This, he argued, was because reasonable foreseeability was required in negligence, and it would be wrong to set a stricter standard for defendants who had interfered with enjoyment of land than that for personal injuries.

The outcome seems to be that a defendant who uses land unreasonably and thereby causes damage to the claimant's enjoyment of land will only be liable if such damage was reasonably foreseeable – while a defendant who is found to be using their land reasonably will not be liable, even if damage was foreseeable (although this seems to ignore the effect of malice, which was not mentioned in **Cambridge Water**).

▶ Who can be sued?

There are three potential defendants in an action for nuisance: the creator of the nuisance; the occupier of the land; and the owner of the land.

The creator of the nuisance

Anyone who creates a nuisance by some act (rather than an omission) can be sued for nuisance, regardless of whether that person owns or occupies the land from which the nuisance originates. Nuisance need not necessarily even come from privately-owned land; in **Thomas *v* National Union of Mineworkers (South Wales Area)** (1985), it was held that striking miners picketing in the road outside a factory could be liable in private nuisance.

The occupier

In the majority of cases, the defendant will be the occupier of the land from which the nuisance comes. An occupier need not be the owner of the land – where land is rented to a tenant, the tenant will usually be considered the occupier, and can be sued for creating a nuisance (in some cases it is also possible to sue the landowner for nuisance caused by the tenant – see below).

An occupier of land is liable for any nuisance caused by themselves, or by their employees, subject to the principles of vicarious liability – see p. 277. In an exception to the usual rules of vicarious liability, they may also be liable for nuisance caused by independent contractors, where the activities of the contractors involve 'a special danger of nuisance'. This was established in **Matania *v* National Provincial Bank** (1936), where the claimant's flat was affected by noise and dust from work done by independent contractors in the defendant's flat above; the activities were held to involve a special danger of nuisance because it was inevitable that they would interfere with the claimant's use of their flat unless precautions were taken.

Occupiers of land may also be liable for nuisance caused on that land by third parties, such as trespassers or previous occupiers, if the occupier is or ought to be aware of the potential for nuisance to be caused and fails to take steps to prevent it. The leading House of Lords case on this issue is **Sedleigh-Denfield *v* O'Callaghan** (1940). The defendants, an order of monks, occupied some land where there was a ditch. The local authority had built a pipe which took water away from the ditch; this was done without the defendants' knowledge, and in legal terms, the workers who built it were considered trespassers. The pipe had a grate to keep out leaves, but it was wrongly placed, and eventually, some three years after the pipe had been laid, it became completely blocked with leaves. As a result, neighbouring land owned by the claimant became flooded. By this time, the defendants knew that the pipe existed, because it drained their own land, and the House of Lord held that an occupier who knows of a danger and allows it to continue is liable, even though they have not created the danger in the first place.

As explained earlier, an occupier can also be liable for nuisance caused by naturally occurring hazards on their land (see p. 219).

The owners

Where land is occupied by someone other than the owner, it is generally the occupier rather than the owner who will be liable for nuisance caused by the occupiers, but there are three circumstances in which the owners may be held liable. First, owners will be liable where a nuisance already existed when the land was let, and they knew or ought to have known about it. Secondly, they will liable where the land is let out, but the lease provides that the landlord has an obligation to repair the premises, or the right to enter and do repairs. This was the case in **Wringe** *v* **Cohen** (1940), where the defendant owned a shop that was let out to tenants. The defendant was responsible for keeping the premises repaired, but failed to do so, and as a result, a wall collapsed and damaged the neighbouring shop which belonged to the claimant. The defendant was held liable.

The third situation in which a landlord can be liable for nuisance caused by the occupier is where the landlord can be said to have authorized the nuisance. The clearest example of this is where the purpose for which the tenancy or lease is created is certain to create a nuisance. This applied in **Tetley** *v* **Chitty** (1986), where the local council allowed a go-kart club to use their land, and the noise from it disturbed local residents. The council claimed they were not liable because they had neither created the noise nor permitted it, but the court held that as such noise was an inevitable result of the activities of a go-karting club, allowing the club to use the land amounted to permitting the nuisance, and the council were liable.

A landlord may be found to have authorized a nuisance if they knew about it and failed to take steps to avoid it. This principle was examined in two recent cases, with contrasting results. In **Lippiatt** *v* **South Gloucestershire Council** (1999), the council had allowed a group of travellers to set up an unofficial encampment on their land. The claimants were farmers on the neighbouring land. They claimed that the travellers had used the land as a 'launching pad' for repeated ventures onto their farm, where they had caused damage, stolen property and behaved aggressively towards them, and they sued the council on the basis that they had authorized the nuisance. The council applied to have the claim struck out, but the Court of Appeal dismissed the application, and held that it was arguable that the council could be said to have authorized the nuisance.

The complaint in **Hussain** *v* **Lancaster City Council** (1999) was essentially similar to that in **Lippiatt**, yet in this case the Court of Appeal reached the opposite conclusion. The claimants owned a small shop and flat on a housing estate owned by the council. They were subjected to continual harassment and abuse by other residents (who were the council's tenants), and had complained many times to the council about this. The council had powers to evict tenants who behaved in this way, but failed to use them, and the claimants argued that this amounted to authorising the nuisance. The Court of Appeal rejected this view, and held that the facts of the case could not give rise to a claim in nuisance, because the harassment did not involve the tenants' use of the land – the fact that they were tenants on the council's land was incidental to what they were doing, whereas in **Lippiatt**, it was emphasized that even though the nuisance actually took place off the defendant's land, the land was being used as a 'launching pad' for the nuisance caused to the neighbours.

▶ Who can sue?

The traditional view was that the claimant had to have an interest in the land affected by the private nuisance in order to succeed in an action. This meant that while owners and tenants could sue, a person who only had the use of the land without possession or any other proprietary interest could not. Thus lodgers, guests and spouses of owners or tenants were excluded.

The position appeared to have been changed in **Khorasandjian *v* Bush** (1994). Here the claimant was a 16-year-old girl who had been friends with the defendant, a 21-year-old man. Their relationship broke down at the end of 1991 and the claimant told the defendant that she did not wish to see him any more. He reacted very badly to this news and over a period of months was violent and threatening towards her; he followed her around and started making menacing phone calls to her home where she lived with her parents. As a result of his threats to kill her he was jailed in May 1992, and he also received fines under the criminal law for the menacing phone calls. Despite these punishments the phone calls continued and the claimant succeeded in bringing a civil action against the defendant in private nuisance, despite the fact that she had no traditional proprietary interest in the family home. Lord Dillon said in the Court of Appeal:

> To my mind, it is ridiculous if in this present age the law is that the making of deliberately harassing and pestering telephone calls to a person is only actionable in the civil courts if the recipient of the calls happens to have the freehold or a leasehold proprietary interest in the premises in which he or she has received the calls.

The view taken in **Khorasandjian** was supported by the Court of Appeal when it considered the case of **Hunter *v* Canary Wharf Ltd and London Docklands Development Corporation** (1995). It stated that there had to be a substantial link between the person enjoying the use of land, and the land itself, but that mere occupation of a home was sufficient to provide this link, and to give the occupant the right to sue for any private nuisance affecting the land. It was no longer right, the Court of Appeal said, to limit the right to sue in nuisance to those who held legal rights in land.

Unfortunately for those without legal rights in land, **Hunter** was appealed in 1997 to the House of Lords, who disagreed. A majority of the House stated that only claimants with a right in land could sue, which (without going into the intricacies of land law) essentially limits the right to sue to those who own or rent land, or for some other reason have exclusive possession of it. The House stated that the change made in **Khorasandjian** had been made for a good reason, as at the time there was no other way to protect the claimant from harassment, but since then the Protection from Harassment Act 1997 had created a new tort to deal with this problem and nuisance was not required to do so.

The House of Lords insisted that there needed to be a clear distinction between nuisance and negligence, and the way to assert this was to maintain nuisance as a tort protecting a claimant's right to use and enjoy land, and negligence as protecting the claimant's bodily security.

In addition, Lord Goff identified practical reasons why the tort should be connected with rights in land. First, in many cases potential claimants and defendants often come to amicable arrangements with each other rather than going to court (for example, those affected by nuisance might agree to it continuing if the party causing it offers payment by way of compensation, or agrees to limit it to certain times). Lord Goff feared that such sensible arrangements would be less likely if the class of potential claimants was made wider. Secondly, it would prove impossible to fix any clear limits if the requirement for rights in land were lifted, and there might be difficult decisions to be made as to the rights of, for example, lodgers, au pairs or employees.

The issue was examined again in **Pemberton** *v* **Southwark London Borough Council** (2000), where the claimant was what is known in legal terms as a 'tolerated trespasser'. She lived in a council flat and had fallen behind with her rent payments. As a result the council had been able to get a court order allowing them to evict her from the flat if they wished to. She then began to pay rent again, and the council decided to let her stay there for the time being; they did not renew her tenancy because this would have meant that they would have to go through the whole court process again if she fell behind with the rent, and they would have been obliged to re-house her if she had been evicted. The flat became infested with cockroaches, which came through the heating ducts from communal areas owned and controlled by the local authority, so she sued the local authority in nuisance. The issue before the court was whether she had a sufficient interest in the land to sue for nuisance, under the principle established in **Hunter**. The Court of Appeal held that she did, because she had exclusive occupation of the premises, and this occupation was not unlawful.

The case of **Delaware Mansions Ltd and Another** *v* **Westminster City Council** (1999) establishes that liability can apply even if the danger is created before the claimant acquires their interest in the land. The claimants in the case suffered damage to a block of flats in which they had a legal interest, caused by roots from a tree on neighbouring land owned by the defendant council. The damage had happened by March 1990; the council knew this, and they could have felled the tree and prevented the need for any work on the flats. The claimants did not acquire their interest in the block until several months later, and the council argued that as the claimants did not have a legal interest at the time the damage was done, and no further damage had been caused after they acquired their interest, they could not sue. The Court of Appeal disagreed; the nuisance was a continuing state of affairs, and while it continued, so did the right to sue.

▶ Defences

It is thought that the general tort defences of contributory negligence, act of God and inevitable accident can apply to private nuisance, though given the lack of legal authority on the point, they seem to have little practical usefulness. The defence of *volenti* is subject to specific rules in nuisance, where it is usually referred to as 'coming to the nuisance', while the two most important defences are the general one of statutory authority, and the nuisance-specific defence of prescription.

Volenti (or 'coming to the nuisance')

As we saw in the chapter on negligence, the defence of *volenti* provides that a claimant cannot sue for injury or loss that he or she consented to. In nuisance, the cases where a consent defence has been put forward are those where the nuisance existed when the claimant came to the land, and defendants have sought to argue that this amounted to consenting to the nuisance (the position is usually known as 'coming to the nuisance'). The courts have, however, repeatedly rejected this argument, and stated that the fact that a claimant has voluntarily come into a situation where a nuisance exists does not provide a defence.

The argument was made in **Sturges** *v* **Bridgman**, the case involving the noisy confectioner and his new neighbour the doctor, discussed on p. 221. The confectioner claimed that the doctor could be considered to have consented to the noise of his business, since it was already in existence when the doctor moved in, but the court held that this was not a defence in private nuisance.

The same view was taken in the more modern case of **Miller** *v* **Jackson** (1977). Here the claimants had moved into a house beside a cricket club. Cricket balls were frequently hit into their garden and they attempted to get an injunction against the cricket club to stop play. The cricket club argued that in moving there, when they were aware of the club, they had 'come to the nuisance', but a majority of the Court of Appeal held that this was not a defence. Lord Denning made a powerful dissenting argument, pointing out that the claimants had come into the situation with their eyes open, and should have had to accept the risks of living beside a cricket ground if that was what they chose to do. This may seem reasonable, but taken to its obvious conclusion, it would mean that a defendant could avoid liability for any activity simply by being there first.

Statutory authority

Where a statute orders something to be done, and doing that thing inevitably creates a nuisance, there will be no liability because the statute is treated as having authorized the nuisance. The leading case on the subject is **Allen** *v* **Gulf Oil Refining Ltd** (1981). Residents in the area where the defendants were operating an oil refinery brought an action claiming that the refinery was causing a nuisance. The company pleaded in their defence that the nuisance was an inevitable result of operating the refinery, which they had power under statute to do. The relevant Act only gave express permission to the company to compulsorily purchase land and to build the refinery but did not expressly give them power to operate it. However, the courts said that it must have been Parliament's intention that they should also operate the refinery, so such a power could be implied. As Lord Diplock pointed out:

> Parliament can hardly be supposed to have intended the refinery to be nothing more than a visual adornment to the landscape in an area of natural beauty. Clearly the intention of Parliament was that the refinery was to be operated as such . . .

Since the alleged nuisance was an inevitable consequence of the operation of the refinery, arising from its ordinary working, the defence of statutory authority succeeded and an injunction against the operation of the refinery was refused.

If a nuisance can be avoided by the use of reasonable care and skill, statutory authority will not offer a defence. The House of Lords in **Allen** pointed out that if the nuisance caused by the refinery was more than the inevitable consequence of the refining process (if, for example, the owners could have taken reasonable steps to make the works less noisy or smelly), it could not be said to have been authorized by statute.

It has been argued that planning permission acts in the same way as statutory authority. This view was rejected by the courts in **Gillingham Borough Council** *v* **Medway (Chatham) Dock Co** (p. 222), though it was accepted planning permission can have a role to play in assessing reasonableness.

Prescription

A defendant may be held to have acquired the right to commit a private nuisance by what is called prescription. This applies where it can be shown that the nuisance has been actionable for at least 20 years, and that the claimant was aware of this during the relevant period.

Note that the fact that an activity has been carried on for at least 20 years may not in itself be enough; it must have amounted to a nuisance for at least that long. In **Sturges** *v* **Bridgman** (1879) the defendant confectioner had been running his business for over 20 years, using heavy machinery, before his new neighbour, the doctor, moved in and was disturbed by the noise. The defendant pleaded the defence of prescription, but the court held that this did not apply; although the noise had been going on for more than 20 years, it did not become a nuisance until the claimant's consulting room was built. Therefore the activity must have been a nuisance to the actual claimant (or any predecessors) for at least 20 years; the fact that it may have been a nuisance to people occupying other property is not sufficient to create a prescriptive right.

Inapplicable defences

There are two circumstances which students often think might provide a defence in nuisance, but which in law do not. The first is public benefit. It may seem reasonable that an activity which provides a public benefit should be less vulnerable to nuisance claims, but this is not the case. In **Bellew** *v* **Cement Co Ltd** (1948), Ireland's only cement factory was forced to close down for causing a nuisance, even though new building works were desperately needed at the time.

However, the courts will take public benefit into account when deciding on remedies, and may deny the claimant the exact remedy they want in order to strike a balance between the claimant's rights and the public benefit. In **Adams** *v* **Ursell** (1913), a fish shop situated in a residential street was held to be a nuisance, even though it was accepted that an injunction forcing it to close would cause hardship to local customers. In this case the court framed the injunction so as to allow the shop to be set up in a different part of the street where the claimant would not be affected by the nuisance.

Similarly, in **Miller** *v* **Jackson** (1977) (p. 230), the Court of Appeal agreed that the cricket club had committed a nuisance, but refused to grant the injunction that the claimants wanted because the usefulness of the club to the local community outweighed the claimants' interest in preventing cricket balls from being hit into their garden.

The second area which is often wrongly believed to offer a defence in nuisance is that of care and skill. Probably because most students spend the largest part of their course studying negligence, and because it is usually the first tort studied, its principles tend to make a big impression, with the result that students almost instinctively feel that a defendant who has used care and skill to avoid committing a nuisance should not be liable if the nuisance happens anyway. As we have seen when we looked at the fault element in nuisance (p. 223). this is not precisely the case. If a defendant's use of land is unreasonable, and damage to the claimant's enjoyment of their own land was the foreseeable result of that, the fact that they have used care and skill to prevent such damage is not a defence.

▶ Remedies

Injunction

Injunction is the main remedy for nuisance, and it aims to make the defendant stop the activity which is causing the nuisance. An injunction may be perpetual, which orders the activity to stop completely, or it may be partial, and for example, simply limit the times at which the activity can be performed. As it is a discretionary remedy, an injunction may be refused even though nuisance is proved.

An example of a partial injunction is **Kennaway** *v* **Thompson** (1980). The claimant owned land near Lake Windermere. A motor-boat club had been organizing boat races and water-skiing on the lake for several years, and the claimant was aware of this when she started building a house on her land, but believed she would not be disturbed by the noise. However, by the time the house was finished, the club had expanded, and was holding more frequent meetings, involving more powerful and noisier boats. It even began running big national and international competitions.

The claimant sought an injunction to restrain the club from causing or permitting excessive noise to come on to her land. The motor-boat club argued that there was a public interest in the facilities of both racing and observing the sport being made available to a large number of people. The Court of Appeal held that the claimant was entitled to an injunction restraining the club from carrying on those activities which caused a nuisance to her in the enjoyment and use of her land, despite the public interest in those activities. However, they framed the injunction so that it limited, rather than completely stopped the club's activities.

Damages

Damages can be recovered for damage to the claimant's land, or the enjoyment of it, and also for injury to the claimant which is associated with loss of enjoyment, such as loss of sleep, or discomfort caused by noise or smells.

Abatement

This remedy involves self-help, and allows the claimant to take steps to end the nuisance, for example by trimming back overhanging foliage. Where the claimant needs to enter the defendant's land for this purpose, notice must be given; if it is not, the abator will become a trespasser.

▶ Problems with private nuisance

Television reception

The outcome of the case of **Hunter *v* Canary Wharf Ltd and London Docklands Development Corporation** (1997) seems particularly unsatisfactory. The reliance on the old authorities refusing liability for the obstruction of a view is unrealistic. Television forms an important part of many people's lives and it seems extremely unjust to remove that leisure activity without providing any compensation. The reality is that such interference is likely to affect the very value of those people's homes. The type of buildings that are likely to cause this interference are tower blocks, the builders of which are likely to be able to afford to pay compensation. The law as it currently stands seems to provide a green light for large property developers to completely ignore the interests of local residents in the areas under development.

The requirement for rights in land

The House of Lords decision in **Hunter *v* Canary Wharf** regarding who can sue for nuisance has been regarded as a backward step by some. In his powerful dissenting judgment, Lord Cooke pointed out that there was no logical reason why those who were actually enjoying the amenities of a home should not be able to sue someone who unreasonably interfered with the enjoyment. The decision was essentially based on policy, and since that was the case, he would have preferred it to uphold justice rather than tidiness.

Certainly some of the arguments of his colleagues seem overstated. There is every reason why people should enjoy special protection when they are inside their homes, whether they own or rent those homes or not. Cases such as lodgers and au pairs may make for tricky decisions, but not impossible ones: time habitually spent on the land would be one useful criteria by which such cases could sensibly be decided.

PUBLIC NUISANCE

Public nuisance, as we said in the introduction to this chapter, is a crime, and those who commit it are generally dealt with by the criminal law, rather than being sued by individuals who are affected by the nuisance. However, there are occasions when a party affected by a public nuisance can sue in tort, and this is the situation that we will be looking at in this section. In some ways it is unfortunate that this crime has been labelled public nuisance, since it is actually quite different from the tort of private nuisance. It need not have any connection with the use of land, either by defendant or claimant, and is as likely to arise from a single act as from a continuing situation.

The leading definition of public nuisance comes from the case of **Attorney-General** *v* **PYA Quarries** (1957). The defendants used a blasting system in their quarry which caused noise and vibrations, and threw out dust, stones and splinters, which affected people living nearby. The Court of Appeal held that this could amount to a public nuisance, which it defined as any nuisance which 'materially affects the reasonable comfort and convenience of a class of her Majesty's subjects'.

This definition has been taken to include a whole range of activities which endanger the public, cause them inconvenience or discomfort, or prevent them exercising their rights. Examples include picketing on a road (**Thomas** *v* **NUM** (1985)); blocking a canal (**Rose** *v* **Miles** (1815)); obstructing a highway by queuing on it (**Lyons** *v* **Gulliver** (1914)); causing noise and disrupting traffic through a badly-organized pop festival (**Attorney-General of Ontario** *v* **Orange Productions Ltd** (1971)); and making obscene phone calls to large numbers of women (**R** *v* **Johnson (Anthony Thomas)** (1996)).

How many people have to be affected in order for them to amount to 'a class of her majesty's subjects'? This question was examined in **PYA Quarries**, where, as there were only 30 houses nearby, the quarry owners argued that they were too few for the problem to amount to a public nuisance. The court stated that the test was whether the nuisance is 'so widespread in its range or so indiscriminate in its effect that it would not be reasonable to expect one person to take proceedings on his own responsibility to put a stop to it, but that it should be taken on the responsibility of the community at large'. The court explained that this would not be the case where only two or three people were affected by it, but agreed that the 30 householders in the case before them were enough. Beyond that, they declined to give guidelines on numbers and said that the issue of whether the number of people affected by a nuisance amounts to a class is a question of fact, to be examined in each case.

The case also establishes that it is not necessary to prove that every member of a class has been affected by the nuisance, so long as it can be shown that a representative cross-section has been affected.

▶ Tort actions for public nuisance

A defendant whose behaviour comes within the definition of public nuisance can be prosecuted, but they can only be additionally sued in tort for public nuisance if a claimant can prove that they suffered 'special damage' over and above the effects on other members of the affected group. A good example of what is meant by special damage can be found in the old case of **Benjamin** *v* **Storr** (1874). The claimant kept a coffee house in the Covent Garden area of London, and the defendant regularly left his horses and carts outside, obstructing the highway and blocking out light from all the shops in the row. The nuisance affected all the shopkeepers, but because of the nature of the claimant's business, he was able to prove that he had suffered special damage, because the smell of the horses put his customers off.

Special damage may also arise when the nuisance costs the claimants money, though the general public only suffers inconvenience. In **Tate & Lyle Food and Distribution Ltd** *v* **Greater London Council** (1983), the defendant council built some ferry terminals in the River Thames, which cause excessive silting on the riverbed. This caused inconvenience to river users in general, but the claimants were more affected than most as access to their jetty was blocked, and they had to spend a lot of money having the riverbed around it dredged. The House of Lords held that this amounted to special damage.

Defences

The general tort defences discussed in the chapter on negligence apply to public nuisance, and statutory authority is the most important. It was used successfully in **Allen** *v* **Gulf Oil Refining Ltd** (see p. 230) in a claim for public nuisance as well as private.

The defence of prescription, used in private nuisance, does not apply in public nuisance.

Remedies

Both injunctions and damages are available for public nuisance, and although a tort action for public nuisance may only be brought by those who have suffered special damage, an injunction can obviously also benefit everyone else who has been bothered by the nuisance.

It appears that damages for personal injury can be fully recovered in public nuisance.

▶ Differences between private and public nuisance

As we explained earlier, these are separate and in many ways quite different torts, but as they often crop up together in problem questions in exams, it is useful to keep in mind the following specific differences.

Private nuisance	Public nuisance
Creates a cause of action in tort even if only one person is affected	Can only be actionable as a tort if a class of people are affected and at least one of them suffers special damage
Claimant requires an interest in land	No interest in land required
Nuisance must arise from defendant's use of land	Can arise from activities not related to use of land
Prescription is a defence	No defence of prescription

ANSWERING QUESTIONS

1 George recently had a swimming pool installed in land at the back of his house. The pool was designed by Harris Associates and the construction work was carried out by Truebuild Ltd. Because of unforeseen problems with the land, the work took much longer than originally anticipated and there was noise, dust and obstruction of the rather narrow lane which gave access both to George's land and to that of four of his neighbours.

When the pool was completed, it soon became obvious that the filter mechanism did not operate efficiently and the water was frequently very cloudy. In one part of the pool, the design created a shallow ledge in an otherwise deep area. While visiting for the first time since the pool was ready, George's brother, Frank, dived into this area and severely damaged his neck and back.

The incident was witnessed only by John, George's neighbour, with whom he was on very bad terms. John rushed over to the pool, jumped in and dragged Frank out. In doing so, John cut his arm on a sharp edge on the tiles of the pool and injured his knee, which was still weak from a recent operation.

(a) Explain what rights George's neighbours may have had in connection with the disturbance caused by the construction work. *(10 marks)*

(b) Consider whether Frank could succeed in an action against Harris Associates and against Truebuild Ltd to recover damages for his injuries. *(10 marks)*

(c) Consider whether John could bring any action to recover damages for the injuries he suffered in going to Frank's aid. *(15 marks)*

(d) Of what legal significance is the fact that Harris Associates is a partnership while Truebuild Ltd is a company? *(5 marks)*

(e) How far do you consider that the law would have ensured a just solution in each of the cases above? *(10 marks) AQA (AEB)*

(a) There may be a public and a private nuisance arising from the disturbance caused by the construction. These are best considered one after the other rather than trying to discuss them together. Looking first at private nuisance, the easiest approach would be to go through the key ingredients in the order considered in this chapter. There must be interference, which could be the noise and dust. This must cause damage: the noise may have caused general discomfort and inconvenience to the neighbours while the dust may have caused physical damage – **St Helens Smelting Co Ltd** v **Tipping**. The interference must have been unreasonable and the issues on locality (**Sturges** v **Bridgman**) and duration are relevant here, but those of sensitivity, malice and public utility are not. It will be a question of degree whether the noise and dust was sufficient to be so unreasonable that it amounted to a private nuisance. The fact that unforeseen problems meant the work took longer than expected may be relevant, given Lord Goff's comments on fault in **Cambridge Water** (see p. 224).

On the issue of who could be sued, both the builders as creators of the nuisance and George as the occupier (**Sedleigh-Denfield** v **O'Callaghan**) could be defendants. As regards the designers, Harris Associates, they can probably not be sued by the neighbours as they are neither strictly the creators of the nuisance nor the occupiers. The neighbours are likely to be able to sue as they have an interest in land (**Hunter** v **Canary Wharf**).

As regards public nuisance, again the easiest approach is to work through the different elements of the tort. First of all it will need to be considered whether a class of the public has been affected. Reference to **Attorney-General** v **PYA Quarries** could be made; it has similar facts with the class affected being local residents. The claimants must also have suffered special damage so George's neighbours would have to show that they were inconvenienced more than the other local residents; this would be easiest to show in relation to obstruction of the narrow lane, as this gave access to their homes.

Note that there is unlikely to be an action under **Rylands** v **Fletcher**, as building a swimming pool would probably not be viewed as an unnatural use.

(b) Here you should consider the liability of Harris Associates and Truebuild Ltd in negligence, dealing with them separately as their positions are slightly different. Looking first at Truebuild Ltd you need to work your way through the elements of negligence: a duty; breach of that duty; and resulting damage to the claimant that is not too remote. Frank's damage is straightforward personal injury, so apply the three-part **Caparo** test (see p. 18). If there is a duty, was it breached? The standard of care required would be that of a reasonably skilled builder of swimming pools. Whether or not they are in breach of that duty depends on whether reasonably skilled builders would rely on the advice of such people as Harris Associates. A key issue here is causation; were the injuries caused by bad design (the ledge), incompetent installation (the filter leaving the water cloudy so Frank could not see the ledge) or both? You will need to consider the cases on multiple causes here.

As regards the liability of Harris Associates, they gave advice as to the state of the pool so they might argue that the appropriate test as to whether they owed a duty is that laid down in **Hedley Byrne**. However, as their statement leads to physical damage the **Hedley Byrne** special relationship probably does not need to be proved. Their relationship to Frank is slightly more distant than the builder's but is probably still sufficiently proximate to give rise to a duty to Frank. Harris Associates will be expected to have the knowledge that they hold themselves out as having when giving their advice – **Bolam v Friern Barnet Hospital Management Committee**. Consideration also needs to be given as to whether Frank was contributorily negligent.

(c) First, John could sue Truebuild or Harris Associates. He would have to prove that as a rescuer, he was foreseeable. Alternatively, he could sue George, either for negligence, or for breach of the Occupiers' Liability Acts. As regards the latter, you would need to consider whether John would be regarded as a trespasser, given that we are told he is on bad terms with George. However, given John's reason for entering the land, he seems unlikely to be viewed as a trespasser. You will need to look at whether by employing a competent contractor and then having the pool inspected, George had met his responsibilities under the Act.

The relevance of the pre-existing weakness in John's knee is that you would need to consider issues of causation and remoteness. Finally, you should cover the defence of *volenti* in the context of rescues.

(d) This part of the question raises issues which are outside the scope of this book, which you will study as part of an English Legal System course. A textbook by the same authors on the English Legal System is available.

(e) Issues you might discuss here include the way in which opposing interests are balanced in the nuisance actions, and how the different remedies can achieve this. As regards Frank's case, you could discuss the extent to which he was to blame, and how the law takes this into account.

You could also bring in some of the alternatives to the tort system for dealing with cases like these, such as no-fault and insurance systems.

10 The rule in **Rylands** v **Fletcher**

The rule laid down in **Rylands** *v* **Fletcher** (1868) is the best-known example of a tort imposing strict liability. In essence, the rule is that an occupier of land who brings on to it anything likely to do damage if it escapes, and keeps that thing on the land, will be liable for damage caused by such an escape.

The defendant in **Rylands**, a mill owner, had paid independent contractors to make a reservoir on his land, which was intended to supply water to the mill. During construction, the contractors discovered the shafts and passages of an old coal mine on the land, some of which joined up with a mine situated on neighbouring land, belonging to the claimant. The contractors could have blocked up these shafts, but did not, and as a result, when the reservoir was filled the water from it burst through the shafts, and flooded the claimant's mine, causing damage estimated at £937.

The defendant himself had not been negligent, since there was no way he could have known about the shafts, and nor could he be held vicariously liable for the contractors, who were clearly not his employees for that purpose. An action for trespass (discussed in the next chapter) was unavailable, because the damage was not direct and immediate, and at the time of the case, the tort of nuisance could not be applied to an isolated escape. Nevertheless, the House of Lords held that the defendant was liable in tort, upholding the judgment delivered in the lower court by Blackburn J, which defined the rule: 'A person who, for his own purposes, brings on his land and keeps there anything likely to do mischief if it escapes, must do so at his peril, and, if he does not do so, he is *prima facie* answerable for all damage which is the natural consequence of its escape.'

The justification for this rule, he explained, was that 'the person whose grass or corn is eaten down by the escaping cattle of his neighbour, or whose mine is flooded by the water from his neighbour's reservoir, or whose cellar is invaded by the filth of his neighbour's privy, or whose habitation is made unhealthy by the fumes and noisome vapours of his neighbour's alkali works, is damnified without any fault of his own . . .'

Despite the fact that the courts claimed a clear foundation for the rule in previous cases, these authorities did not go nearly as far as the decision in the case, and it is generally regarded as establishing a completely new principle at the time. Cases decided subsequently restricted the tort by imposing so many conditions to its application that its role had until recently become very limited. However, in the most recent House of Lords case, **Cambridge Water** v **Eastern Counties Leather** (1994), the way was opened for the tort to play a greater role, particularly as a means of protecting the environment.

▶ Elements of the tort

The defendant must control the land

The tort will only apply where the land on to which the dangerous thing is brought is in the control of the defendant. In **Smith** v **Scott** (1973), a local authority let a house to a homeless family, on condition that they promised not to make any trouble. This promise was disregarded by the family once they moved in, and their behaviour was so intolerable that their next-door neighbour tried to sue the local authority on the basis of **Rylands** v **Fletcher**. However, it was held that the rule could not be applied to the landlord of tenants, as control of the land would lie with the tenants.

A defendant can also incur liability for bringing a dangerous thing on to the highway, if it then escapes on to someone's land. In **Rigby** v **Chief Constable of Northamptonshire** (1985), police attempting to capture a dangerous psychopath fired CS gas into the shop where he was, which was set on fire by the gas. It was decided that the rule did apply to the escape of things from the highway.

Bringing or accumulating for unnatural use

The dangerous thing must have been accumulated or brought on to the defendant's land in the course of some unnatural use of the land; the rule does not apply to damage caused by anything which naturally occurs there (for such problems there will often be an action in nuisance or negligence). There has been much debate over what does amount to natural and non-natural use of land. It is clear that a defendant will not be liable for damage caused by trees or plants which grow naturally, nor for the escape of water which is naturally present on the land. In **Giles** v **Walker** (1890), the defendant ploughed up forest land, with the result that a large crop of thistles grew there. The seeds from these blew on to neighbouring land, causing the same problem on that land. The defendant was held not liable under **Rylands** v **Fletcher** because thistles grew naturally, and had not been introduced by him.

An activity that may be considered natural in one context may be unnatural in another. Planting trees, for example, might well be a natural use in many cases, but in **Crowhurst** v **Amersham Burial Board** (1878), it was held not to be on the facts of that case. The defendants planted a yew tree on their land, and once it grew, branches protruded over into neighbouring land, where the claimant kept cattle. The cattle ate some of the yew leaves, which are poisonous to some animals, and died. The defendants were found to be liable under **Rylands** v **Fletcher** on the grounds that on the facts planting a yew tree was not a natural use of the land.

From the late nineteenth century, increasing industrialization in Britain led the courts to hold, in a series of cases, that industrial activity was a natural use of land, so that problems arising from such activity could not be dealt with under **Rylands** v **Fletcher**.

In **Rickards** v **Lothian** (1913), the defendant leased the upper part of a building. A tap there was turned on by an unknown person and caused a flood, which damaged stock kept by the claimant on the floor below. The defendant was held not liable, since he was making an ordinary and proper use of the building. The Court of Appeal defined non-natural use as: 'some special use bringing with it increased danger to others. [It] must not merely be the ordinary use of the land or such a use as is proper for the general benefit of the community.'

In a similar vein was **British Celanese** v **A H Hunt** (1969), where the defendants owned a factory on an industrial estate in which they manufactured electrical components. Strips of their metal foil escaped from the factory and blew on to an overhead cable, causing a power failure which stopped production at the claimant's factory. The defendants were held not liable under **Rylands** v **Fletcher**, because given where their factory was sited, theirs could not be called a non-natural use of land. There were no special risks attached to the storage of foil and the use was beneficial to the community. On the other hand, the defendants were held liable in both negligence and nuisance.

Such cases seemed to suggest that **Rylands** would be of little use in the field of environmental protection. However, **Rickards** and **British Celanese** have to be reconsidered in the light of the most recent House of Lords judgment on the subject: **Cambridge Water** v **Eastern Counties Leather** (1994). The defendants had carried out a leather manufacturing business for many years. In the tanning process they had used a particular chemical solvent until 1976, when they changed to another method of tanning. In carrying out the old tanning process there were frequent spillages of the solvent on to the concrete floor, amounting to over 1,000 tons of solvent over many years. This then seeped through the concrete floor and into the soil below. It polluted an area where the claimants, a water company, had their pumping station, extracting water for domestic consumption.

The pollution was only discovered in 1983 when changes in EC regulations forced the water company to make tests for such pollution. On discovering the problem the water company were forced to move their pumping station further upstream at a cost of over a million pounds.

They sued the leather manufacturers for the expenses they had incurred. The claim failed because the damage suffered was held to be too remote, but the importance of the case lies in what Lord Goff had to say on the issue of unnatural use. He stated that the storage of chemicals on industrial premises was a 'classic case of non-natural use'. Just because the activity benefited the community in that it created employment did not render such use of the land natural.

The dangerous thing

The thing which is brought on to the land must be likely to do damage if it escapes, even though it might be quite safe if not allowed to escape. Examples of 'dangerous things' from decided cases include gas (**Batchellor** v **Tunbridge Wells Gas Co** (1901)); electricity (**National Telephone Co** v **Baker** (1893)); poisonous fumes (**West** v **Bristol Tramways Co** (1908)); a flag pole (**Shiffman** v **Order of St John** (1936)); tree branches (**Crowhurst** v **Amersham Burial Board** (1878)) and one of the chairs, complete with occupant, from a fairground 'chair-o-plane' ride (**Hale** v **Jennings** (1938)).

Essentially this is a standard of foreseeability – the defendant will not be liable for damage caused by something which nobody could have foreseen as causing damage if it escaped. However, because this is a tort of strict liability, the fact that the possibility of escape was not foreseeable offers no defence.

Escape

The tort only covers damage caused when a dangerous thing escapes from the defendant's land; damage caused to someone else while they are on the defendant's land is not applicable. In **Read** v **Lyons** (1946), the claimant was an inspector of munitions, visiting the defendants' munitions factory. A shell being manufactured there exploded, injuring her, and because there was no suggestion that the defendants had been negligent, she claimed under **Rylands** v **Fletcher**. The defendants were held not liable, on the grounds that although high-explosive shells clearly were 'dangerous things', the strict liability imposed by **Rylands** v **Fletcher** requires an escape of the thing that caused the injury. The court defined an escape as occurring when something escapes to outside a place where the defendant has occupation and control.

It was traditionally thought the term 'escape' meant that the release of the dangerous thing had to be accidental. In **Crown River Cruises Ltd** v **Kimbolton Fireworks Ltd** (1996), however, it was suggested that **Rylands** could be extended to cover intentional releases of dangerous things (in that case letting off fireworks as part of a display), although the defendants in the case were not held liable under **Rylands**.

Damage

The tort is not actionable *per se*, so the escape of the dangerous thing must be proved to have caused damage. Obviously in most cases this will take the form of damage to land or other property. There are conflicting cases on whether damages are available in **Rylands** for personal injury, but the latest House of Lords' view, given in **Hunter** *v* **Canary Wharf**, is that they are not; however, since the remarks were *obiter* (because there was no personal injury in **Hunter** *v* **Canary Wharf**), the issue is still not regarded as entirely certain.

The claimant must prove causation under the normal rules (see p. 92). It was made clear in **Cambridge Water** *v* **Eastern Counties Leather** that the test for remoteness of damage in **Rylands** is reasonable foreseeability.

▶ Who can sue?

It seems likely, though there is some conflicting *dicta*, that the claimant must have some interest in the land on to which the thing escapes. In **Read** *v* **Lyons** (1946) the rule in **Rylands** *v* **Fletcher** was stated to be simply 'a principle applicable between occupiers in respect of their land'. Lord Simonds held that like nuisance, it could only be relied upon by someone who had suffered an invasion of some proprietary or other interest in land. Similarly, in **Weller & Co** *v* **Foot and Mouth Disease Research Institute** (1966), a virus escaped from the defendants' premises, with the result that a ban was placed on the movement of livestock locally. The claimants, who were cattle auctioneers, sued the defendants for loss of income, but it was held that they had no action under **Rylands**, because they had no interest in any of the land on to which the virus escaped.

Liability is strict

As we said at the beginning of this chapter, **Rylands** *v* **Fletcher** is the best-known example of a tort of strict liability. This means that the defendant may be liable even if they did not know that there was a danger, and/or could not have done anything to prevent it. However, this does not mean that liability is absolute; there are defences, and where liability is imposed, the defendant is only expected to pay for those consequences which were foreseeable.

▶ Defences

The general defences of *volenti*, contributory negligence, and statutory authority are applicable to **Rylands** *v* **Fletcher**, along with the related defences of common benefit and default of the claimant, and other specific defences discussed below.

Volenti and common benefit

Consent to the dangerous thing being on the claimant's land is a defence, and such consent can be implied or express. Consent will be implied where the presence of the thing offers some benefit to the claimant, as in the case of, for example, water tanks and pipes in a block of flats (some authorities treat this as a separate defence called common benefit).

Contributory negligence and default of the claimant

Where a claimant contributes to causing the escape of the dangerous thing, their damages can be reduced under the normal rules of contributory negligence. A further defence, known as default of the claimant, applies if the escape of the dangerous thing is completely the fault of the claimant, or, more commonly, if the escape only causes damage because of some abnormal sensitivity on the part of the claimant's property. This was the case in **Eastern and South Africa Telegraph Co** *v* **Cape Town Tramways Co** (1902), where the defendants were held not liable when a very minor escape of electricity caused by them affected the claimants' extremely sensitive power cables.

Statutory authority

Defendants may escape liability under **Rylands** *v* **Fletcher** if the terms of a relevant statute clearly authorize their actions. However, many Acts which permit the performance of dangerous activities do not specify whether the rule should apply, and the question then becomes one of interpretation of the particular statute. In **Green** *v* **Chelsea Waterworks Co** (1894), a water main laid by the defendant burst, flooding the claimant's premises. The Court of Appeal held that the company was not liable, because they were not only permitted, but obliged by statute to maintain a water supply, and occasional bursts were an inevitable result of such a duty. By contrast, in **Charing Cross Electricity Co** *v* **Hydraulic Co** (1914), which featured similar facts, the defendants were found not to have a defence of statutory authority, because the relevant statute did not oblige them to provide a water supply, but only gave them the power to do so.

Act of a stranger

A defendant will not be liable where the damage is done by a third party who is not acting under the defendant's instructions (note that that person need not literally be a stranger; the fact that the defendant knows them does not prevent the defence applying). This defence was applied in **Box** v **Jubb** (1879), where defendants were held not liable for damage done when their reservoir overflowed, because the flooding was caused by a third person who had emptied his own reservoir into the stream which fed the defendants' reservoir.

Where a defendant avoids liability under **Rylands** because the harm was caused by the act of a stranger, there may nevertheless be liability for negligence, if the act of the stranger was such that the defendant should have foreseen it and taken precautions against it.

Act of God

This defence is available when the escape is caused purely by natural forces, in circumstances which the defendant could not have been expected to foresee or guard against. In **Nichols** v **Marsland** (1876), the defendant dammed a natural stream in his land, in order to create three artificial lakes. The whole thing was well built, and precautions against flooding were quite adequate for all normal circumstances. However, an exceptionally heavy thunderstorm – described by witnesses as the heaviest in living memory – burst the banks of the lakes, and the resulting rush of water down the stream swept away four bridges on the claimant's land. The defendant was held not liable, because the thunderstorm was an act of God which he could not reasonably be expected to predict, and without it, the lakes would have been secure.

On the other hand, in **Greenock Corporation** v **Caledonian Railway Co** (1917), which involved similar facts, the defence was unsuccessful, even though the rain was exceptionally heavy. The corporation had built a concrete paddling pool for children, and in the process had changed the flow of a stream. After unusually heavy rainfall, the stream overflowed, and water poured down a public street into the town, damaging the claimant's property. The House of Lords concluded that the rainfall was not an act of God, and therefore the corporation were liable. Clearly these two decisions are difficult to reconcile, and the later case suggests that the availability of the defence will be rarer than the earlier case would imply.

▶ Relationship to other torts

Nuisance

The rule in **Rylands** v **Fletcher** has its origins in nuisance; in the case itself, the claimants relied almost exclusively on authorities from the law of nuisance. Now the two torts overlap to a certain extent. **Rylands** v **Fletcher**, however, has a more restricted application than nuisance, because of the specific requirements of accumulation, and of a substance likely to cause injury if it escapes, neither of which are necessary for liability in nuisance. In addition, the requirement of a non-natural use, though similar to the unreasonable user in nuisance, normally involves some degree of exceptional risk, which the unreasonable user does not. Nevertheless, in many factual situations, claimants will succeed equally well under **Rylands** v **Fletcher** or in nuisance.

Negligence

In **Rylands** v **Fletcher**, the degree of care taken by the defendant to avoid the escape continues to be irrelevant, since liability is strict. However, where the defendant puts forward the defences of act of God, act of a stranger, common benefit or statutory authority, the courts must examine not only the reasonableness of the accumulation, but also the defendant's responsibility for its actual escape, and although the steps to their decision may be different from those where negligence is alleged, the result is likely to be the same, as suggested in **Mason** v **Levy Auto Parts of England Ltd** (1967).

Trespass

On occasion judges have regarded the rule in **Rylands** v **Fletcher** as a kind of trespass (discussed in the next chapter), but the main difference is that in most **Rylands** v **Fletcher** cases the damage done is not direct.

▶ The role of Rylands **v** Fletcher

When **Rylands** v **Fletcher** was first decided, the tort could have been interpreted by future courts as a broad cause of action, imposing strict liability and available not just to injuries related to land but also to those concerning personal injury. However, with decisions such as **Read** v **Lyons** the courts chose not to move down this road, preferring the fault-based tort of negligence for most purposes. **Rylands** v **Fletcher** could still have had an important role to play as a tort that was aimed primarily at protecting the environment. But the range of restrictions that have been imposed before liability can be found has until recently limited its usefulness even in this role. The decision of **Cambridge Water** v **Eastern Counties Leather** has led some to hope that with the broadening of 'non-natural user' to include industrial activities the **Rylands** v **Fletcher** tort could now serve to protect the environment.

Some might argue that the rule in **Rylands** v **Fletcher** could be abolished altogether and reliance could be placed on other torts such as nuisance and negligence where it currently applies. But another view is that **Rylands** *v* **Fletcher** is still needed as a general action to deal with harm caused by hazardous activities, when the claimant for some reason cannot succeed under such fault-based torts as negligence. Judges may dislike the idea of strict liability in such cases, but the alternative is leaving an innocent claimant to bear the loss. **Read** *v* **Lyons** is a clear example of the injustice caused in such cases, when the restrictions placed on the rule in **Rylands** *v* **Fletcher** mean that in the absence of negligence, the injured claimant has no redress at all. Given that these days insurance against most types of liability is commonplace, it does not seem especially demanding or harsh to expect anyone who undertakes activities which may be hazardous to others to be responsible for any harm done.

Proposals for reform

The Royal Commission on Civil Liability and Compensation for Personal Injury proposed that the rule under **Rylands** *v* **Fletcher** should be abolished. It recommended that a new statute should give a Government Minister the power, with the aid of an advisory committee, to list in delegated legislation specific dangerous activities which would be held to incur strict liability. The statute would expressly provide for compensation for personal injuries caused by the listed activities.

Clearly this idea would allow for more predictability than under the present law, but there remains the problem of injuries caused by hazardous activities which were not listed, leaving claimants with no redress unless negligence could be proved. The rapid development of technology and science means it would be difficult for the list to keep pace with new hazardous activities, and it is highly likely that influential pressure groups – particularly in industry – would use behind-the-scenes pressure on Government to try to keep their own hazardous activities off the list. This problem could be dealt with to some extent by keeping the rule in **Rylands** *v* **Fletcher**, to run alongside the statutory scheme.

The Law Commission report on Civil Liability for Dangerous Things and Activities proposed the introduction of the concept of 'special danger', which could cover activities constituting an above-average risk of accidents or a risk of more than ordinary damage if accidents in fact occurred. This could provide the basis for new legislation replacing **Rylands** *v* **Fletcher**, which could impose strict liability on anyone who carries out 'abnormally dangerous' activities, without the problematic conditions and restrictions which currently apply.

A problem with this proposal would be knowing how the judiciary might interpret it, given their dislike of strict liability. This could give rise to considerable uncertainty.

Other protections against hazardous activities

Many of the activities which potentially could come under the rule in **Rylands** *v* **Fletcher** (and nuisance) are in fact regulated by statute, a recognition of the fact that an increasingly technological society brings risks as well as benefits. Some of these statutes impose strict liability for the escape of certain dangerous things, such as the Reservoirs Act 1975 regarding accumulated water, the Nuclear Installations Acts 1965 and 1969, which cover the escape of ionizing radiation, and the Consumer Protection Act 1987, which imposes strict liability for injuries caused by defective products.

ANSWERING QUESTIONS

1 **Give a critical explanation of the tort created in the case of** Rylands **v** Fletcher **(1868).**
Here you need to give the elements of the tort, explaining in what circumstances it is used, and detailing the defences to it, but at each step, you must go further than simply describing the tort, and include some comment on it. Issues to discuss include whether the tort has been too restrictively defined, whether it could and/or should play a greater role in protecting the environment, and to what extent it is and should be a tort of strict liability. A good way to sum up at the end might be by considering the tort's place in the wider law – does it fill a necessary gap? – and its possible future.

11 Trespass

There are three categories of trespass: trespass to the person, trespass to goods, and trespass to land. They protect claimants against interference with their bodies, their property and their land respectively.

All three are actionable *per se*, which means that the claimant only has to prove the tort has been committed; it is not necessary to prove that the trespass caused damage. For example, unwanted physical contact can constitute trespass to the person even though the claimant suffers no physical injury. The personal integrity and rights over property which the tort protects are considered so important that any infringement of them is a wrong, regardless of the damage caused.

Trespass requires an act which is direct and physical; where the rights protected by tort are infringed by an indirect act, there may be a remedy in a tort such as nuisance or negligence, but not in trespass. For example, if the defendant throws a brick which hits the claimant, this can be trespass; if, however, the defendant leaves bricks lying around and the claimant falls over them, the act would not be sufficiently direct to amount to trespass, though it might constitute the tort of negligence.

TRESPASS TO THE PERSON

There are three torts of trespass to the person: battery, assault and false imprisonment. All of them aim to protect an individual's right not to have their body touched, or freedom of movement interfered with, except where they have given consent.

▶ Battery

A battery is the direct and intentional application of force to another person without their consent.

Force

The force can consist of any physical contact with the claimant's body, or clothing being worn at the time; there is no requirement for violence or injury. For example, in **R** *v* **Chief Constable of Devon and Cornwall** (1982), it was pointed out that an unwanted kiss may be a battery; and in **Nash** *v* **Sheen** (1953) a hairdresser who caused a skin complaint by applying the wrong kind of chemical to a customer's hair was held to have committed a battery. Performing a surgical operation or even a haircut without consent may amount to battery, as may spitting at someone or throwing something at them (provided it hits them).

The contact must be direct and physical, so that, for example, obstructing a person's way without actually touching them is not a battery.

The mental element

It was once thought that battery was a strict liability offence, but modern cases make it clear that intention is the required mental state. The defendant must intend the act of touching the claimant; doing so carelessly is not sufficient.

In **Letang** *v* **Cooper** (1965) the claimant was sunbathing on a piece of grass outside a hotel, where cars were parked, and the defendant drove his car over the claimant's legs. The court held that the defendant had certainly been negligent, but had not intended to run the claimant over; therefore the appropriate action was negligence, and not trespass to the person.

It is only the physical contact that must be intentional; the defendant does not have to intend any resulting damage. In **Wilson** *v* **Pringle** (1986) the defendant, a schoolboy, admitted pulling the claimant's bag from his shoulder, which made the claimant fall over and injure himself. The act of pulling the bag was intentional, so he was held liable.

Hostility

In **Wilson** *v* **Pringle** the Court of Appeal held that the physical contact in a battery should have some element of hostility. Whether this element was present would be a question of fact in each case. The court said hostility need not necessarily mean malice or ill-will, but did not make clear exactly what hostility did mean.

The effect of a requirement of hostility is that in practice, it would mean that the claimant had to prove lack of consent. If there is no requirement of hostility, the defendant bears the burden of proving consent as a defence.

It appears from later cases that the **Wilson** *v* **Pringle** approach has not found favour, and therefore that hostility is not required. In the House of Lords case of **F** *v* **West Berkshire Health Authority** (1989) (the facts of which are not relevant here), Lord Goff expressed his disapproval of the idea of a requirement for hostility, explaining that it appeared to place unacceptable limits on the traditional principle that any touching of another person's body without lawful excuse was a trespass. This view has been supported in a number of recent cases, including **T** *v* **T** (1988), **R** *v* **Brown** (1994) and **R** *v* **Broadmoor Special Hospital Authority** (1997).

▶ Assault

When we speak of an assault in ordinary language, we generally think of someone being violent to someone else – hitting or punching them for example. As far as tort law is concerned, this sort of behaviour comes within the definition of battery, while assault has its own precise legal meaning. In tort, assault is defined as an act which causes another person reasonably to apprehend immediate violence to their person – **Collins** *v* **Wilcock** (1984). In practice, the two torts commonly arise together, the assault being closely followed by the battery.

Although the defendant need not touch the claimant, there must be some movement. In **Innes** *v* **Wylie** (1844) a police officer stood still and barred the claimant's way; this was held not to amount to assault.

Immediate violence

A threatening or frightening act will not constitute an assault unless its nature and the circumstances in which it occurs are such as to put the claimant in fear or apprehension of immediate violence. This has been taken to mean that there must be some likelihood of the person making the threat being able to carry it out immediately; it may be an assault to raise your hand at someone right in front of you, but probably not to do it from 200 yards down the street.

This rule was applied in **Thomas** *v* **National Union of Mineworkers** (1985), a case arising from the 1984 miners' strike. The claimant was a miner who refused to join his colleagues on strike, and was among a number of such workers who were brought into the pit by bus, past the picket lines. As the bus passed through, the striking miners made violent gestures at those inside it, but it was held that such acts could not constitute assault. The pickets were held back by a police cordon, and the claimant was inside the bus; he had no reasonable grounds for believing that the pickets could use immediate violence on him.

A contrasting case is **Stephens** *v* **Myers** (1830), which involved a parish meeting at which the Christian spirit was decidedly thin on the ground. The claimant was chairing the meeting when the defendant, who was sitting six or seven places away from the claimant, started shouting. A majority of the people present voted that the defendant should be expelled from the meeting, at which point he approached the claimant with a clenched fist. He was restrained by the churchwarden, who was sitting between him and the claimant, but was nevertheless held liable for assault.

Since the essence of the tort is that the claimant should fear that the defendant will use violence, threatening behaviour that the claimant is unaware of cannot amount to assault.

Words

It was traditionally thought that words alone could not be sufficient to amount to an assault, a principle established in the old case of **R v Meade** (1823). However, it has always been difficult to see a rational basis for the distinction; the whole essence of the tort is that it induces fear in the claimant, and words are as capable of doing this as acts – it may be no less frightening to hear someone say 'I'll kill you' than to see them raise their fist. The distinction has been abolished within the criminal law, where it was held in **R v Costanza** (1997), that the words of a stalker could amount to a criminal assault; it was also held in **R v Ireland and Burstowe** (1997) that a criminal assault could be comprised of making silent phone calls. It is thought likely that the civil law will also abolish this distinction when an appropriate case comes before the courts.

In some cases, an act which would otherwise amount to an assault may be prevented from doing so by the words which accompany it. An example occurred in **Turberville v Savage** (1669), where the defendant had reached for his sword and told the claimant, 'If it were not assize time, I would not take such language from you.' Since it was assize time (which meant that the judge was in town), the words prevented the act of reaching for his sword from being an assault, because they meant that the claimant knew there was no danger of immediate violence.

The mental element

There must be an intention to frighten the claimant, but there need be no intention or even power to use the threatened violence. In **R v St George** (1840) it was held that pointing a gun at someone in a threatening manner was an assault, even though the defendant knew it was not loaded. The result would probably be different if the claimant also knew it was not loaded, since they would not apprehend immediate violence.

Criminal law

Assault and battery constitute criminal offences as well as torts. Under the Offences Against the Person Act 1861, some relatively minor criminal proceedings prevent any additional civil proceedings arising from the same incident.

▶ False imprisonment

False imprisonment can be defined as the unlawful prevention of another from exercising their freedom of movement. In this context, 'false' really means wrongful.

Imprisonment

The tort is not limited to actually locking someone away; the claimant merely has to be completely deprived of their personal liberty for any length of time, no matter how short. Depriving someone of their clothes could amount to false imprisonment, as could holding their arm so they cannot walk away, or unlawfully arresting them.

However, the defendant must have prevented the claimant from moving in any direction; there is no false imprisonment where the claimant is prevented from going in some directions, but left free to go in others. This point was made in the case of **Bird** *v* **Jones** (1845). A boat race was to be run along the Thames. The defendants fenced off part of the public footway on Hammersmith Bridge, put seats in it, and charged for admission. The claimant demanded to be allowed to walk along the footpath as usual, and climbed into the closed-off area without paying. The defendants would not let him walk on across the enclosure, and said he could go back on to the road, and cross to the other side of the bridge. He was not prepared to do this, and sued the defendants for false imprisonment. They were held not liable.

Where one way is blocked but others left open, those left open must be reasonable in all the circumstances of the case, and it is unlikely that a defendant will escape liability for false imprisonment if the only available ways are dangerous.

The claimant must actually have been deprived of their liberty; the fact that a defendant had both the power and intention to do so, but had no need to because the claimant stayed voluntarily is not sufficient. This was the situation in **R** *v* **Bournewood Community and Mental Health NHS Trust, ex parte L (Secretary of State for Health intervening)** (1998). A profoundly mentally handicapped man had become agitated during a visit to a day centre, and when his carers could not be contacted, he was taken to hospital on the advice of a doctor. The psychiatrist there decided that he was in need of in-patient treatment, and he was admitted. The hospital could have used powers available under the Mental Health Act 1983 to detain him against his will, but as he did not resist admission, there was no need to do so, and he was placed on an unlocked ward. However, nurses were instructed to keep him under constant observation, and it was clear that if he had tried to leave, the hospital would have used the statutory powers to prevent him from doing so. Did this amount to imprisonment for the purposes of a claim for false imprisonment? The Court of Appeal held that it did, but the House of Lords disagreed. They said that the deprivation of liberty must actually have happened in order for there to be an 'imprisonment'; the fact that the hospital could and would have detained him if he had tried to leave was not enough.

A positive act

The false imprisonment must be caused by a direct, positive act, and not merely someone's carelessness. In **Sayers** *v* **Harlow Urban District Council** (1958) the claimant was trapped in a toilet cubicle by a defective lock, and injured herself trying to escape. It was held that lack of a direct act meant there could be no liability for false imprisonment. Instead the council were found to be negligent. However, there need not be any force, and in fact false imprisonment can be achieved by words – for example, a threat to the effect of 'Stay there or I'll kill you.'

An interesting issue arose in the recent Court of Appeal case of **Davidson** *v* **Chief Constable of North Wales** (1994). The claimant's friend had bought a cassette tape from a shop and then chatted with the claimant before leaving the shop. The store detective saw the two of them leave and formed the mistaken belief that they were leaving without having paid for the cassette. She therefore rang the police and on their arrival she pointed out to them the claimant and his friend, saying that the claimant had taken the cassette without paying. The police approached the two of them and the friend was unable to prove that he had paid for the cassette because he had thrown away the receipt. They were arrested and taken to the police station but then released two hours later after a message was received from the shop assistant who remembered serving the friend.

Following this incident the claimant brought an action against the store detective's employers for false imprisonment. The police had a defence of lawful arrest, but the store detective fell outside those provisions, because as a private citizen and not a police officer, she only had a power of arrest (and therefore also of imprisonment) where an offence had been committed; it was not sufficient that she had reasonable grounds to believe that one had been committed. The defendants therefore argued that it was the police who had done the positive act of carrying out the arrest and not the store detective, she having merely provided the relevant information. However, there was evidence that the police always arrested whenever she provided such information and she considered that such arrests were carried out on her behalf.

The court held that the test was 'whether the defendant has merely given information to a properly constituted authority on which that authority may act or not as it decides or whether he has himself been the instigator, promoter and active inciter of the action that follows'. The store detective would be treated as having carried out the arrest and therefore of wrongly imprisoning the claimant if she had done something that 'went beyond laying information before the police officers for them to take such action as they thought fit and amounted to some direction, or procuring, or direct request, or direct encouragement that they should act by way of arresting these defendants'.

The court concluded that on the evidence it was the police who had carried out the arrest and the action for damages therefore failed as the police had a defence to the claim of false imprisonment.

Knowledge of the detention

In the past it was considered that the claimant had to be aware of the false imprisonment at the time it occurred. In **Herring** *v* **Boyle** (1834) a child who had been kept behind at school because his parents had not paid the fees was held not to have been falsely imprisoned, because he was unaware of the detention.

However, more modern cases suggest that a defendant may be liable even though the claimant is unaware of the false imprisonment. In **Meering** *v* **Grahame-White Aviation Co Ltd** (1920) the defendants suspected the claimant, their employee, of stealing paint. He was not told of their suspicions, but was asked to go with two police officers to his employer's offices. Without the claimant's knowledge, the officers remained outside the door while he was questioned. The claimant sued for false imprisonment, and the defendants argued that he had been unaware of any detention, and believed he was quite free to leave if he wanted to, but merely did not want to. The Court of Appeal held that the defendants were liable, because as soon as the claimant came under the influence of the police, he could not be said to be a free agent, and knowledge of the detention was irrelevant to whether the tort had been committed; in fact it was held the tort could even be committed while the claimant was asleep.

This approach was affirmed, *obiter*, by the House of Lords, in **Murray** *v* **Ministry of Defence** (1988). However, where a person was completely unaware of being detained, and suffered no actual harm from it, only nominal damages would normally be awarded.

The mental element

The case of **R** *v* **Governor of Brockhill Prison** (2000) makes it plain that false imprisonment is a tort of strict liability; if the claimant is imprisoned and there is no lawful excuse for that imprisonment, the defendant will be liable, even if there was nothing they could have done to prevent the imprisonment. The claimant in the case had been convicted for a number of criminal offences, and had been sentenced to different lengths of time in prison for them, but the sentences were to run concurrently (rather than one after the other). She had already served time in prison on remand for some of the offences, and so the calculation of how long she should serve in prison after sentencing was a complicated one. In working it out, the prison governor used rules set down in case law, but the claimant disagreed with the outcome, and went to court, arguing that she had been imprisoned for longer than was lawful. The court agreed with her calculation, and ordered her immediate release; she then sued the prison governor for false imprisonment during the time she was held in prison after the date on which she should have been released. The House of Lords stated that although the governor had had no choice about the way he made his calculations, since he was obliged to follow decisions which at the time were thought to represent the law, he was nevertheless liable because false imprisonment was a tort of strict liability.

Defences

The most important general defence in trespass to the person is *volenti*. Contributory negligence, statutory authority and inevitable accident also apply, and there are some specific defences.

Volenti

The normal rules on the defence of *volenti* (discussed at p. 111) apply. It is important to note that consent will frequently be implied, rather than expressed. When you sit down in a hairdresser's chair, for example, you consent by implication to having your hair touched, and consent is implied to such physical contacts that are a reasonably necessary and ordinary consequence of everyday life, such as touching someone on the shoulder to attract their attention, or accidentally bumping into someone in the street (**Collins** *v* **Wilcock** (1984)).

There are, however, areas where the issue of implied consent can cause difficulties – this is the main reason why the courts have suggested a requirement of hostility in battery, because consent cannot be implied where the touching is obviously hostile.

In **Herd** *v* **Weardale Steel Coke and Coal Co** (1915), a miner, employed by the defendants, went down the mine to start his shift as usual. During the shift, a dispute arose, and he demanded to be returned immediately to the surface. His employers refused to allow him use of the lift, and he was left there for 20 minutes, before they relented and brought him out. The House of Lords held that this was not false imprisonment, even though the motive might have been to punish the claimant. The defence of *volenti* applied because all the miners had, by implication, consented to stay underground until the end of the shift, and no one was entitled to be taken to the surface until then.

In **Robinson** *v* **Balmain Ferry Co Ltd** (1910) the claimant paid one penny to cross a river in one of the defendant's ferries. He entered the defendants' wharf but having just missed the ferry he decided not to wait for the next one, which would leave in 20 minutes, and wanted to leave the wharf. A notice stated that there was a one penny exit charge, and the defendants refused to allow him through the turnstile unless he paid this. The court held that this was not false imprisonment. The condition that a penny should be paid was reasonable, and the claimant had contracted to leave the wharf by another way. The basis of the decision seems to be consent; the claimant consented to a contract which restricted his movements, and therefore reasonable limitations on his movement could be imposed. One implication of these cases is that travellers on public transport cannot insist on getting off except at a scheduled stop.

Consent is always limited to the act for which permission is given. In **Nash** *v* **Sheen** (1953), the claimant had asked her hairdresser for a perm, but in fact the hairdresser applied a colourant, which caused a skin complaint. The hairdresser was held liable for battery; this would not have been the case if a perm had in fact been applied, and had caused the skin complaint, because the customer had consented to a perm.

Any medical or surgical treatment administered without consent may amount to trespass, though consent can often be implied and sometimes doctors will have the defence of necessity, in emergency situations.

The issue of consent often arises in the context of sports. For example a competitor in a game of rugby might argue that he was assaulted by another player, or a spectator hit by the ball at a football match might make this claim. As with negligence (see p. 115), the approach of the courts is that players and spectators accept the risks of contact and injury that occur during the course of the game being played according to the rules, but not if the rules were breached, for example if the tackle on the rugby player amounted to a foul.

Some writers have suggested that these sports cases can be better explained on the basis that while the sport is being carried out according to its rules, no tort has actually been committed so there is no need to fall back on a defence such as consent.

Contributory negligence

The normal rules on contributory negligence apply in cases of trespass to the person (see p. 108).

Statutory authority

There are a number of statutes which authorize trespass to the person in particular circumstances. One of the most important is the Criminal Law

Act 1967, which in s. 3(1) provides that no trespass to the person is committed when a reasonable amount of force is used to lawfully arrest a person, prevent a crime or assist in the lawful detention of a person unlawfully at large (such as an escaped prisoner). A sentence of imprisonment passed by a court provides a complete defence to an action for false imprisonment.

The question of when an arrest will be lawful for the purposes of the defence was addressed in **Percy** *v* **Hall** (1996). The claimants had been arrested for breach of certain byelaws. They argued that the byelaws were invalid (for reasons which are derived from public law, and not important here). The court said that the byelaws were in fact valid, but even if they had not been, this would not have prevented the defence of statutory authority, so long as the arresting officers had acted in the reasonable belief that the claimants were committing an offence.

Statutes also authorize certain medical examinations and tests, such as the breathalyser test under the Road Traffic Act 1988, and blood tests under the Family Law Reform Act 1969. If taken without consent, any of these tests would normally amount to battery, but statutory authority provides a defence.

Inevitable accident

A defendant will not be liable in trespass to the person for an event over which they had no control, and could not have avoided by using even the greatest care and skill. In **Stanley** *v* **Powell** (1891), the defendant was part of a shooting party, and the claimant was employed to carry their cartridges. The defendant fired a shot in the usual way, but through no fault of his own, the bullet ricocheted off a tree and injured the claimant. It was held that the injury was an inevitable accident and the defendant was not liable.

Self-defence

A defendant is covered by this defence when using reasonable force for self-protection, or to protect another person or property. What constitutes reasonable force will be a question of fact in each case, but the basic principle is that the degree of force must be balanced against the seriousness of the attack. So, for example, a degree of force which would be considered reasonable to protect life might be thought unreasonable where only property was at risk.

Lane *v* **Holloway** (1968) concerned a dispute between neighbours. The claimant had been drinking, and was standing talking to a friend outside his house, when the defendant's wife yelled out at them, 'You bloody lot.' The claimant replied, 'Shut up you monkey-faced tart.' Hearing this, the defendant came out and said he wanted to see the claimant alone. Believing he was about to be hit, the claimant smacked the defendant on the shoulder, and the defendant responded by punching the claimant in the eye, causing a wound which needed 19 stitches. Although it was accepted that the defendant had cause to defend himself, his blow was held to be out of proportion to the danger, so that he was not covered by the defence of self-defence.

Ejection of a trespasser

An occupier of land, or any other person with the authority of the occupier, may use a reasonable degree of force to prevent a trespasser from entering, or, after entry, to control a trespasser's movements or eject them. However, before an ejection will be justified, the trespasser must have been requested to leave, and given a reasonable opportunity of doing so peaceably.

Parental authority

Parents may exercise reasonable restraint or chastisement on their children, without being guilty of trespass to the person.

▶ The role of trespass to the person today

Trespass to the person has now lost most of its significance in personal injury litigation. There are three main reasons for this: the existence of the Criminal Injuries Compensation Scheme; the power of the criminal courts to grant compensation orders against defendants, which often remove the need for a civil action; and the development of negligence, which has become the principal vehicle for litigation concerning personal injuries, with the approval of the courts. In **Sidaway** *v* **Governors of Bethlem Royal Hospital** (1985), for example, it was held that the appropriate tort for personal injuries resulting from medical treatment is not battery but negligence.

Trespass to the person now arises mainly in the area of civil liberties, often associated with allegedly improper police conduct. Although in some such cases no real physical harm is done to the claimant, the possibility of exemplary damages to mark disapproval of the defendant's conduct can mean that damages in these cases may be very substantial.

▶ Other protections from physical harm

There are two further torts concerned with causing intentional harm to the person, which are usually discussed alongside trespass to the person, even though they differ from it in important respects. The first is a common law tort, defined in the case of **Wilkinson *v* Downton**, and the second is the statutory tort of harassment created in the Protection from Harassment Act 1997, which we discuss later on in this chapter.

The tort in Wilkinson **v** Downton

In the case of **Wilkinson *v* Downton** (1897), the defendant, who clearly had a dubious sense of humour, had played what she saw as a practical joke on the claimant, by telling her that her husband had been seriously injured in an accident. The claimant believed her and suffered serious psychiatric illness as a result. The defendant could not be liable for trespass to the person, as there was no direct interference with the claimant's person. However, the court found that she was nevertheless liable in tort. The judge explained the basis for the ruling as:

> The defendant has . . . wilfully done an act calculated to cause physical harm to the plaintiff . . . and has in fact thereby caused physical harm to her. That proposition, without more, appears to me to state a good cause of action, there being no justification for the alleged act.

The ruling has only been followed in one other English case, **Janvier *v* Sweeney** (1919). The claimant was engaged to a German, and the defendants threatened that unless she stole a particular letter from her employer and gave it to them, they would tell the authorities that her fiancé was a spy. Although this was not true, the political climate at the time, just after the end of World War 1, made this a frightening threat, and she suffered a nervous illness as a result. The Court of Appeal held that the defendants' behaviour fell within the tort explained in **Wilkinson *v* Downton**.

The tort also appeared to attract judicial approval in the more recent case of **Khorasandjian *v* Bush** (1994), where the claimant had been harassed by telephone calls and threats from a former boyfriend. The case was actually decided on the basis that the behaviour constituted a nuisance, but the Court of Appeal also expressed the opinion that the behaviour complained of was covered by **Wilkinson *v* Downton**. This view was then backed up by the House of Lords in **Hunter *v* Canary Wharf** (1997), where they overruled the decision that the situation in **Khorasandjian** could amount to nuisance (because the claimant did not have sufficient interest in land – see p. 228), but said that the defendant's behaviour in that case was still tortious, and 'must be seen as a case of intentional harassment'.

Elements of the tort

Because of the lack of decided cases, it is not easy to establish the boundaries of liability for the tort in **Wilkinson *v* Downton**. We do know from the definition in **Wilkinson** that there must be harm to the claimant, so the tort is not actionable *per se*, but the issues open to question concern the defendant's behaviour, the kind of harm caused to the claimant, and the mental state of the defendant.

As far as the first issue, the defendant's behaviour, is concerned, we know from the two decided cases that threats and false statements fall within the tort; however in principle there seems to be no reason why other acts which are calculated to cause physical harm and do cause such harm should not be covered, such as perhaps shocking the claimant with a loud noise, or even intentionally infecting them with a contagious disease (but remember that a direct act which causes harm would be more likely to be sued as a trespass). Similarly, a true statement rather than a false one might be sufficient, so long as the person making it intended to harm the claimant by doing so.

With regard to the harm caused, the term used by the court was 'physical harm'; this clearly included psychiatric harm, since that was the damage in the case, but use of the broad term suggests actual physical harm would also be included. The case of **Khorasandjian** has been taken by some commentators to suggest that the harm covered may go beyond actual psychiatric damage and include mental distress. The claimant in the case had not actually suffered psychiatric damage, but had been put under enormous stress and emotional upset, and was asking for an injunction to prevent the harassment that caused this. It could be argued that therefore the damage aimed at was still actual psychiatric injury, in that the stress was likely to lead to such injury, and the injunction was therefore designed to prevent it. However, the practical result was that the claimant could obtain a remedy against stress and upset, whereas in negligence this is not actionable damage; the distinction, if it exists, may be justified given that the acts in **Wilkinson** are intentional.

What about other types of harm? In an Australian case, **Smith** *v* **Beaudesert Shire Council** (1966), an attempt was made to extend the tort to cover economic loss, but the House of Lords firmly ruled this out in **Lonrho Ltd** *v* **Shell Petroleum** (1982).

Finally, what is the mental element of the tort in **Wilkinson**? The term generally used is that the behaviour must be 'intentional', but what does this mean? Does the defendant have to intend harm, or merely intend the behaviour which in fact causes harm? If viewed as normal everyday language, the phrase 'calculated to cause physical harm' used in **Wilkinson** suggests the former explanation, but the facts of the case lean more towards the latter, and the question was unfortunately not an issue in either **Janvier** *v* **Sweeney** or **Khorasandjian**.

The Protection from Harassment Act 1997

This Act was passed following public concern over the problem of 'stalkers', after a number of much-publicized cases in which individuals became obsessed with an ex-girlfriend or boyfriend, a celebrity or even a mere acquaintance, and subjected them to constant and often long-term harassment. It imposes both criminal and civil sanctions for 'harassment'. Civil remedies allowed under the Act include injunctions and damages; damages can be claimed for mental distress and even pure economic loss resulting from the harassment.

The Act does not define harassment. Section 1 states that the offence consists of pursuing a 'course of conduct' which amounts to harassment, and which that person knows or ought to know amounts to harassment. The phrase 'ought to know' is explained as applying where a reasonable person, who knows what the defendant knows, would think the behaviour amounted to harassment. Harassment is said to include alarming someone or causing them distress, and conduct can include speech; a 'course of conduct' must involve harassment on at least two occasions.

Clearly the statutory tort of harassment under the 1997 Act has considerable potential overlap with the tort in **Wilkinson** *v* **Downton**, which, along with the fact that **Wilkinson** is so rarely used, has led to some suggestions that it will now quietly wither away; Lord Hoffmann is one who has suggested that the 1997 Act means that there is no longer any need for the common law to develop in this area. However, it can also be argued the tort in **Wilkinson** still has a role to play in dealing with intentional, indirect harm which might not be covered by the term harassment – an example being the conduct in **Wilkinson** itself, which, being limited to one occasion, would not amount to a 'course of conduct' as required by the Act.

TRESPASS TO GOODS

This is sometimes called interference with goods. It covers intentional, direct and unlawful injury to, or interference with, goods in the possession of another. Examples of trespass to goods might include riding someone else's bicycle without permission, taking the stereo from someone's car, or throwing someone's book out of the window.

As the tort, like the other forms of trespass, is actionable *per se*, the goods need not be damaged, nor does the claimant have to be permanently deprived of them – merely moving or touching them may suffice. In **Kirk** *v* **Gregory** (1876), the defendant's brother-in-law had died, and she moved his jewellery from one room to another, where she thought it would be safer. It was then stolen by an unknown person, and the deceased's executor successfully sued the defendant for trespass. However, the damages awarded were nominal.

Where damage is caused, the defendant will only be liable to compensate for that damage which was reasonably foreseeable. This was established in **Kuwait Airways Corporation** *v* **Iraqi Airways Co (No 5)** (2000), where the court held that trespass to goods should be subject to the same rules on remoteness of damage as negligence (see p. 99).

▶ Elements of the tort

Intentional and direct interference

Purely accidental interference with goods is not actionable in trespass (though it may be in negligence, if damage is caused). Actual physical contact is not necessary, but the defendant must have done some form of direct act, on purpose.

Goods in the possession of another

The claimant need not actually own the goods, only have possession of them at the time of the trespass. Someone who has borrowed or hired goods will be regarded as being in possession of them, as will what is called a bailee of goods, such a shoemaker with shoes sent for repair, or a garage with a car brought in to be fixed. This means that in such cases the owner of the goods cannot sue the party in possession for trespass. Even wrongful possession may be sufficient against a trespasser who does not have better title to the goods.

▶ Defences

Statutory authority

The police commit no trespass to goods when they exercise their lawful powers of search and seizure, as they have a defence of statutory authority.

Necessity

Provided that the conduct is reasonable in the circumstances, the defence of necessity provides that it is lawful to interfere with or damage goods in order to avert immediate danger to people or property. As usual with this type of defence, the degree of interference or damage must be balanced against the threatened harm. In **Cresswell** *v* **Sirl** (1948), the defendant was responsible for shooting the claimant's dog, which had been worrying the defendant's pregnant sheep. Although the dog was not attacking the sheep at the time, it was held that shooting it was justified by the threatened harm, and therefore lawful.

Volenti

Consent to a trespass may be implied from the claimant's conduct. In **Arthur** *v* **Anker** (1996) a company which clamped a car parked on private land was held to have a defence of consent. Notices displayed prominently had warned that anyone parking without authorization would be clamped, and by parking there, the claimant was deemed to have accepted that risk.

This issue was addressed again in **Vine** *v* **Waltham Forest Borough Council** (2000). The facts were similar, but the claimant maintained that the defence should not apply because she had not seen the warning notices. On the day in question, she had been driving home from a hospital appointment when she began to feel sick. She had parked her car hurriedly, not seeing a sign on the wall behind, walked some distance away from the car and then vomited. When she got back to the car a few minutes later, it had been clamped.

The Court of Appeal said that it in order to be protected by the defence, the defendant had to prove that the claimant was aware of the consequences of parking her car on the land concerned, and this meant establishing that the claimant had seen and understood the warning sign. This did not mean that the claimant necessarily had to read all the details; seeing the notice and realizing what it was about could be enough, even if the claimant had not bothered to read it properly and find out exactly what would happen to cars parked on that land. However, where a claimant had not even seen the sign, they could not be said to have been aware of the consequences of parking on that land, and so the defence could not apply.

TRESPASS TO LAND

Trespass to land involves unjustifiable interference with land which is in the immediate and exclusive possession of another. Again, it is not necessary to prove damage to land; the tort is actionable *per se*.

▶ Elements of the tort

Land

Land includes not only the soil itself, but things under it, any building that is fixed to the surface, and such airspace above as is needed for the normal use and enjoyment of the land and the structures on it. This means that trespass may arise from tunnelling under land in possession of another, even though neither end of the tunnel is on that land, or from invading the air above it. In **Anchor Brewhouse Developments** *v* **Berkley House (Docklands) Developments** (1987), the arms of tower cranes situated on the defendants' land occasionally crossed the airspace above the claimants' land; the defendants were held liable for trespass, even though the cranes were at a height which meant that the normal use of the land was not affected.

The Civil Aviation Act 1982 provides that there is no trespass where civilian aircraft fly over property at a reasonable height; however, the Act imposes strict liability for damage caused by the taking off or landing of such aircraft, or by anything falling from them.

Possession

The defendant need not own the land, but must be in possession of it. In this context, possession means the right to exclude others from the land. Such possession must be immediate (meaning that it must exist at the time the trespass is committed). Therefore, for example, if someone trespasses on rented premises, it is the tenant who has the right to sue for trespass, and not the landlord.

Simply being on the land does not amount to possession for the purposes of trespass, and because possession must be exclusive, a lodger in someone's house or a guest in a hotel will not usually have possession in this context.

Interference

The interference must be direct and physical; indirect interference may give rise to an action for negligence or nuisance, but not for trespass. So if, for example, your next-door neighbour prunes their roses and throws the clippings into your garden, that may be trespass. However, if they simply fail to prune them, so that they overhang your garden, that may be nuisance, but is not trespass.

Interference covers entry on to land which is in the immediate and exclusive possession of another, remaining on such land when asked to leave or when permission to be there expires, abusing a right of entry to such land, and placing or throwing something on to such land.

Entering land

Even the slightest crossing of a boundary can suffice here, such as putting your hand through a window.

Abuse of right of entry

A person who has permission to enter land, but does something which goes beyond what has been allowed, may be guilty of trespass. An example would be where students in a hall of residence have permission to go into their own rooms, and use the communal areas, but would commit trespass by going into another student's room without permission. Abuse of right of entry also applies where someone is allowed on to land for a certain purpose and then does something unrelated to that purpose – for example, if you allow someone into your home to paint the kitchen, and they then go and have a look round the bedrooms without your permission.

Remaining on land

A person who has lawfully entered land in the possession of another, and then remains there after the permission expires, or after being asked to leave, commits a trespass.

Placing things on land

It is a trespass to throw or place anything on to land occupied by another. It is not necessary that the boundaries are crossed, so long as there is some physical contact with the claimant's property, so trespass could arise from, for example, planting a vine so that it grows up the claimant's wall, piling rubbish against a fence, or leaning a bike against a shop window.

A common example of such trespass occurs when livestock stray on to land. In **League Against Cruel Sports** *v* **Scott** (1985) the defendant was the master of a hunt, and the claimants, an anti-bloodsports organization, owned certain areas of Exmoor, which they had purchased for the purpose of creating sanctuaries for wild deer. On seven occasions, the hunt's hounds strayed on to the sanctuaries, and the court granted an injunction. It was held that persistent hunting near the prohibited land, when there was no effective way of preventing the hounds from straying on to it, could be evidence of an intention to trespass.

Trespass on highways

The owners of the soil on which a highway rests are treated as having possession of it for the purposes of trespass. There is no trespass where a person uses a highway to get from one place to another, or for anything which is incidental to that, such as stopping to look in a shop window, or consult a map.

It was traditionally thought that anyone who uses the highway for any other purpose becomes a trespasser. In **Hickman** *v* **Maisey** (1900) the claimant owned land on which racehorses were trained. A highway crossed this land, and while the horses were undergoing trials, the defendant, who owned a racing newspaper, spent two hours walking up and down, watching the horses and taking notes on how well they were performing. It was held that this went beyond using the highway for its normal purpose, and he was liable for trespass.

However, the case of **DPP** *v* **Jones** (1999) has changed the law in this area. The case was actually a criminal one, in which a group of people were charged with the offence of trespassory assembly under the Public Order Act 1986, but it has relevance for tort law because the offence requires that the defendants have committed a trespass within the meaning of the tort. The defendants in the case had staged a demonstration at the side of the road adjoining the fence around Stonehenge. None of them were behaving in a destructive or violent way, and nobody else using the highway was obstructed by their presence. On the traditional view that it is trespass to do anything on the highway that amounts to more than getting from one place to another or the activities stemming from that process, the defendants would have been committing the tort of trespass. However, Lord Irvine, giving the leading judgment, held that this approach had become outdated. He presented a more modern test, concluding that:

> . . . the public highway is a public place which the public may enjoy for any reasonable purpose, provided that the activity in question does not amount to a public or private nuisance and does not obstruct the highway by unreasonably impeding the primary right of the public to pass and repass; within these qualifications there is a public right of peaceful assembly on the highway.

The case makes it clear that there is a right to do more than simply pass along the highway, but quite what that right can comprise is unclear. Lord Irvine stated that in each case, it will be for the trial court to decide whether the use of the highway is reasonable, and consistent with the right of other people to pass along it.

Continuing trespass

Trespass is said to be 'continuing' and can justify a series of legal actions for as long as it lasts. This arises mainly in cases of objects placed on the land, where the trespass continues until they are removed. In **Holmes** *v* **Wilson** (1839), the highway authorities had built a road which was supported by buttresses on the claimant's land. Building these buttresses was held to be a trespass, and they had to pay damages. However, they did not take the buttresses away, and so were found liable in a subsequent action for trespass.

Trespass by relation

A person who has a right to take immediate possession of land, and enters it in order to exercise that right, is regarded as having been in possession ever since the right of entry accrued. They may therefore sue for any trespass committed since the right of entry accrued. This principle allows a tenant to sue for any trespass committed between the time when the tenancy was agreed, and the time when they entered in pursuance of it; this is known as trespass by relation.

Trespass *ab initio*

Where a person's entry on to land is permitted by statute or common law, rather than merely by permission of the occupier, and the person does a wrongful act while there, that act makes the original entry a trespass, and not just the wrongful act. This is known as trespass *ab initio*. It was first defined in the old case of **The Six Carpenters** (1610). Here six carpenters went into an inn (which they had a lawful right to do), ordered bread and wine, and paid for it. Later, they ordered more wine, and this time refused to pay. The court held that a wrongful act committed at this stage could retrospectively render their original entry unlawful. However, the defendants were not held liable because they had not committed an act, only an omission, which does not suffice.

The doctrine allows the claimant to recover damages for the entire transaction, and not just for the wrongful part of it. In modern times it arises principally in connection with the exercise of police powers, and recent cases make it clear that the wrongful act will only render the original entry unlawful where it takes away the entire basis for the lawful entry. In **Elias** *v* **Pasmore** (1934), police officers wanted to arrest a man and had legally entered the claimant's land in order to do so. While on the land they seized a number of items, some lawfully and some unlawfully. It was held that they had committed trespass only with regard to the documents unlawfully removed; their wrongful act did not disturb the main purpose of entry, which was to make a lawful arrest.

This approach has taken away much of the power of the *ab initio* doctrine, and in **Chic Fashions (West Wales) Ltd** *v* **Jones** (1968), the Court of Appeal criticized the very existence of the doctrine, saying it ran counter to the principle that subsequent events cannot make an act unlawful if it was lawful when it was originally carried out. In this case the police were searching the claimant's premises for stolen goods, and seized goods which they wrongly thought to be stolen. The seizure was held to be lawful, because police entering premises with a warrant have authority to remove anything which they believe has been stolen.

This criticism was ignored in the later case of **Cinnamond** *v* **British Airports Authority** (1980) where the principle was applied to mini-cab drivers who were unlawfully touting for business.

▶ The mental element

Most trespasses are obviously intentional, and so the state of mind of the defendant is rarely an issue. However, the decision in **League Against Cruel Sports** *v* **Scott** (above) suggests that trespass to land can be committed negligently.

Where a person trespasses accidentally, either being unaware that the land is private, or mistakenly believing it is their own, liability is incurred nevertheless. However, it is well established that where a defendant unintentionally enters land adjoining the highway (perhaps where a car leaves the road as a result of an accident), the claimant must prove negligence (**River Wear Commissioners** *v* **Adamson** (1877)).

Defences

Licence

Where the person in possession of land gives someone permission, express or implied, to be on that land, there is no trespass, so long as the boundaries of that permission are not exceeded. This is called giving a person licence to be on the land.

Some licences are irrevocable and some statutes lay down restrictions on the revocation of licences such as residential licences, in order to protect the security of a person's home. However, a licence which is given without valuable consideration (that is, it is given rather than sold) can be revoked at any time. Where a licence is given by contract, it can also be revoked at any time, though this may result in liability for breach of contract. Once a licence is revoked, the person to whom it was granted must be allowed a reasonable time in which to leave and remove their goods; after that, they become a trespasser.

Justification by law

People sometimes avoid liability for trespass because the law provides some justification for their conduct. For example, much of the conduct of the police would amount to a trespass but for the provisions of the Police and Criminal Evidence Act 1984. Section 17 of this Act allows a police officer to enter and search premises in order to carry out an arrest.

Jus tertii

A defendant may have a defence to an action for trespass if it can be shown that the land rightfully belongs neither to the person in possession nor to the person claiming the land, but to a third person. This was established in **Doe d. Carter** *v* **Barnard** (1849).

There is one exception to this rule. If a tenant takes a lease, and it turns out that the landlord had no right to grant the lease, the tenant cannot set up the defence of *jus tertii* against the landlord.

Necessity

Necessity has been allowed as a defence to trespass, for example in **Esso Petroleum Co** *v* **Southport Corporation** (1956), where a sea captain was forced to discharge oil, which then polluted the shoreline, in order to prevent his ship breaking up and endangering the crew after it ran aground. Similarly, in **Rigby** *v* **Chief Constable of Northumberland** (1985), the defendant successfully pleaded necessity after causing a fire by releasing CS gas into a shop in an attempt to eject a dangerous psychopath.

However, the courts have traditionally kept a tight rein on the use of necessity as a defence (in all torts, not just nuisance), and an example of this can be seen in **Monsanto Plc** *v* **Tilly** (1999). The claimant, Monsanto, is a multi-national firm which has spearheaded the development of genetically modified food. As part of this process, they were growing genetically modified crops on test sites throughout the UK. The defendant was a member of a group which considers genetically modified crops to be potentially harmful to the environment and to public safety, and they conducted a campaign in which they entered land where the trial crops were growing and uprooted part of them. When sued for trespass, the defendants claimed the defence of necessity, on the basis that their actions were designed to protect public health and the environment, but the Court of Appeal refused to accept this argument. They recognized that there might be occasions when pulling up a whole crop might be justified to protect others, in this case however, the defendant's group had only pulled up part of the crop as a symbolic gesture, and it was clear that the main purpose of the actions was to attract publicity for their campaign.

▶ Remedies

As well as the usual remedies of damages and injunction, the tort of trespass to land allows some specific remedies.

Self-help

The person with the right to possession can enter or re-enter the land. This is a form of self-help as the courts are not involved. But self-help is not encouraged by the courts and therefore there are considerable restrictions on when it can be resorted to. Only reasonable force can be used. In **Collins** *v* **Renison** (1754) the defendant found a trespasser up a ladder on his land. He said that he had reacted by gently shaking the ladder, which was a low one, and 'gently overturned it and gently threw the claimant from it upon the ground'. This amount of force was found to be unreasonable. Even where the force is reasonable and no tort has been committed, the person may still find that they have committed a statutory criminal offence.

Action for the recovery of land

This is sometimes called ejectment. It allows a person who has lost possession of their land to get possession back, provided they can establish an immediate right to possession. With the problems caused by squatters particularly in mind, a special summary procedure has been devised, which allows the claimant quickly to obtain an order for possession, and a writ for its enforcement, against anyone in occupation of their land, who has entered or remained there without licence. This can be done even though the claimant cannot identify those in possession.

Mesne profits

An action for mesne profits is a type of action for trespass. It allows the claimant to claim profits taken by the defendant during occupancy, damages for deterioration, and reasonable costs of regaining possession. An action for the recovery of land can be joined with a claim for mesne profits, and in this case it is unnecessary to have entered the land before suing. If the actions are brought separately, the claimant will have to enter the land before bringing the claim for mesne profits.

Distress damage feasant

Where an object placed or left unlawfully on the claimant's land causes damage, the claimant can keep it until the damage has been paid for. So if, for example, you hit a tennis ball through a neighbour's window, they are entitled to keep the ball until you pay to have the window replaced.

A qualification to this principle was highlighted in **Arthur *v* Anker** (1996). The claimant had parked his car on private property and it had been clamped. The clamping company argued that it was practising distress damage feasant, but the Court of Appeal rejected this. In clamping the car, they were continuing the very damage they sought to prevent (the presence of the car on the land) and distress damage feasant could not be used in this way. Furthermore, the car had not actually caused any damage (none of this, however, made the clamping illegal, because the claimant was deemed to have consented to the risk).

▶ Trespass in the criminal law

In the past, despite signs on land saying 'Trespassers will be prosecuted', trespass was only a civil wrong and not a crime. However the Criminal Justice and Public Order Act 1994 has created certain limited circumstances when trespass will now be a criminal offence as well as a tort. The

Act was aimed at such people as animal activists opposed to hunting, and has been heavily criticized as increasing criminalization and giving the police unnecessary powers.

ANSWERING QUESTIONS

1 Diana and Celia are the stars of the local tennis club and are deadly rivals. They are due to play the finals of the singles championship next Saturday. Recently Celia has proved to be the better player. Diana wants to make sure that Celia does not turn up for the match so that she, Diana, will be champion. On Saturday, Diana and her friend, Edward, manage to lure Celia into a garden shed where they lock her in, intending to leave her there for the rest of the day. Celia eventually discovers that she can get out by breaking a small window and climbing through it. She manages to arrive at the tennis club just in time for the match.

In the course of the game, Celia deliberately hits the ball straight at Diana's head and succeeds in hitting her several times. Eventually Diana loses her temper, leaps over the net and punches Celia in the face, giving her a nosebleed. Celia pushes Diana away, causing her to fall and break her ankle.

Consider the liability, if any, in tort of Diana, Celia and Edward. *OCR*
Diana and Edward could be jointly liable for false imprisonment. On whether there was actually an imprisonment consideration would need to be given to **Bird** v **Jones** as Celia had a means of escape, though the facts can probably be distinguished from those in that case. The imprisonment is caused by a positive act. There is no problem as regards knowledge of detention as Celia is fully aware that they have tried to lock her in. Point out that as they are jointly liable, so Celia can choose whether to sue both of them or just one of them.

Celia may be liable for assault and battery. The elements of these offences need to be considered and the issue of the defence of consent in sports looked at. As regards the later push causing Diana to break her ankle, you also need to discuss self-defence. Diana could additionally be liable for assault and battery.

2 **Analyse the elements of the tort of false imprisonment.** *OCR*
This is a fairly straightforward question in that you can use most of the material on the law of false imprisonment. This would not be sufficient in itself, as examiners generally want critical analysis as well as a summary of the law. You could also use the material in the section headed 'The role of trespass to the person today', discussing how important the tort is in practice.

12 Joint and several liability

In some cases, a claimant suffers damage as a result of the activities of more than one person. An example might be where two drivers are involved in a crash, each being negligent, and the claimant is a pedestrian injured as a result. In such cases, there are three ways in which liability may be divided among the defendants: independent liability; several liability; and joint liability.

Independent liability

This occurs where the victim suffers damage which is caused by two completely separate torts, as, for example, where a lorry is involved in two completely separate accidents, each causing damage. In such cases, each tortfeasor is liable for the damage they inflict, and has no connection with the other tortfeasor.

Several liability

Where two or more tortfeasors act independently, but the result of their acts is damage to the claimant for which they are both responsible, they are severally liable. The example in the introduction of two careless motorists crashing and injuring a pedestrian would be covered by several liability. The practical result is that each tortfeasor is separately liable for the whole of the damage, so the claimant may choose which to sue, but cannot get damages twice.

Joint liability

Where the same wrongful act is committed by two or more people, they are described as joint tortfeasors, and are jointly and severally liable. This means that the claimant can sue both (or all) of them, or recover the whole amount from just one, regardless of the extent to which each participated. Even where all are sued, judgment will be given for a single sum, and this may be enforced in full against any one of them. The claimant can only get damages once.

The two situations in which joint liability mainly arises are vicarious liability (see Chapter 13), where an employer and employee may be held jointly liable for the employee's negligence, and where the tortfeasors had a common design. The latter covers cases where the defendants are acting together, with the same purpose in mind. In **Brooke** *v* **Bool** (1928) the claimant had leased a shop from the defendant. A lodger in the shop smelt gas, so the lodger and the defendant went to investigate whether there was a gas leak. The defendant told the lodger to light a match, which he did, and there was an explosion. They were held jointly liable for the damage caused by the lodger's negligence.

Three situations can cause problems in the areas of joint and several liability: where successive actions are brought by the claimant; where one of the tortfeasors is released from liability; and where the question of contribution arises.

Successive actions

Where more than one tortfeasor has caused loss or injury to the claimant, there may be circumstances where it is difficult or impossible to sue them all in the same action. In the past, under common law, a claimant could sue each in turn where there was several liability, but not where there was joint liability; in that case only one action could be brought in respect of the injury or loss in question. However, this distinction has now been removed by statute. Under the Civil Liability (Contribution) Act 1978, s. 3, if a claimant has already successfully sued a joint tortfeasor, but has been unable to enforce the judgment, they can still sue any remaining joint tortfeasor, whether liability is joint or several.

Clearly, as far as the courts are concerned, it is preferable that a claimant should, if possible, sue all the tortfeasors who are liable for the same damage in one action. To encourage this, s. 4 of the 1978 Act provides that if successive actions are brought, the claimant can only recover costs in the first action, unless the court decides there were reasonable grounds for bringing the separate action(s).

Where a claimant settles out of court with one tortfeasor, this can have the effect of extinguishing any claims against other tortfeasors, so long as the settlement is intended by the parties to be a full and final settlement. This was the case in **Jameson** *v* **Central Electricity Generating Board** (1999). The claimant, Mrs Jameson, was the wife of a man who had contracted a fatal lung disease at work. There were two potential tortfeasors liable for the injury; his own employer and the owners of the power station where his employer sent him to work. Mr Jameson reached an out-of-court settlement with his employer, worth £80,000, but he died before the money could be paid, and it was inherited by his widow. She then brought a claim under the Fatal Accidents Act 1976 against the power station owners, this claim being worth £142,000. The House of

Lords held that this claim could not be successful unless it was clear that the earlier settlement had only ever been intended to settle part of Mr Jameson's claim. Given that the parties had said it was to be 'in full and final settlement', this could not be that case, and therefore settling the claim with the first tortfeasor meant there could be no further claim against the second one.

Release of a joint tortfeasor

If the potential claimant agrees that one of the joint tortfeasors will not be liable for a tort committed, all the others are released too, even though this may not have been the intention of the parties. The reasoning behind this rule is that in cases of joint liability, only one tort has been committed, and there is only one cause of action. If this cause of action is terminated, everyone's liability must be terminated. By contrast, where liability is several, the release of one tortfeasor does not affect the liability of the others. The harshness of this rule for claimants in cases of joint liability has been reduced by the courts distinguishing between a mere agreement not to sue, in which the other tortfeasors remain liable, and a release by contract, which extinguishes the liability of the other tortfeasors.

Contribution

The Civil Liability (Contribution) Act 1978 provides that where there is joint or several liability and one tortfeasor is sued and pays damages, they may recover a contribution or indemnity from any other who is liable in respect of the same damage. This is a matter between the defendants and does not affect the claimant, who remains entitled to recover the whole loss from whichever defendant they choose.

Where an out-of-court settlement is reached, a contribution can still be sought, provided it was an honest settlement.

In each case, the court will decide the contribution to be claimed on the basis of what is just and equitable regarding each tortfeasor's proportion of responsibility for the damage, though the contribution recoverable will not exceed the amount that the claimant could have recovered from that particular defendant. The courts appear to take a similar approach to this issue as they do in relation to the reduction of an award of damages for contributory negligence (see p. 108). In **Fitzgerald** *v* **Lane** (1988), the claimant walked out on to a busy road, and was hit by a vehicle, which pushed him into the path of another vehicle. Both drivers were found to have been negligent. The House of Lords held that the claimant's behaviour had to be considered in the light of the totality of the two drivers' conduct. The claimant was considered to be 50 per cent to blame, and the court then had to decide how much contribution had to be made. It was held that both drivers were equally to blame, and should contribute equal shares of the remaining 50 per cent of the damage.

The Limitation Act 1980 provides that the contribution must usually be sought within two years of the original award or settlement.

ANSWERING QUESTIONS

The issues raised in this chapter are unlikely to form the main subject of an exam question, but they do sometimes arise as a small part of problem questions. Therefore whenever a problem talks about two people causing the same damage to a claimant, you should consider whether there are issues of joint and several liability.

13 Vicarious liability

There are some cases where one person will be held liable for torts committed by someone else; such liability is said to be vicarious. Vicarious liability only arises where there is a particular relationship between the two, usually (in fact almost exclusively) that of employer and employee. An employer is considered to be responsible for many of the acts of their employees. Vicarious liability is a form of joint liability as both the person who committed the tort and the person having vicarious liability for the tort can be sued. In practice, it is usually just the employer who is sued, simply because they are more likely to be covered by insurance.

It is necessary to distinguish between vicarious liability, in which the defendant is held liable for another's acts, and primary liability, which arises from the defendant's own acts. When a tort is committed by an employee, their employer will often be both vicariously liable for the tort and have primary liability for a separate tort, for example, for negligently failing to provide adequate supervision.

▶ Employers and employees

Employers are vicariously liable for the torts committed by their employees, if they were acting in the course of their employment.

Who is an employee?

An employer will generally only be liable for the acts of an employee (sometimes called a servant), and not those of an independent contractor. In many cases the distinction will be obvious; in a factory, for example, a staff member who works full-time helping to produce whatever the factory produces is likely to be an employee, whereas someone called in from time to time to fix the plumbing, and who works elsewhere the rest of the time, is probably an independent contractor. However, there are areas where the distinction is blurred, especially now that many employers like to give themselves maximum flexibility by employing casual, freelance or temporary staff.

The control test

In the past the usual way of deciding whether a person was an employee was to look at the degree of control exercised over that person's work by the supposed employer. Where the employer had control over the work, and was in a position to lay down how and when tasks should be done, the person doing the work would be an employee. If, on the other hand, the person was engaged to do a particular task, but allowed discretion as to how and when to do it, they would be an independent contractor.

However, as many types of work became increasingly skilled and specialized, the test became less useful. In industry, for example, many managers would have no idea how their computer technicians should do their work, and so are not in a position to give directions on the subject, yet it is obvious that in common-sense terms, this does not make a salaried computer technician an independent contractor.

Other tests

The control test is still used, but clearly, in the light of these developments, it can no longer be conclusive. The courts now accept that no single test could cover the variety of work situations, and instead they look at all the circumstances of the particular case, including the level of control.

In **Ready Mixed Concrete (South East) Ltd** *v* **Minister of Pensions** (1968) it was stated that a contract of service would exist if the following three criteria were satisfied. First, that the employee agrees to provide work and skill for the employer in return for payment. Secondly, that the employee agrees (expressly or by implication) to be subject to the employer's control. Thirdly, that the other terms of the contract are consistent with the existence of a contract of service. Terms which would be inconsistent with such a conclusion might be that the person is required to pay for their own materials, or is allowed to employ staff to help do the job. Another factor frequently taken into account is who owns the tools and equipment used to do the job; independent contractors are likely to own their own.

The courts may find that a person is an employee even in the face of an express contractual term describing them as self-employed. This was the case in **Ferguson** *v* **Dawson** (1976), where it was held by the Court of Appeal that a building labourer was an employee and therefore protected by certain safety legislation, on the basis of the type of work done and the degree of control exercised over it. This was despite a specific contractual term stating that he was self-employed.

A test that has grown in popularity with the courts is whether a worker was in 'business on his own account'. This was used by the Court of Appeal in **Hall** *v* **Lorimer** (1992). The case was concerned with whether the defendant, a freelance television technician, was an employee for the of tax law; as an employee he would have had to pay more tax than if he was self-employed. The Inland Revenue argued that he was an employee because he was subject to the control of the television companies in that they told him where, when and for how long to work. The Court of Appeal took a slightly different approach. They held that the crucial factor was that he was not in business on his own account. Workers will be viewed as in business on their own account if, for example, they provide their own equipment, take financial risks (such as doing work on credit), hire helpers, have managerial and investment responsibilities, charge varying amounts for different jobs, send out invoices for their work and have quite a few clients.

Nolan LJ said in **Hall** *v* **Lorimer** that just because people do highly-skilled work does not mean they are more likely to be self-employed, for a brain surgeon is usually an employee while a window cleaner is usually self-employed. Nor, in this day and age, does the fact that a person is on short-term contracts with different employers matter. He pointed out that the label that people give themselves is relevant but never decisive. He concluded that the 'business on their own account' test is not the exclusive test in deciding whether workers are employees:

> [T]he question whether the individual is in business on his own account, though often helpful, may be of little assistance in the case of one carrying on a profession or vocation. A self-employed author working from home or an actor or a singer may earn his living without any of the normal trappings of a business . . . The extent to which the individual is dependent on or independent of a particular paymaster for the financial exploitation of his talents may well be significant.

The loan of an employee

In some cases, one employer may 'lend' another the services of an employee. If an employee who is on loan commits a tort, who will incur vicarious liability for it?

This question was addressed in **Mersey Docks and Harbour Board** *v* **Coggins & Griffiths (Liverpool) Ltd** (1947). The Harbour Board had hired out one of their crane drivers, with his crane, to Coggins, a company of stevedores. As a result of the crane driver's negligence, someone was injured, and it was necessary to decide who was the crane driver's employer (and therefore who was vicariously liable). According to the terms of the contract between the Harbour Board and Coggins, he was an employee of Coggins, but the Harbour Board paid his wages, and retained the power to sack him. The House of Lords held that this meant that the Harbour Board was his employer, and in doing so, they laid down three principles to be used in deciding future cases:

1 The terms of any contract between the two potential employers are not decisive.
2 The permanent employer is presumed liable, unless they can prove otherwise.
3 Where employees alone are lent, it is easy to infer that the hirer is the employer. If equipment as well as the employee is hired then this will be less easy to infer as the hirer may not have control over the way the equipment is used.

On the facts of this case, the Harbour Board had failed to rebut the presumption, and remained the driver's employer for the purposes of vicarious liability.

▶ In the course of employment

An employer will only be responsible for torts committed by their employees if those torts are committed in the course of the employment, rather than, as the courts have put it, when the employee is on a 'frolic of his own'. The tort will have been committed in the course of employment if the act which comprises the tort is one which has been authorized by the employer, even if the employee performs the act in a manner which was not authorized by the employer.

An employer may also be liable for acts done by employees (but not independent contractors) where their behaviour has not been authorized, but is sufficiently connected with authorized acts that it can be regarded as merely an improper way of committing the authorized acts. In the past this has allowed for a wide interpretation of the phrase 'in the course of their employment'.

In **Century Insurance** *v* **Northern Ireland Road Transport** (1942), the defendants' employee, a petrol tanker driver, was unloading petrol from his tanker to underground storage in the claimant's garage, when he struck a match to light a cigarette and then dropped the lighted match on to the ground. This caused an explosion, damaging the claimant's property. The defendants were found to be vicariously liable for his negligence, on the basis that what he was doing at the time was part of his job, even if he was doing it in a negligent way. It was agreed that the match was struck for his own purposes, not those of the employer, but nevertheless, in the circumstances in which it was done it was still in the course of his employment.

In **Bayler** *v* **Manchester Railway Co** (1873), a railway porter employed by the defendants thought the claimant was on the wrong train and, meaning to be helpful, pulled him off it by force. The defendants were held vicariously liable, because the porter was trying to do what he was authorized to do, in helping a passenger to get to his destination, even though he was doing it so badly as to have completely the opposite effect.

An employer will not be responsible for acts committed by employees which have nothing to do with their employment, even though those acts may be committed in the workplace during working hours, or even using the employer's equipment. In **Heasmans *v* Clarity Cleaning Co** (1987) the employee of a cleaning contractor was employed to clean telephones, and while doing so, used the phones to make private long-distance calls from clients' premises. The defendants were held not vicariously liable; the Court of Appeal held that the unauthorized use of the telephone was not connected with cleaning it, and could not be regarded as the cleaning of it in an authorized manner.

In **Hilton *v* Thomas Burton (Rhodes) Ltd** (1961), four workmen were out in their employer's van, which they were allowed to use for travelling to work on a demolition site out in the country. After half a day's work, they decided to stop and go to a cafe seven miles away for tea. They were nearly there when they changed their minds and started back again. On their return journey there was an accident, and one of them was killed through the negligent driving of another. The employer was held not to be vicariously responsible, as the men were not acting in the course of their employment; the court described them as 'on a frolic of their own'.

Employees travelling within work hours are more likely to be found to be acting in the course of employment. Thus, in **Whatman *v* Pearson** (1868) the employee had an hour lunch break when he was forbidden to go home or to leave his horse and cart unguarded. Despite the ban, he went home for lunch, which was a quarter of an hour away from his workplace. While having his lunch he left his horse in the street and it ran off, damaging the claimant's property. The employee was found to be acting in the course of his employment, as he was still within the general scope of his job, which included guarding the horse and cart all day.

This can be contrasted with the case of **Storey *v* Ashton** (1869). Some employees had finished delivering wine for their employers and were on their way back after their official work hours were over. They decided to take a detour to visit a relation of one of the employees. On the way there they negligently ran over the claimant. His attempt to sue their employer failed as they were treated as being on a 'new and independent journey' from their work trip at the time of the accident.

Express prohibition

An employer who expressly prohibits an act will not be liable if an employee commits that act. However, the employer may be liable if the prohibition can be regarded as applying to the way in which the job is done, rather than to the scope of the job itself. In **Limpus *v* London**

General Omnibus Co (1862) a bus driver had been given written instructions not to race with or obstruct other buses. He disobeyed this order, and while racing another bus, he caused a collision with the claimant's bus, which damaged it. The court held that he was doing an act which he was authorized to do: driving a bus in such a way as to promote the defendants' business. This meant that he was within the course of his employment, even though the way he was doing the job was quite improper and had been prohibited. The defendants were vicariously liable.

A common situation arising in this area has been that of employees giving lifts to people. In **Twine** *v* **Bean's Express Ltd** (1946), the defendants' employee gave the claimant's husband a lift in a van, and as a result of the employee's negligence, he was killed. The driver had been told not to give lifts to anyone who was not within a group of authorized passengers, and there was a notice on the side of the vehicle stating who could be carried. The deceased was not among them. The defendants were held not to be vicariously liable, because the driver was doing an unauthorized act and was therefore outside the course of his employment.

By contrast, in **Rose** *v* **Plenty** (1976) a milkman had been told by his employer not to permit passengers on his float, nor to let children help him deliver the milk. He disregarded these orders, and paid the claimant, who was 13, to help him. The claimant was injured while riding on the vehicle, as a result of the milkman's negligent driving. The defendants were held vicariously liable, because the prohibition did not affect the job which the milkman had to do, only the way in which he should do it. He was doing his allocated job of delivering the milk, even though in a way that his employers disapproved of. Certainly there is a very fine division between this case and **Twine**. The majority of the Court of Appeal pointed to the fact that in **Twine** the lift was not given for a purpose which would benefit the employer, but in **Rose** the boy was helping with deliveries, and therefore furthering the employer's business. However, it is likely that the court was influenced by the fact that compensation for the child could only be secured by making the employer's insurance available to meet the claim.

Criminal acts

Criminal acts alleged to be done in the course of employment tend to take the form of either violent assaults or property offences such as theft. In the case of assaults, the courts are very unlikely to find that the employee acted in the course of employment. In **Warren** *v* **Henley's Ltd** (1948), the employee worked at a petrol station. He accused a customer of intending to drive away without paying, and the customer threatened to report him to the police and to his employers. The employee responded by punching the customer on the nose. The court held that this was not done within the course of his employment; it was an act of personal vengeance.

The case of **S-T** *v* **North Yorkshire County Council** (1999) indicates how far the courts will go in avoiding imposing vicarious liability for any kind of physical assault. The claimant in the case was a mentally handicapped teenager, who had severe epilepsy. On a school trip to Spain, it was arranged that the deputy headmaster would share a room with the claimant, who needed attendance during the night because of the fits he had. On several nights during the holiday, the deputy headmaster sexually assaulted the boy. He was later convicted of sexual assaults on several other boys. The claimant claimed damages against the council, on the ground that as the deputy headmaster's employer, it was vicariously liable for his acts. It was agreed that the mere fact that his work had provided the opportunity to commit the assaults was not sufficient to establish that they were committed in the course of his employment, but the claimant argued that the situation went further than that: the reason why the deputy headmaster had been sharing his room in the first place was because he was responsible for the claimant, and the assaults had arisen as a result of that responsibility. The Court of Appeal rejected that argument, and stated that where an employee does something which actually negates the employer's duty to the claimant, the employer cannot be vicariously liable; in other words, an act cannot be considered to be committed in the course of someone's employment where that act goes against the purpose for which that person is employed. That was clearly the case here, and so the council was not liable.

Where a property offence has been committed, there is more flexibility, and the courts will look at whether the employment merely provided the opportunity for the dishonesty, or whether the dishonest conduct was actually part of the work for which the employee was engaged. Only in the latter case should the employer be liable, though the case of **Lloyd** *v* **Grace, Smith & Co** (1912) suggests that the courts look unfavourably on employers whose lack of supervision provides an opportunity for dishonesty. The defendants in that case were a firm of solicitors who employed a managing clerk and allowed him to carry out conveyancing work unsupervised. The claimant owned some cottages, which she rented out. Feeling that they generated insufficient income, she went to the defendants' firm and spoke to the clerk. He persuaded her to give him instructions to sell the cottages, and told her to complete two documents in connection with the sale. In reality the effect of the documents was to convey the cottages to the clerk.

The House of Lords held that the defendants were vicariously liable for the clerk's fraud, and made much of the fact that it was the defendants' lack of supervision which had given him the means to commit the fraud. They held that as he was paid to do conveyancing, and that was what he had done, he was acting within the course of his employment. Before this case, it had been supposed that where an employee committed a fraud, or some other dishonesty, for their own benefit, rather than the employer's, the employer could not be held vicariously liable. The House of Lords, however, held that so long as an employee is acting within the scope of their employment, the employer is liable, regardless of whether the employer has any financial interest in the fraud.

In **Credit Lyonnais Bank Nederland** *v* **Export Credit Guarantee Department** (1999), a fraud amounting to the tort of deceit had been committed against the bank by a Mr Chong, who was helped by a Mr Pillai, an employee of the defendant. By the time the bank was able to take action, Mr Chong had disappeared and Mr Pillai had died, so they attempted to sue the defendants as being vicariously liable for Mr Pillai's part in the fraud. However, Mr Pillai had not actually committed the tort, merely helped Mr Chong to do so, and even his acts of assistance had not all been committed within the course of his employment. The House of Lords held that the defendants could only be vicariously liable where all the features which are necessary to make the employee's behaviour amount to a tort have occurred in the course of their employment.

Employer's indemnity

Because vicarious liability makes employer and employee joint tortfeasors, each fully liable to the claimant, an employer who is sued on the basis of vicarious liability is entitled to sue the employee in turn, and recover some or all of the damages paid for the employee's tort. This is called an indemnity, and the employer's entitlement to sue may derive either from the provisions of the Civil Liability (Contribution) Act 1978, or in common law under the principle in **Lister** *v* **Romford Ice and Cold Storage** (1957). In that case, a lorry driver drove negligently in the course of his employment, and ran over his father, who was also employed by the company. The father recovered damages on the basis of the employer's vicarious liability for the driver's negligence; the damages were paid by the employer's insurers. The employer then exercised its right to sue the driver for an indemnity. The House of Lords held that the lorry driver's negligent driving was not only a tort against his father, but also a breach of an implied term in his employment contract, to the effect that he would exercise reasonable care in performing his contractual duties. It was decided that the employer was entitled to damages equivalent to the amount which it had had to pay to the father.

The House justified the decision on the basis that the employee who had committed the tort should not be able to avoid paying damages for the wrong. But the case was widely criticized as undermining the whole principle of vicarious liability, which is based on the assumption that employers are best placed to take out insurance, and therefore to meet the risk. Allowing insurers effectively to reclaim money from the employee means that the employers are paying premiums for a risk which may cost the insurance company nothing. In fact, since **Lister** was decided, companies providing insurance to employers have informally agreed that they will not pursue their rights under the **Lister** principle unless there is evidence that employer and employee colluded together, or evidence of other misconduct with regard to the insurance cover.

Independent contractors

An employer is generally not liable for the acts of an independent contractor, as opposed to an employee. However, there are circumstances in which the acts of an independent contractor may give rise to the employer having primary liability, because the employer was breaching their own duty to the claimant. The employer will then be liable as a joint tortfeasor with the independent contractor. The type of duty that the employer must have breached is described as a non-delegable duty. This means that while the work can be delegated to someone else, the liability for it cannot be delegated. For example, a water authority may have a non-delegable duty to repair a burst main. If it arranges for a private firm to carry out that repair, rather than its own employees, the firm will be its independent contractors. Should that firm then carry out the repairs negligently so that several homes are seriously flooded, the firm can be liable for negligence, but the water authority will also be liable.

Whether a duty is delegable or not is always a question of law, but the answer is not always obvious. Strict liability torts tend to involve non-delegable duties, and in other cases the position may be clear from statutory provisions. For example, the Occupiers' Liability Act 1957 provides that an occupier may delegate the duty of care to make premises reasonably safe when a competent independent contractor is employed to deal with a potential risk, such as electrical maintenance. However, there are many situations where it is not clear whether a duty is delegable.

An employer can also be liable for the torts committed by an independent contractor where they have delegated a delegable duty but failed to take reasonable steps to find a competent person to do the work, or make sure it was done properly. In this situation the employer will incur primary liability for this failure.

Where there is potential liability for something done by an independent contractor, the employer will only be liable if the act was part of the work the contractor was engaged to do. Acts which are completely outside their employment as an independent contractor (called collateral negligence) impose no liability on the employer. In **Padbury** *v* **Holliday and Greenwood Ltd** (1912), sub-contractors were employed by the defendants to do work on the windows of a house the defendants were building. While doing this, the sub-contractor placed on the window sill an iron tool, which subsequently fell off and injured the claimant in the street below.

Placing the tool on the window sill was not part of the ordinary course of doing the work which the sub-contractor was employed to do, and so it was held that the claimant's injuries were caused by an act of collateral negligence, for which the builders were not liable. In order to make them liable, the negligence would have had to be central to the work the sub-contractors were doing for them, not merely casually connected to it.

▶ Why is vicarious liability imposed?

Vicarious liability obviously conflicts with a basic principle of tort, that wrongdoers should be liable for their own actions. Why then do we have it? Various explanations have been put forward, including the following.

Control of employees

It has been pointed out that the employer is in control of the conduct of employees, and therefore should be responsible for their acts. While this may have been persuasive in the past, in modern industrial society, with its increasingly sophisticated division of labour, it is very difficult to believe. In many cases employees may have technical skills and knowledge not shared by their employers; to say, for example, that the manager of a hospital controls the work of a surgeon is simply not true. However, the modern application of this principle can be seen in the fact that employers set profit targets, either formally or informally, and if these mean that there is insufficient time or staff to do a job properly, with the result that someone is, for example, injured by negligence, it is the employers who should be responsible.

Benefits to employers

Employers benefit from the work of their employees, and so ought to be liable for any damage the employee may cause in its performance. This is linked to the point about profit targets above; it would be very unfair if employees were sued for negligence when effectively they had been forced to be negligent by a cost-cutting employer, who would thereby profit from that negligence.

Resources

It is obvious that in the majority of cases, an employer will be in the best financial position to meet a claim, either because its resources are simply greater than those of an individual employee, or, more often, because it has relevant insurance cover. Many employers are large companies; placing liability on them effectively means that losses can be transferred to the consumer through higher prices, and so spread very thinly over a lot of people, rather than imposed on one.

Preventing negligent recruitment

It has been suggested that commission of a tort by an employee in the course of their employment implies that the employer was negligent in selecting that employee, and incurs liability on that basis. There is, however, no evidence that the courts approach the issue in this way, and in any case, one negligent act does not necessarily mean that an employee is unfit for the work.

Promotion of care

There is some evidence to show that the imposition of liability on employers encourages them to take care to prevent work practices that could result in accidents; there could be a temptation for employers to 'turn a blind eye', especially if the practices have a benefit to themselves, if they knew liability would be restricted to the employee.

ANSWERING QUESTIONS

1 Adrian has been employed for five years by Daily Deliveries Ltd as a delivery man. It is a term of Adrian's employment that he may not carry any person other than employees of Daily Deliveries Ltd on his van. In fact, since his employment started, Adrian has been helped on Saturdays, and during school and college holidays, by his son James, who is 19. James has never been employed by Daily Deliveries Ltd and is aware of the restriction in Adrian's contract of employment. Last month James was helping Adrian as usual when, owing to Adrian's negligent driving of the delivery van on their lunch break, there was an accident in which James was seriously injured. Daily Deliveries has now told James that the company has no liability to pay damages to him.

Advise James. *OCR*

In James' situation, there are two possible options: to sue his father for negligence, or to sue Daily Deliveries Ltd (DDL) on the basis of their vicarious liability for his father's negligence. It will only be worthwhile sueing his father if he has some form of insurance on his own behalf. If he has, there is no problem, since as a passenger James was clearly owed a duty of care, we already know that Adrian had fallen below the standard of care and there was damage within the rules of causation and remoteness.

However, given that Adrian is an employee, he is unlikely to have taken out his own insurance, which leaves James with his possible claim against DDL. Are they correct in asserting that they have no liability towards him? In order to establish that DDL was vicariously liable for Adrian's negligence, James must establish that Adrian is an employee and that he was acting in the course of his employment. We are told that Adrian is an employee, so there is no problem there, but there are difficulties with establishing that he was acting in the course of his employment. You need to consider the effect of the rule that no passengers who were not DDL employees were to be carried; the cases of **Twine** v **Bean's Express Ltd** and **Rose** v **Plenty** should be discussed here. Clearly DDL will want to argue that **Twine** applies, whereas in advising James you will want to look for reasons why **Rose** should be followed. You also need to consider whether the fact that the pair were on their lunch break might make a difference, discussing **Whatman** v **Pearson** and **Storey** v **Ashton**.

If DDL are liable to James, they may be covered by the defence of *volenti*, since James knew that his father was not allowed to take him as a passenger and therefore that he was taking the risk if there was an accident. However you should point out the provisions of the Road Traffic Act 1988, and the fact that cases like **Pitts** v **Hunt** (1991) (see p. 114) suggest that the courts will prevent *volenti* from being used against passengers as a result.

You should also mention the issue of employer's indemnity, pointing out that the possibility of DDL reclaiming any compensation from Adrian still exists, even though it is unlikely these days to be used.

14 Remedies in tort

So far, we have looked at the rules on whether a defendant can be liable in tort. In this chapter, we look at the remedies that are available to the claimant once that liability is proved. The main remedies in tort are damages, which aim to compensate the claimant financially, and injunctions, which aim to stop or prevent the behaviour which comprises the tort. There are also a number of other remedies which are specific to particular torts; these have been discussed in the relevant chapters.

DAMAGES

In the vast majority of cases where damages are claimed, they are what is known as compensatory (there are some types of non-compensatory damages, which are discussed at p. 303). The principle behind compensatory damages is that they should put the claimant in the position they would have been in if the tort had never been committed. An award of compensatory damages may be composed of either general or special damages, or both. General damages are designed to compensate for the kinds of damage which the law presumes to be a result of the tort, such as pain and suffering from a personal injury, and loss of future earnings where the claimant's injuries mean they cannot return to a previous employment, or cannot work at all. Obviously, the amount of such damages cannot be calculated precisely, but the courts use the awards given for similar injuries in the past as a guideline.

Special damages are those which do not arise naturally from the wrong complained of, and must be specifically listed in pleadings, and proved in court. They generally cover the claimant's financial loss up until the date of trial, and any expenses incurred up to that point, and are therefore susceptible of more exact calculation.

Note that special damages are not the same as the special damage referred to in connection with slander or public nuisance.

▶ Calculating compensatory damages

The principle of restoring the claimant to the position they would have held if the tort had not been committed is called *restitutio in integrum*. Obviously, it is easiest to achieve where the loss is financial (usually known as pecuniary loss), since the difference in financial position can be precisely calculated. So, for example, in an action for negligence, pecuniary loss will be calculated by comparing the financial position the claimant was in before the negligent conduct, with their position after its occurrence. Even so, there are cases where the loss is purely financial, but the issue of what will amount to *restitutio in integrum* is not straightforward. In **Gardner** *v* **Marsh & Parsons** (1997), the claimants had bought a leasehold flat after having it surveyed by the defendants. The surveyor was negligent, failing to discover a serious structural defect, which did not come to light for three years. The lease contained a clause making the freeholder responsible for structural repairs, and the freeholder eventually repaired the defect, but not until two years later. The claimants sued the surveyors for negligence, claiming the difference between the price they paid, and the lower market value of the flat with the defect, but the surveyors claimed that no damages were required since the defect had been repaired, albeit not by them, and there was no loss.

The Court of Appeal disagreed, stating that loss could not be avoided by the claimant's own actions, unless those actions flowed from the original transaction between the parties, and were really part of a continuous course of dealing arising from it. In this case the claimants were only able to put right the problem because they had a contract with the freeholder, and even then they had had to go to the trouble of hassling the freeholder to do the repairs; they had also waited a long time for them to be done, during which time they could not sell the flat. The means by which they solved the problem were too remote to be taken into account when deciding the defendants' liability.

In **South Australia Asset Management Corporation** *v* **York Montague Ltd** (1996), the House of Lords heard three appeals, each arising from similar facts: the defendants had each negligently valued a property, and the claimants lent money for the purchase of the property on the strength of those valuations. Soon afterwards, property prices dropped, and the borrowers in each case defaulted on the loan, leaving the lenders with a property worth less than the money they were owed on it. Each of the lenders gave evidence that they would not have granted the loans if they had known the true value of the property, and claimed that therefore their damages should include the loss that they had made through the general drop in property prices, since if they had not made the loan, they would not have made that loss either. For our purposes, the details of one of the cases is sufficient: here the lenders lent £1.75 million on a property that was valued at £2.5 million, but was actually worth £1.8 million. By the time the property market had dropped, it was only worth £950,000.

The Court of Appeal analysed the cases on the basis of whether the loans would have been granted if the true valuations had been known, and said that where the lenders would not have gone ahead with the loans had it not been for the negligent valuation, the lenders were entitled to recover the difference between the sum lent, and the sum recovered when the property was sold, together with a reasonable rate of interest, so that they would be compensated for the drop in market prices. Where a lender would still have gone ahead with the loan even if the correct valuation had been given, but lent a smaller sum, they would only be able to recover the difference between what they actually lost and what they would have lost had they lent a lesser amount; any fall in the market could not be compensated.

The House of Lords rejected this argument. Their Lordships said that in order to calculate damages for breach of a duty of care, it was first necessary to determine exactly what the duty consisted of; a defendant would only be liable for consequences arising from negligent performance of that duty. In this case, the defendants did not have a duty to advise the claimants whether or not to make the loan; their duty was to inform the claimants of the value of the property offered as security, and so their liability was limited to the consequences of that advice being wrong, and not to the entire consequences of the loan being made. The consequence of the advice being wrong was that the claimants had less security for the debt than they thought, and that loss should be compensated; in the case detailed above, the correct figure would be £700,000. This would give the claimants the amount of security they thought they had at the time the loan was made, but would not compensate for the drop in property prices, since this was not a consequence of the negligent valuation, but would have happened anyway. If the defendants had had a duty to advise the claimants whether or not to make the loan, they would have been liable for all losses arising from the fact that the loan was made, including the drop in property prices, but here their duty did not extend that far so their liability could not either.

In a case with similar facts, **Platform Home Loans Ltd** *v* **Oyston Shipways Ltd** (1999), the House of Lords held that where part of the loss was due to the claimants' own negligence in making the loans in the first place without adequately assessing the borrowers' ability to repay it, the damages could be reduced for contributory negligence.

In **Patel** *v* **Hooper & Jackson** (1998) the Court of Appeal allowed the buyer of a residential property, who was unable to live in it as a result of a negligent survey, to claim the cost of alternative accommodation up until such time as the house could reasonably be expected to have been sold, as well as the difference between the true value of the house and the price paid as a result of the negligent survey. The court held that in the circumstances the cost of alternative accommodation was part of the reasonable cost of the buyer extricating himself from the purchase. However, he could not claim compensation for the mortgage payments and insurance premiums he had paid, since he would have had to pay these even if he had bought a different property instead of the defective one.

Where loss is non-pecuniary (such as pain and suffering), *restitutio in integrum* is even more difficult, and the general aim is to provide fair and reasonable compensation for the damage done, taking into account all the circumstances. In each case, the exact calculation of damages is a question of fact, and the judge has discretion over whether to allow counsel to refer to decisions in previous similar cases. In practice, such references are frequent.

Mitigation

A person who falls victim to a tort is expected to take reasonable steps to mitigate any loss; the defendant will not be liable for compensatory damages in respect of any losses that could have been prevented by such steps. However, since the situation is the fault of the defendant, not the claimant, the standard of reasonableness is not particularly high, and the claimant is certainly not required to make huge efforts to avoid a loss that is the defendant's fault.

In **Emeh** *v* **Kensington Area Health Authority** (1985), the claimant underwent a sterilization operation carried out by the defendants' employees, but afterwards became pregnant. The defendants rather bizarrely argued that she could have mitigated her financial loss by having an abortion, and therefore saving the cost of bringing up the child. Rejecting this argument, the court accepted that in the circumstances it was reasonable to refuse to have an abortion.

▶ Compensation for personal injuries

Damages for personal injury (which covers physical or psychiatric harm, disease and illness) raise problems not encountered with other types of loss. In the case of damage to property, for example, financial compensation is both easy to calculate and an adequate way of making good the loss, by allowing the claimant to buy a replacement or pay for repairs. It is not so easy to calculate the value of a lost limb, or permanent loss of general good health, and even if it were, money can never really compensate for such losses. In addition, the court may be required to estimate the amount of future earnings which will be lost, and the future development of the injury; even though personal injury cases may take years to come to trial, the degree of recovery to be expected may still be unclear, and new symptoms may not appear until years later.

Damages for personal injuries are divided into pecuniary and non-pecuniary losses. Pecuniary damages are those which can be calculated in financial terms, such as loss of earnings, and medical and other expenses, while non-pecuniary damages cover less easily calculable damages, such as loss of physical amenity, pain, shock and suffering.

Pecuniary losses

The courts have divided financial losses made by claimants in personal injury cases into the following 'heads of damage'.

Pre-trial expenses

The claimant is entitled to recover all expenses actually and reasonably incurred as a result of the accident up to the date of the trial. This includes, for example, loss of, or damage to, clothing and any medical expenses.

Expenses incurred by another

The most common example here is where a claimant has had to be looked after by a partner or relative, who has had to give up paid work as a result. Such carers cannot bring an action themselves directly against the defendant to seek compensation. But in **Donnelly** *v* **Joyce** (1972) the Court of Appeal recognized that the claimant could normally claim for this loss as part of his or her own claim. In that case the claimant was a child and his mother had to give up work to look after him when he was seriously injured by the defendant's negligence. The claimant succeeded in claiming for the financial loss that his mother had suffered as a result of caring for him.

The House of Lords recently decided in **Hunt** *v* **Severs** (1994) that any damages received under this head are awarded to the claimant to compensate the carer and not the claimant. When the claimant received this award he or she should hand the money over to the carer and until he or she did so the money was held under an obligation to do so, known as being held on trust. On this point the House of Lords reversed **Donnelly** *v* **Joyce**, which had viewed such an award as being to compensate the claimant's loss and therefore placing him or her under no legal obligation to hand it over to the carer (for the facts of **Hunt** *v* **Severs**, see p.301).

This conclusion runs counter to the approach preferred by the Pearson Commission, which argued that damages should be the absolute property of the claimant. They pointed out that any duty to hand some of it over to someone else, such as a carer, would be extremely difficult to supervise. It might also constitute an incentive for members of a family not to help each other but to employ people from outside the family to care for their relations.

Where a spouse provides services in a business context, the courts have decided that there must be an actual loss before the claimant can claim for the cost of the services. In **Hardwick** *v* **Hudson** (1999), the claimant was injured in a car accident. He was a partner in a garage business, and while he was recovering, his wife took over his role at work, without being paid. The claimant argued that this was comparable to carer services supplied free by a relative, but the Court of Appeal disagreed. The claimant's wife was supplying services which the business would otherwise have had to pay for, and in doing that, she could be seen as providing a benefit to the business and actually preventing the claimant from suffering the loss he would have done if he had paid someone to do the work. In fact, the couple would have been better off if the wife had been properly employed and paid by the business, under an express or implied contract, as then there would have been a loss and, the court said, the claimant could have claimed this from the defendant.

The same principle applies to other benefits provided by third parties. In **Dimond** *v* **Lovell** (2000), the claimant was involved in an accident for which the defendant was responsible, and as a result, she had to hire a car. Due to irregularities with the hire contract, it was held to be unenforceable and she ended up not having to pay the hire charges, but she attempted to claim them from the defendant anyway, on the basis that she had had to hire the car because of his negligence. The court compared the situation with that in cases where care was provided free by, for example, a partner, as in **Hunt** *v* **Severs**, and held that the same rule applied. Where a claimant has received services from a third party at no cost to themselves, the court can award damages to be held in trust for that third party – but where it is not possible to impose a trust for the third party, the damages cannot be awarded to the claimant instead. In this case, imposing a trust for the benefit of the car hire company would have amounted to enforcing an unenforceable contract, and the court could not impose a trust for this purpose.

Pre-trial loss of earnings

The claimant can receive damages for the loss of the earnings or profits which would otherwise have been earned up to the date of the judgment. The amount awarded will be that which the claimant would have taken home after tax and National Insurance contributions have been deducted. Both pre-trial expenses and pre-trial loss of earnings are considered to be special damages (see p. 289).

Future loss of earnings

Claims for future pecuniary loss are almost always comprised of loss of future earnings, and are regarded as general damages. Obviously they are difficult to calculate, since there is no real way of knowing what the future would have held for the claimant if the accident had not happened. It has been made even more difficult in recent years by high levels of unemployment, which make it difficult to predict whether or not a claimant could have expected to remain employed had the accident not happened.

Damages are usually awarded as a lump sum, but obviously the purpose of damages for loss of future earnings due to personal injury is usually to give the claimant an income to replace the one they would have had if the injury had not happened. The courts therefore calculate a figure which, given as a lump sum, would be sufficient to buy an investment called an annuity that would give the claimant the right level of income for life, or however long the effects of the injury were expected to last (an annuity is an arrangement under which a lump sum is invested so as to produce an income).

The starting-point for calculating future loss of earnings is the difference between income before the accident and afterwards, which is called the net annual loss. Obviously in some cases the claimant may be so badly injured that no income can be earned, but the principle also covers those who can work, but at lower paid employment than before. Predicting future earnings can be a matter of guesswork, as the case of **Doyle** *v* **Wallace** (1998) shows. In this case the claimant was badly injured in a road accident and was unable to work. She had been planning to train as a drama teacher if she could get the necessary qualifications, and if not, she planned to get a clerical job. Her income would have been substantially higher as a teacher than as a clerk, but at the time of the accident it was too early to know whether she would have obtained the necessary qualifications. The trial judge found that she had a 50 per cent chance of qualifying as a drama teacher, and calculated the damages for loss of future earnings on the basis of an income that was half-way between that of a drama teacher and that of a clerical worker. The Court of Appeal upheld this approach.

The court adjusts the net annual loss to take into account factors which might have altered the claimant's original earnings, such as promotion prospects, and the figure that they reach as a result of doing so is called the multiplicand. The court then takes the number of years that the disability is likely to continue, and reduces this number by taking into account what are called the 'contingencies (or vicissitudes) of life' – basically, the fact that even if the accident had not happened, the claimant might not have lived or worked until retirement age.

At this stage, the court has before it the annual amount that will compensate the claimant, and the number of years for which this amount should be payable. However, simply to multiply the first figure by the second would actually over-compensate the claimant. If we take, for example, an annual loss of £10,000, to be payable over 20 years, simple multiplication of these figures gives us £200,000. But a claimant does not actually need a lump sum of £200,000 to produce an annual income of

£10,000 over 20 years, because the assumption is that the lump sum is invested and so makes more money during the 20 years, with the result that the claimant would end up over-compensated. To avoid this, the court assumes that the investment will earn a particular rate of return (called the discount rate), and reduces the lump sum to one which, on the basis of the assumed rate of return, will provide the right rate of compensation, nothing more and nothing less. The sum arrived at is called the multiplier, and the multiplicand multiplied by the multiplier gives the sum necessary to compensate the claimant for loss of future earnings.

Within these calculations, the rate of return on investments that the court assumes is very important – the higher the assumed rate of return, the smaller the lump sum, and if for some reason the claimant in practice is unable to achieve this rate of return on their investments, they will be under-compensated.

Until recently, the courts generally assumed a rate of interest of 4–5 per cent per year. This practice was criticized by, among others, the Law Commission in its 1995 report *Structured Settlements and Interim and Provisional Damages* (Law Com No 224). It said that the assumed rate of interest was an arbitrary figure; it was possible to achieve this rate of interest, but only with a relatively sophisticated understanding of investments which few claimants would possess, and so many claimants were likely to end up under-compensated. The Commission recommended that the courts should use as their guideline the return given to investors on a type of investment called an Index Linked Government Security (ILGS), which would give a more accurate picture of the kind of returns claimants could hope to get on their lump sums. The practical effect of this would be that multipliers would go up and so, as a result, would damages.

The Damages Act 1996 responded to this recommendation by providing that the Lord Chancellor can prescribe a rate of interest for the purposes of calculating multipliers. At the time of going to press, no new discount rate had in fact been set by the Lord Chancellor; instead the House of Lords stepped in to deal with the issue in **Wells** *v* **Wells** (1998). They acknowledged the problem, and agreed that with the Law Commission that the calculations should be based on the rate of return available on ILGS. After looking at that rate and allowing for deductions of tax, they held the assumed rate of return should be three per cent.

However, although the case is a clear step towards better compensation for claimants, it has not delivered quite as much flexibility as might appear at first sight. The House of Lords could simply have stated that the ILGS rate should be the basis for calculations, so that courts in later cases would have been able to reflect movements up or down in that rate, and therefore avoid the out-of-date assumptions that had caused the problem **Wells** set out to correct. Instead they held that three per cent was not only the correct figure at the time of the case, but also a guideline for future cases. Lord Lloyd, who delivered the judgment, did emphasize the need for flexibility to change the figure if, for example, the ILGS rate changed 'significantly', but it would appear from the subsequent case of **Warren** *v* **Northern General Hospital Trust** (2000) that this is to be interpreted quite narrowly. The claimant in the case argued that, as the ILGS rate had fallen since **Wells** was decided, three per cent was too high. This view was rejected by the Court of Appeal. They emphasized that there was a need for certainty in this area, otherwise out of court settlements might become less likely, and that it was undesirable to introduce a degree of flexibility in the rate that would lead to enormous amounts of evidence from financial experts being put before the courts. They also pointed out that the Lord Chancellor had recently issued a consultation paper on the subject, and it would not be appropriate for them to alter the rate before he had acted.

Non-pecuniary losses

These are losses which are not financial, although the courts can only compensate for them in a financial way. They do this by reference to guidelines produced by the Judicial Studies Board, based on awards in previous cases. The Law Commission's 1995 Report No 225, *How much is enough?*, argued that compensation paid for these losses had fallen behind inflation and should be substantially increased. The Commission suggested that there was no real problem with the very smallest awards, those currently under £2,000, but that above that, claimants were being under-compensated.

In **Heil** *v* **Rankin and Another and Other Appeals** (2000), the House of Lords took the opportunity to look into this claim, and agreed with the Law Commission that there was a problem. However, they held that only those awards currently worth £10,000 or more needed adjustment, with the biggest problem being at the very top end of the scale, with the compensation for what the House of Lords called 'catastrophic injuries'. Where previously £150,000 had been regarded as the top level, this should be raised to £200,000; below that, there should be a tapering scale of increases down to awards of £10,000 or less, which would stay at current levels. The latest Judicial Studies Board guidelines, published in 2000, follow the line taken in this case.

Non-pecuniary losses fall into the following heads of damage.

The primary injury

Damages for the actual injury are usually calculated with reference to a tariff so that recognized values are placed on similar injuries. There are set awards, for example, for the loss of a limb or of sight.

Pain and suffering

Damages will be awarded for any pain and suffering which results from the injury itself, or from medical treatment of that injury. The claim may cover pain which the claimant can expect to suffer in the future, and mental suffering arising from the knowledge that life expectancy has been shortened or that the ability to enjoy life has been reduced by disability resulting from the injury.

Where the injury has caused a period of unconsciousness, that period will be excluded from any claim for pain and suffering, as it is assumed that an unconscious person is unaware of pain.

Loss of amenity

Loss of amenity describes the situation where an injury results in the claimant being unable to enjoy life to the same extent as before. It may include an inability to enjoy sport or any other pastime the claimant enjoyed before the injury, impairment of sight, hearing, touch, taste or smell, reduction in the chance of finding a marriage partner, and impairment of sexual activity or enjoyment. Calculation of these damages is based on a tariff laid down by the Court of Appeal, though the tariff figure can be adjusted to take into account the claimant's individual circumstances.

Damages for loss of amenity are not affected by whether the claimant is actually aware of the loss, so unconscious claimants may claim damages as if they had not been unconscious. This was the case in **West & Son** *v* **Shephard** (1964). The claimant was a married woman, who was 41 when she was injured. Serious head injuries left her at least partially unconscious, and paralysed in all four limbs. There was no hope of recovery, and her life expectancy was only five years. She was unable to speak, but there was evidence to suggest that she had some awareness of her circumstances. An award of £17,500 for loss of amenity was upheld by a majority in the House of Lords.

Interim awards and provisional damages

Unless there is a statutory provision to the contrary, damages are usually awarded as a once-only lump sum. This can cause problems in personal injury cases, where long after the case is tried, the injury may turn out to have consequences which could not have been foreseen. In order to deal with this situation, the Supreme Court Act 1981 gives the courts power to award provisional damages. Where there is a possibility that the injured person will, as a result of the tort, develop a serious disease, or serious physical or mental deterioration in the future, the court can award initial damages based on the claimant's condition at the time of trial, but retain the power to award further damages if the possible future deterioration does in fact happen. The award can only be adjusted once.

A further problem with damages for personal injury is that delays in coming to trial often mean the claimant has no financial help when it is actually needed most. The Supreme Court Act 1981 also provides some mitigation of this situation, by allowing the courts to award interim damages before trial, where the defendant admits liability, and is only contesting the amount of damages claimed. The defendant must also be insured, or be a public body or have the resources to make an interim payment. Because there is often a long delay between being injured and receiving damages, the Supreme Court Act 1981 makes it mandatory for courts to award interest where damages are more than £200, unless there are special reasons not to do so.

In **Wadey** *v* **Surrey County Council** (1999), it was decided that courts should disregard any social security benefits received by the claimant when they calculate the interest due on the damages.

Structured settlements

Many compensation payments for personal injury are made in the form of structured settlements. Instead of one lump sum, the claimant receives an initial payment, covering losses up to the date of settlement, and the rest of the damages are paid as a pension, providing a regular income which will usually last for the rest of the claimant's life, and designed to cover future loss of income, medical expense and future non-pecuniary losses, such as pain and suffering.

The courts cannot order damages to be paid in this way, so it is a matter for the parties to agree between themselves the appropriate terms of such a settlement. One of the main reasons for their current use is that they provide tax advantages.

The Law Commission has reviewed the use of structured settlements and has recommended their continued existence on a voluntary basis. While they recognized their value to both claimants and defendants they were not prepared to recommend that the courts should have the power to order their use, primarily because this would raise too many practical problems as to when such settlements should be ordered and what should happen if they were breached. It recommended certain administrative changes such as that money from the settlement should be paid direct to the claimant rather than the current arrangement whereby the money is paid first to the defendant or the defendant's insurance company. The Damages Act 1996 aims to encourage the use of structured settlements.

Set-offs

As we have said, tort damages are generally calculated to put the claimant in the position they would have enjoyed if the tort had never been committed. They are not designed to put the claimant in a better position than if the tort had never been committed, and so the courts will generally take steps to make sure that any other money paid as a result of the injury will be deducted from the damages: this is known as a set-off. The following principles are followed.

Tax

Where a claimant is awarded damages for loss of earnings, the amount payable will be what the claimant would have earned after paying tax and National Insurance (**British Transport Commission** *v* **Gourley** (1956)).

Payments by an employer

Sick pay from an employer is taken into account in assessing damages, and damages are reduced accordingly. In **Hussain** *v* **New Taplow Paper Mills Ltd** (1988) the House of Lords stated that long-term sick pay from the employer according to the terms of the employment contract could be deducted, as such payments were the equivalent of receiving a salary.

Social security benefits

When the social security system was first set up, the Law Reform (Personal Injuries) Act 1948 provided that the value of certain social security benefits received by claimants should be deducted from the compensation payable to them, and as time went on, the courts extended this approach, so that all benefits were covered by the rule. This prevented claimants being double-compensated, but it meant that the social security system (and therefore the taxpayer) was in effect subsidizing defendants. From the late 1980s, new legislation was enacted, which deducted the value of social security benefits from the compensation received, but gave it to the state, rather than back to the defendant. The situation is now covered by the Social Security (Recovery of Benefits) Act 1997. This provides that the value of social security benefits received by the claimant during the five years immediately following the accident or until the making of the compensation payment (whichever is the earlier) should be deducted from the compensation ordered by the court, and paid to the Secretary of State. The Act treats compensation as having three elements – loss of earnings, cost of care, and loss of mobility – and the value of benefits received can only be set off against the corresponding element in the damages award. This means, for example, that if a claimant who has received £7,000 in income support and £3,000 in attendance allowance is awarded £10,000 for loss of earnings and £2,000 for cost of care, they will end up with £3,000, because the Scheme will not take the outstanding £1,000 in attendance allowance from the sum awarded for loss of earnings. In addition, no part of the value of social security benefits can be deducted from damages awarded for pain and suffering. The previous legislation did not apply to awards of up to £2,500, but the 1997 Act brings such payments within the Scheme.

Exceptions

Apparent exceptions to the rule that damages should not make a claimant better off than they would have been if the tort had not been committed are made in the case of disability pensions paid by a claimant's employers, insurance pay-outs and payments made on a charitable basis. This was established in **Parry v Cleaver** (1970), where Lord Read explained the decision on the grounds that set-offs of these kinds of payments would discourage charity and sensible investment in insurance, and might allow tortfeasors to benefit.

The rule has been criticized by the Law Commission in its 1997 consultation paper *Damages for Personal Injury: Collateral Benefits*. The Commission argued that it over-compensates victims, which is both contrary to the aims of tort law, and a waste of resources. It doubted that anyone would be put off buying insurance by the prospect of set-offs, since people buy insurance against income loss generally, not just loss as a result of a tort, so they would still want the cover.

However, in **Longden v British Coal Corporation** (1998), the House of Lords ignored such criticisms. The claimant in the case had suffered an injury at work which meant he had to retire at 36. Under a scheme run by his employers, he became entitled to receive a disability pension from that point, instead of the ordinary pension he would have started receiving when he became 60. The defendants accepted that they could not set off the disability pension against the damages for loss of earnings, following **Parry v Cleaver**, but argued that the disability pension could be set off against the claimant's claim for loss of the pension he would have started receiving at 60. The House of Lords held that the amounts he would receive from the disability pension after he reached 60 could be set off against the claim for loss of the normal pension, but the payments he received before he was 60 could not.

Benefits provided by the tortfeasor

In **Hunt v Severs** (1994), the claimant was very seriously injured in a car accident caused by her fiancé, who she went on to marry. She sued him (which may seem odd, but bear in mind it would actually be his insurance company that stood to pay damages), and the issue arose of whether she could claim the cost of care that had been provided by him, and would continue to be given by him in the future. There is usually no problem with compensating the cost of care, even if that care is provided by a relative and so not actually paid for, but in this case the House of Lords held that such compensation could not be awarded, because it would amount to double compensation, just as if the defendant had, for example, given the claimant a wheelchair and then been asked to pay compensation for the cost of it.

Fatal accidents

When a claimant dies as a result of a tort, the claim they would have had against the tortfeasor passes to their estate, meaning that it becomes part of what is inherited as a result of the death. Whoever inherits the estate can recover the losses that the claimant would have claimed for the period between the injury and the death, provided that it is not too brief – Law Reform (Miscellaneous Provisions) Act 1934, s. 1. So if, for example, someone is injured in an accident and dies six months later, the estate can claim damages for pecuniary and non-pecuniary losses, based on the usual principles, for that six-month period.

In addition, the Fatal Accidents Act 1976 establishes two further claims: a claim by dependants of the deceased for financial losses and a claim for the bereavement suffered. As well as the spouse and children of the deceased, dependants can include other relatives, so long as they can prove financial dependence on them. A partner who lived as husband or wife with the deceased for at least two years is also classed as a dependant. Dependants will only have a claim if the deceased would have had one, and any defence which could have been used against the defendant can be used against them.

Dependants can claim for financial losses to themselves caused by the death, including earnings spent on the dependants, savings made for their future use, non-essential items such as holidays, and the value of services rendered. So, for example, a man who loses his wife can claim the value of any domestic services she provided for the family. In **Martin and Browne** *v* **Grey** (1998), a 12-year-old girl was awarded a record amount of damages for loss of the services provided by her mother, who had been killed. The court held that in calculating the award it was necessary to look at the cost of providing the services a mother would normally provide, whether or not these services had actually been replaced; this might include, for example, the costs of employing a housekeeper, or the loss of earnings of the father if he gave up work.

Assessing the loss can be a difficult task, and in **Davies** *v* **Powell Duffryn Associated Collieries Ltd** (1942), Lord Wright laid down some guidance. The court must start with the earnings of the deceased; from this it deducts an amount estimated to cover the deceased's personal and living expenses. The sum left will be the multiplicand. This is then multiplied by the multiplier, which is calculated using the rules described at p. 295, except that the multiplier runs from the date of the death. Benefits received by the dependants, such as social security or insurance payments, are not deducted.

The second claim allowed by the Fatal Accidents Act 1976 is for a fixed award of £7,500 damages for bereavement, which is designed to provide some compensation for the non-pecuniary losses associated with bereavement. It is only available to the husband or wife of the deceased, or, if the deceased was unmarried and a minor, to the parents. It does not give children a claim for the death of a parent.

▶ Non-compensatory damages

As we have seen, compensatory damages are carefully calculated to put the claimant in the position they would have enjoyed if the tort had never been committed. In some cases however, damages may be awarded for different reasons, and these may be less, or much more, than is required to compensate the loss directly. There are four types of non-compensatory damages: contemptuous, nominal, aggravated and exemplary.

Contemptuous damages

Where a court recognizes that the claimant's legal rights have technically been infringed, but disapproves of their conduct, and considers that the action should never have been brought, it may order contemptuous damages. These will amount to no more than the value of the least valuable coin of the realm (currently 1p). A claimant awarded contemptuous damages is also unlikely to recover costs. Contemptuous damages are not commonly awarded; their main use is in defamation actions.

Nominal damages

An award of nominal damages is normally made where there has technically been an infringement of a person's legal rights but no actual damage has been done. It comprises a small sum of money, normally £20, and tends to arise in relation to torts which are actionable *per se*, such as trespass and libel. Its purpose is to acknowledge that the defendant has violated the claimant's rights, rather than to compensate for loss.

An example of nominal damages being awarded is **Constantine v Imperial London Hotels** (1944), where the claimant, a famous West Indian cricketer, was only awarded damages of five guineas, after the defendants wrongfully refused to allow him into one of their hotels, though they allowed him to rent a room in another of their hotels.

A claimant who secures nominal damages will not necessarily be awarded costs as well.

Aggravated damages

Where a defendant has behaved in such a way that the claimant has suffered more than would normally be expected in such a case, the court can show its disapproval by awarding damages which are higher than would normally be appropriate. These are called aggravated damages. A recent example of the kind of case where aggravated damages are considered appropriate is **Khodaparast** *v* **Shad** (1999). The claimant, an Iranian woman, had sued her ex-boyfriend for libel after he created photo-montages that appeared to show her advertising pornographic telephone lines, and distributed the images throughout the local Iranian community. As a result, the claimant lost her teaching job at an Iranian school, and had little or no prospect of finding further work within the Iranian community; as her English was poor, this had been her main source of employment. In his pre-trial statements, and later in court, the defendant persisted in denying that he had created the montages, and insisted that they were real pictures of the claimant and quite likely to have come from pornographic magazines; in support of this allegation, he made a number of other untrue claims, including that she 'slept around', associated with prostitutes, and had had 'an improper relationship' with her solicitor. As a result of this behaviour, the trial judge awarded aggravated damages, and his decision was upheld by the Court of Appeal.

Exemplary damages

Exemplary damages also involve paying the claimant more than would normally be appropriate, but they differ from aggravated damages in that their purpose is actually to offer a serious punishment to the defendant, and to deter others from behaving in the same way.

The punitive nature of exemplary damages means that they stray into an area which is generally thought to be more appropriate to criminal law, where of course there is a higher standard of proof. As a result, their use is very carefully controlled, and in **Rookes** *v* **Barnard** (1964), the House of Lords laid down strict rules about when they could be ordered. The case must fall within one of the following categories.

Statutory authorization
There are a few cases in which exemplary damages are expressly allowed by statute.

Conduct calculated to make a profit
There are clearly some cases, usually involving defamation, where a defendant may calculate that it is worth committing a tort, even at the risk of being sued, because the profit to be made will exceed the cost of

compensating the claimant if they do sue. For example, an unscrupulous newspaper may calculate that the revenue from increased sales may make it worthwhile to print libellous stories.

It is not necessary for the defendant precisely to calculate the potential profit and compensation, so long as they deliberately risk causing damage in order to make a profit. This was the case in **Cassell & Co Ltd** *v* **Broome** (1972). The claimant was a retired naval officer, and the defendants published a book about a wartime convoy with which the claimant was involved. The claimant successfully sued for libel and was awarded £25,000 exemplary damages. This was upheld by the House of Lords, taking into account the profit which the defendant would have made.

Oppressive conduct by government servants

Exemplary damages may also be awarded where there has been oppressive, arbitrary or unconstitutional action by government servants, which includes people exercising governmental functions, such as police officers. The purpose here is to mark the fact that government servants are also supposed to serve the community, and must use their power accordingly.

An example of such a case is **Huckle** *v* **Money** (1763). The claimant was detained under a search warrant. The detention was for six hours, and involved no ill-treatment; in fact food and drink were provided. Even so, the court upheld an award of £300 damages, stating that entering a person's home with a search warrant that did not have his name on it was a serious breach of civil liberties, and 'worse than the Spanish Inquisition'.

Modern cases have involved local authorities which have practised sexual or racial discrimination in recruiting employees, such as **Bradford City Metropolitan Council** *v* **Arora** (1991).

In addition to falling within one of these categories, it must be clear that the case is one where compensatory damages would be insufficient, and if there is a jury, the members must be fully and carefully directed. Later cases have shed more light on the nature of the direction to be given to juries in particular types of case. In **John** *v* **Mirror Group Newspapers** (1995), the Court of Appeal stated that in defamation cases, the jury should be told that an award of exemplary damages could only be made if the publisher had no genuine belief that the published information was true, and in **Thompson** *v* **Commissioner of Police of the Metropolis** (1997), the Court of Appeal stated that in cases of unlawful conduct by the police, juries should be told that they can award damages at a level designed to punish the defendant. Such damages were unlikely to be less than £5,000, and might be up to £50,000 where officers of at least the rank of superintendent were directly involved.

A further restriction on the use of exemplary damages was established in **AB** *v* **South West Water Services Ltd** (1993), in which it was stated that they could only be applied to torts for which exemplary damages had been awarded in at least one case before **Rookes** *v* **Barnard**.

▶ Problems with damages

Lump sums

As we have seen at p. 298, the fact that damages are paid in a lump sum has disadvantages for the claimant, particularly where the effects of injury worsen after the award is made. The introduction of provisional damages has gone some way towards dealing with this problem, but still does not cover cases where at the time of trial there is no reason to believe that further deterioration will occur.

As well as the future prospects of the claimant's health, the lump sum system requires the court to predict what the claimant's employment prospects are likely to be; in reality this can never be known, so the compensation may well turn out to represent much more or less than the claimant should have had. Perhaps more importantly, it is impossible to predict the result of inflation on the award, so that when inflation is high, the award's value can soon be eroded.

A further problem is that there is no way to ensure that the claimant uses the lump sum in such a way as to make sure it provides a lifelong income, where necessary. If the money is used unwisely, the claimant may end up having to live on state benefits, which partly defeats the object of making the tortfeasor compensate for the damage caused.

These issues were considered by the Pearson Commission (1978), which recommended that in cases of death or serious, long-term injury, claimants should be able to receive damages in the form of periodic payments. Assuming that the defendant was insured, the insurer would be responsible for administering the payments, which would be revalued annually to reflect average earnings. In addition, the Commission recommended that the courts should be able to vary awards where changes in the claimant's medical condition affected the level of pecuniary loss. These recommendations were not taken up by the Government.

Degrees of fault

Because the aim of tort damages is to compensate the claimant, rather than punish the defendant, compensation does not take into account the degree of fault involved in the defendant's action. As a result, a defendant who makes a momentary slip may end up paying the same damages as one who shows gross carelessness. The system as it stands seems unable to provide justice for the claimant without injustice to some defendants.

West & Son *v* Shephard **and loss of amenity**

The case of **West & Son** *v* **Shephard** (1964), and the principle that a person who is unaware of their loss of amenity can still be compensated for it, has been strongly criticized. The main criticism is that the compensation cannot actually be used by the unconscious person, and in most cases will simply end up forming part of their estate when they die. This being the case, it seems inequitable that relatives in this situation may end up with considerably more than the relatives of someone killed immediately as the result of a tort. But if no such award was made the court would be treating the claimant like a dead person.

The Law Commission has recommended that this aspect of the law should be kept, but the Pearson Commission suggested that awards for non-pecuniary loss should no longer be made to unconscious claimants. The Pearson Commission recommendation has not been implemented.

The role of exemplary damages

Despite the restrictions imposed by **Rookes** *v* **Barnard** (see p. 304), exemplary damages continue to cause concern, notably in high-profile cases such as the libel actions involving the ex-MP Jeffrey Archer, and Sonia Sutcliffe, the wife of the murderer known as the Yorkshire Ripper. These were seen as examples of juries 'punishing' newspapers beyond what was deserved by the particular libels, and instead using the cases to show their disapproval of newspapers generally.

Critics of the idea of exemplary damages argue that they go beyond the purpose of tort law, and that they introduce the potential for punishment without the safeguards built into the criminal legal system (such as the standard of proof beyond reasonable doubt). Some steps have been taken to meet these criticisms, for example, in the case of **John** *v* **Mirror Group Newspapers** (see p. 211), but there is still a strong body of opinion that would like to see the problem avoided by taking the calculation of damages away from juries, so that in cases where juries are used (in practice this is usually defamation cases), the jury would deliver only a verdict, with the job of deciding damages left to the judge (as sentencing is in the criminal system).

INJUNCTIONS

Injunctions are the other main remedy the courts can order in tort cases, and are mainly used to deal with continuing or repeatable torts such as defamation and nuisance. In issuing an injunction, the court prohibits the defendant from committing, continuing or repeating a particular tort. Injunctions are an equitable remedy, and therefore issued at the discretion of the court, where it is considered to be 'just and convenient'

(Supreme Court Act 1981, s. 37). An injunction will not be granted where damages would be an adequate remedy.

Most injunctions prohibit the defendant from doing something: these are called, not surprisingly, prohibitory injunctions. Injunctions may also be mandatory, in which case they order the defendant to do something. In **Redland Bricks Ltd** *v* **Morris** (1970), the defendants had been digging on their own land, and this work had caused subsidence on the claimants' land, and made further subsidence likely if the digging continued. The claimants were awarded damages for the damage that had already been done, and a mandatory injunction ordering the defendants to restore support to their land. This restoration work was to cost more than the total value of the claimants' land, and the defendants appealed against the injunction.

The House of Lords allowed the appeal and laid down some general guidelines on the issue of mandatory injunctions, although they stressed that the decision on whether to grant such an order remained one for the courts' discretion, bearing in mind the individual circumstances of a case. In general, they said, mandatory injunctions should be ordered only where damages would not be adequate to remedy the harm done to the claimant. Where the defendant has acted reasonably, though wrongly, the fact that carrying out a mandatory injunction would, as in the case of **Redlands**, be very costly may be a reason not to grant such an injunction; however, if the defendant has acted unreasonably, and particularly if the defendant has in some way tried to gain an advantage over the claimant or the court, the cost of carrying out the injunction should not be taken into account. Should a mandatory injunction be ordered, the court must ensure that the defendant knows precisely what is to be done, so that accurate instructions for carrying out the work can be given.

Interlocutory injunctions

In some cases a court may order an injunction (which may be either mandatory or prohibitory) before the case is actually heard. This is called an interlocutory or interim injunction, and is designed to prevent potential harm, or continued harm, during the period before the case comes to court (an injunction granted as a result of a decided trial is called a perpetual injunction).

The fact that an interlocutory injunction has been granted does not mean that the claimant has won; when the case is tried, the defendant may be found to have been in the right, and the injunction unjustified. For this reason, the courts do not give interlocutory injunctions easily, and in some cases the claimant may be required to give an undertaking in damages – a promise to pay damages for any loss incurred by the defendant while the injunction was in force, should the claimant lose the case. In **American Cyanamid Co** *v* **Ethicon Ltd** (1975), guidelines for the use of interlocutory injunctions were laid down. The claimant does not have to establish a *prima facie* case, but the court should be satisfied that there is a 'serious question' to be tried. If damages are an adequate remedy for the alleged wrong, no interlocutory injunction should be granted. On the other hand, if the adequacy of damages is questionable, the court should decide on the basis of the balance of convenience, weighing what the claimant stands to gain from an interlocutory injunction against what the defendant stands to lose.

One of the most obvious potential uses for interlocutory injunctions is that of libel cases, as clearly once a statement has been made public, the damage can never truly be undone. However, in assessing whether to allow interlocutory injunctions in libel cases, the courts are very aware of the need to protect free speech, and such injunctions are in practice uncommon in libel cases.

Damages in lieu of injunction

The High Court has a discretion to order damages instead of an injunction. In **Shelfer *v* City of London Electric Lighting Co** (1895), it was stated that this discretion should generally be exercised where an injunction could have been issued, but would be oppressive to the defendant, and the harm done to the claimant is minor, and capable of being calculated in and compensated by money.

Damages in such cases would generally be calculated using the normal principles discussed at the start of the chapter.

An example of the way the courts apply **Shelfer** can be seen in **Daniells *v* Mendoca** (1999). The parties were neighbours, and Ms Daniells had had a bathroom extension built on her property. Some years later, she went away for three months, and when she came back, she discovered that Mr Mendoca had built an extension too, which was supported by the wall of hers and joined to her roof. The London Building (Amendments) Act 1939 requires that neighbours be informed of plans to build, but Ms Daniells had known nothing of the work that was taking place while she was away. Mr Mendoca admitted trespass, but the issue of remedies could not be agreed; Ms Daniells wanted an injunction, but Mr Mendoca argued that this was a case where **Shelfer** suggested that damages should be ordered instead. Applying the **Shelfer** principles, the court allowed the injunction: it was true that the extent of trespass was small, but this was offset by the fact that it was permanent, and other additions were planned; the injury could be compensated for by money, but this would not be a small amount, given the nuisance, the fire danger and the risk of structural damage; and the injunction could not be said to be oppressive to the defendant, given his own behaviour in building the extension in the first place, and failing to comply with the Act.

·
ANSWERING QUESTIONS

1 When Oliver recently moved into a new flat, he was aware that it was situated very close to a stadium (owned by Sara) in which speedway (motorcycle) racing was held. However, he had not realized that race meetings were held on three evenings per week between 7 pm and 10 pm and he was totally unprepared for the degree of noise generated and for the general disruption and noise caused by spectators going to and from the stadium (including problems of litter, car parking and slamming of car doors).

Peter was a regular spectator at race meetings but, on this occasion, he had not brought enough money to pay to enter. Even so, he was able to force entry at a little-used part of the stadium where the wooden fencing was particularly weak. He then took up a position close to the steel mesh fencing which separated spectators from the race track.

During the first race of the meeting, one of the riders took a bend far too quickly, lost control of his motorcycle and crashed into the fence. Though having been tested by stadium staff earlier that evening, the fence gave way and Peter suffered severe injuries when he was struck by the motorcycle.

(a) Discuss what rights Oliver may have in connection with the noise and other disturbance. *(10 marks)*

(b) (i) Explain the rules in the law of tort which impose obligations on Sara in respect of the safety of the spectators and participants in the speedway racing. *(10 marks)*

(ii) Explain how those rules would be modified in the case of Peter, given his manner of entry, and consider whether he would succeed in an action for compensation against Sara. *(10 marks)*

(c) In the event of legal action by either Oliver or Peter, a judge would have a very important role to play in the resolution of the dispute. Critically discuss the appointment of judges and their suitability to perform their role. *(10 marks)*

(d) How satisfactory are the remedies provided by English law in cases such as those of Oliver and Peter? *(10 marks) AQA (AEB)*

(a) Any rights Oliver has here will arise from the law on nuisance. Considering first private nuisance, three things need to be proved: an indirect interference with enjoyment of land; damage to the claimant; and that the interference was unreasonable. It seems fairly clear that the interference is substantial, though remember that the courts will balance this against Sara's right to use her land as she chooses. Damage also seems fairly straightforward, since it can include discomfort or inconvenience. The critical point will be whether the interference was unreasonable, and an obvious factor here may be public utility, as explained in **Kennaway v Thompson** and **Miller v Jackson**.

Note that the fact that the meetings were already taking place when Oliver moved into the area will not give Sara a defence, since 'coming to the nuisance' does not have this effect, as explained in **Sturges** *v* **Bridgman**. You might want to point out that although in practice it will be Sara who is sued, technically Oliver could sue the spectators, as the creators of the nuisance.

Public nuisance is also a possibility, if the problem is also affecting others in the locality, as the residents living near a nuisance have been accepted as a class of persons for the purposes of public nuisance. However, Oliver would have to prove that he suffered special damage over and above that suffered by others in that class, and we are not told whether or not this is the case.

(b) (i) Here you should deal with the spectators and the riders in turn. Taking the spectators first, the relevant rules here are those concerning occupiers' liability, because the spectators are obviously visitors. Note that the occupier's duty is to 'take such care as is reasonable'. It is therefore not an absolute duty, and the fact that the fence was tested might be held to reach a reasonable standard of care. We are not told whether the spectators include children, but you could point out that if so, special rules will apply. Note too that there are special rules concerning spectators of sports events and the defence of *volenti*, as discussed in the case of **Wooldridge** *v* **Sumner** (see p. 115). You should also discuss the fact that Sara may be vicariously liable for any tort done by her employees to the spectators.

As regards Sara's obligations to the participants, occupiers' liability is also relevant here, as the riders are visitors to the premises, but Sara may also have a duty of care towards them as an employer – this will depend on whether they are in fact employees or independent contractors. Again, the rules concerning the defence of *volenti* and participants in sports will apply, as explained in **Simms** *v* **Leigh Rugby Football Club** (see p. 115).

(ii) The main difference between Peter and the other spectators is that he has entered as a trespasser. Under the Occupiers' Liability Act 1984, Sara will owe a duty to Peter only if she knew or had reasonable grounds to suspect that a danger existed, that a trespasser might be in the vicinity of it, and that the risk was one against which in all the circumstances she could reasonably be expected to offer some protection. If this is deemed to be the case, she may have taken the appropriate steps by inspecting the rail earlier.

(c) This part of the question raises issues which are outside the scope of this book, which you will study as part of an English Legal System course. A textbook by the same authors on the English Legal System is available.

(d) Oliver's possible remedies are abatement, injunction and damages, while for Peter, the choice will be damages. Abatement has obvious problems in a case like this, and in practice, would be useless to Oliver. Injunction may be the most appropriate remedy for Oliver, but as the case of **Kennaway** shows, where the activity causing the nuisance has some public utility, an injunction may not stop it completely.

As far as damages are concerned, there are a number of problems discussed in this chapter. Those particularly appropriate here include the difficulties with calculating damages, lump sums, deduction of social security benefits, and failure to match degrees of fault to the level of compensation. You should discuss the attempts which have been made to address these problems, such as structured settlements.

Appendix: Answering examination questions

A t the end of each chapter in this book, you will find detailed guidelines for answering examination questions on the topics covered. Many of the questions are taken from actual A-Level past papers, but they are equally relevant for candidates of all law examinations, as these questions are typical of the type of questions that examiners ask in this field.

▶ General guidelines

Citation of authorities

One of the most important requirements for answering questions on the law is that you must be able to back the points you make with authority, usually either a case or a statute. It is not good enough to state that the law is such and such, without stating the case or statute which says that that is the law.

Some examiners are starting to suggest that the case name is not essential, as long as you can remember and understand the general principle that that case laid down. However, such examiners remain in the minority and the reality is that even they are likely to give higher marks where the candidate has cited authorities by name; quite simply, it helps give the impression that you know your material thoroughly, rather than half-remembering something you heard once in class.

This means that you must be prepared to learn fairly long lists of cases by heart, which can be a daunting prospect. What you need to memorize is the name of the case, a brief description of the facts, and the legal principle which the case established. Once you have revised a topic well, you should find that a surprisingly high number of cases on that topic begin to stick in your mind anyway, but there will probably be some that you have trouble recalling. A good way to memorize these is to try to create a picture in your mind which links the facts, the name and the legal principle – the more bizarre the image, the more likely you are to remember it.

Knowing the names of cases makes you look more knowledgeable, and also saves writing time in the exam, but if you do forget a name, referring briefly to the facts will identify it. It is not necessary to learn the dates of cases, though it is useful if you know whether it is a recent or an old case. Dates are usually required for statutes.

You need to know the facts of a case in order to judge whether it applies to the situation in a problem question. However, unless you are making a detailed comparison of the facts of a case and the facts of a problem question, in order to argue that the case should or could be distinguished, you should generally make only brief reference to facts, if at all – long descriptions of facts waste time and earn few marks.

When reading the 'Answering questions' sections at the end of each chapter in this book, bear in mind that for reasons of space, we have not highlighted every case which you should cite. The skeleton arguments outlined in those sections must be backed up with authority from cases and statute law.

There is no right answer

In law exams, there is not usually a right or a wrong answer. What matters is that you show you know what type of issues you are being asked about. Essay questions are likely to ask you to 'discuss', 'criticize', or 'evaluate', and you simply need to produce a good range of factual and critical material in order to do this. The answer you produce might look completely different from your friend's but both answers could be worth 'A' grades.

Breadth and depth of content

Where a question seems to raise a number of different issues – as most do – you will achieve better marks by addressing all or most of these issues than by writing at great length on just one or two. By all means spend more time on issues which you know well, but at least be sure to mention other issues which you can see are relevant, even if you can only produce a paragraph or so about them.

The structure of the question

If a question is specifically divided into parts, for example (a), (b) and (c), then stick to those divisions and do not merge your answer into one long piece of writing.

Law examinations tend to contain a mixture of essay questions and what are known as 'problem questions'. Tackling each of these questions involves slightly different skills so we consider each in turn.

▶ Essay questions

Answer the question asked

Over and over again, examiners complain that candidates do not answer the question they are asked – so if you can develop this skill, you will stand out from the crowd. You will get very few marks for simply writing all you know about a topic, with no attempt to address the issues raised in the question, but if you can adapt the material that you have learnt on the subject to take into account the particular emphasis given to it by the question, you will do well.

Even if you have memorized an essay which does raise the issues in the question (perhaps because those issues tend to be raised year after year), you must fit your material to the words of the question you are actually being asked. For example, suppose during your course, you wrote an essay on the advantages and disadvantages of limiting compensation for nervous shock, and then in the exam, you find yourself faced with the question 'Should compensation for nervous shock be subject to the same rules as for physical damage?' The material in your coursework essay is ideally suited for the exam question, but if (after briefly explaining what the rules on compensation for physical damage and for nervous shock are) you begin the main part of your answer with the words 'The advantages of limiting compensation for nervous shock include . . .', or something similar, this is a dead giveaway to the examiner that you are merely writing down an essay you have memorized. It takes very little effort to change the words to 'There are a number of good reasons why compensation for nervous shock should not be subject to the same rules as physical damage . . .', but it will create a much better impression, especially if you finish with a conclusion which, based on points you have made, states that special rules are a good or bad idea, the choice depending on the arguments you have made during your answer.

During your essay, you should keep referring to the words used in the question – if this seems to become repetitive, use synonyms for those words. This makes it clear to the examiner that you are keeping the question in mind as you work.

Plan your answer

Under pressure of time, it is tempting to start writing immediately, but five minutes spent planning each essay question is well worth spending – it may mean that you write less overall, but the quality of your answer will almost certainly be better. The plan need not be elaborate: just jot down everything you feel is relevant to the answer, including case names, and then organize the material into a logical order appropriate to the question asked. To put it in order, rather than wasting time copying it all out again, simply put a number next to each point according to which ones you intend to make first, second and so forth.

Provide analysis and fact

Very few essay questions require merely factual descriptions of what the law is; you will almost always be required to analyse the factual content in some way, usually highlighting any problems or gaps in the law, and suggesting possible reforms. If a question asks you to analyse whether individuals are adequately protected by the law on defamation, you should not write everything you know about defamation and finish with one sentence saying individuals are or are not adequately protected. Instead you should select your relevant material and your whole answer should be targeted at answering whether the protection is adequate, by, for example, pointing out any gaps or problems in it, and highlighting changes which have improved protection.

Where a question uses the word 'critically', as in 'critically describe' or 'critically evaluate', the examiners are merely drawing your attention to the fact that your approach should be analytical and not merely descriptive; you are not obliged to criticize every provision you describe. Having said that, even if you do not agree with particular criticisms which you have read, you should still discuss them and say why you do not think they are valid; there is very little mileage in an essay that simply describes the law and says it is perfectly satisfactory.

Structure

However good your material, you will only gain really good marks if you structure it well. Making a plan for each answer will help in this, and you should also try to learn your material in a logical order – this will make it easier to remember as well. The exact construction of your essay will obviously depend on the question, but you should aim to have an introduction, then the main discussion, and a conclusion. Where a question is divided into two or more parts, you should reflect that structure in your answer.

A word about conclusions: it is not good enough just to repeat the question, turning it into a statement, for the conclusion. So, for example, if the question is 'Are the rules on compensation for negligence causing economic loss satisfactory?', a conclusion which simply states that the rules are or are not satisfactory will gain you very little credit. A good conclusion will often summarize the arguments that you have developed during the course of your essay.

▶ Problem questions

In problem questions, the exam paper will describe an imaginary situation, and then ask what the legal implications of the facts are – usually by asking you to advise one of the parties involved.

Read the question thoroughly

The first priority is to read the question thoroughly, at least a couple of times. Never start writing until you have done this, as you may well get halfway through and discover that what is said at the end makes half of what you have written irrelevant – or at worst, that the question raises issues you have no knowledge of at all.

Answer the question asked

This means paying close attention to the words printed immediately after the situation is described. If a question asks you to advise one or other of the parties, make sure you advise the right one – the realization as you discuss the exam with your friends afterwards that you have advised the wrong party and thus rendered most of your answer irrelevant is not an experience you will enjoy. Similarly, if a question asks about possible remedies, simply discussing whether a tort has been committed will not be enough – you need to say what the injured party can claim as a result.

Spot the issues

In answering a problem question in an examination you will often be short of time. One of the skills of doing well is spotting which issues are particularly relevant to the facts of the problem and spending most time on those, while skimming over more quickly those matters which are not really an issue on the facts, but which you clearly need to mention.

Apply the law to the facts

What a problem question requires you to do is to spot the issues raised by the situation, and to consider the law as it applies to those facts. It is not enough simply to describe the law without applying it to the facts. So in a question raising issues of negligence, for example, it is not enough to say what constitutes a duty of care and breach of it. You need to say whether, in the light of those rules, there was a duty of care and breach of it in the situation described in the problem.

Do not start your answer by copying out all the facts, or keep referring to them at great length. This is a complete waste of time, and will gain you no marks.

Unlike essay questions, problem questions are not usually seeking a critical analysis of the law. If you have time, it may be worth making the point that a particular area of the law you are discussing is problematic, and briefly stating why, but if you are addressing all the issues raised in the problem you are unlikely to have much time for this. What the examiner is looking for is essentially an understanding of the law and an ability to apply it to the particular facts given.

Use authority

As always, you must back up your points with authority from case or statute law.

Structure

The introduction and conclusion are much less important for problem questions than for essay questions. Your introduction can be limited to pointing out the issues raised by the question, or, where you are asked to 'advise' a person mentioned in the problem, what outcome that person will be looking for. You can also say in what order you intend to deal with the issues. It is not always necessary to write a conclusion, but you may want to summarize what you have said, highlighting whether, as a result, you think the party you have advised has a strong case or not.

There is no set order in which the main part of the answer must be discussed. Sometimes it will be appropriate to deal with the problem chronologically, in which case it will usually be a matter of looking at the question line by line, while in other cases it may be appropriate to group particular issues together. If the question is broken down into clear parts – (a), (b), (c) and so on – the answer can be broken down into the same parts.

Whichever order you choose, try to deal with one issue at a time. Jumping backwards and forwards gives the impression that you have not thought about your answer. If you work through your material in a structured way, you are also less likely to leave anything out.

Glossary

Act of God. An event can only be an Act of God if it is caused entirely by natural forces, with no human intervention. There is no liability in tort for acts of God.

Actionable per se. In the case of a tort which is actionable *per se*, the claimant only has to prove that the tort has been committed; they do not have to prove damage.

Assault. In tort, assault is defined as an act which causes another person reasonably to apprehend immediate violence to their person.

Battery. This is the direct and intentional application of force to another person without that person's consent.

Breach of contract occurs when two parties make a contract, and one of them fails to do what they promised to do.

'But for' test. In order to decide whether a defendant's breach of duty was, as a matter of fact, a cause of the damage suffered by the claimant, the question to be answered is whether the damage would not have occurred but for the breach of duty. This is known as the 'but for' test.

Compensatory damages. The majority of damages awards in tort are compensatory, i.e. they are designed to compensate the claimant for damage done by the defendant. The basic principle behind them is that, so far as possible, the claimant should be put into the position they would have enjoyed if the tort had never been committed.

Contemptuous damages. Where a court recognizes that the claimant's legal rights have been infringed technically, but disapproves of their conduct and considers that the action should not have been brought, it may order contemptuous damages. These will amount to no more than the value of the least valuable coin of the realm (currently 1p).

ntract damages. Unlike most tort damages, these generally try to put claimant in the position they would have enjoyed if the contract had en performed as agreed.

Contribution. The Civil Liability (Contribution) Act 1978 provides that where there is joint or several liability, and one tortfeasor is sued and pays damages, they may recover a contribution or indemnity from any other person who is liable in respect of the same damage. This is a matter between the defendants and does not affect the claimant, who remains entitled to recover the whole loss from whichever defendant they choose.

Contributory negligence. A claimant who it has been shown has, by their own lack of care, contributed to the harm done to themselves, will be considered contributorily negligent. In such a case the damages can be reduced, at the discretion of the court, to take account of the contributory negligence involved.

Defamation. This is the publication of a statement which tends to lower a person in the estimation of right-thinking members of society generally, or which tends to make them shun or avoid that person. There are two types of defamation, libel and slander.

Dependant. For the purposes of a claim under the Fatal Accidents Act 1976 by the dependants of the deceased, the word 'dependant' can include not only the spouse and children of the deceased but also other relatives, provided that they can prove financial dependence on the deceased.

Distress damage feasant. Where an object placed or left unlawfully on the claimant's land causes damage, they can keep it until the damage has been paid for.

Duress. A claimant who can prove that they were physically compelled by another person to commit a tort is covered by this defence.

Economic loss. In tort the term is usually used to cover losses which are 'purely' economic, i.e. those where a claimant has suffered financial damage but has incurred no personal injury or damage to property.

'Egg-shell skull' rule. This states that defendants must take their victims as they find them, including any health problems which make the harm suffered more serious than it would otherwise be.

Ex turpi causa non oritur actio (Latin for 'No right of action arises from a base cause'). This is a defence that may be used against a claimant whose claim arises from their own criminal actions.

Exemplary damages. Also known as punitive damages, these are awarded, in addition to compensatory damages, when a court wishes to mark its extreme disapproval of the defendant's conduct and to deter both that defendant and others from similar conduct in the future.

False imprisonment. This is the unlawful prevention of another from exercising their freedom of movement. In this context 'false' really means wrongful.

Fault principle. Most torts require some element of fault, i.e. in addition to proving that the defendant has committed the relevant act or been guilty of an omission (and, where necessary, that damage has been caused as a result) it is necessary to prove a particular state of mind on the part of the defendant (for example, malice or negligence).

Intention. This has various meanings depending on the context but essentially it involves deliberate and knowing behaviour.

Interim damages. Under the Supreme Court Act 1981 the court can award interim damages before trial, where the defendant admits liability and is only contesting the amount of damages claimed.

Interlocutory injunction. The court may award an interlocutory (or interim) injunction before the action is heard. It is designed to prevent potential harm, or continued harm, during the period before the case comes to court.

Joint tortfeasors. Where the same wrongful act is committed by two or more people, they are described as joint tortfeasors and are jointly and severally liable. This means the claimant can sue both (or all) of them, or recover the whole amount from just one, regardless of the extent to which each participated. Even where all are sued, judgment will be given for a single sum and this may be enforced in full against any one of them. The claimant can only recover once.

Jus tertii (Latin for 'The right of a third party'). A defendant may have a defence to an action for trespass if it can be shown that the land rightfully belongs neither to the person in possession of it nor to the person claiming it but to a third person.

Libel. This is the publication of a defamatory statement about a person, made in some permanent form. This usually means in printed or written form, but it also covers films, pictures, broadcasts, statues and effigies.

Licence. Where the person in possession of land gives someone permission, express or implied, to be on that land, there is no trespass, provided the boundaries of that permission are not exceeded. This is called giving a person licence to be on land.

Limitation of actions. The Limitation Act 1980 lays down time limits within which tort actions must be brought. The standard limitation periods are three years in a case which involves personal injury or death and six years in other tort actions.

Loss of amenity. This term describes the situation where an injury results in the claimant being unable to enjoy life to the same extent as before. It may include an inability to enjoy sport or any other pastime they engaged in before the injury, impairment of sight, hearing, etc., reduction in the chance of finding a marriage partner or impairment of sexual activity.

Malice. In tort, to act maliciously means acting with a bad motive. Normally malice – and motive in general – is irrelevant in tort law but there are a few torts (e.g. malicious prosecution) where it is an essential ingredient. It may also be relevant to the calculation of damages, making them higher than they would otherwise be if the same act was committed without malice.

Mesne profits. An action for mesne profits is a type of action for trespass. It allows the claimant to claim profits taken by the defendant during occupancy, damages for deterioration and reasonable costs of regaining possession. An action for recovery of land can be joined with a claim for mesne profits, and in this case it is unnecessary to have entered the land before sueing. If the actions are brought separately, the claimant will have to enter the land before bringing the claim for mesne profits.

Mitigation of loss. A person who falls victim to a tort is expected to take reasonable steps to mitigate any loss; the defendant will not be liable for compensatory damages in respect of any loss which could have been prevented by such steps.

Necessity. This defence applies where a defendant intentionally causes damage in order to prevent greater damage. It may turn out that the defendant need not have taken action at all, but so long as the action taken was reasonable in the circumstances the defence will still apply.

Negligence. (1) As a state of mind, this generally means carelessness – doing something without intending to cause damage, for example, but not taking care to ensure that it does not. (2) It is also a tort, which concerns the breach of a legal duty of care, with the result that damage is caused to the claimant.

Neighbour principle. In **Donoghue** *v* **Stevenson** the House of Lords attempted to lay down a general criteria as to when a duty of care in negligence would exist. Lord Atkin stated that the principle was: 'You must take reasonable care to avoid acts or omissions which you can reasonably foresee would be likely to injure your neighbour.' He said that by 'neighbour' he meant 'persons who are so closely and directly affected by my act that I ought to have them in contemplation as being so affected when I am directing my mind to the acts or omissions which are called in question'.

Nervous shock. Lawyers often use the term 'nervous shock' to describe psychiatric damage caused by a person suffering a sudden or unexpected shock. Such illnesses include anxiety neurosis, clinical depression and post-traumatic stress disorder. In this book we usually use the term 'psychiatric injury'.

Nominal damages. An award of nominal damages is normally made where there has technically been an infringement of a person's legal rights but no actual damage has been done. Such damages are for a small sum (normally £2) and tend to arise in relation to torts which are actionable *per se* (such as trespass and libel).

Non-pecuniary damages. These cover damages which are not always easily calculable, such as loss of physical amenity, pain, shock and suffering.

Novus actus interveniens (Latin for 'A new act intervening'). If the chain of causation between a defendant's act and the damage done is broken by the intervening act of a third person, the defendant will not be liable for the damage unless it could be foreseen that it would necessarily follow from their original act.

Occupier. For the purposes of the Occupiers' Liability Acts 1957 and 1984 an occupier is the person who controls the premises. They do not have to be the physical occupier nor the owner; the critical issue is whether they exercise a sufficient degree of control to allow or prevent other people entering.

Pecuniary damages. This kind of damages can be calculated in financial terms, such as loss of earnings and medical and other expenses.

Personal injury. This term covers physical or psychiatric harm, disease or illness.

Prescription. A defendant may be held to have acquired the right to commit a private nuisance by prescription. This applies where it can be shown that the nuisance has been actionable for at least 20 years and that the claimant was aware of that during the relevant period.

Provisional damages. The Supreme Court Act 1981 gives the court power to award provisional damages. Where there is a possibility that the injured person will, as a result of the tort, develop a serious disease, or serious physical or mental deterioration in the future, the court can award initial damages based on the claimant's condition but retain power to award further damages if the possible future deterioration does in fact happen. The award can be adjusted only once.

Punitive damages. *See* **Exemplary damages**.

Recklessness. For the purposes of the tort of deceit, recklessness means that the defendant must have been consciously indifferent as to whether a statement which they have made was true or not. Mere negligence, in the sense of failing to make sure it was true, is not enough.

Remoteness of damage. This term is used to describe a lack of a sufficiently direct connection between the wrong complained of and the injury alleged to have been sustained.

Res ipsa loquitur (Latin for 'The facts speak for themselves'). Where, in negligence cases, it is clear that the harm caused was such that it could not possibly have arisen unless the defendant was negligent, the court may be prepared to infer that the defendant was negligent without hearing detailed evidence of what was or was not done.

Restitutio in integrum. This is the principle of restoring the claimant to the position which they would have held if the tort had not been committed.

Rylands *v* **Fletcher, rule in**. The rule is that an occupier of land who brings onto it anything likely to do damage if it escapes, and keeps it there, will be liable for damage caused by such an escape.

Several liability. Where two or more tortfeasors act independently, but the result of their acts is damage to the claimant for which they are both responsible, they are severally liable. The practical result is that each tortfeasor is separately liable for the whole of the damage, so the claimant may choose which to sue, but cannot recover twice.

Slander. Defamatory statement about another made in a transitory form, i.e. orally or by gestures, not in writing or in print.

Special damage. (1) In an action for slander, the claimant must normally prove that the slander has caused some actual damage (known as 'special damage') over and above the loss of reputation, usually a financial loss. (2) In a tort action for public nuisance, special damage means damage beyond that suffered by other members of the affected group.

Special damages are those which do not arise naturally from the wrong complained of and must be specifically listed in pleadings and proved in court. They generally cover the claimant's financial loss up until the date of trial, and any expenses incurred up to that point.

Strict liability. A tort of strict liability is committed simply by the performance of the relevant act or omission. The claimant does not have to prove the defendant's state of mind at the time.

Tort. In general terms a tort occurs where there is a breach of a general duty fixed by civil law.

Tortfeasor. The wrongdoer, i.e. the person who committed the tort.

Trespass *ab initio*. Where a person's entry onto land is permitted by statute or common law, rather than merely by permission of the occupier, and the person entering does a wrongful act while there, that act makes the original entry a trespass. This is known as trespass *ab initio*.

Trespasser. A trespasser is someone who goes onto private land without any kind of permission to do so.

Vicarious liability. There are some cases where one person will be held liable for torts committed by someone else; such liability is said to be vicarious. It only arises where there is a particular relationship between the two, usually (in fact, almost exclusively) that of employer and employee. An employer is vicariously liable for the torts committed by his employees if they are acting in the course of their employment.

Visitor. For the purpose of the Occupiers' Liability Act 1957 a visitor is someone who has express or implied permission from the occupier to enter premises. Where permission to enter is given and then withdrawn while the entrant is still on the property, they are allowed a reasonable time in which to leave; once that expires, they become a trespasser.

Volenti non fit injuria (Latin for 'No injury can be done to a willing person'). This defence applies where the claimant has consented to what was done by the defendant, on the grounds that they have voluntarily assumed the risk of injury. An obvious example is a boxer, who, by the fact of entering into a match with an opponent, voluntarily consents to be hit.

Index